Language vs. Reality

Language vs. Reality

Why Language Is Good for Lawyers and Bad for Scientists

N. J. Enfield

The MIT Press
Cambridge, Massachusetts
London, England

The MIT Press would like to thank the anonymous peer reviewers who provided comments on drafts of this book. The generous work of academic experts is essential for establishing the authority and quality of our publications. We acknowledge with gratitude the contributions of these otherwise uncredited readers.

This book was set in Stone Serif and Stone Sans by Westchester Publishing Services. Printed and bound in the United States of America.

Library of Congress Cataloging-in-Publication Data

Names: Enfield, N. J., 1966– author.
Title: Language vs. reality : why language is good for lawyers and bad for scientists / N. J. Enfield.
Description: Cambridge, Massachusetts : The MIT Press, 2022. | Includes bibliographical references and index.
Identifiers: LCCN 2021010579 | ISBN 9780262046619 (hardcover)
Subjects: LCSH: Communication—Social aspects. | Cognition. | Psycholinguistics.
Classification: LCC P95.54 .E54 2022 | DDC 401/.9—dc23
LC record available at https://lccn.loc.gov/2021010579

10   9   8   7   6   5   4   3   2   1

Contents

Preface and Acknowledgments

The world as we know it is saturated with language: our minds, our systems of knowledge and belief, our patterns of reasoning, our values, our narratives, our relationships. For us, these things could not develop as they do, in sustained and intensive social interaction, if language did not provide moorings for us to coordinate around. In aiming to understand how this works, my research has taken me to worlds far from the one I grew up in. There has been no better lesson than to be shaken from the idea that my background assumptions—including the kind of language I grew up speaking—are adequate as reference points for all of humanity. Eighty years ago, the linguist and anthropologist B. L. Whorf advocated the study of diverse languages—especially, Indigenous languages—precisely for the purpose of gaining insight into our own cognitive and cultural prejudices and limitations. He asked us to imagine ourselves as a people with "the physiological defect of being able to see only the color blue." Such a people "would hardly be able to formulate the rule that they saw only blue," he wrote. "In order to formulate the rule or norm of seeing only blue, they would need exceptional moments in which they saw other colors." The quest to see other colors has led me to spend years in the wilds of mainland Southeast Asia working with languages and cultures quite unlike my own. This book draws in part on lessons I have learned in the upland rainforests of central Laos and similar lessons that others have learned looking for new colors with speakers of sometimes radically different languages of the world. But I also draw on many other areas and methods of language science—from controlled psychology experiments to media and narrative analysis—without which there would be no hope of reaching a comprehensive understanding of language, our species' most unique combination of art and instinct.

*

This work has had many inspirations. I mention just three here.

First, in 1997, my PhD adviser, Nick Evans, handed me a book edited by Esther Goody, *Social Intelligence and Interaction*. That book set the coordinates for most of the questions I have asked about language in the quarter century since. Among many gems in the book is a chapter by Ed Hutchins and Brian Hazlehurst, titled "How to Invent a Shared Lexicon: The Emergence of Shared Form-Meaning Mappings in Interaction." In trying to understand language, Hutchins and Hazlehurst wanted to "push the boundaries of a genuinely cognitive unit of analysis out beyond the skin of the individual." They grapple with the question: How can a cognitively shared language arise among members of a community when there is no telepathy? They planted this question in my mind, and the question has guided, in one way or another, most of the research I've done since. This book is another of my efforts to provide an answer.

Second, on an evening in 2003, Steve Levinson hosted a research retreat for the Language and Cognition Department of the Max Planck Institute for Psycholinguistics in the Netherlands. We were deep in discussion about the properties of language, both its strengths and weaknesses: How is it that the distinctions languages make for describing the world are so minimal compared to the many fine distinctions we can perceive with our senses? The average human language has only five or six basic color words, yet the human senses are able to discriminate some 2 million or more distinct colors.[1] Steve remarked: "Language is hopelessly blunt for capturing the details of reality".[2] Tanya Stivers—now Professor of Sociology at UCLA—retorted: "Yes, but it's exactly as sharp as it needs to be for managing social relations." In the years since, I have worked on trying to understand both of those contentions (which are, essentially, the two contentions in the subtitle of this book: language is too blunt for scientists but just right for lawyers), working together with many of the people who were there in the room that evening. In time, I have become convinced that the concept of language as a social coordination device helps to explain why—and how—both Steve and Tanya are right. In the subsequent years that I spent collaborating with them and other incomparable colleagues and visitors—especially Melissa Bowerman,

Mark Dingemanse, Paul Kockelman, Asifa Majid, and Jack Sidnell—I have explored language in ways that shed light on both of these ideas.

Third, in a more distributed way, I have been inspired by more than two decades of interactions, real and virtual, direct and indirect, with an incredible array of researchers and thinkers beyond those just named. These include (but are not limited to!) Paul Bloom, Penny Brown, Eve Clark, Herb Clark, Emma Cohen, Sotaro Kita, Betty Couper-Kuhlen, Daniel Dor, Robin Dunbar, Nick Evans, Dan Everett, Susan Goldin-Meadow, Bill Hanks, John Heritage, Chris Knight, Hugo Mercier, Seán Roberts, JP de Ruiter, Manny Schegloff, Michael Silverstein, Marja-Leena Sorjonen, Dan Sperber, Mike Tomasello, Anna Wierzbicka, and Chip Zuckerman.

For generous comments and suggestions on the manuscript of this book, which have greatly helped improve it, I am grateful to Emma Cohen, Kensy Cooperrider, Daniel Dor, Robin Dunbar, Margie Enfield, Phil Laughlin, Weijian Meng, Hugo Mercier, Susan Perry, Danielle Pillet-Shore, Jack Sidnell, Oliver Traldi, Tom van Laer, Samantha Williams, and three anonymous readers for MIT Press.

For their expert and professional assistance, I thank Gus Wheeler (who prepared the figures), Weijian Meng (who assisted with preparation of the manuscript), Naomie Nguyen (who assisted with proofs), and Angela Terrill at Punctilious Marvelid for compiling the index.

I am sincerely grateful to my agents, Katinka Matson and Max Brockman, for their guidance and support and to my editor at MIT Press, Phil Laughlin.

And finally, with love, I thank the other Ns at Goldie—Na, Nyssa, and Nonnika—for brightening the locked-down world in which this book was written.

*

I dedicate this book to Nyssa and Nonnika. May they be good lawyers and better scientists.

Introduction

Language is the knife with which we cut out facts.
—Friedrich Waismann (1945)

When primate scientist John Gluck began his research career in the 1960s, he was taking newborn rhesus monkeys from their mothers and raising them alone in bare steel containers, to study the effects of social isolation. In time, he came to question why he was doing this, and would soon deeply regret the harm and suffering he had caused. In the midst of a successful scientific career, Gluck abandoned his research and applied himself instead to promoting animal welfare. With hindsight, he identified one factor of special importance in explaining how a good man can do bad things. That factor is language.

As a young scientist starting out, Gluck liked the language of the branch of psychology known as behaviorism because it signaled an intellectual stand. The behaviorist does not say that an animal is frightened, only that it is *avoidant*. He does not say that it is smart, only *accurate*. He does not say that the animal is hungry, only that it is *food deprived* or has a *latency to consumption*. That stand became part of Gluck's identity within the culture of scientists doing animal experiments. By using the idiom of his teachers and peers, Gluck had elided—some might say *erased*—the inner experiences of the animals he worked with. "If you must sanitize the language that is used to describe the procedures in regular use," Gluck wrote, "you have entered morally perilous territory."[1]

On his path into that perilous land, Gluck had exploited the power of language for two purposes. One was sense making: to create a version of reality that cohered with his chosen purposes and actions. The other was rationalization: to provide justifications for those actions. When he came to understand the power of words in creating a world and defending it, John Gluck discovered something fundamental. Just as language cannot create physical reality, it cannot merely reflect physical reality as it is. It always imposes a doubly-subjective vision, consisting of the views encoded in the language being spoken and the view of the speaker who chooses the words being used. Language is shaped by our subjective, purpose-calibrated view of reality. And in turn, our view of reality is shaped by language. Just as Gluck's old worldview was enabled by the language he used, so too would language play a role in recasting that worldview, in bringing about his personal and professional redemption. Gluck's story invokes one of the central ideas in this book: *We create our worlds by the language we use.*[2]

In this book, I explain what this means, but let me say here what it does *not* mean. Words do not give us direct control, magical or otherwise, over brute reality. For instance, in my time on Earth, nothing I could say would change the fact that I am subject to the force of gravity. We create worlds with language but this does not exempt us from being accountable to physical reality. This is why truth seeking—a quest that requires us to be maximally mindful of the biases that language and reasoning introduce—must be our highest calling.

Researchers of mind have long known that human rationality is not an ideal tool for truth seeking. Our patterns of perception and reasoning fall constant victim to an array of biases and shortcomings.[3] Much of this book is about the role that language plays in this. In their 2017 book, *The Enigma of Reason*, cognitive scientists Hugo Mercier and Dan Sperber argue that this doesn't mean human rationality is poorly adapted to its purpose. That conclusion would follow only if the evolved purpose of reason were to arrive at objective truth. Instead, Mercier and Sperber argue that reason evolved for another purpose. Human reason is the way it is—"flawed" if seen as a tool for classical logic in the privacy of your mind—because it is a *social* tool. Reason evolved for convincing and persuading other people, winning arguments with other people, defending and justifying actions and decisions to other people. These functions may be achieved regardless of whether the content of a proposition is true. I can benefit from convincing someone of something even when that thing is false.[4]

This is the tension between the "scientist" and the "lawyer" in the subtitle of this book. It is often said that human reasoning is not as balanced or dispassionate as we would like to think it is, that our inner scientist is in fact an inner lawyer.[5] The scientist seeks to know the truth, while the lawyer seeks to persuade. And in persuading, the lawyer seeks not to get at the truth but to get her way (or to get the way of those who pay her fee). She seeks not to explain but to defend. And notice that while the scientist may sometimes work alone, the lawyer's job is a necessarily social one, and language is her primary tool.

The idea that language is an infrastructure for social coordination and not for the transfer of information per se will help us understand some of its shortcomings, which we shall encounter in the first two parts of this book: why language seems to fail us in the ways it does, why it is so ambiguous and approximate, why it distracts and detracts, why it falls short when we try to describe an experience or capture an innermost feeling. At the same time, the idea that language is a coordination device will help us understand why it can be so good at the things it is good at: directing people's attention, framing situations in arbitrary ways, playing to people's biases, tuning our interactions, managing reputations, and regulating social life.

Arguments for the social function of human intellect go back to pioneering ideas in evolutionary psychology,[6] and language is central to those ideas. In this book, I focus not on the natural history of language's role in socially oriented reasoning but rather on the properties of language that shape its functions today. Language excels at reason giving, storytelling, and sense making: the quintessentially social qualities that characterize our species.

One of the most dangerous properties of language is that it allows us to say things that aren't true. The danger is not just that people may be misled, but that falsehood may be more effective than truth. Truth becomes a collateral victim of human sociality. The strength of human commitment to beliefs in supernatural entities and conspiracy theories—a kind of commitment found in human groups worldwide—draws precisely on the disconnect between a statement and the reality it claims to describe. If a group of people collectively state a belief in something that is likely to be false, then the statement, far from seeding doubt, will work as an honest signal of each individual's commitment to the group.[7] Author Curtis Yarvin explains the attraction of improbable ideas in building social movements. For the purpose of social allegiance, it's actually better if the belief that people coordinate around is patently false: "Nonsense is a more effective organizing tool than the truth. . . . To believe in nonsense is an unforgeable demonstration of loyalty. It serves as a political uniform. And if you have a uniform, you have an army."[8] This is all very well if your only goal is to secure loyalty in defending a position, but reality will come for you at some point. While real soldiers may pledge allegiance to magical ideas, they are ultimately in the business of physical force, not magic but brute reality par excellence. Once a bullet is flying, neither words nor the beliefs they express can stop it.

This is why you cannot say that there is no reality beyond our ways of talking, or that reality is whatever we say it is. That caricature of postmodernist thought—as if anybody really lived by it—makes no sense in a world in which our species evolved by natural selection, in which we depend on food, air, water, light, and avoidance of injury to live through each new day. Those who claim to doubt objective reality will still defer to that reality in lawful and predictable ways. As the philosopher David Hume quipped, if you are skeptical that a real world exists, then you are welcome to leave via the second-floor window.[9]

But heeding physical reality as a matter of survival is quite a different matter from coordinating around reality for social purposes. When we talk, our words create the *versions of* reality—whether social or physical—that we agree to coordinate around, for example, when we want to affiliate with someone, influence someone, recruit somebody's help, or collectively evaluate a situation and work out what has happened, why, and what action to take. It's only through our publicly *shared versions* of reality that social coordination is possible. And it is always just *one* version of reality that we coordinate around at a time. That version is the one we create with words.

*

Do you control language or does language control you? Does your act of describing an experience alter that experience forever? Are you putty in the hands of a compelling narrative or can you think for yourself? In this book, we find answers to these questions in far-apart fields of the cognitive and social sciences. We delve into research in linguistics, anthropology, cognitive psychology, sociology, and communications to find out what language is good for, what it does for us, and what it does *to* us. We discover some of the many ways in which language giveth and taketh away.

In part I (chapters 1 to 3), we begin with the question of how words relate to physical reality. There is, of course, a reality beyond human perceptions and beliefs. But as evolved creatures, we have access to only a thin slice. Our perceptual systems deliver a massively stripped-back version of the real world. This is good because it reduces the computational complexity involved in interacting with our surroundings. Simplifying matters—without oversimplifying them—is necessary. It gives us the information we need for survival without being overloaded or paralyzed. Right now you are surrounded by electromagnetic radiation on a spectrum ranging from the shortest gamma rays to the longest radio waves, but you can only perceive a tiny band of that radiation, visible to you as the color spectrum. In turn, human language imposes on this tiny band a second radical simplification. We *name* only a fraction of the perceptible distinctions available in that already-narrow range.

We shall see that the two processes of abstraction—from reality to perception and from perception to language—serve different functions. While perception reduces reality to make it easier to navigate the physical world, word meanings further reduce complexity for navigating the *social* world. If perceptual categories provide individuals with anchors to reality, *linguistic* categories provide shared moorings for social coordination in groups. Perception is private; language is public.[10] The two things provide solutions to very different kinds of problem.

Using language to simplify reality is not only the business of ordinary social sense making; it is also important in scientific progress. When a scientist makes a breakthrough, they yield a sharable narrative about some piece of reality. This narrative reduces the work involved in making predictions about that piece of reality. In turn, it enables people to coordinate around questions of how to intervene in our environment in useful ways. Language is key. We use it to reduce computational complexity in features of our world—real and imagined—when we need to coordinate around those features.[11]

All human languages categorize natural phenomena ranging from plants and trees to colors to smells to the structure and movements of the human body. As we shall see, the languages of the world show a form of *constrained diversity*. All languages capture only a tiny part of reality, and they do so in similar ways—up to a point. Beyond that point, languages can vary widely in what they capture. Constrained diversity means that languages can vary but not without limit. Words for physical objects and events—from plant species names to color terms to kinship terms to words for parts of the body and human emotions—will always show some degree of respect for the structure of physical reality.

In part II (chapters 4 to 7), we explore how language can tamper with our perceptions, memories, and processes of reasoning, in sometimes surprising ways. More than a century of ingenious experimentation in the psychology of language reveals that the meanings of words do not have transparent or straightforward links to the reality they describe nor to the mental images and ideas they denote. Far from it. We shall see that not only do our words simplify and skew our perceptions, they can alter and overwrite them, changing our memories and beliefs about things we've experienced firsthand. Choice of words can prime us, directing our attention toward some things and away from others. And the effects of misdirection are profound. They underpin the incorrigible biases that characterize human decision making, and in turn they can be exploited in influencing people's attention and reasoning. One of our most important weapons against misinformation is to be aware of these biases, in others and in ourselves. Language is *choice architecture* for thinking and social action.[12] We may yield to it quite unknowingly or we may take control of it through mindful attention to its design. And because different languages feature different kinds of meanings and structures—different architectures—this introduces the possibility of *linguistic relativity*: the idea that if a language can nudge our thoughts and perceptions then different languages can nudge us in different ways.

These effects of nudging and skewing our thinking at a microlevel can be viewed as bugs from the point of view of the person who is affected. But they are also features because they reduce the costs involved in processing language, and because they can be exploited in influencing people. Nowhere is this more apparent than in the use of framing, a key tool of persuasion.

In part III (chapters 8 to 11), we scale up, examining the power of framing, stories, and narratives in persuasion, sense making, and social cohesion. We open with two powerful principles in the manipulation of information. One is the tendency to use language strategically, in an artful form of "conjugation" described by the philosopher Bertrand Russell. We might say, *I am firm*, but *He is pig-headed*, choosing markedly different ways to describe the same quality in two people. A corollary of Russell's principle is that when you choose a framing, that choice reveals something about *you*. By a principle of inversion noticed by the philosopher Ludwig Wittgenstein, we can use a person's words as a measure not of the thing this person describes but as a measure of their stance toward that thing, and thereby as a measure of the person. Through the chapters of part III, we explore the power of these principles in public discourse, first through case studies of strategic wording in media language and then through an examination of the structure and power of storytelling and narrative.

We shall see that storytelling is central to human affairs, not only in the creative arts but in the everyday narratives that pepper our conversations. Narrative informs us, transports us, and engages us through emotional connections that attract and hold our attention and bind us socially with our co-audience members. Stories convey the practical and cultural wisdom of myths and teachings and help us make sense of our social worlds. And more locally, we use storytelling to manage reputations, an important part of our species' particularly complex and intense form of social group organization.

In the book's concluding chapter, we reflect on implications of what we've learned about the things that language does for us and to us. These are implications for human agency and freedom of thought and action in a physical world that demands our respect. In order to coordinate around reality for social and practical purposes, we rely on language for shared moorings. Most importantly, I think, the implications of language's shortcomings concern our obligations to ourselves and to our fellow users of humankind's most powerful and transformative invention.

I Mapped by Language

1   Coordinating around Reality

Solving a problem simply means representing it so as to make the solution transparent.

—Herbert Simon (1981)

The scene is a tropical dry forest floor in the Lomas de Barbudal Biological Reserve, northwest Costa Rica.[1] Two wild white-faced capuchins—a smallish species of monkey around a foot and a half tall and weighing about the same as a newborn baby—scuttle along looking for food. They stop and together turn their attention to something nearby. One hops on the other's back, and they form the overlord posture, their little heads stacked one on top of the other like a totem pole.[2] As one, they scream at their common focus of attention.[3] This coordinated action is how capuchins signal and build coalitions in their societies. Once coalition-mates have built a bond, they may later protect each other or call on each other for help when needed. But who—or what—are these two capuchins threatening?

It's a patch of dirt. As it happens, capuchin monkeys engage more often in pseudo-aggressive incidents than in real encounters. When they get together to display aggression toward something harmless like dirt or an eggshell, this shows us that the function of coordination is not just about defeating a threat but also about building a social structure.[4] When individuals build coalitions through coordination, they become merged as agents. They work as one. To achieve this, they need landmarks to coordinate around. Even a patch of dirt will do.

This is one sense of *coordination* that we will encounter in this book: adopting a common stance toward a landmark, a shared focus of attention. Many species engage in this, but we humans have remarkable capacities to use such landmarks as cognitive tools for achieving coordination even in the absence of communication, in a kind of virtual mind reading.

Imagine you are a parachutist coming down in unknown territory. You are with another parachutist who is somewhere in the same area, but neither of you knows where the other has landed. You have no way of communicating. But you need to find each other, and fast, if you are going to be rescued. Your one chance is the map shown in figure 1.1.[5]

You are both in possession of the map, and you each know that the other has it. Can the two of you figure out how to coordinate your movements and meet in the same place? 'Does the map suggest some particular meeting place so unambiguously that each will be confident that the other reads the same suggestion with confidence?'[6] Where would *you* go to meet the other parachutist?

The scenario and map are from a 1960 study by economist Thomas Schelling. In Schelling's experiment, most people said they would meet at

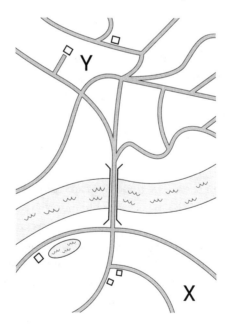

Figure 1.1
Schelling's map: Two parachutists, at points X and Y, must coordinate and find each other by going to where they think the other will go, each knowing that the other has the same map. After Thomas C. Schelling, *The Strategy of Conflict* (Cambridge, MA: Harvard University Press, 1960), 55.

the bridge.[7] It doesn't seem like rocket science, but it's actually remarkable that we can pull this off so reliably. We appear to be the only species that can achieve entirely ad hoc coordination of this kind *without communication.*[8] This demands a certain kind of "mind reading" or, more accurately, not reading but imagining or speculating.[9] We take into account what the other person knows, what we believe that person knows about what we know, and how that mutual knowledge should factor into our current shared task of trying to coordinate our behavior. The things we say provide landmarks of this kind, and we actively imagine where our minds are supposed to meet. If you hear someone say, *It was too slow,* this vague proposition could mean a million things, but if you know the context, you will readily use the words as a map to arrive at a much more specific understanding. We have a subjective sense that everything comes through in the words, that the words themselves carry all the meaning. But in truth, our words are as sketchy as Schelling's hand-drawn map, leaving out almost every feature of the landscape, and requiring us to imagine where in the world we are supposed to come together.

This is a second sense of *coordination* that we will encounter in this book: when we use language in interaction, we draw on landmarks to infer common solutions to the problem of converging in thought and action. The reason we are forced to rely on inference is that we have no recourse to telepathy. When we coordinate around the maps that language draws for us, we naturally fill in the details by imagining what must be there. Language is a portable device for constructing such landmarks at will.

As a coordination device, language is a tool of human *agency*, both individual and shared. Agency can be defined as our capacity to do things and make things happen, where this capacity entails some degree of control and some degree of accountability. Words are our most powerful tools. Students of the Stanislavski acting method are taught to regard their every spoken line—along with their every move on stage—as pursuing a task, solving a problem, carrying out an action. At every point, an actor must ask: What am I trying to make the other person *do*? With words, we act both *on* other people and *with* other people, for agency is situated in the individual *and* is distributed across individuals.

We find it natural to think of ourselves as individuals when it comes to our personal agency. By coordinating socially, separate individuals may mutually influence one another, but in reality, our agency is distributed.

At every step, we enhance our individual agency using person-extending technologies from levers and wedges to bicycles and smartphones. These technologies are *interfaces* that translate or transform our actions beyond what our bodies alone could do.

An interface for coordination requires mutual tuning between those who would coordinate. Here is an example of such tuning in the natural world. In the jungles of Kibale National Park in southwestern Uganda, primates and birds play a special role in the ecology. These day-active creatures are the primary seed dispersers for rainforest plants, eating ripe fruits and spreading the seeds in droppings. Three thousand kilometers away, an entirely different ecology is found in the rainforests of Ranomafana National Park, across the Mozambique Channel in southeastern Madagascar. There, the main seed dispersers are lemurs. They are different from Kibale's primates and birds in a specific way: they are active at night and are red-green color-blind. A team of biologists measured the color contrast between ripe fruits and leaf backgrounds in the two parks and found a difference: "Fruits in Uganda have higher contrast against leaf background in the red–green and luminance channels whereas fruits in Madagascar contrast more in the yellow–blue channel."[10] What explains this? The answer is evolution by natural selection. If an individual plant's fruit happens to be more visible to the animals that would eat it and thereby disperse its seed, then that plant is more likely to have its seeds dispersed. As long as differences in fruit color are genetically inherited by each generation of plants, the fruits in time will become more clearly visible to the relevant seed-dispersing animals in each area.

The Madagascar fruits are *tuned to* the local lemurs' visual systems. The fruits show higher color contrast in the yellow-blue channel because that's what makes them more easily noticed by the red-green color-blind lemurs. The fruit's color is an evolved interface between the seed-bearing edible fruits and the visual systems of the lemurs. By producing fruits of a certain color, these forest plants use light waves to go beyond their skins, influencing another species at a distance, in this case for mutual benefit. With the fruit-color interface, these two life forms—the plants and the lemurs—can coordinate.

We humans show a similar form of interdependence for coordination. Among the resources we mobilize to extend our agency are other people. Language is our interface with them and our tool for mobilizing them. Language is the most flexible, powerful, and all-pervasive agency-extending technology we have. Many would say that language is a way of conveying experience and ideas to other people, but it does not transfer the contents of what we have in mind. Rather, it invites people to imagine what we have in mind.[11] As with the Madagascan forest fruits, the interface of language is tuned to exploit our audience's habits of attention and interest.[12] We use language to create purpose-built landmarks for coordination, whether we are trying to enlist somebody's help for our ends, offer them help for their ends, or come together with someone for shared goals. Coordination does not always mean mutual benefit or altruistic motives. Two top tennis players have to coordinate around the rules of tennis and the play of the ball, yet they are fighting tooth and nail to defeat one another. Two people may be having a bitter disagreement, but to have it out, they will still need to coordinate around the words they are using and around the turn-taking rules of social interaction.

Language allows us to coordinate with each other in movement and action, as well as in value and identity. It does this by exploiting a rarefied sort of social cognition, likely only found in humans. When a surgeon turns to her assistant and says "Scalpel," this one-word linguistic act—we might call it a command or a request—is, first and foremost, an instruction for mutual coordination.[13] The key to understanding this is that when you use language, you are never just saying something. You are doing something. With words, you act on those around you, to help them, influence them, build affiliations with them.

Think of language like the interface that allows you to operate your car. We drive along, with near-zero effort, pressing pedals and buttons, turning wheels and levers. In ways that are mysterious to most of us, these actions control the inner workings of the car. With language, we control the inner workings of other people. Things are happening under the hood that few of us have any idea about. The interface of words hides most of the underlying reality that it operates on. But there's a catch: when you control the device, the device controls you. You don't just use the pedals and buttons to operate on another person. The same pedals and buttons are operating on you in return.

One job of the interface of language is to deal with the inner workings of conversation, the to-and-fro of turns and moves, interactional systems of turn taking, sequence organization, and repair. This is the infrastructure for interaction.[14] In this book, I focus more on the interface built from the meanings of our words, constructions, phrases, and stories—meanings that we create and put into each other's environment when we use language. In the chapters that follow, we examine how language captures information; how it plays on our attention, our thoughts, and our understandings; and how it helps us make sense of the world, of ourselves, and of each other through the meanings that language allows us to coordinate around. At the core of this will be the link between language and reality.

Language has a complicated relationship with reality. One reason is that reality comes in two kinds. *Brute reality*—in the realm of natural causes—can be captured by language only in the most partial, subjective, and fragmentary ways. It isn't affected by whether we talk about it or by how we choose to describe it or frame it. By complete contrast, *social reality*—the realm of rights, duties, and institutions—cannot exist without language.[15]

Another reason is that language itself has a foot in both realities. Languages rely on brute reality to be possible at all. If it is going to be learned, used, and transmitted, any piece or system of language must be carried by physical reality—for instance, on light waves and sound waves—in order to be perceived. Language can be used to *describe* both brute reality and social reality, but the tools it uses to do so—essentially, word meanings—are bits of social reality in the classic sense. The line between my property and my neighbor's property has the meaning it has because linguistic acts have made it so, and we all agree to abide by those acts (which are, by the way, ultimately backed up by the state's monopoly on force—back to brute reality). In other words, my property is mine because we all agree that it is, and we act in accordance with that agreement. If my neighbor trespasses on my property, she will not be surprised if, when caught, I am surprised at her actions and may even want to hold her to account. In the same way, the English words *dog, table,* and *walk* refer to the things they do because we agree that they do, or at least we act as if we had made such an agreement. We similarly anticipate that others will be surprised and even disposed to sanction us if we fail to keep to that agreement (for example, by using the word *dog* to refer to a cat).

Brute reality is unaffected by our norms. It is not negotiable in the same way that property rights or word meanings might be. Brute reality is "that which, when you stop believing in it, doesn't go away."[16] These words by author Philip K. Dick capture the incorrigible existence of a real, physical brute world. Gravity pulls you down. Water boils when you heat it. Matchsticks snap when you bend them. A dose of cyanide will kill you. You can say what you like about these statements but your beliefs or opinions will have no effect on whether they are true. This is not to say that our grip on reality isn't subjective. Of course, how you access reality depends on what kind of body you have.[17] Thanks to the nature of the human auditory system, the average person can't hear sounds at a frequency of 30 kHz. But this doesn't make those sounds any less real. A dog can hear them just fine. We might say that they *aren't real for humans*. They don't affect us, and so they can't interest us or influence our decisions, at least not in everyday life. It's the things we can detect that have captured our attention and interest to our advantage through our species' evolutionary history: voices, hailstorms, rocks, bears, breakages, heat, earth, wind, fire, water, chairs, guns, parties, and especially, other people.

Let's see just how narrow a slice of reality we normally have access to. We are each of us surrounded by electromagnetic radiation, with wavelengths that vary by many orders along a continuous spectrum. Through our evolved visual systems, our bodies deliver only a small slice of that reality, the slice that we call visible light. The rest is literally invisible to us (figure 1.2).

Perception is a simplified user interface between us and the world.[18] Our perceptions "have not been shaped to make it easy to know the true structure of the world but instead to *hide its complexity*."[19] They "have been

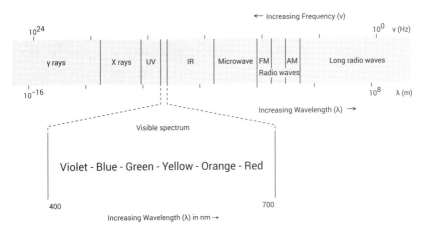

Figure 1.2
The spectrum of electromagnetic radiation, highlighting the part that is directly perceivable by humans. Image adapted from https://upload.wikimedia.org/wikipedia /commons/3/30/EM_spectrumrevised.png.

shaped by natural selection to make it easier for us to act effectively in the world."[20] This means that it is more important for our perceptions to be useful than to be true. Of course, it is more useful to know the truth than to believe a lie. But it's also often more useful not to know the *whole* truth. We are better off knowing only know what we *need* to know.

Think back to your car's user interface. You don't engage directly with the engine, the hydraulic system, the electrical system. You engage with much simpler mediating structures: the gas pedal, the brake pedal, the steering wheel, the indicator lever. The user interface is many orders simpler than the true workings of the car. You don't need to know how the movements of your feet and hands cause the car to slow down or speed up, reverse or turn. In fact, you are better off not knowing those things, at least for the purpose of driving around. The simpler the interface, the fewer demands it makes on us, freeing us up for other things. It reduces cognitive cost. Our senses of sight, smell, hearing, taste, and touch—designed by the merciless processes of evolution—follow this principle.

With vision, do we see what is actually there? "The frog does not detect flies, it detects small, moving, black spots of about the right size."[21] Vision scientist David Marr explains why evolution might result in perceptions that do not present reality as it is. The perception need only provide an organism with "sufficient information for it to survive":[22] "Natural selection is a search procedure that yields *satisficing* solutions, not optimal solutions."[23] Satisficing can be defined as motivated stopping:[24] When you've arrived at a solution that's *good enough*, you cut your losses and move on to the next thing.

If our systems of perception provide interfaces that simplify reality in order that our decision making may be more efficient, this would explain why our *perception* delivers such sparse mapping of our world, but it wouldn't explain the *linguistic* facts. While our perceptions capture only a small set of possible distinctions in brute reality, words make *many orders fewer distinctions* again. The visible spectrum of light is a tiny slice of the full spectrum of electromagnetic radiation, though even within that spectrum, more than 2 million distinctions in color can be discerned.[25] In turn, our vocabularies for color reduce that number of distinctions by many orders, usually coming down to only a handful of words for basic color categories (*red, green, blue*) or at best a few dozen or so technical words for color distinctions in a language (see figure 1.3).

Figure 1.3
Two layers of simplification: reality is reduced by perception, perception is reduced by language.

Why have two interfaces that successively simplify and hide reality? Because the two interfaces serve two different purposes.

Perception is an interface between reality and an individual. It delivers a version of reality that is good enough for individual decisions and action—good enough for *individual agency*. Perception simplifies reality in a way that reduces costs for individuals, without reducing these costs so much as to cause an intolerable level of error in our interactions with the real world.

In turn, and by contrast, language is an *interface between individuals*. It delivers a rendition of reality that is good enough for coordinating *joint* decisions and actions. Good enough for *distributed* agency. Language simplifies our perceptions and concepts in a way that reduces costs, yet without reducing those costs so much as to prevent us from coordinating successfully in our interactions with other people. A system for social coordination can serve its function with information that is much more abstract and partial than what is needed for individual decision making and action. The two interfaces—perception as an interface with the world and language as an interface between people—successively simplify reality.

It's difficult to overstate how poor language is at capturing brute reality, or at transferring the richness of people's perception or experience. Suppose I say to you, *Jo drives a red car*. Now, what if I ask you to do a painting of the car as you see it in your mind? Which exact shade of red do you choose?

What sort of car is it? What if I asked you to pick out Jo's car in a parking lot? Could you do it? Not likely if there were ten red cars of slightly different shades. Or suppose I describe Jo's face. Would you be able to pick her out from a lineup of ten similar-looking people, based solely on my verbal description? Even assuming you are a skilled portrait artist, could you draw her face accurately from my words alone? Language provides nowhere near the required level of information for the task. And not only that, as we'll see, language distracts us in various ways. It can divert our attention and mess with our memories.

Now let's turn to the relation between language and the second type of reality: social reality. A true statement about brute reality—for example, *These potatoes will fall if I drop them*—will remain true no matter what people believe. By contrast, a statement about *social* reality—for example, *These potatoes belong to me*—is a statement about my rights and duties. The statement is entirely dependent on people's beliefs. It is true *because of* an agreement among people to treat it as true, whether that agreement is tacit or explicit. I can sell the potatoes or give them away. These are both ways of transferring the rights and duties I have over them, and thus of rendering untrue the statement that "they belong to me".

The philosopher Elizabeth Anscombe introduced this distinction between brute and social reality by comparing two ways of describing a single situation.[26] She imagines that someone delivers a shipment of potatoes to her house. Two descriptions are: (1) *He had potatoes carted to my house and left there* and (2) *The potatoes came into my possession*. The first sentence is a physical description of a person's movements in relations to some objects and places. It describes brute reality—things that can be physically observed. The second sentence describes a different kind of reality. You would not be able to tell by physically examining the potatoes who they belonged to. The potatoes are edible when cooked. They can block someone's path. These are matters of brute reality. But when we say that somebody has the right to cook and eat them or the duty to move them out of the way, we are talking about social reality. My right to eat them or my duty to remove them is not caused by brute facts but by social, interpersonal agreements about ownership—agreements that are created by, or at least backed up by, language.

The philosopher Wilfred Sellars presented a similar contrast using the example of chess.[27] One situation, two descriptions: (1) *There is an open diagonal space between this white piece of wood and that red piece of wood*, (2) *My bishop is checking his king*. The first describes a physical situation and could be roughly rendered in any language and understood and evaluated by anybody in the world on the basis of the words in the one-sentence description (assuming we know what the words *diagonal, wood, white, red,* mean). But the second requires knowledge of the regulations of chess and of the social rights and duties that chess entails. Not only that, but the facts at hand—what a bishop can do, how check is defined—are true only because people agree to treat them as being true. People can stop Sellars's second statement from being true if they simply change the rules of the game—for example, by deciding to agree that bishops cannot move diagonally. But no form of agreement would stop the first one from being true (unless, of course, the meanings of the words in the statement are changed in meaning; we will encounter examples of this later in the book). Whatever the game's rules, the white piece of wood will stand in the same spatial relationship to the red one.

The relation between the two realities is not symmetrical. Legalities are a classic example of social reality. How are laws upheld? By the threat of physical force. Brute reality. This is why political power—mostly a matter of institutionalized rights and duties—is ultimately grounded in physical facts. A baton to the head will hurt, no matter who you vote for. The political sociologist Max Weber defined the state as an entity with a monopoly on the legitimate use of physical force.[28] Whether force is legitimate can be contested (as social reality), but the physical effects of the force cannot. The effects of force are in the realm of brute reality. They are not affected by our interpretations or our perspectives, and this is what makes physical facts the ultimate arbiter of power in human affairs. In this sense, brute reality is the bedrock of all of our social institutions.

It is sometimes argued that brute reality is trumped by social power, that "facts" are illusory, as if anyone with power can decide what is true and what is not. But social power can only change social facts. Ownership, for example, can readily be negotiated—rendered untrue, if you like—by the use of force and its nonnegotiable effects. If someone with a knife deprives me of my rights to the cash in my wallet, this works because of the physical fact that the knife would cause me harm. A mugger's power to overturn the social fact of ownership comes directly from physical facts. I can contest it by producing a bigger knife. Or if I threaten the mugger with prosecution, this again is based in physical facts—the brute denial of physical freedom by imprisonment.

Research in the cognitive science of meaning in language has been primarily concerned with the relationship between language and brute reality. When linguistic anthropologist John Lucy asked, "Does the particular language we speak influence the way we think about reality?"[29] by "reality," he means brute reality, as in statements like, *This stone is next to that stone* or *There is snow on Mount Everest*.[30] Of course, physical facts exist without language, but we cannot coordinate around those facts—for example, to agree on them—unless we put them into words. Take a simple statement like, *There are two fish in this pond*. If a cod and a grouper are in the pond, the statement is true—but not if the creatures are a cod and a squid. Or at least, not if we are speaking *English*. If the statement were translated into the Lao language, the word *paa* (fish) would in fact cover squid. So the statement *There are two fish in this pool* (in the Lao language: *sa nii mii paa sòòng too*) would be true. (In the same way, $2+2=11$ is true but only if we're using base 3.) How we evaluate the truth of a statement about brute reality must depend on the language we are using to describe that bit of reality. There are some seven thousand languages in the world, and so there is plenty of scope for failure to calibrate on even the most basic facts.[31]

If you want to bring something into shared reality for the purpose of social coordination—whether it's to inform somebody, cooperate with somebody, or influence somebody—you have to describe it, or at the very least label it. Even the ideally objective pursuit of science is unable to escape the framing effects of language. Like all cumulative culture, science is constructed on report, reason, debate, negotiation, justification, consensus, and, most important, coordination. And all of these things depend on language. Even something as fundamental as particle physics depends on language in a particular way. I don't mean that particle physics wouldn't exist if we didn't describe it. Particle physics is part of brute reality and so it will carry on independent of any human agreement or understanding of what it is. But consider this remark by computer scientist Michael I. Jordan, referring to the "infinite potential well" model in quantum physics, which studies how a single particle behaves in a small, enclosed space:[32] "A particle in a potential well is optimizing a function called the Lagrangian function. The particle doesn't know that. There's no algorithm running that does that. It just happens. It's a description mathematically of something that helps us understand as analysts what's happening."

Jordan's remark calls to mind long-held debates on the relation between reality and our descriptions of it by physicists through the twentieth century and beyond. Niels Bohr, in the context of his famous debates with Einstein a century ago, stated: "There is no quantum world. This is only an abstract physical description. It is wrong to think that the task of physics is to find out how nature is. Physics concerns what we can *say* about nature."[33] David Bohm argues that human thought is "fragmented" in a way that reality is not, and that we mistake our linguistically structured patterns of thought for reality itself rather than as "merely convenient features of description and analysis."[34] David Deutsch writes that "languages are theories" which are "invented and selected for their ability to solve problems."[35] Douglas Hofstadter and Emmanuel Sander explore the extraordinary importance of analogy in scientific thinking, made possible by the "categorization engine" we call language.[36] And Sean Carroll says that our ways of talking are "an absolutely crucial part of how we apprehend reality."[37]

As these ideas all recognize, if we are going to achieve a collective understanding, it is not enough for someone just to understand a piece of reality.[38] We need ways to *coordinate around* that understanding of reality, and for that, we need words. We need *descriptions* of what we are going to coordinate around, even if we cannot perfectly capture the truth. We don't need to capture the truth—at least not the whole truth. What we need are conceptual landmarks to coordinate around, so that we may succeed in our shared objectives. A verbal description is not necessary for an individual analyst to understand something, but it is necessary for an individual analyst to *convey* or *share* that understanding, for example in reporting it, teaching it, or inviting somebody to coordinate around it. The "us" in Jordan's comment—"it's a description of something that helps *us* understand"—is a group of people with shared goals, a corporate agent, such as a team of scientists who are building a new technology.

This is why language can be called a *collective cognitive activity*, in the words of cognitive scientists Edwin Hutchins and Christine Johnson.[39] Language gives us a way to couple with others in interaction, but not through direct physical connection (as when a coffee mug couples me with my coffee)[40] or direct, lossless transfer of information (as when you press Send and the text on your phone screen appears in identical form on mine). Language is unlike either of these things because it is neither direct physical manipulation[41] nor direct reading or replication of a mental state. Any plausible explanation of how language works has to appeal to nature and not magic. Hence, a *no-telepathy assumption*: "No mind can influence another except via mediating structure."[42] In the case of language, that mediating structure is provided by words, gestures, and the rules of grammar. It is a shared structure for calibration and coordination of thought and action. Individuals must of course still individually process and represent meanings in language.[43] Ultimately, when we have learned a language, our minds have become "organized by structure created by other individuals."[44] We are all mutually implicated in the collective significance of our languages.

2 Schelling's Game

Every living creature is in fact a sort of lock, whose wards and springs presuppose special forms of key.

—William James (1884)

Imagine you are participating in an experiment. The experimenter puts you in a room on your own and tells you that you have a partner in the experiment, someone you've never met, who is sitting in a room nearby, also on his own. You have no way to communicate with that person. Here is your instruction:

> You are to divide $100 into two piles, labeled A and B. Your partner is to divide another $100 into two piles labeled A and B. If you allot the same amounts to A and B, respectively, that your partner does, each of you gets $100; if your counts differ from his, neither of you gets anything.

Can you guess what the most popular solution is? That's right. Ninety percent of people in Schelling's experiment converged on the obvious: fifty-fifty.

Schelling's coordination problems are famous for showing that strangers are able to converge in brand-new situations with no discussion or conferral. But the situation that Schelling put his subjects in is just one special case of coordination problem.[1] The philosopher Margaret Gilbert explains: "Where it is not possible for the parties to make an agreement about who will do what, or otherwise to communicate their intentions, and there is no special background knowledge, the parties have a genuine problem: Should each make a random choice of action, the chances of achieving the desired coordination of actions are not good."[2] But of course, most of the time we do have the opportunity to make an agreement, and we do share relevant background knowledge. Most of the time we are able to follow convention. Take the case of traffic rules. The most important traffic rule of all tells us which side of the road to drive on. As the philosopher David Lewis wrote, "It matters little to anyone whether he drives in the left or the right lane, provided the others do likewise."[3] We don't leave this to chance.[4] It is a convention, codified in law.

Whether we rely on conventions, laws, or clever guessing, coordination has two crucial elements. First, whether one person's action is the correct one will depend on what the other person does. In the case of the parachutists, your choice to go to the bridge will be the right decision only if the other parachutist also goes to the bridge. Second, the two people involved have aligned incentives: they will both prefer it if they succeed in meeting in the same place on the map, regardless of what place that is.[5]

Schelling's findings led him to a *theory of interdependent decision*:[6]

> People *can* often concert their intentions or expectations with others if each knows that the other is trying to do the same. Most situations—perhaps every situation for people who are practiced at this kind of game—provide some clue for coordinating behavior, some focal point for each person's expectation of what the other expects him to expect to be expected to do. Finding the key, or rather finding *a* key—any key that is mutually recognised as the key becomes *the* key—may depend on imagination more than logic, it may depend on precedent, accidental arrangement, symmetry, aesthetic or geometric arrangement, casuistic reasoning, and who the parties are and what they know about each other.

There are many more examples of these kinds of coordination problems.[7] Here are some:

- Call "heads" or "tails." If you and your partner call the same, you both win a prize.

- Circle one of the numbers listed in the line below. You win if you all succeed in circling the same number.

  7   100   13   261   99   555

- Name some amount of money. If you all name the same amount, you can have as much as you named.

- Suppose you and I are talking on the telephone and we are unexpectedly cut off after three minutes. We both want the connection restored immediately, which it will be if and only if one of us calls back while the other waits. It matters little to either of us whether he is the one to call back or the one to wait. We must each choose whether to call back, each according to his expectation of the other's choice, in order to call back if and only if the other waits.

We are so practiced at solving coordination problems like these that we hardly notice we are solving them at almost every turn.

Solutions to Schelling's games have something in common: the thing that people coordinate around will always have "some kind of prominence or conspicuousness."[8] That conspicuousness should be apparent to both parties. Recall that there is only one bridge on the map in figure 1.1. It is near the center of the image, and most roads lead to it. People readily see it as the best thing to coordinate around. This is not just because people find the bridge prominent. It is because they understand that anybody else would also recognize this prominence.

When openly or mutually prominent solutions to coordination problems are available, then people can not only increase the likelihood of successful coordination; they also reduce the costs. Schelling's coordination games are remarkable because people solve them without needing any kind of communication at all. These sorts of solution relieve us of the need for explicit bargaining or negotiation so that we may get on with whatever is next in the stack of things to deal with.

You might wonder how often in everyday life you are faced with a coordination game of this kind. The answer is: all the time. Every time you talk to somebody. Language is our most important tool for achieving social coordination, and using language is itself a coordination game.[9] Becoming highly practiced at using language means recognizing the prominent features that word meanings provide, just as the parachutists' map provides prominent landmarks for anyone who looks. And with language, as with the parachutists, the map is shared and known to be shared. When it comes to using language, we are all, as Schelling put it, highly practiced at this kind of game.

This point underpins one of the central ideas I want to convey in this book. The idea is that words and other bits of language are none other than *highly practiced solutions to coordination games*.

Take a simple word like *spoon*. Imagine the sentences I might use it in. *Can you pass me a spoon? This spoon's dirty. You need a fork and spoon to eat spaghetti.* If the function of this word were to capture a piece of reality, it would be a rather blunt tool for that. The examples of *spoon* that you just read gave you only the most schematic information about the objects I might have been referring to. Was I referring to metal or plastic spoons? Stainless steel or silver? What size? What color? Damaged or in mint condition? The word *spoon* alone gives you none of this, although I might have all those details in mind. The word's function cannot be to convey the details of my mental image—or at least it would be inadequate for that function. But if the function of the word were to provide a useful landmark for us to coordinate around, it would be just good enough.[10] If you're fetching a spoon for me, you scan the possibilities for something that will fit the description and provide the solution to the coordination problem at hand. The word *spoon* abstracts from the differences between individual spoons and is a historically practiced solution to the frequently occurring need for coordinating our behavior around the things we agree to call spoons. This is what psychologist Roger Brown meant when he said that the meaning of the English word *spoon* is grounded in "the community-wide practice of treating spoons as equivalent but different from knives and forks." The word is a coordination device.[11]

What information does a word like *spoon* need to encode? It needs to hit a happy medium between being not so vague as to result in a failure to coordinate but no more specific than that. A basic level of meaning is "just right." Just right for what? For achieving coordination with others in social interaction. Most of our words are established coordination devices, and when we use them, we receive immediate feedback on how effective they have been in context. That feedback is not incorporated into purely referential views of meaning because they focus on the links joining word, mind, and thing, and they bracket out the actual functional context for words as public entities.

For frequently recurring coordination problems, words like *spoon* are so easy to access and use that we often feel as if the word simply encodes the information we have in mind. We don't notice how imprecise the word is because it is so well tuned to the situations we use it in. Those situations occur over and over. But there are still plenty of situations that aren't just repeats of what we've seen before. You know the feeling of wanting to say something and having trouble finding the right word. That's when the problem of coordinating through language comes to the surface.

Suppose you are on the phone with a friend and you want to mention someone you both know. You need to agree on who you're talking about. As it happens, we have well-practiced solutions to this coordination problem. Personal names serve the function.[12] But what happens when you can't remember a person's name? Here is an example from a recording of a phone conversation:[13]

Ann: I heard you were at the beach yesterday. <u>What's her name—oh, you know, the tall redhead that lives across the street from Larry? The one who drove him to work the day his car was</u>—

Ben: Oh! Gina!

Ann: Yeah, Gina. She said she saw you at the beach yesterday.

Ann can't remember Gina's name, but they solve the coordination problem by means of other landmarks. She's tall. She's a redhead. She lives across the street from Larry. She drove him to work once. Now these are not just facts about Gina; they are also things that Ann figures Ben also knows about. They are *mutually conspicuous* landmarks in Ben and Ann's common knowledge.[14]

This example shows that when we need to coordinate on something but don't have access to practiced solutions such as personal names, we can still manage pretty well, and we can quickly converge on efficient solutions if given the chance. In an experiment designed to tap into this process,[15] two people sat in the same room but were separated by a screen and could not see each other. One of the people had the role of director. In front of the director was an array of tangram figures, laid out in a set order (see figure 2.1 for an example).

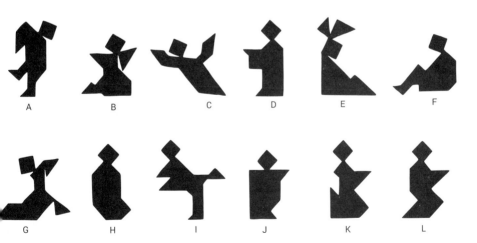

Figure 2.1

Array of tangram figures arranged by directors and matchers. After Herbert H. Clark and Deanna Wilkes-Gibbs. "Referring as a Collaborative Process." *Cognition* 22, no. 1 (1986): 1–39, https://doi.org/10.1016/0010-0277(86)90010-7.

The other person had the role of matcher. The matcher had the same set of tangram figures in front of her but laid out in a different order. The director's task was to instruct the matcher to lay the figures out in the order that he could see. As you can see in figure 2.1, the figures all evoke a human form. English vocabulary isn't much help in differentiating these, and so on their first attempt at getting matchers to pick the right figures, directors came up with pretty convoluted descriptions. See if you can identify which figure the director is referring to here:

> All right, the next one looks like a person who's ice skating, except they're sticking two arms out in front.

This worked. The director and matcher were able to coordinate on item I using this overt form of communication. But as you can see, it wasn't the most elegant or concise wording. The same director-matcher pairs then had to simply repeat the procedure, over and over. After the first round, the pairs quickly converged on more streamlined ways to solve the problem. They were able to achieve coordination through interdependence at lowest cost. Here are the words used to identify item I on the next five rounds from this director-matcher pair:

Round 2. Um, the next one's the person ice skating that has two arms?

Round 3. The fourth one is the person ice skating, with two arms.

Round 4. The next one's the ice skater.

Round 5. The fourth one's the ice skater.

Round 6. The ice skater.

By round 4, the phrase "the ice skater" alone was enough to get the matcher to identify item I in figure 2.1. The words *ice skater* served as an instruction to the matcher for how to select the correct item.[16] But take note: when the director chose the words *the ice skater* from round 4 on, he didn't just do so because that phrase happened to contain information that would successfully lead somebody to the referent. The phrase was specifically designed for this person, in this context, and it had already worked. The successful phrasing became simpler over the course of the experiment. The director and matcher were able to solve the problem through successively more efficient means because of the convention that they had established.

In this seemingly simple situation, one person's choice of words results in another person's successful actions. One way to interpret what is going on is that the speaker is helping the listener. He is giving the listener what she needs in order to solve the problem of picking the right item. Another way to think about it is that the speaker is influencing or manipulating the listener, using words to direct or even control the listener's thinking and behavior. The difference between these two views depends on whose goals we are focusing on. If we are concerned with the matcher's goal of picking the right item, then it's natural to think of the director as helping that person. If we see the selection of the correct item as essentially the director's goal, then the matcher is the means toward that end.

But surely both of these things are true. It's not my goal versus your goal. The people in this interaction share a goal. As in any other coordination game, they have aligned incentives, so the director is helping the matcher precisely *by* influencing her. This is how language works.

A corollary of the minimalist language that emerges when coordination problems are solved is our tendency to use simplified descriptions when possible. Imagine you are in an experiment and you have been asked to read this paragraph:[17]

Rachel parked her car outside the supermarket. She got out of her car, collected a grocery cart and wheeled it inside. She checked her list and went down the aisles. She put the items that were on her list into her grocery cart until she had them all. Then Rachel went to the checkout where she joined the fastest line. She waited in the line, and then unloaded her items onto the belt. The cashier rang up the items on the till and told Rachel the total. Rachel gave the cashier some money and the cashier gave Rachel her change. Rachel put the shopping into the bags and put the bags into the grocery cart. She wheeled the grocery cart out to her car and put the bags into the boot before driving away.

The experimenter asks you to write down what you can remember from what you've just read. Here's what you write:

Rachel went shopping, parked her car at the supermarket, got out of the car, got a grocery cart, went into the supermarket and collected the food she wanted. She went to pay for the goods, gave the cashier the money, he gave her change and a receipt. Then she took the grocery cart back and then drove off in her car.

Now your paragraph is given to the next person in the experiment, who in turn is asked to write what she can remember from it. This is then passed on to another person, and another person. Here is how the experiment plays out:

Round 2. Rachel drove to a supermarket, parked her car, got a grocery cart, and chose some food. Then she went to the cashier to pay for her food. The cashier gave her some change. Then she put back the grocery cart and drove away.

Round 3. Rachel drove to the supermarket, parked her car, got a grocery cart, and chose some food. She paid the cashier and drove home.

Round 4. Rachel went to the supermarket, got some food, and went home.

Each round has the same ever-simplifying language we saw in the ice skater experiment. But there is an important difference. In this supermarket story task, each contribution is an act of recall, not an instruction to a matcher who has to pick from alternatives. In the tangram study, the phrase that resulted from a series of rounds—*the ice skater*—emerged because it was the phrase that worked for solving the coordination problem at hand. All of the unnecessary stuff was whittled away over the course of each round. Now, note that the first version of the supermarket story features twenty-one distinguishable events. In the end, almost all of them are captured with a single phrase: *she went to the supermarket*. It's no accident that this phrase ended up as the description of the original complex description. Why? Because the phrase *go to the supermarket* is a landmark on the Schelling map of cultural knowledge that is already shared by everybody in a particular slice of human culture and society. Unlike the ice skater case, the solution wasn't worked out on the spot. This particular solution has been worked out over generations of community language use: if you say that someone went to the supermarket, that conveys all of the usual stuff that one does—you park your car, get out of your car, collect a grocery cart, wheel it inside, and so on—as laid out blow-by-blow in the first version in this experiment.

The truth is that people would hardly ever say anything like the first version of the supermarket story. The reason we have phrases like *go to the supermarket* is precisely to save us that trouble. We so often need to coordinate around the idea of going to the supermarket and all it entails—for example, when I say, *I'm going to the supermarket. Do you want me to pick anything up?*—that we have converged on a simple and brief convention: the phrase *going to the supermarket*. The details of that complex chain of events—for example, whether I used a grocery cart or a hand basket, whether I pay by cash or card, whether I put the bags in the trunk or on the passenger seat—seldom matter to the basic function of the phrase that describes it, so the convention is not to mention them at all. And in fact, when we do mention them, this departure from the normal economy of expression signals to our addressee that we are adding this detail for a reason.

Consider this line in the first version of the story: *She joined the fastest line.* Of course she joined the fastest line. If I was talking about a trip to the supermarket, why would I even mention this? It would have to be specifically relevant to what I'm telling you. From what we know of how people actually talk, the most likely reason to mention this detail would be as a prelude to some kind of disruption to normal expectations. (We get into this in chapters 9 to 11 on storytelling and sense making.) Maybe the line looked as if it would be the fastest one, but then there was some delay and it turned out I had to wait longer than I would have at any other line. That could be the basis of the kind of everyday anecdote we tell each other all the time. But if I'm not launching a narrative about how something went differently from normal, I should stick to the simple, default way of referring to the situation and leave out the details. That's why in the tangram experiment, you can be sure that if they kept playing, players would stick to the phrase *ice skater*, never again bothering to mention that the skater happens to be sticking two arms out in front. And it's why (at least in English) when we refer to people in conversation, we tend to stick to personal names—like *Gina*—rather than more roundabout ways of referring.[18]

When we optimize coordination through language in these ways, we are following principles of *recipient design*[19] and *mutual responsibility*. As Herbert Clark and Deanna Wilkes-Gibbs, the authors of the tangram study, put it, "The participants in a conversation try to establish, roughly by the initiation of each new contribution, the mutual belief that the listeners have understood what the speaker meant in the last utterance to a criterion sufficient for current purposes."[20] What those "current purposes" are will vary depending on the community of people who are conversing. When certain kinds of coordination problem recur in a community, then rich, culture-specific concepts can emerge, like *going to the supermarket*. These concepts will "accurately portray crucial relations in the thinker's physical world."[21] This explains why specialist terminology exists in various subcultures. Consider this example of 1980s' surfer terminology from psychologists Earl Hunt and Mahzarin Banaji:

> Surfers speak of waves as being "hollow" or "walled." A hollow wave is one that breaks sequentially along its crest, so that the wave break may roll roughly parallel to the beach for perhaps a mile. A good surfer will ride a hollow wave just in front of the break, moving almost perpendicular to the wave's path towards the beach. By contrast, a walled wave has a nearly vertical rise, and breaks simultaneously at all points. A wall can only be ridden directly towards the beach. These concepts have functional distinctions. Surfers can perform acrobatics on their boards while riding hollow waves, so beaches with hollow waves are considered more desirable for surfing. The ability to manipulate hollow waves, however, depends upon the design of one's surfboard. In the 1950's, before surfing technology developed, surfers did not speak of hollow and walled waves, for all waves were ridden directly toward the beach. The surfer example is an example of a situation in which a single referent can be used to describe a whole sequence of events. A surfer's statement "I rode hollow waves all day" implies a whole style of surfing in addition to specifying a wave form. The concept has obvious predictive utility; saying the waves are hollow informs the surfer of the sort of day, type, and probably intensity of surfing. Indeed, one of the benefits of having a single word for a schema is that two surfers can, briefly and succinctly, explain to each other why they are not going to work or class: "It's hollow."[22]

Hunt and Banaji argue that concepts "are culturally satisfactory if they succeed in explaining and predicting the problems that a culture faces."

The key insight is not about how individual people think or behave. It is about how groups of people coordinate in their thinking and behavior. This point pushes back against an individual-centered view of language that has dominated cognitive science for decades.[23]

In chapter 4, we discuss the idea of basic-level categories in language, a degree of specificity in referring to things that captures a sweet spot between too general and too specific. As with maps, there is a Goldilocks principle in getting the resolution just right: providing not too much information, and not too little, for the purposes at hand. People categorize things at the basic level (for example, "He was bitten by a dog," not "by a mammal" or "by a pug") in order to optimize the benefits of information, while minimizing the cost of gathering and holding on to that information. Now note that this argument is about categories we *think with* rather than categories we *communicate with*. Cognitive scientists have emphasized that this trade-off is to "the organism's advantage," focusing on the individual.[24] But words are not for individuals. They exist for achieving convergence among two or more people. If we are talking about word meanings—and not just any concepts—then our unit of analysis needs to be the dyad, the two people whose aligned incentives are met by the unique solution that a basic-level category provides. Our examples of *the ice skater, going to the supermarket, hollow wave,* and *dog* aren't just ideas inside our minds. They are publicly shared. They exist only because they have successfully functioned in the history of certain communities as landmarks for social coordination.[25]

*

If our words capture concepts for explaining and predicting things, they do this in order to share explanations and to *coordinate* around shared predictions. As we'll see, words capture only a tiny slice of all the things that one might conceivably perceive or think. Language is not good for capturing and transmitting the details of reality. What it's good for is providing landmarks we can coordinate around. Unlike with any other communication system, with language we can tell people about things that they have not experienced themselves. We can use language to update people on unseen realities. But this does not mean that our experiences are literally transferred to others simply to be downloaded and viewed or experienced. We are now going to examine the limitations of language in its function of describing reality. Not only are there oak trees, fir trees, and spruce trees; we have words for them. But the link between words and the world is not direct. Our minds must provide that link.

3   Language and Nature

Words do not express thoughts very well. They always become a little different immediately after they are expressed, a little distorted, a little foolish.

—Hermann Hesse (1922)

There is only one planet Venus, but it has more than one name. We call it the Morning Star when it hangs in the East at sunrise. In the West after sunset it is the Evening Star. The two phrases point to the same physical object, but they give our minds different ways to get there. It's easy to think of a million other examples: New York versus the Big Apple, twelve versus a dozen, half an hour versus thirty minutes, orca versus killer whale. The nineteenth-century German philosopher Gottlob Frege gave us some terminology to keep track of this.

Frege's best-known distinction is between *reference* and *sense*. Consider the difference between half an hour and thirty minutes. The reference of the two expressions is identical. I can use both expressions to refer to the same exact length of time, equal to 1800 seconds or one 48th of a day. But the sense of the two expressions is not the same. They have different senses because, as Frege put it, they use different "modes of presentation," The sense of a word is the instruction it gives the listener to use for reaching the reference. It's like route directions to a location. Different paths are always possible. (I could say, *Go straight for two blocks, then turn right* or *Go west for two blocks, then head north.*) Of course, the instructions presuppose that you already understand the terms used (*straight, right, west, north*). If you say *half an hour*, I can get to the intended reference because I have the concepts of "half" and "hour" and I can combine them. If you say *thirty minutes*, this gets me to the same place using the concept of minute and the common counting system. Same reference, different senses.

The contrast between *twelve* and *a dozen* is internal to English. There are also sense-to-reference contrasts *across* languages. Suppose I am telling you the time, and it is 1:20 p.m. In English, both *one twenty* and *twenty past one* would get you there. Dutch speakers have another option: they can use a mode of presentation that works just as well but makes no sense in English. The phrase *tien voor half twee* literally means "ten before half (of) two."[1]

The sense of linguistic expressions is stripped back and partial in comparison to the richness of either the references or the ideas that those senses correspond to.[2] As the psychologist Dan Slobin notes:

> Language evokes ideas: it does not represent them. Linguistic expression is thus not a straightforward map of consciousness or thought. It is a highly selective and conventionally schematic map.[3]

So, the mode of presentation—the word's sense, or content—gives instructions for reaching the idea or thing being described. Words with different senses but ostensibly the same reference—think *freedom fighter* versus *terrorist*, *half empty* versus *half full*—is the essence of framing, a powerful principle in language's capacity as a tool for influence.

Language links to the world in highly flexible ways. How this works has been the most studied question in the psychology of language for at least the past 175 years.[4] Researchers have asked: How do our words relate to things in the world? How do we identify objects from their names? What is the link between our knowledge of objects and their linguistic labels? They have found that words and other bits of language touch on virtually every element of our mental and social lives. As cognitive scientists George Miller and Philip Johnson-Laird put it in their landmark 1976 book, *Language and Perception*:

> The meaning of a word can tell you what is, and what is not, an entity that can be labeled with that word. . . . [It] can tell you the function or purpose of the entity that the word labels. [It] can lead you to all you know about an entity. It has access to encyclopaedic information in long-term memory. [It] can tell you about relations between what the word labels and what other words label. [It] can tell you about what other sorts of words can occur with it in sentences. It can place syntactic and semantic constraints on other words.[5]

Through their meanings, words connect to:

1. The physical world of objects and events[6]
2. The concepts and images in our minds
3. The social situations in which words are used
4. The texts we build with words
5. The linguistic system that the words are embedded in

This implies a thick and textured mesh of interrelations between language and our ways of thinking and interacting.

We are going to focus on points 1 and 2: reference and sense, respectively. What is the relation between them? One view is that our sensory perception provides the essential connection between reference and sense. According to psychologist Greg Murphy, "You couldn't distinguish the words *chair* and *stool* if you didn't perceive the difference between these kinds of things and have that difference represented in your concepts of furniture."[7] But there are many differences in choice of words that don't correspond with any perceptible difference at all. If I have a pet dog, you could refer to it with the basic term *dog*, but you could also say *mammal* or *pug*. You could call it a *mutt*. You could call it a *pet*. Any of these might accurately label the same individual animal. Nothing in your perception would tell you which of the words is correct by looking at this one dog. This dog may be a pug, but there's nothing in my perception of the dog that makes *pug* the right word for it (as opposed to *dog*, *mammal*, or *pet*). I get to decide how specific I want to be. So perception in itself is going to go only so far in explaining how and why we use certain words for things.

*

Language is often seen as a link between a person and the world.[8] But this overlooks something important about how language works. When you use the word for something, there is not only a link between the word and the thing you are referring to, but also, and always, a link between you and the person you are talking to. Yet through most of the history of research in the psychology of language, speaker and hearer have been studied separately. Researchers of language production look at what happens in the mind when people say things. When you show someone a photograph of a dog, what has to happen in order for that person to successfully call up the word *dog* and say it out loud?[9] Then there is research on language comprehension (also called language perception).[10] When someone hears the word *dog*, what has to happen in her brain and mind in order for her to successfully select the photograph of the dog?[11]

If the function of language is to refer to things, how good is it for this function? Let's take up this question.

It is early one evening in 2004, during my first field research expedition to the village of Mrkaa, a network of hamlets dotted along the snaking Nam Noy river in a remote hilltop valley of central Laos. I am working with a middle-aged man named Mun, a senior figure in the community. Mun is one of a few hundred people who make up the entire population of speakers of Kri, a language that has not previously been documented or put in writing. Mun is teaching me Kri words, helping me to compile a written vocabulary of the language.

I balance a field notebook on my knee as I try to get comfortable sitting on the bamboo-slat floor of Mun's home, which like all other Kri dwellings has no tables or chairs. Like all residents of Mrkaa at the time, Mun built his house entirely by hand, with a machete as his only tool, and solely from forest products: bamboo and light timber, lashed together with lengths of rattan cord and thatched with giant palm leaves.[12] For Mun and his fellow villagers, the rainforest is a pantry, hardware store, hunting ground, and highway. Mrkaa is located deep within one of the most biodiverse places on the planet. The tropical Northern Annamites Rain Forests area is one of the World Wildlife Fund's Global 200 most outstanding and representative areas of biodiversity.[13] Kri speakers are intimately familiar with this biodiversity, and so in my search for new Kri vocabulary, I soon turn my attention to words for natural kinds.

That evening, I ask Mun to tell me any names for tree species that he can think of. He starts with a quick list of a dozen or so trees that first come to mind, much as I might start with go-to tree names like *oak, pine, birch, fir, ash,* and *eucalyptus* in English. Mun's initial list includes trees found in abundance around the village, ones that he frequently encounters and frequently makes use of. Then a pause for breath and another quick dozen or so, as he casts his mind to sites around the village that he would visit on his daily travels through nearby groves. Another pause, and then another dozen or more species. In a few minutes, he has given the names of fifty types of tree in Kri.

It goes on. And on. Within ten minutes, Mun has named more than a hundred tree species. By this time, his ten-year-old son has joined us. Together, Mun and his boy are able to prompt each other for tree names in their area, and in little more than twenty minutes, they have given me the Kri names for more than two hundred distinct timber and bamboo species. During that expedition, I would learn that all adult Kri speakers have a similarly vast vocabulary for plant and tree names. I would also learn that having such a rich set of names is part of a larger pattern of language knowledge in the community. Residents of Mrkaa have extensive vocabularies for the many biological distinctions found in their immediate environment: not just the plants but the fish, reptiles, birds, and insects.

The Kri are typical of many human groups whose lifestyles involve cultivation of plants and close proximity to nature in everyday life.[14] The Warnindhilyagwa people of Australia live on Groote Eylandt, a low-lying island in the Gulf of Carpentaria off the northeastern tip of Australia's Northern Territory. They traditionally engaged in a hunter-gatherer lifestyle, typical of many Australian Aboriginal groups. Their considerable knowledge of the plant ecology is encoded in their language, Anindilyakwa. A comprehensive study found 199 words for distinct generic plants.[15] Twelve thousand kilometers away, in the northwestern plateau along the Columbia River and its tributaries in the northwestern United States, speakers of the Sahaptin language—also practicing a hunter-gatherer livelihood—supplied anthropologist Eugene Hunn with 213 generic plant names.[16]

These examples are typical of indigenous hunter-gatherer peoples around the world. The mean number of generic plant labels in these languages is around 200, ranging from 137 terms in Lillooet, spoken on the Fraser River in British Columbia, to 310 terms in Seri, an indigenous language of the Gulf of California in Sonora, Mexico.

Two hundred words for plant species might seem like a lot, but it is fewer than half the size of the vocabularies for plants found in languages spoken by traditional cultivator peoples.[17] In riverine villages straddling the thickly forested borderlands of French Guiana and Brazil, speakers of the Wayampí language have at least 516 generic plant terms. This is the global average plant vocabulary size for cultivator peoples.[18] An even greater number of words for plants is found in the Aguarana language, spoken along the Marañón River—the source of the Amazon—in northern Peru. Aguarana has at least 598 terms for generic plants.[19] Some cultivator peoples have fewer labels than this, though hardly less impressive: Quechua speakers in Peru were found to have 238 terms (overlapping with the top of the range of terms among hunter-gatherer peoples).[20] And speakers of Ndumba, living on the northern slopes of Mount Piora in the rugged Kratke Range in the Eastern Highlands Province of Papua New Guinea, have at least 385 generic plant terms in their language.[21] Toward the high end of the scale, there is Hanunóo, an indigenous language of the south of Mindoro Island in the Philippines. Hanunóo has an established total of 956 generic plant terms. And in the Ifugao language of northern Luzon, also in the Philippines, legendary anthropologist Harold Conklin described more than two thousand separate words for distinct plant types.

Now contrast these with the most impoverished known human vocabularies for natural kinds. Urban dwellers in the United States typically know only a handful of plant names and often aren't even able to identify the plants if they see them. Many urban dwellers can't tell a fir tree from an ash, let alone a fir from a spruce or a pine.[22]

Cognitive anthropologists Scott Atran and Doug Medin recount an interview with an honors student at Northwestern University in Illinois who had expressed surprise that Atran and Medin were asking three- and four-year-old Mayan children about their knowledge of plants:

Interviewer: Tell me all the kinds of trees you know.

Student: Oak, pine, spruce, . . . cherry . . . evergreen, . . . Christmas tree, is that a kind of tree? . . . God, what's the average here? . . . So what do kids say, big tree, small tree?

No. Even four-year-olds in Mayan cultivator communities have extensive knowledge and vocabulary of the plant world. A Mayan child has a solid capacity to name nature with far greater breadth and accuracy than the average urban US adult.[23]

I have to admit that my own place in this scale is well toward the impoverished end. I grew up in the suburbs of an Australian city. So that evening, seated on a bamboo-slat floor in the village of Mrkaa, my elicitation session with Mun was exhilarating. I witnessed the extraordinary intimacy that people can have with their natural surroundings. I felt the finesse with which a language can encode that intimate knowledge. I naturally wanted to know: Why do speakers of Kri in Mrkaa have so many words for types of plants?

We will get to that, but first there is another question, a less obvious one. Kri speakers know a lot of words relative to a suburban dweller from afar.

But relative to the full extent of diversity in their environment, we may ask: Why do they have so *few* words? There are nearly five thousand scientifically documented vascular plants in Laos, and—on a highly conservative estimate—more than a thousand in the province of Khammouan, where Mrkaa is situated.[24] There are some 60,000 known tree species in the world and nearly 400,000 vascular plants.[25] And these are just the ones known to science. Yet few languages name more than a few hundred. Why do people have words for just a subset of the plant life in their environment?

One answer is that we hone in on the aspects of nature that are most striking to us. The natural world is not just mush that can be cut and labeled any old way. Nature has structure. Different species look different to us in obvious ways. There are discontinuities in natural systems, like joints, branchings, markings, and edges. These forms of structure guide our attention to certain distinctions in the world and not others. This doesn't mean that all human groups will explicitly name those distinctions. To see more clearly how the structure of the physical world may account for commonalities across languages, let's look at a much simpler case than the biodiversity of tropical rainforests. Consider the simple distinction between walking and running.

The human body is a complex biomechanical system with defined possibilities for movement and action. And these limits and possibilities are independent of culture or language, or of where we happen to live in the world. Of course, people of different human groups may sometimes move their bodies in conventionalized ways, for example, in diverse practices of dance performance, gesture, and posture. But in everyday life, there is one universal and particularly abrupt border that separates modes of moving: the line between walking and running.

Imagine someone walking on a slowly moving treadmill. She paces forward—left then right then left then right—always with her weight firmly on one or the other foot. If we gradually increase the speed of the treadmill, at a certain point she will break into a run. This is an abrupt and simultaneous change in multiple aspects of bodily movement, including the length of each stride, the energy expended, and the length of time each foot is on the ground. The line between walking and running is a natural distinction supplied by the nature of the human body.[26]

All human bodies respect this distinction. Do all languages respect the distinction? Do they all have distinct words, like English *walking* versus *running*? Psychologist Barbara Malt and her colleagues investigated this question by designing a set of short video clips of exactly the scene just described—a person on a treadmill, moving at different speeds, with different gaits—and asking people to describe what they see.[27] They wanted to know: Is the sharp biomechanical break between a walking gait and a running gait labeled in all languages? They showed the clips to speakers of English, Dutch, Spanish, and Japanese and asked them simply to say what the person in the clip was doing. They found some variation across the languages. For example, English has some highly specific terms for locomotion such as *stroll, saunter, jog,* and *sprint.* These words do not have direct equivalents in all languages. But the main finding of the experiment was that the most easily seen and easily felt distinction in human locomotion—that between walking and running—was captured in languages that are otherwise unrelated and different in type.

This doesn't mean that all languages in the world have two words that mean exactly the same as the English words *walk* and *run.* What it does mean is that whatever words a language has for making distinctions in this domain, they won't overlook the walk/run boundary.[28] Barbara Malt and colleagues take this to be evidence that not all naming distinctions in language are arbitrary cultural constructions. They show that in some areas at least, diverse human communities are not simply free to carve up external reality any way they like when using language to label things.[29] It is evidence that languages can converge in how they name a piece of reality because they respect the structure of that piece of reality.

The walk/run distinction is a simple and clear place to establish this point, as it provides a neat binary distinction relating to perhaps the most important piece of structure that exists for all people: the human body. Most, if not all, languages have a word that refers to the body as a whole, that is, the thing that is left when a person dies. What about the words for parts of the body? English has words like *arm, leg, hand, foot, finger, toe, elbow, knee, head, neck, belly, face, eye, nose, mouth, chin, cheek,* and *wrist.* Do all languages make the same distinctions?

In my research as part of a large team together with Asifa Majid and other colleagues[30] at the Max Planck Institute for Psycholinguistics in the Netherlands, we looked at how different languages label parts of the body. The approach we took was similar in its logic to the study on walking and running. Instead of asking, "What's the word for hand/arm/leg/etc. in language X?" we showed an unlabeled image of the body to speakers of various languages and asked them to provide their own labels as relevant. This method avoids bringing in biases from other languages. Team members took line drawings of the human body and ran the study in field sites with diverse languages, spoken in places from Aboriginal Australia to Surinam to Pakistan to the Solomon Islands.

Given that the human body features sharp discontinuities—such as the joints—we might expect all languages to have words that respect these features, by analogy with the walking/running study. For example, in English, the words *hand* and *arm* refer to those parts of the body that are separated by the *wrist*, a prominent piece of structure in the body. The *leg* and *foot* are separated by the *ankle*. This might seem entirely natural to English speakers,[31] but it turns out that not all languages have separate words for *hand* and *arm* (see figure 3.1). Some languages have a single word that refers to the entire limb. Speakers of Savosavo, spoken in the Solomon Islands, use the word *nato* to refer to the whole lower limb, including the foot. In Lavukaleve, also spoken in the Solomon Islands, there is an even more general term, *tau*, which means limb and can refer to either the whole arm or whole leg, including the foot. (The Lavukaleve word *fe* can sometimes refer to the foot as distinct from the rest of the leg.) Yélî Dnye, spoken on Rossel Island at the southeastern tip of New Guinea, has two terms for the parts of

	Upper Arm	Lower Arm	Hand	Upper Leg	Lower Leg	Foot
Jahai	*bliŋ*	*prbɛr*	*cyas*	*blɨ$^?$*	*gor*	*can*
Punjabi	*baa*		*hatth*	*lətt*		*pœr*
Dutch	*arm*		*hand*	*been*		*voet*
Japanese	*ude*		*te*	*ashi*		
Yélî Dnye	*kêê*			*kpââli*	*yi*	
Indonesian	*tangan*			*kaki*		
Savosavo	*kakau*			*nato*		
Lavukaleve	*tau*					*fe*

Figure 3.1
Variation in terms for parts of the body across eight languages. From Simon Devylder et al., "Carving the Body at Its Joints: Does the Way We Speak about the Body Shape the Way We Think about It?" *Language and Cognition* 12, no. 4 (2020): 577–613, https://doi.org/10.1017/langcog.2020.13; adapted from Asifa Majid and Miriam van Staden, "Can Nomenclature for the Body Be Explained by Embodiment Theories?" *Topics in Cognitive Science* 7, no. 4 (2015): 570–594, https://doi.org/10.1111/tops.12159.

the lower limb, but instead of respecting the ankle joint, as in the English distinction between *leg* and *foot*, it respects the knee. The Yélî Dnye word *kpââlî* refers to the upper leg, above the knee, while *yi* refers to the whole lower part of the limb from the knee down: foreleg and foot together. And in Jahai, spoken in the highlands of Peninsular Malaysia, there are three terms for parts of the lower limb: *bliʔ* for upper leg, *gor* for lower leg, and *can* for foot.

In our global study of vocabularies for parts of the body, we found that people speaking different languages show a similar kind of constrained diversity that we saw in the labeling of plant species, though the range of variation is narrower. A language typically has a vocabulary of between 100 and 150 words for parts of the body, including parts of the face and the internal organs. This number is much smaller than the number of possibly nameable parts of the human body. Words in different languages show a lot of overlap in the kinds of discontinuities they respect, but the systems are far from identical in their details.

Variations across languages in their body part terms aren't due just to the number of terms supplied or where the lines are drawn. There are other kinds of difference too. For instance, the Yélî Dnye language of Rossel Island in Papua New Guinea has special substitute words for parts of the body in the "in-law vocabulary," a set of words that one uses just when talking with one's in-laws.[32] Such avoidance terms are found in many languages and are usually more general in meaning than their everyday language counterparts. In English, for example, in polite speech we might use intentionally vague terms for parts of the body such as *private parts*, which can refer equally well to the distinctly unalike genitalia of men and women. Similarly, in avoidance speech in Yélî Dnye, both male and female genitalia are referred to using the same word, *tapa* (which literally means boulder). In another example of in-law vocabulary, the words *kpââlî* (upper leg) and *yi* (lower leg, including foot) are avoided, and a single term for the whole limb is used instead: *péépi*.

The surface descriptions of the human body that language labels give us do not necessarily give a direct read-off of people's mental image of what the words refer to. In the context of our project on words for parts of the body, Asifa Majid and Miriam van Staden developed a test that tapped into people's visualizations of their language's body vocabulary. People were given an outline drawing of a person's body and were asked to color in the part of the body labeled by a given word. The researchers compared the words for arm in three languages: Dutch (*arm*), Japanese (*ude*), and Indonesian (*tangan*). Both Dutch and Japanese have distinct words for hand and arm, as in English, but Indonesian has a single word, *tangan*, that covers both the hand and the arm. When the coloring-in responses were layered on top of each other into a single image for each language, there was some consensus (see figure 3.2). The coloring is darker where more speakers colored in that part and lighter where fewer included that part.

Figure 3.2 shows us that the Indonesian speakers are consistent with each other and with the terminology of the Indonesian language. All the Indonesian speakers colored in the hand and arm together as a single field, consistent with the idea that *tangan* refers to the hand-and-arm as a whole. This is a clear contrast from the Japanese speakers, who mostly colored in the arm from the shoulder down to the wrist, that is, not including the hand. Meanwhile, most of the Dutch speakers included the hand in the scope of their word *arm*, like the Indonesian speakers for *tangan*. This test

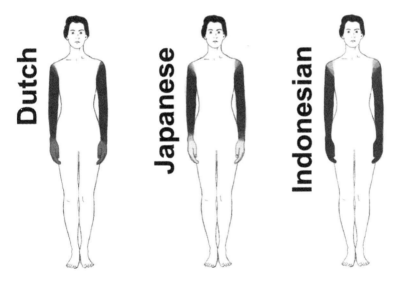

Figure 3.2
Coloring-in shows people's interpretations of the meaning of the words most closely translatable as "arm." Image from Asifa Majid, "Words for Parts of the Body," in *Words and the Mind: How Words Capture Human Experience*, ed. Barbara Malt and Phillip Wolff (Oxford: Oxford University Press, 2010), 68, https://doi.org/10.1093/acprof:oso /9780195311129.001.0001.

shows that just because two languages appear to have directly equivalent translations of common words, this does not mean that people will have the same understanding of what exactly these words refer to, even within the same language. Dutch and Japanese have the same surface distinction in vocabulary—separate words for hand and arm—but this coloring-in task suggests an underlying difference in conceptualization or at least mental imagery. For the majority of the Japanese speakers in the study, "'arm" does not include "hand," while for the majority of Dutch speakers, it does.

Languages around the world show a lot of variety in how they label the parts of the human body, but this doesn't mean there are no universal tendencies. Languages may differ in how many words they have for parts of the lower limb. But as we've seen, those words usually respect obvious features of the structure of that limb (i.e., knee and ankle). In a study of language universals, the anthropologist Cecil Brown allowed that a language need not have a word that means "hand," but he suggested that if it did, then it would be a simple word (like English *hand*) and not a complex one (like English *fingernail*, with two parts, *finger* and *nail*).[33] The linguist E. S. Andersen made similar predictions.[34] For example, if any language has a word that means foot, then it will also have a word that means hand. If there are words for individual toes, there will be words for individual fingers.[35]

The upshot is that diverse languages of the world label prominent features of the human body in similar ways—for example, with words like *head, hand, arm, finger, elbow, neck, eye, mouth, nose*—but there is plenty of variation too. In fact there are few strong universals in this domain.

The human body is part of every culture, but the tools and technologies we wield with our bodies vary widely. Let's turn to an area of everyday reality, which is more obviously going to vary depending on differences in technology and cultural practice.

People in all cultures engage in various actions of cutting, breaking, snapping, slicing, chopping, hacking, and so on—for example, in the course of cultivation, food preparation, or construction. Do different languages label these kinds of events in the same ways? To answer this question, together with a large research team led by my colleagues Asifa Majid and Melissa Bowerman, we developed a set of sixty-one video clips showing people carrying out various actions of separation. Some were typical, everyday, recognizable situations that you would likely see anywhere in the world. A person takes a twig and snaps it in two. Someone uses a knife to slice a piece of fish, chops a carrot with a cleaver. Other clips were designed to test the limits of people's flexible use of language by presenting unlikely events that people probably hadn't seen before. For example, a person breaks a carrot in two with a karate chop. The study looked at twenty-eight diverse languages, spoken in twenty-three countries.[36]

Again, the results reveal constrained diversity. On the one hand, languages vary in the meanings of words they provide for describing the scenes. The English word *cut* is very broad in meaning. It can refer to quite different actions—among them, cutting hair with scissors, cutting grass with a lawnmower, and cutting grooves into meat or fish before grilling. It might seem surprising, but many languages don't have a word with the exact same meaning as *cut*. In the Lao language, spoken in Laos, the word *tat* is usually translated as "cut," but as this study showed, there is an important difference from English. In Lao, the word *tat* can be used only if a part of the thing being cut is fully separated from the whole. So, really it means "sever" or "cut off." If I cut grooves in something, the Lao word *tat* doesn't describe this.

The study was able to discern some underlying similarities between diverse languages in how their vocabulary distinguishes types of action or events. For example, any language will be highly likely to give distinct names to events like slicing a carrot versus snapping a twig.[37] Both involve separation, but in the case of slicing, the person directly controls the exact place and moment where separation should take place. Another way in which languages are quite consistent is that they are likely to have a distinct word meaning "tear" or "rip"—the act of separating something such as cloth, bark, or paper by pulling on it. But beyond these general similarities, different words in different languages described the scenes differently. For example, the Miraña language of the Colombian Amazon has a word that people use to describe the act of ripping something, but they also use that same word to describe scenes that involved destruction with a sharp blow (for example, chopping at cloth with a hammer, splitting a melon with a whack of a machete, smashing a plate with a hammer).[38] In the Yélî Dnye language of Papua New Guinea, the verb that people used to describe ripping was also used to describe events in which an object is separated along the grain, as when a carrot is cut lengthwise.[39]

The cutting/breaking study shows that languages from around the world have sets of words for specialized reference to distinct types of cutting, breaking, tearing, chopping, and separating. The specific meanings of these words can differ greatly across languages. But at an abstract level, these sets of words are organized in a similar way. The commonalities are harder to see than, say, a universal distinction between words for running and walking or a common respect for the body's joints in words for parts of the body. But they are there. The cutting/breaking study shows more evidence of constrained diversity in the ways that word meanings link to the real world.

Another area of reality in which language universals have been tested is color. The smooth and continuous gradation of colors in a rainbow suggests that there are no natural points of discontinuity between colors—like the joints in a body—that could lead different languages to have similar naming systems. Are languages free to divide up the color space in unlimited ways?

The Dani language is spoken in the Biliem Valley of the tropical Western Highlands of Irian Jaya, Indonesian New Guinea. Speakers of Dani have the leanest imaginable vocabulary for naming colors: two words, *mili* and *mola*.[40] Together, these two words cover the entire color spectrum. The word *mili* can refer to black, green, or blue and any shade in between. These are the cool shades. *Mola* is warm: white, red, yellow. Many languages around the world have this kind of two-term system for labeling color.

Then there are languages, for example Italian, that have up to twelve basic words that divide the color spectrum more finely: *verde* (green), *azzurro* (light blue), *viola* (purple), *blu* (dark blue), *rosa* (pink), *giallo* (yellow), *marrone* (brown), *arancione* (orange), *rosso* (red), *bianco* (white), *grigio* (gray), and *nero* (black).

Over the past fifty years, researchers have combed through languages of the world to understand the differences in their systems for naming colors. They have found that color is a field of reality in which, again, languages show constrained diversity. The range from two to twelve basic color terms might seem like a radical contrast, but as cognitive anthropologists Brent Berlin and Paul Kay discovered, there is a highly limited set of possible systems for naming color between the extremes of Dani and Italian.[41] Comparing languages to the simplest two-term system found in Dani, they found that when a language divides the color space more finely than the simplest two-way divide between warm (white/red/yellow) and cool (black/green/blue), it is done in a highly constrained and predictable way. Berlin and Kay described this as a system of evolutionary stages, from stage I to stage V (see figure 3.3).

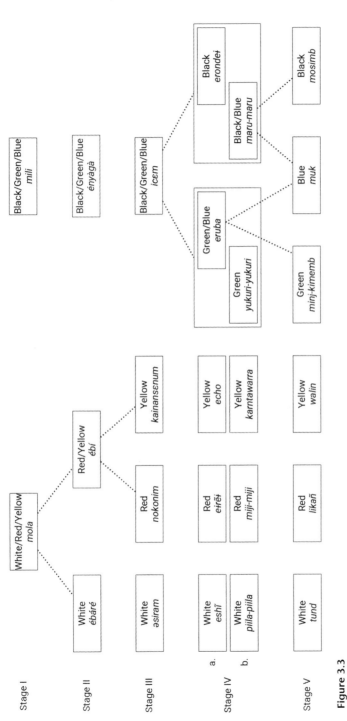

Figure 3.3

Hypothesized stages at which different languages divided up the color space into distinct terms (Example color words are from the following languages: stage I = Dani, stage II = Ejagham, stage III = Kwerba, stage IVa = Sirionó, stage IVb = Martu-Wangka, stage V = Kalam.

The Dani language, with its two basic color words meaning white/red/ yellow and black/green/blue, is an example of a stage I language. A stage II language, for example, the Ejagham language of Nigeria and Cameroon, builds on this by splitting one of the two categories. Ejagham has a black/ green/blue category like Dani but splits the warm category into two: white versus red/yellow. [42] The Kwerba language, spoken in the Upper Tor River area of Irian Jaya, is a stage III system, featuring a further split, dividing the red/yellow category into red and yellow (while retaining the compound black/green/blue term). The Sirionó language, spoken in the eastern Beni and northwestern Santa Cruz departments of the Bolivian lowlands, is a stage IV language. It has distinct terms for four fundamental color categories: white, red, yellow, and black. In this system, the black/green/blue part of the color space—labeled by a single term in the Kwerba language system—is split off into two terms—one for black, the other for the green-blue composite. Martu-Wangka, spoken in the Western Desert region of western Australia, is also a stage IV language, but black/green/blue is split in the other direction, into green versus black/blue. And Kalam, a trans–New Guinea language spoken in the Hagen District of the Western New Guinea Highlands, has a stage V system, in which the white/red/yellow and black/ blue/green spaces are fully split into distinct categories. The result is distinct words for each of the six fundamental color categories.

Many languages with stage V systems have more than these six terms. In English, for example, the eleven basic color terms include the same six fundamental color categories found in Kalam, along with five secondary terms: *brown, purple, pink, orange, gray.*

The way that humans perceive color is a crucial part of this story. In human color perception, color is not just an undifferentiated gradient. We experience certain hues as focal. Think of the colors that can fit the description of *red*. It is a broad range, but within that range we can pick out "real red"—something like the color of arterial blood or a fire engine.[43] Our sense that certain colors are focal comes from the way our visual system delivers color vision to our brains. Because all humans share the same brains and visual systems, color vision serves as a kind of map, with focal color experience as a landmark and a potential mooring for social coordination.

There is a lot more to the linguistics of color reference in the world's languages than this simple step-wise set of distinctions between types of languages—stages I to V—grounded in Brent Berlin and Paul Kay's pioneering work, starting in the 1960s. Hundreds of studies of languages around the world have since honed and challenged our understanding of the possible kinds of color vocabulary, and these studies have presented counterexamples and refinements to the generalizations just given. Of course, these sets of basic color terms—such as the set of eleven terms in English—contain only a small number of the many words that people can use when talking about color. English has many words for highly specific colors beyond the eleven just mentioned. We have words like *fuchsia, teal,* and *alizarine.* We can refine our descriptions of color with multiword phrases like *dark red* or *sky blue.* And we can appeal to common knowledge of the colors that things typically have—for example, *fire engine red* or *canary yellow.* But these words are not basic in a technical linguistic sense.[44]

There are several reasons that a word like *red* is considered basic and words like *fuchsia* and *fire engine red* are not. We use basic terms like *red* more frequently than nonbasic terms. Basic terms tend to be shorter. They don't have multiple elements (unlike *dark red* or *sky blue*). In tests, people are faster at naming colors using basic terms than nonbasic terms. And people who speak the same language will tend to agree closely on the core meanings of basic terms but may differ in their understanding of nonbasic ones.[45]

There are special situations in which people may know dozens, if not hundreds, of distinct words for colors. The Dulux brand of house paints has more than two thousand colors in its commercial palette.[46] Many of these are labeled with unique (and decidedly nonbasic) English names: *violet posy, wing commander, Aztec tan.* But even allowing nonbasic terms and even allowing the highly specialized vocabulary of the paint industry, the distinctions that languages make in the color space are astronomically small in comparison to well over *2 million* distinctions in color that the human eye can discern.[47] Even in highly specialized, technical vocabularies, the total inventory of color terms in use makes less than one-tenth of 1 percent of the discernible distinctions in color that the human visual system can make. The everyday vocabulary that most people use will be one hundred times less than that again. Our perceptual experience is rich, but our language comes nowhere close to that richness. If you think that language is good for capturing perceptual experience, think again.

The aspects of reality we have considered so far in this chapter have been things we can see. These are perhaps the most tangibly public distinctions we make: things or events that people can literally point to, and to a large extent agree on, and know that they are agreeing on. What about a more subjective, seemingly less tangible domain? Let's look at words for smells.

If European languages are any guide, odors are more difficult to capture in words than experiences in any of the other senses. Researchers have long argued that "olfactory abstraction is impossible" and that "humans are astonishingly bad at odor identification and naming."[48] The *Cabinet of Grammatical Rarities*, a research resource published by linguist Frans Plank, says that it's hard to find a good vocabulary for smells in any language.[49] But this conclusion has been based on a skewed sample of languages. English appears to fit the description of a system in which odors defy description.

English speakers have only a few vague everyday expressions that refer to smells. Possibly the only dedicated, abstract forms of basic reference to odor in English are *It smells* and *It stinks*. These are both extremely broad in meaning, and both refer to a bad smell of some kind. For good smells, we have the word *fragrant*, but it is not a basic term. Normally we just say that something *smells good*. And mostly when we talk about odors, we use metaphors (e.g., extending from flavors such as sweet or minty) or we construct wordy, nonbasic descriptions using reference to concrete things that have the smell in question (*smells like a wet dog, old socks, roses, fresh apple pie,* and so on).

But not all languages are like this.[50] The Totonac language is spoken along the Gulf of Mexico in Mesoamerica. In the 1940s, linguist Herman Aschmann noted the special vocabulary for smells: "In Totonac there is no general word to indicate that a thing smells. The exact shade of smell must be taken into account and a word chosen giving it."[51] The distinct terms in Totonac fall under eight headings:

Bad smells

Sour smells

Artificial smells

Air-permeating smells

Body and animal smells

Vegetation and good smells

Medicinal and aromatic smells

Smells that leave a taste in the mouth

Totonac speakers use a variety of words based on these categories to refer to smells as diverse as the "smell of mint, parsley, tobacco and other herbs," the "savoury smell of garlic," "smell of mould," "smell of citrus fruit skins," and "intense skunk smell."

There have been similar reports from other languages, including the Seri language of coastal Sonora, Mexico, the Xóõ language of Botswana and Namibia, the Tarok language of plateau Nigeria, the Kapsiki/Higi language of Cameroon and Nigeria, Boholano in the Philippines, the Amis language of eastern coastal Taiwan, and the Matsigenka and Yora (Yaminahua) languages of Amazonian Peru.[52]

Cognitive scientist Asifa Majid and linguist Niclas Burenhult have systematically investigated a special vocabulary for smells in Jahai, an indigenous language of upland Peninsular Malaysia, spoken by a hunter-gather community there. The language has a dozen basic terms for smells (see figure 3.4).

Majid and Burenhult, along with other colleagues, carried out a controlled experiment and analysis to compare the smell vocabulary of Jahai with that of Dutch, spoken 10,000 kilometers away in the Netherlands.[53] Dutch was

Odor Terms	Approximate Translation
cŋəs	"to smell edible, tasty" e.g., cooked food, sweets
crŋir	"to smell roasted" e.g., roasted food
harɨm	"to be fragrant" e.g., various species of flowers, perfumes, soap (Malay loan; original Malay meaning "fragrant")
ltpɨt	"to be fragrant" e.g., various flowers, perfumes, bearcat
haʔɛ̃t	"to stink" e.g., feces, rotten meat, prawn paste
pʔus	"to be musty" e.g., old dwellings, mushrooms, stale food
cŋɛs	"to have a stinging smell" e.g., petrol, smoke, bat droppings
sʔĩŋ	"to have a smell of human urine" e.g., human urine, village ground
haɲcĩŋ	"to have a urine-like smell" e.g., urine (Malay loan; original Malay meaning "foul odor, stench")
pʔih	"to have a blood/fish/meat-like smell" e.g., blood, raw fish, raw meat
plʔeŋ	"to have a blood/fish/meat-like smell" e.g., blood, raw fish, raw meat
plʔɛŋ	"to have a bloody smell that attracts tigers" e.g., crushed head lice, squirrel blood

Figure 3.4
Smell terms in the Jahai language of Peninsular Malaysia. List from Asifa Majid and Niclas Burenhult, "Odors Are Expressible in Language, as Long as You Speak the Right Language," *Cognition* 130, no. 2 (2014): 266–270, 269, https://doi.org/10.1016/j.cognition.2013.11.004.

chosen to represent the kind of standard average European language that has been taken as evidence for a supposed pan-human hopelessness at encoding smells in language.

The researchers prepared a set of special felt-tip pens soaked in different test odors.[54] The thirty-seven different odors included both pleasant smells—for example, acetoin (butter, cream), cyclotene hydrate (caramel), and nerol (sweet, floral, rose)—and unpleasant ones—for example, skatole (fecal), trimethyl amine (fishy), and 2-methyl-1-butane thiol (bloody, sulfurous).[55] People in the experiment had to smell each odor and simply state what smell it was.

The responses from Jahai and Dutch speakers couldn't have been more different. Recall that the Jahai speakers have a set of words that denote smells in an abstract sense. In the experiment, the Jahai speakers consistently used these words to describe the test smells. They independently agreed on which Jahai words should be used for each smell. This conformed with Majid and Burenhult's earlier findings about Jahai speakers' tendency to describe smells quickly and without hesitation: "Contrary to the widely-held belief that people universally struggle to describe odors, Jahai speakers name odors with ease. . . . Jahai speakers could name odors with the same conciseness and level of agreement as colors."[56] By contrast, the Dutch speakers struggled with their inadequate vocabulary. Their responses were meandering: "Yes, it is something cinnamon-like, but I can, no, I can, erm, not specifically, erm, say what it is."[57]

Dutch speakers grappled for ways to describe what they were perceiving. Most of the time they named something that might give off the smell (flowers, ammonia, manure) or a scenario associated with the smell ("house that isn't aired," "if you ride along or stand behind a garbage truck"). These speakers showed a lower level of agreement with each other than Jahai speakers did. And their words were mostly focused on concrete descriptions. The Dutch language actually does have some abstract smell terms. Five were used in the study—*stinkt* (smelly), *stinkt niet* (not smelly), *muf* (musty), *ranzig* (rancid smell), and *weeïg* (sickly smell)—but these made up only 2 percent of responses in the experiment.

The comparison of Jahai and Dutch shows that odors can be far more expressible in human language than some have supposed. But these findings are relative to a baseline of a language like English, which has almost the most primitive imaginable vocabulary for smells. Jahai or Totonac, when compared to English, can be said to have highly refined vocabularies for smell. So when it comes to capturing our experience of reality, some languages are indeed better than others. But that said, no language is particularly good for capturing the details of human experience. In the context of our capacity for actually perceiving distinctions in smells in our surroundings, these linguistic systems only discern and label the tiniest subset of reality. The human nose is capable of an extraordinary number of distinctions in odor. It has been claimed that there are "at least *one trillion* olfactory stimuli."[58] Biochemist Caroline Bushdid and colleagues write, "The human olfactory system, with its hundreds of different olfactory receptors, far outperforms the other senses in the number of physically different stimuli it can discriminate."[59] So we can't say that languages like Jahai or Totonac, with a dozen or so words for odors, are particularly good at capturing distinctions in this domain of reality. A language with a dozen words for smells is considered elite among human languages, but even such a language would make fewer than one ten-millionth of 1 percent of the distinctions that our individual sensory perception can make. No matter the language being spoken, when words try to capture a sensory impression, they strip most of it away.

*

How good are human languages at capturing details of the real world? The examples we've looked at in this chapter have shown a recurring pattern of *constrained diversity*: languages vary, but only within the same narrow range. In the domain of names for plant life in a local environment, languages vary but in roughly predictable ways. Urban populations tend to have only a small number of names for life forms, say a couple of dozen, and have trouble identifying them in nature; hunter-gatherer communities have a much larger knowledge set, with people knowing some two hundred or so names for plants they can recognize; and cultivators can name and identify around five hundred distinct types of plant. Languages universally encode a distinction between walking and running. They label parts of the body similarly, typically having a hundred or so words for body parts, where the distinctions made will tend to respect the perceptually prominent joints of the body. Words for actions of cutting and breaking vary in details but respect certain prominent underlying causal distinctions. Words for colors are limited in number and tend to capture perceptual focus points. Words for smells may make finer distinctions in some languages than others, but they make more distinctions among bad smells and only ever make the tiniest fragment of the distinctions we can individually perceive.

Why do languages make such coarse distinctions in reality compared to how finely we are able to make distinctions through our senses? Why do they do this in similar ways across languages? And why does the observed variation appear to be conditioned by social and cultural practices? It is because the true function of language is not to capture and communicate our experience of reality. If it were, it would have to be better than it is at this job. The function isn't to transmit information per se (though it does do that) but rather to provide for social coordination. The labels found in the words of languages are not for mirroring or depicting reality. They are practiced solutions to coordination problems in social life.

Languages have developed in such a way that they draw on available sources of mutual prominence. Recall that for people to be readily able to coordinate around something, two criteria must be met: the thing should be somehow prominent and this prominence should be assumed to be shared among the people who would coordinate. One of these sources of prominence is our pan-human perceptual system. If something is visually prominent to you, then you can assume it is visually prominent to everyone else. If that landmark happens to be useful for people in solving a recurrent coordination problem, then it will likely become encoded in the main toolbox of language: the vocabulary. Another source of shared prominence is common cultural interest or values. If we all share an interest in some aspect of reality, then we can assume that its prominence will be noticed by all, and thus will be available as a landmark to coordinate around. Sometimes, of course, in a certain cultural context, people have their awareness heightened to certain things that in another cultural context would be overlooked. Perception and cultural interest are distinct sources of mutual prominence, but clearly they can combine. The meanings encoded in words for distinctions in perceptible reality tend to be focused on the things that stand out as landmarks on a Schelling map. Seen in this way, both human color vision and local cultural practices around color—say, in the production of paints, dyes, or cosmetics—interact in charting a collective map for members of a community to coordinate around colors. Similarly, both human perception of the structures of plants and culture-specific practices of plant collection or cultivation interact in charting a community-wide map for coordinating around certain plant species. And so on for the entirety of our collective cultural troves of knowledge.

*

Words capture only a tiny fraction of what we can distinguish with our senses. If you have an experience and you try to put it into words, much will be lost in the process. If the only information someone has about a scene is in the words you've used to describe it, that person will hardly be able to recover anything of what you have in mind, let alone the details of the scene itself. We've seen in this chapter that words make many orders fewer distinctions in reality than our perception can make (which itself already hides much of how the world actually is).[60] Recall the two-layered simplification of the world shown in figure 1.3: first, reality is reduced by perception; then, perception is reduced by language. If perception hides things from us, then language makes things almost disappear. And as we are about to see, language doesn't only strip away reality. It also distracts us and misleads us as to what we think is even there.

II Nudged by Language

4 Priming and Overshadowing

Just as a wing performs its normal function by working on the air, so a signal performs its normal function by working on another animal.

—J. R. Krebs and R. Dawkins (1984)

Humans are fast. We can think and act in a split second. The way we process language is a prime example. Suppose I show you a picture of a guitar.[1] How fast can you label it by uttering the word *guitar*? You have to visually process the image and recognize what it is. You have to retrieve the word for it in your mind. Then you have to initiate and execute the fine motor programs for pronouncing the word. People can do all this in 600 milliseconds, little more than half a second.[2]

That's fast but there is a weird trick to do it faster. Suppose that just before you see the guitar, I show you a different image. If that image shows something related to the guitar, say a tennis racket (which has a similar shape to a guitar), then you become *primed*. When you see the similar shape in advance, this makes you able to say the word *guitar* slightly faster than normal (experiments show a speed advantage of 35 milliseconds). And if the previewed image resembles a guitar both visually and functionally—for example, a violin—then you can react faster still (125 milliseconds faster). This effect also occurs when the prime is a written word. If you are primed with a word related to the image you need to name, or especially if you see the word for the object itself, then you will be faster in naming the object when it appears.

But while priming can speed us up, it has downsides too. It can make us overconfident about what is coming next. In one of the earliest experiments in the psychology of language, published in 1897, American psychologist Walter Pillsbury wanted to know how well people could detect errors or distortions in written words under different conditions.[3] He showed people lists of words, some spelled correctly (for example, *father*), others with errors (for example, *fathex*), and tested how well they would detect errors. In one part of the experiment, just before showing people the test word, Pillsbury would call out another word. Some of the time, the word he called out was related to the test word. For example, before seeing *fathex*, people would hear the word *son*; before seeing *fashxon*, they would hear *style*; before *verbati*, they would hear the phrase *word by word*. When people were primed like this with related words, they were less likely to notice the misprints and errors. The priming made them anticipate the test word at some level, and so they were less likely to pay careful attention to what they were seeing.[4] The prime provided a kind of off-switch for their attention. This effect shows that priming can cause us to move too fast, to become too certain about what's there, and to overlook errors we might otherwise have seen.

In this chapter, we look at some ways in which language interferes with how we think and act. Interference from priming and other contextual effects can be viewed positively or negatively, depending on your perspective.[5] Because two parties are involved whenever language is used, an exploitable vulnerability in the system can be seen as a feature from one side of the equation and a bug from the other. It depends on whether you are the player or the played.

The image in figure 4.1 is based on one of the most famous experiments in the history of cognitive psychology, carried out in Nashville in the 1930s by American psychologist John Ridley Stroop.

Look at the image in figure 4.1 and imagine you're a subject in the experiment. All you have to do is say the color of each shape—black, white, or gray—as fast as you can. People can do this pretty quickly and accurately. Try it.

In the next part of the experiment, you just have to read out words for colors, from a list like the one shown in figure 4.2. People can do this even faster.

Figure 4.1
Name the colors as fast as you can.

Figure 4.2
Read the words as fast as you can.

Figure 4.3
Name the colors as fast as you can. (Ignore the words!)

Now, naming a color and reading out a word are quite different kinds of task, and Stroop wondered what would happen if the two tasks were in competition. Look at figure 4.3.

Don't read the words. Ignore them. Just say the color that each word is written in, as quickly and accurately you can. There is an irresistible form of interference due to language. This task takes twice as long as naming the colors of shapes (as in figure 4.1). Even with training, it's almost impossible to overcome this interference from language. The Stroop effect is one way in which language can mess with our performance in a quite direct sense.

Priming affects more than our speed of response; it can also affect the *kind* of response we give. By controlling where people direct their attention, it's possible to literally control a person's linguistic choices. Linguist Russell Tomlin conducted an experiment in which participants watched a simple video clip featuring two fish. In the clip (see figure 4.4), a black fish and a white fish swim in from opposite sides of the screen, approaching each other directly. As they get close to each other, a small arrow flashes above one of the fish, and then when the fish meet in the middle, one swallows the other whole, and swims on.

In the scene shown in figure 4.4, the black fish eats the white fish. But that's just one way to describe this scene, using the active voice. Another option in English is the passive voice: *The white fish gets eaten by the black fish.* The two strategies describe the same event, but in the active version, the agent in the scene (the black fish) is the subject of the sentence, while in the passive version, the patient (the white fish) is the subject. Tomlin found that when an arrow draws people's attention to one of the fish immediately

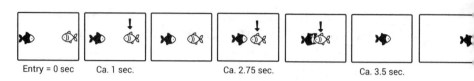

Entry = 0 sec   Ca. 1 sec.   Ca. 2.75 sec.   Ca. 3.5 sec.

Figure 4.4
Still images from the film used in Tomlin's attention experiment. (Figure created by
Gus Wheeler, after Tomlin 1995.)

before the eating event takes place, it doesn't matter whether that fish is
the eater or the eaten; people will put it in the subject position when they
describe the scene. In figure 4.4, where the arrow points to the white fish,
people consistently said, "The white fish got eaten," even though it would
have been equally accurate to say, "The black fish ate the white one." The
experiment shows that you can directly determine whether people choose
an active or passive description of a scene as long as you can determine
where their attention is directed at the key moment. The effect isn't just
strong; it is "invariant and automatic."[6] And not only does it work in English, it has been found to work in other languages, including Burmese,
Indonesian, and Mandarin Chinese.[7]

Language is directly influenced by where our attention happens to be fixed.
So the way we talk can *reveal* our current focus of attention. Language, then, is
good not just for specifying the elements of a scene (black fish, white fish) but
also for conveying information about the speaker's perspective on that scene.

Tomlin's experiment used the simplest way to direct somebody's attention:
a pointing arrow. Another way to direct people's attention is to use language
itself as the arrow, working less directly but with essentially the same effect.
Have a look at figure 4.5. and imagine how you might describe what you see.

Like the scene with the two fish, you could describe figure 4.5 in at least
two ways. If you say, "The church is being struck by lightning," you are focusing on the church. You have put it in subject position, at the beginning of the
sentence. Notice that when you put the church first like this, there is another
effect: you need to put the sentence in the passive voice ("is being struck by").

An alternative would be to reverse the focus. You could say, "Lightning
is striking the church." What makes people choose between these alternatives? Psychologist Kay Bock discovered a way to bias people toward one or
the other option using an indirect way of diverting their attention to one or
another part of the image. The method is called *semantic priming*.

Figure 4.5
Image from Bock's semantic priming experiment. What do you see? After J. Kathryn Bock, "Meaning, Sound, and Syntax: Lexical Priming in Sentence Production," *Journal of Experimental Psychology: Learning, Memory, and Cognition* 12, no. 4 (1986): 374. https://doi.org/10.1037/0278-7393.12.4.575.

Suppose that you ask people to say what is happening in figure 4.5. If you prime them with the word *worship*, a concept related to *church*, this makes them more likely to put the church in the subject position (and thus also use the passive voice) when they describe the scene. The concept of worship acts like a mental pointer to the concept of church. By contrast, if you prime people with the word *thunder*—drawing their minds toward the associated concept of lightning—they will tend to describe the scene by putting the word *lightning* in the subject position.[8]

Maybe it makes no difference how we frame our description of the event. Does it matter if the sentence is about the church rather than about the lightning? Either way, it accurately describes what happened. In the fish-eats-fish and lighting-strikes-church experiments, people all saw the same depiction of reality, and they know what they saw, irrespective of how they happen to describe it with words. Right?

Actually, no. Language doesn't just affect how fast we respond or the kinds of sentences we produce, as we've seen in these priming studies. Language can also affect our beliefs about what we think we've seen.

In 1922, gestalt psychologist Friedrich Wulf published an experiment that tested people's memories. He showed people a set of simple, abstract line drawings, and asked them to remember the drawings and then later redraw them.[9] Figure 4.6 gives some of the images people saw.

When people later redrew the images from memory, Wulf found that they would omit certain details and exaggerate others. People "normalized" the images, as Wulf put it. They would alter the images to better resemble familiar shapes or objects. For example, some curved lines were redrawn to look more like a bridge with pillars. Sometimes different speakers would interpret a single abstract image differently.

Participants in Wulf's experiments didn't just normalize the original images in their redrawings; they reflected this normalization in the words they used to describe the redrawn forms that they created. For example, when people redrew the form in figure 4.7, their descriptions ranged from "two triangles" to "the letter *W*" to "mountains".

Wulf's study inspired psychologist J. J. Gibson to dig deeper into people's linguistic commentary on the figures they drew. In a 1929 study, Gibson

Figure 4.6
Abstract images after Wulf's 1922 memory experiments. From Friedrich Wulf, "Beitrage Zur Psychologie Der Gestalt; vi. Über Die Veranderung von Vomellungen (Gedachtnis Und Gestalt)," *Psychologische Forschung* 1 (1922): 333–373.

Figure 4.7
Image after Wulf's 1922 memory experiments. Image from Wulf, "Beitrage Zur Psychologie Der Gestalt," 374.

created similar line images to Wulf's and told each participant "simply to look carefully at each figure and at the end of the series to draw as many figures as he remembered in any order he wished." As people worked away, with the experimenter sitting by them, they were "encouraged to comment" on their reproductions:

> A reproduction would be made with some unusual change, and in reporting on the reproduction the observer would mention casually (of his own accord or on questioning) that the figure looked like a particular object, e.g. a maid's apron, a fish's tail or a geological formation. It would at once become clear that the change had been of such a nature that the reproduction conformed more closely to the object than did the original. . . . The reproduction which followed was altered in the direction of the verbal memory.[10]

Figure 4.8 shows Gibson's abstract image (at left) which was redrawn variously as *star*, *bird*, and *arrow* (from left to right).

In figure 4.9, Gibson's image (at left) was altered in line with the labels *hourglass* and *tilted anvil* (left to right).

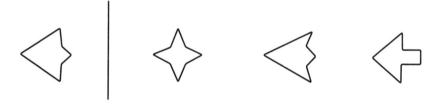

Figure 4.8
Star/bird/arrow image after Gibson's memory experiment (at left of line) with redrawings to the right. After James Jerome Gibson, "The Reproduction of Visually Perceived Forms," *Journal of Experimental Psychology* 12, no. 1 (1929): 13.

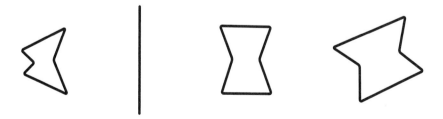

Figure 4.9
Hourglass/anvil image after Gibson's memory experiment (at left of line) with redrawings to the right. Gibson, "The Reproduction of Visually Perceived Forms,"13.

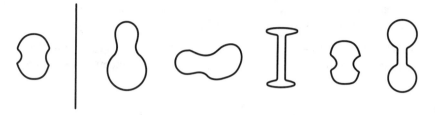

Figure 4.10
Torso/footprint/dumbbell/violin image after Gibson's memory experiment (at left of line) with redrawings to the right. Gibson, "The Reproduction of Visually Perceived Forms," 14–15.

And in figure 4.9, the image at left was redrawn variously as *woman's torso, footprint on the sands of time, dumbbell, violin,* and *dumbbell* (from left to right)

These examples suggest that when people need to remember things, they can use their existing knowledge of familiar objects as a reference point. In this sense, language is good for helping us remember things. But there is a cost. People were not making perfect mental recordings of the images for later reference. Instead, they were grounding their specific memory of what they saw in more general points of reference, established concepts—such as those encoded in the words *hourglass* or *anvil*—that could be tagged with a readily available English word.

Are the labels in these redrawing experiments an effect of subjects' non-linguistic mental processes of distorting the images in memory? Or are they a *cause* of those distortions? The two scenarios are these:

1. See X, choose words to describe X. (cause) → Form Y, an altered concept of X. (effect)

2. See X, form Y, an altered concept of X. (cause) → Choose words to describe Y. (effect)

What do words have to do with the distortions that people made in redrawing these images? Maybe the distortions were taking place in people's minds, independent of language, and the words that people offered were simply effects of those distortions. But it's also possible that people were using language in their minds as a tool when remembering the images, and this use of language was a cause of the changes of shape in their memories of the images. If I see a nondescript image and say to myself that it is like an anvil, then this act of labeling may actually be overwriting the details of my memory.

Could this mean that language is good for influencing people at a subliminal level? One way to find out is to see if words can be used to directly manipulate people's redrawings in the Wulf/Gibson experiments. This is what psychologist Leonard Carmichael and colleagues did in a 1932 study. The idea was to prime people with different words as they were shown the images and see if this priming affected their memory in the direction of the word given. Figure 4.11 shows some of the images used in the experiment. The images are deliberately ambiguous.

Three groups of people saw the images and were told they had to remember them and redraw them later. One group saw the images without any label, as in the earlier studies by Wulf and Gibson. A second group was given one label (for example, *curtains in a window, bottle, crescent moon*), and a third group saw another label (*diamond in a rectangle, stirrup, letter "c"*). As expected, most of the time (more than 90 percent) when people redrew the images, there were major changes to the original. When people were primed with a label, they would usually (74 percent of the time) redraw it to look more like that label. Figure 4.12 shows some examples of the redrawn figures, in the left and right columns, alongside the words that primed these distortions.

This experiment shows that words can cause distortions in people's memory of what they've seen.[11] Whether this effect is something that language is "good for" depends on your perspective. With language, we can either play other people or be played by them. What's needed is to understand these effects and be mindful of them.

These experiments establish a clear relation between language and our memory for visual images. Would these effects matter in the real world? The answer is yes. Consider the legal domain of eyewitness accounts of accidents or crimes.

Imagine you are walking down the street and you see two cars collide right in front of you. Later you are called to give witness testimony in an insurance case. You are asked to estimate how fast you think the cars were going. Could language be used to prime and bias your answer? Psychologists Elizabeth Loftus and John Palmer tested this question in a 1974 study that transplanted the dumbbell/eyeglasses experiment into an incident–eyewitness scenario.[12] Those in the experiment saw a film clip of two cars colliding and were later

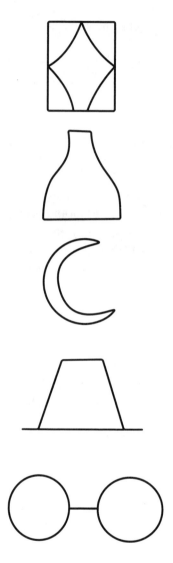

Figure 4.11
Deliberately ambiguous images from the Carmichael et al. 1932 study on language and memory. After L. Carmichael, H. P. Hogen, and A. A. Walter, "An Experimental Study of the Effect of Language on the Reproduction of Visually Perceived Form," *Journal of Experimental Psychology* 15, no. 1 (1932): 75, https://doi.org/10.1037/h0072671.

| Reproduced figures | Word list 1 | Stimulus figures | Word list 2 | Reproduced figures |

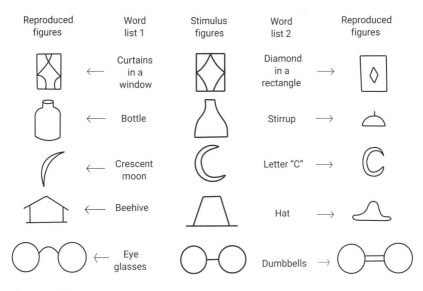

Figure 4.12
The 1932 memory study by Carmichael and colleagues showed that ambiguous images are remembered and reproduced differently depending on the words used to describe them. After Carmichael, et al., "An Experimental Study," 80.

tested on their memory of the scene. The key twist was that different people heard different words in the test questions.

For one group, the test question was, *How fast were the cars going when they bumped into each other?* For another group, the question was, *How fast were the cars going when they smashed into each other?* Depending on which word was used, people had slightly different memories of the scene later. People who had heard the scene described as *smashed into* estimated a higher speed than those who heard *bumped into*, even though both groups saw the exact same scene. Also, people who heard *smashed into* rather than *bumped into* were more likely to report that there was broken glass on the ground. (There wasn't.) Again, we see that the words we use to talk about a scene can directly affect what people believe they have seen with their own eyes.[13]

As these examples show, language can push people's beliefs and memories in different directions by pointing them toward different targets. What is the mechanism?[14] At the core of it is the psychological process of *categorization*, which at best is an economical way to generalize and at worst a kind of off-switch for the mind.

Every object, event, person, or situation we come across in the real world is unique in some way. But when we give something a label, we are grouping it in the set of all things that can also be given that label. To categorize something is to treat it as being the same as other things that belong in the category, and thus to ignore any differences. So when we see the event and say that the cars *smashed into* each other, we have grouped the event together with all other events that could be labeled in that way, and for the moment, we ignore the differences among them. Categorization is one of the most general and powerful mechanisms by which word meanings do their work. It is the basis of everything we discussed in the previous chapter.

By its very nature of treating a set of unalike things as being the same, the mechanism of categorization strips away distinguishing information. If I tell you that I bought a chair, the English word *chair* tells you something about the thing I bought, but it leaves out a lot of distinguishing information. From the word *chair*, you can be pretty sure of the approximate size and shape that the thing will have, but a lot of the detail (color, material, exact construction) is stripped away in my description. From my general description of it as a *chair*, you don't have anything remotely like the detailed image that I have of the specific chair I bought. After all, I have seen it with my own eyes. Words strip away the details. But we assume that the person who saw the chair is not affected by this linguistic stripping away of information. I know what I saw, right? Not so fast.

In a 2008 experiment by cognitive scientist Gary Lupyan, people saw images of household objects, such as chairs and lamps. The experiment had two phases. In the first phase, participants in one group were asked to say whether they liked each object, while another group was asked to categorize the objects by name. If they saw a chair, they had to press a *chair* button; if it was a lamp, they pressed a *lamp* button. In the second phase of the experiment, participants saw more images of objects and simply had to say whether they had seen the images already. Here is what Lupyan found. The people in the group who had categorized the objects according to their label—using the English words *chair* or *lamp*—were worse at remembering exactly what they'd seen. As Lupyan wrote, "Labeling a familiar image distorts its encoded representation."[15]

So here is one thing that language does to you: when you label the things you experience, that very act of labeling strips away information you might have registered about those things. The stripping-away effects of categorization are not just felt on the receiving end of the path of communication.[16]

When we label the things we see, our own memories of what we've seen become depleted. Our choice of words doesn't just affect other people's minds. When we describe things in certain ways, we also mess with our own minds.

This effect isn't necessarily bad. Categorization simplifies matters. It makes our complex world more conceptually manageable. It can focus our attention on things that matter most for whatever purposes are at hand. This helps when we are learning our first languages. Words help infants to pay better attention to objects, find contrasts between the words they are learning, and look for similarities and differences between things in the environment.[17] But there are downsides as well, as Lupyan's chair study shows for memory tasks. We saw in the car crash study that eyewitnesses' memory of what they've seen can be skewed by words that they hear, for example, in the questions they are asked about what they saw. Lupyan's chair/lamp study suggests that people's *own* descriptions of a scene can skew their beliefs about what they've witnessed. Let's return to the problem of eyewitness memory and consider what this means.

Psychologists Jonathan Schooler and Tonya Engstler-Schooler coined the term *verbal overshadowing* for when our use of language overwrites our own memories.[18] In an experiment, they showed people a set of slightly different hues, like paint color sample cards in a hardware store. Some people were asked to describe the colors they saw, using whatever words they could. Another group saw the same colors but did not verbally describe them. Later, when participants were shown more colors and were asked to say if they'd seen the colors already, the people who had put the colors into words were worse at later identifying the exact color they had seen. By describing what they were seeing, those in the first group were allowing language to deplete or alter their mental representation of the original experience.

The same effect holds for human faces. In another part of the experiment, participants saw a thirty-second video clip depicting a bank robbery, with a prominent character in action. People in one group were asked to describe the face they had seen, while another group did not describe the face. The participants who had described the face in words were later less accurate in telling whether they had seen the face earlier, just as in the chair/lamp study. Further studies have shown the same effects with people's memories for cars and wines.[19]

Verbal overshadowing is real. It arises especially with respect to things that "defy linguistic description" such as colors, faces, and tastes.[20] These are domains for which no language makes distinctions anywhere nearly as finely as our visual discrimination can (see the previous chapter). But as the chair/lamp experiment shows, the effect is there even for everyday objects that are easy to name.

Think about this. When you see something and then name it, by the very act of giving it a name, you are stripping out information from your own perception of what you experienced. You are doing this literally every time you speak.

Does this matter? It depends on what type of task you are trying to perform. In the chair/lamp memory experiments, people were required to "recognize having seen exact members of a particular category":[21]

> Classification using category labels was detrimental to this task. But while recognition of particular category members is undoubtedly important, as when one searches for one's own car rather than just a car, most categorization tasks are best performed at a higher, more general level that requires abstracting over idiosyncrasies of particular category members.[22]

This suggests that the simplifying, stripping-away effects of linguistic categories may well be adaptive, as should be expected from any biologically evolved system. But what could be the value of language redirecting our thinking, and even overwriting our first-person experiences?

There's a need in everyday life to think at just the right level of specificity. Between too vague and too specific, there is a sweet spot, which psychologist Roger Brown called the *level of usual utility*:

> Many things are reliably given the same name by the whole community. The spoon is seldom called anything but *spoon*, although it is also a piece of silverware, an artifact, and a particular ill-washed restaurant spoon. The community-wide preference for the word *spoon* corresponds to the community-wide practice of treating spoons as equivalent but different from knives and forks. There are no proper names for individual spoons because their individuality seldom signifies. It is the same way with pineapples, dimes, doors, and taxi cabs. The most common name for each of these categorizes them as they need to be categorized for the community's nonlinguistic purposes. The most common name is at the level of usual utility.[23]

Roger Brown's point is that if our language captures this sweet spot in the level of specificity we usually use to describe things, then a loss of information will be a feature, not a bug. This is the insight behind basic level categorization (which we met in chapter 2), an idea developed in the 1970s by Brown's student Eleanor Rosch and colleagues. An object can be categorized at different levels of abstraction. We might call the same object a *vehicle*, a *car*, or a *convertible sports car*, but only one of these options is basic in their sense. The word *car* balances the trade-off between stripping away too much information (as in *vehicle*, which could be anything from a Mini Minor to a Mack truck) and including information that is so specific as to be "irrelevant for the purposes at hand."[24]

For Rosch and colleagues, the phenomenon of basic-level categorization concerns individual cognition. Using basic-level concepts—concepts that are not too general and not too specific—is most efficient for our private thought processes. But Brown's original idea was that a basic level of naming was useful not (only) for the individual mind but for the public, social interactions by which words circulate. His conception of "usual utility" links people's preferences for choice of words to their goals and interests in social interaction. It is about creating maps and landmarks that are just right for achieving social coordination among people.

Think back to the priming experiments in which we saw that people can be influenced by pointers, either actual arrows or words that direct our attention. We saw the effects of words on memory eyewitness testimony. Now let's ask whether the simple grammatical choice between active and passive might also have potential for influence in legal contexts. Remember the lightning-strikes-church and fish-eats-fish experiments, which showed that an attention-directing prime could determine whether people used an active or passive description of an event. These experiments showed the effects of priming on people's use of language. Like this:

Speaker receives active prime. (cause) → Speaker produces active framing in language. (effect)

Speaker receives passive prime. (cause) → Speaker produces passive framing in language. (effect)

Could these effects also become causes in turn? Could perspective-changing options in language, like the choice of active versus passive descriptions, in turn, affect people's understanding of a situation?[25] Like this:

Speaker produces active framing in language. (cause) → Hearer understands event in active terms. (effect)

Speaker produces passive framing in language. (cause) → Hearer understands event in passive terms. (effect)

Let's see how this might work. Consider this scene from Joseph Conrad's 1907 novel *The Secret Agent*, in which Mrs. Verloc murders her husband after learning that he was responsible for the death of her brother Stevie:

> She remained thus mysteriously still and suddenly collected till Mr. Verloc was heard with an accent of marital authority, and moving slightly to make room for her to sit on the edge of the sofa.
>
> "Come here," he said in a peculiar tone, which might have been the tone of brutality, but was intimately known to Mrs. Verloc as the note of wooing.
>
> She started forward at once, as if she was still a loyal woman bound to that man by an unbroken contract. Her right hand skimmed slightly the end of the table, and when she had passed on towards the sofa the carving knife had vanished without the slightest sound from the side of the dish. Mr. Verloc heard the creaky plank in the floor, and was content. He waited. Mrs. Verloc was coming. As if the homeless soul of Stevie had flown for shelter straight to the breast of his sister, guardian and protector, the resemblance of her face with that of her brother grew at every step, even to the droop of the lower lip, even to the slight divergence of the eyes. But Mr. Verloc did not see that. He was lying on his back and staring upwards. He saw partly on the ceiling a clenched hand holding a carving knife. It flickered up and down. Its movements were leisurely. They were leisurely enough for Mr. Verloc to recognize the limb and the weapon.

If this paragraph leaves you with the impression that Mrs. Verloc is "'not fully in control of the situation," "unaware of her actions," and "detached," you are not alone.[26] The literary style of this passage is part of a higher-level atmosphere of "moral anarchy" in Conrad's novel.[27] Mrs. Verloc comes across as somehow not responsible for the murder. Where does this impression come from? Look closely at Conrad's language. *Mr. Verloc was heard,* not *She heard Mr. Verloc.* We picture *a clenched hand holding a carving knife,* not *Mrs. Verloc clenching a carving knife.* And during the deed, *its movements were leisurely* not *She stabbed him leisurely.* Conrad's language consistently moves Mrs. Verloc out of the role of actor or agent, even though in the scene, she is committing one of the most agentive acts imaginable: killing somebody with a carving knife.

Discourse analyst Louise Nuttall wanted to test whether readers interpreted Conrad's text in the same way literary scholars do. She rewrote the passage by making the nonagentive parts of Conrad's text as agentive as she could, mostly by putting Mrs. Verloc (or *she*) in the subject position in the sentence. Here is her rewritten version, with the changes underlined:[28]

She remained thus mysteriously still and suddenly collected till she heard Mr. Verloc with an accent of marital authority, and moving slightly to make room for her to sit on the edge of the sofa.

"Come here," he said in a peculiar tone, which might have been the tone of brutality, but Mrs. Verloc knew it intimately as the note of wooing.

She headed toward him at once, as if she was still a loyal woman bound to that man by an unbroken contract. She stroked the end of the table slightly with her hand, and as she passed the table towards the sofa she took the carving knife without the slightest sound from the side of the dish. Mr. Verloc heard the creaky plank in the floor, and was content. He waited for her. Mrs. Verloc was coming to him. As if she sheltered the homeless soul of Stevie, flown straight to the breast of his sister, guardian and protector, she grew to resemble her brother more with every step she took toward him, even to the way she drooped her lip, even to the way she diverted her eyes slightly. But Mr. Verloc did not see that. He was lying on his back and staring upwards at the ceiling. He saw partly on the ceiling Mrs. Verloc clenching a carving knife. She thrust the knife up and down into Mr. Verloc. She stabbed her husband leisurely. She stabbed him leisurely enough for him to recognize the limb and the weapon.

Nuttall ran an experiment in which people were asked to read either Conrad's original, detached, nonagentive version or Nuttall's revised, agentive one. She found that when people read the revised text, they give higher ratings to a number of statements about the text: that Mrs. Verloc was "in control of her actions," that she was "acting intentionally," and that she was "able to influence the outcome of her situation."[29] The two passages ostensibly describe the same events. Nuttall's experiment shows that differences in linguistic choice (of grammatical construction, not just of word choice) can change people's impressions of the forces underlying the events, such as an actor's intentions and agency.

Think about what this means. We aren't just talking about literary style. Changes in language lead to changes in our impression of a character's agency. It would stand to reason that this in turn could lead to a difference in the kind of treatment that Mrs. Verloc might receive in a court of law.

Could agentive language influence legal decisions? Psychologists Caitlin Fausey and Lera Boroditsky looked at the language used in nearly 200,000 legal trials held between 1674 and 1913 at London's central criminal court.[30] They focused on a few key verbs, including *burn* and *break*. Consider the difference between saying *It burned down* (less agentive) versus *Someone burned it down* (more agentive).[31] Fausey and Boroditsky found that if an event was described in an agentive way (as in *They burned it* or *They broke it*), a guilty verdict was more likely than if it had been described in a nonagentive way (as in *It burned* or *It broke*).

As in the studies that inspired the dumbbell/eyeglasses redrawing experiments, this raises a question of causal direction. Did the choice of words simply follow from differences in how the events took place in reality? Like this:

Observe and interpret events of a certain kind. (cause) → Describe them as they are. (effect)

Or did the choice of words cause different understandings of that reality? Like this:

Describe events in a certain way. (cause) → Form a belief that they are that way. (effect)

And if those understandings then resulted in criminal convictions, how often did the choice of words alone make the difference between an innocent versus a guilty verdict? Even if the more agentive language had only a slight effect on the proportion of guilty judgments, this would have affected a good number of people's lives over the course of two and a half centuries of court cases at the Old Bailey. It's hard to imagine a more consequential question for the innocent person who goes to jail or the guilty one who goes free.[32]

Fausey and Boroditsky designed an experiment to test whether these linguistic choices might influence legal reasoning. They asked people to read a report about a fire incident. One group saw this version of the story:

> Mrs. Smith and her friends were finishing a lovely dinner at their favorite restaurant. After they settled the bill, they decided to head to a nearby café for coffee and dessert. Mrs. Smith followed her friends and as she stood up, she flopped her napkin on the centerpiece candle. She had ignited the napkin! As Mrs. Smith reached to grab the napkin, she toppled the candle and ignited the whole tablecloth too! As she jumped back, she overturned the table and ignited the carpet, as well. Hearing her desperate cries, the restaurant staff hurried over and heroically managed to put the fire out before anyone got hurt.

Another group read a nonagentive version, with minimal but important changes (underlined):

> Mrs. Smith and her friends were finishing a lovely dinner at their favorite restaurant. After they settled the bill, they decided to head to a nearby café for coffee and dessert. Mrs. Smith followed her friends and as she stood up, <u>her napkin</u>

flopped on the centerpiece candle. The napkin had ignited! As Mrs. Smith reached to grab the napkin, the candle toppled and the whole tablecloth ignited too! As she jumped back, the table overturned and the carpet ignited as well. Hearing her desperate cries, the restaurant staff hurried over and heroically managed to put the fire out before anyone got hurt.

The only difference between the two versions is that the agentive version has Mrs. Smith as the subject of various sentences while the nonagentive doesn't (*she toppled the candle* versus *the candle toppled*). It's just like the two versions of Conrad's Mrs. Verloc scene.

All of the participants in the experiment were asked to rate Mrs. Smith's culpability and assign a dollar amount to the damages she should be asked to pay the restaurant. The result was that "a subtle difference in language caused a big difference in dollars." People who read the agentive report ruled on average that Mrs. Smith should pay $935 in fines. That was nearly $250 more than the average fines suggested by the participants who saw the nonagentive reports. The experiment shows that language can be decidedly effective in nudging people's reasoning.

In 2018, Christie's auction house sold the world's first AI-generated painting, created by a deep-learning algorithm trained on Renaissance masters. The artwork sold for half a million dollars, forty times Christie's initial estimate. It was a distributed effort: one team built the machine-learning architecture, another built the algorithm, a technologist trained it, and curators printed and marketed the work. Yet the algorithm alone was credited as the artist, and the money went solely to the curators. The case raises fundamental questions about human agency, creativity, control, credit, and responsibility in the context of teamwork and transformative technology. It also gave researchers a chance to test the effects of language on our interpretation of distributed agency. Computational social scientist Ziv Epstein and colleagues found that people reasoned differently depending on the language used: when the algorithm was described as "a tool," people attributed more credit to the person who trained it than when it was described as "an agent."[33] The finding that language influences perceived agency in the context of distributed roles has profound implications for the legal and moral agency of machines and of the people who design and use them. These implications are not confined to modern technology but will also be observable wherever human agency is distributed, either across people in groups or with nonhuman entities.

Do the results of controlled experiments like these translate into real-world consequences? The answer is yes. Minor differences in wording sometimes result in different responses with potential life-and-death consequences.

Picture an elderly woman standing with her partner at home by the bathroom sink. She turns to him and says *I feel funny*. She collapses into his arms; he sits her on the floor and calls 911. The call taker says to him:[34]

Tell me exactly what happened

Here's how he responds (transcribed from a recorded call):[35]

Uh my partner who has Alzheimer's and has had it for a while, I took her to the toilet and we're in the bathroom and uh washing her hands and she was drying her hands and she's turned to me and said "I feel funny" and she collapsed. And of course I was able to catch her. She hasn't hit her head or anything else like that and she is sitting unconscious if you like but breathing. And she breathes for a few minutes or say thirty seconds.

The call continues, and soon an ambulance is dispatched.

Now compare this to a different case but a similar situation. This time, the call taker says:

Tell me exactly what's happened

Here is the caller's response:

It seems like she's collapsed. She's had a stomach ache for the last couple of days and all of a sudden she just can't get out of bed.

There is a clear difference in how these callers respond to the scripted prompt from the call taker. The first caller gives a *narrative*: a blow-by-blow account of what led to the situation, how it played out. The second caller's response is more of a *report*: briefer and simpler, focusing more on the situation at hand. This difference between callers' responses to the call taker's prompt is no accident. It is triggered by a subtle but real difference in how the scripted prompt was delivered in the two cases. Did you notice it?

In a study of nearly two hundred emergency calls for cardiac arrest in the city of Perth, Australia, emergency care researcher Marine Riou and colleagues found that more than half of the time, the emergency call takers would deviate slightly from the prescribed script. The Medical Priority Dispatch System Protocol stipulates that after a call taker gets the location and phone number of a caller, she should say, *Tell me exactly what happened*. But 60 percent of the time, call takers would instead say, *Tell me exactly what's happened.* The phrase *what happened* features a simple past form of the verb. But in *what's happened* (short for "what *has* happened"), the verb is in the present perfect form. The first option focuses our attention on a chain of events in the past, while the second focuses on the situation as it is now.

Just as the examples show, in the real-life emergency calls that Riou and colleagues examined, people responded to *What's happened?* with brief reports, while they responded to *What happened?* with narratives that went on average for twice as long as the reports (18 seconds versus 9 seconds). The narrative-type responses provided more detailed contextual information but also delayed the time it took to dispatch ambulances to assist cardiac arrest patients: 58 seconds versus 50 seconds on average. An 8-second delay might not seem like long to you, reading this now. I think it would if you were breathing what could be your last breaths.

Now imagine you've been through a period of feeling generally unwell. A few things are wrong. You're often tired. You're getting occasional discomfort in your chest. One day you get a bad skin rash and you go to the doctor to get it checked out. The doctor takes a look at the rash and prescribes a medicine. At the end of the visit, she asks, *Do you have any other concerns you would like to discuss today?* This is a common question. But unfortunately, people who really do have other concerns often say no to this question and go on their way. If your doctor was given the additional information about your occasional chest pain, your frequent tiredness, she might look to diagnose a deeper and more serious problem. (Taken together, these symptoms can point to heart disease.) Failing to mention these other concerns could be a dangerous omission.

A team of medical sociologists wondered if this problem could be remedied. They conducted a study in acute care consultation rooms in California and Pennsylvania.[36] Doctors were given scripts to use in the consultation. One group asked the question I have just described: *Do you have any other concerns you would like to discuss today?* Another group was given a script with one crucial difference. The word *any* was replaced by *some*: *Do you have some other concerns you would like to discuss today?* What difference might this make? Well, *any* is what linguists call a negative polarity item. We say *I don't have any cash on me,* not *I don't have some cash on me.* By contrast, *some* is a positive polarity item. It occurs in positive contexts. We say *There were some funny scenes in that film,* not *There were any funny scenes.* This little difference between *any* and *some* makes a big difference when it comes to asking questions in English. The question *Do you have any other concerns?* sets up an expectation that the answer will be no. This doesn't mean the answer must be no. It means that a *no* answer is in a sense easier to give. In the study, researchers spoke to patients after the consultations were completed, to find out for sure whether they actually did have more than one health concern going in to the consultation. They compared how those patients had responded to the doctors' scripted questions. The researchers found that when doctors asked *Do you have any other concerns?* only around half of the patients said yes. This rate of response was the same as cases in which the doctor didn't ask anything about further concerns at all. In other words, asking *Do you have any other concerns?* is as likely to elicit more concerns as not saying anything at all. But when *any* was replaced by *some*, the proportion of patients reporting their other concerns went up to 90 percent, a huge improvement in remedying unmet concerns, with clear public health implications.

In one more example, a study of the language used by UK police negotiators combed through more than thirty hours of audio-recorded hostage and crisis negotiations.[37] When trying to engage in dialogue with people in crisis, police negotiators tend to use one of two words: *talk* (as in "Can you just talk to me") and *speak* (as in "Just speak to me please"). (The word *talk* is used about twice as often as *speak* in these situations.) But there was a difference in the effectiveness of this choice: "When negotiators propose to *talk* to persons in crisis, they are more likely to face explicit rejection than when they propose to *speak*."[38] The two words are near-synonyms, but *speak* has less of a focus on two-way exchange, and hence may seem less confronting in the context of a crisis negotiation.

In the what's-happened, some/any, and speak/talk studies, a simple choice in language—one that we might easily think of as too subtle to make any real difference—turns out to have definite consequences for how people respond. It shows one thing that language is good for: nudging people's behavior in a certain direction.

As we've seen, sometimes these nudges can play a role in shaping social accountability. The matter of culpability and language is central to some of the most famous examples put forward to support the view that language can direct our reasoning, and in turn our behavior.

The early twentieth-century linguist Benjamin Lee Whorf once worked for a fire insurance company. He analyzed hundreds of reports of circumstances surrounding the start of fires.[39] At first, he focused on physical causes, such as defective wiring or air spaces. But he came to realize that "the meaning of that situation to people was sometimes a factor, through the behavior of the people, in the start of the fire."[40] Whorf suggested that the clearest factor in the meaning of a situation was "a linguistic meaning, residing in the name or the linguistic description commonly applied to the situation." Here is Whorf's best-known example:

> Thus, around a storage of what are called "gasoline drums", behavior will tend to a certain type, that is, great care will be exercised; while around a storage of what are called "empty gasoline drums", it will tend to be different—careless, with little repression of smoking or of tossing cigarette stubs about. Yet the "empty" drums are perhaps the more dangerous, since they contain explosive vapour. Physically the situation is hazardous, but the linguistic analysis according to regular analogy must employ the word "empty", which inevitably suggests lack of hazard. The word "empty" is used in two linguistic patterns: (1) as a virtual synonym for "null and void, negative, inert", (2) applied in analysis of physical situations without regard to, e.g., vapor, liquid vestiges, or stray rubbish, in the container. The situation is named in one pattern (2) and the name is then "acted out" or "lived up to" in another (1), this being a general formula for the linguistic conditioning of behavior into hazardous forms.

Whorf gives more examples. An insulation covering was known as *spun limestone*. To people's surprise, when they left it exposed to excessive heat, the insulation burned vigorously: "Behavior that tolerated fire close to the covering was induced by the use of the name 'limestone,' which because it ends in '-stone' implies non-combustibility."[41] And the case of *scrap lead*: "Beside a coal-fired melting pot for lead reclaiming was dumped a pile of 'scrap lead'—a misleading verbalization, for it consisted of the lead sheets of old radio condensers, which still had paraffin paper between them. Soon the paraffin blazed up and fired the roof, half of which was burned off."[42]

These passages, and the concept being expressed, have been interpreted widely as a claim that language determines thought. But Whorf is less focused here on thought than on behavior. By labeling physical situations in certain ways, we are led to act in certain ways. The behavior is "induced by naming," within a framework of understanding that is "to a large extent unconsciously built up on the language habits of the group."[43] Whorf argued that our choices of words result in a kind of "behavioral compulsiveness."

*

Let's recap some of what we've discovered in this chapter. Language can direct people's thought processes and, in turn, our actions and reactions. Whether this is a good thing, and if so who it is good for, will depend on the situation. But the effects can be exploited. Our beliefs, understandings, and memories of things we have experienced can be affected by language. Instructions using language (even as instructions to self) are handy and reduce effort, but they result in the discarding of information. They shut down our processes of attention so that we may turn to the next thing. An effect of this is that if we describe a person, event, or object when we see it, this makes us less likely to accurately remember what we saw. And the words we hear to label or pre-empt things we experience can interfere with our psychological processing of the experience. As Whorf wrote, people "describe situations to themselves" and these notes to self in turn lead us to certain actions and interpretations. In this way, language can be a self-directed coordination device. It can bridge the gap between me now and myself later.[44]

This chapter has examined the phenomenon of priming and related contextual effects on our thought and behavior. These effects somewhat complicate the question of what language is good for. On the face of it, if language interferes with our interpretations and memories of reality, this would seem to be a disadvantage. But these effects can be viewed as advantages in more than one way. For one thing, it can be to our advantage to overlook details of a situation if a global understanding (derived from language) is more useful. For another, someone who understands the cognitive effects of language might find ways to exploit them to their advantage in social interaction. In any case, the better we understand these effects, the more mindful of them we may become, and the better we may be able to take control of the effects, either by wielding them to affect others or by recognizing and taming them in ourselves.

With several of the studies we've looked at, we have already begun to explore the phenomenon of linguistic *framing*. We talk about framing at length later in the book. But first, we turn to an important corollary of the power of language to influence thought and action, one that arises from the fact that different languages have different systems of meaning.

5 Linguistic Relativity

By carefully choosing your words, you can distract me, slow me down, speed me up, and even strip away the details of my very perceptions. In the previous chapter, we looked at choices in English like *eyeglasses* versus *dumbbells* and *The church was struck by lightning* versus *Lightning struck the church*. These choices had effects on behavior: how fast we respond to something, the way we respond, or the kind of judgment or decision we make.

Now think about this in light of the fact that languages differ—sometimes radically—in the choices they provide. Languages can have very different sets of words and grammatical rules. If choice of words influences thought and action—as we saw in the previous chapter, which mostly dealt with English—then it follows that different languages influence thought and action in different ways.

If a language did not have a way to distinguish between agentive and nonagentive sentences—as in English, *She burned it* versus *It burned*—then we might not expect to see effects like those discussed in the previous chapter. The Akan language of West Africa lacks a choice of the passive/active.[1] When Tomlin tested that language in his fish-eats-fish study, the little arrow pointing at one of the two fish at the key moment had no effect on people speaking Akan.

The idea that different languages have different kinds of influence on people's thought and behavior is known as *linguistic relativity*.[2]

Would people who speak different languages behave differently in the kinds of experiments we reviewed in the previous chapter? Remember that in one study, people suggested different penalties depending on whether an incident was described as *she toppled the candle* versus *the candle toppled*. Psychologist Caitlin Fausey and colleagues followed up on this study to test whether the effects applied differently when different languages were involved. They compared English and Japanese.

The experiments featured a set of video clips in which actors played out events that were either accidental or intentional. Among the intentional events: a person crumples a can by stepping on it; someone faces a table and knocks a box off it; someone pours rice into a measuring cup. Accidental events included these: someone turns to walk and crumples a can by stepping on it; a person gestures and knocks a box off the table (then reaches to grab it); someone spills rice while pouring it into a measuring cup. In the first part of the experiment, English and Japanese speakers watched the video clips and simply had to describe what they saw. When they saw intentional events, speakers of both languages used agentive language, as in *She broke the vase* (as opposed to *The vase broke*). But when they saw the accidental events, speakers of the two languages behaved differently.

In describing accidental events, English speakers used agentive language more often than Japanese speakers did. Imagine a person accidentally bumping a vase and knocking it over. To describe this, Japanese speakers were more likely to say something like *The vase got knocked over*, while many English speakers would tend to say *She knocked the vase over*. Does this mean that English speakers have a more generally heightened awareness of and interest in agents than Japanese speakers do, regardless of whether the agents' actions are intentional or accidental? To probe this question, the experimenters asked people to watch the video clips and simply remember what they saw, without overtly describing it. In line with the fashions of speaking observed in the description part of the study, English and Japanese speakers described intentional events in the same agentive terms, and also were equally good at remembering the agents of intentional events. But when it came to *accidental* events, English speakers remembered the agents of accidents better than Japanese speakers did. This difference in how people remember what they've seen fits with the observed difference in linguistic description: English speakers *described* accidents in more agentive terms and also *remembered* them in more agentive terms.[3]

What's going on here? It looks as if these English and Japanese speakers are thinking in line with the unalike habits of their languages, even when they are doing tasks that don't require them to use language. But if language is a persistent part of the broader context for our cognitive life, then maybe we shouldn't be too surprised by these results. If context affects how we think and if our language is part of our broad context for thinking, then our background knowledge of language may broadly affect how we think.[4]

In turn, differences between languages can be exploited in priming people's behavior differently. In another part of their study, Fausey and colleagues found that they could manipulate people's attention to agents in the scenes they had to remember. When English speakers were primed with agentive sentences—even when these were unrelated to the scenes they had to remember—for example, *He burned the toast, He unfastened the necklace*—they were better at remembering the individuals involved in the causal event.

The effects shown in this contrast between English and Japanese concern patterns of attention and focus on objectively distinct elements of a situation. But the effects of language differences arguably go deeper, into our very perceptions. Let's see how.

Dutch and German are closely related languages. Both have words distinguishing the colors yellow and orange, but they use them differently in one prominent context. The middle traffic light, between red and green, is referred to in Dutch as *oranje* (orange) and in German as *Gelb* (yellow). But the objective color of that light is the same in the two countries. It must be, to conform to European legal norms. Psychologist Holger Mitterer and colleagues created images with subtly different hues and showed them to Dutch and German speakers. They asked people to label the colors. In one part of the experiment, people saw a picture of a traffic light and were asked to label the color of the middle light. They adjusted the color to a hue exactly halfway between typical yellow and typical orange. Dutch and German speakers were influenced in different directions by their different social conventions of naming traffic lights. Although they saw the exact same orange-yellow hue, German speakers were more likely to call it "yellow" while Dutch speakers were more likely to call it "orange."

This shows that a habit of naming can affect people's judgments in a broad, top-down way. The finding is similar to an earlier discovery by Mitterer in a study with psychologist Jan de Ruiter. They used the same yellow-orange hue to color an image of both a banana and a carrot. When people saw the banana, they were more likely to call the ambiguous color "yellow," and when they saw the carrot, they would call the exact same color "orange." In both studies, contextual information appears to override direct perception. The traffic light study shows that "contextual information" includes knowledge of language and conventional practices of naming. As Mitterer and colleagues put it, "It's not what things look like, it's what you call them."[5]

These kinds of linguistic effects do more than affect people's judgments about where the line between categories lies—for example, between yellow and orange; they may even affect people's very ability to detect a perceptual distinction at all. As we saw in the previous chapter, hunter-gatherers of the Malay Peninsula have comparatively rich vocabularies for referring to smells. They are also better at identifying and distinguishing among odors. This ability is arguably linked to their possession of an appropriate vocabulary.[6]

A more general kind of effect of language differences on our cognition comes from differences between languages in how sentences are constructed. Most languages of the world are either right-branching or left-branching in their grammatical structure. Without getting into the technicalities of what this means, basically in a right-branching language (such as English), the ordering of elements in a sentence tends to be subject-verb-object (*They ate rice*). In a left-branching language such as Japanese, the basic order tends to be subject-object-verb (*They rice ate*). These different ways of organizing sentences imply different requirements for cognitive processing. Suppose you are listening to somebody talking. Processing language happens fast, and you have no time to waste. So to understand what they are trying to say, you will begin by processing the first thing you hear (or see, if it's sign language), and you will incrementally process what comes in, relying heavily on working memory as you go. (The term *working memory* refers to the short-term storage of information in the mind, where it can be quickly accessed for decision making.) The way your language orders things can affect the way you process and remember the things people say. Different languages imply different cognitive strategies for understanding in the rapid flow of conversation.

A team of researchers tested the implications of different types of ordering for cognitive processing.[7] They worked with speakers of four right-branching languages (Oshiwambo, spoken in Namibia; Khmer, spoken in Cambodia; Thai; and Italian) and four left-branching languages (Sidaama, spoken in Ethiopia; Khoekhoe, spoken in Namibia; Korean; and Japanese). Speakers of these eight languages were given a set of working memory and short-term memory tests involving various strings of numbers, pictures, or words. Their job was to recall these strings in the order that they were presented.

The goal of the study was to find out if the difference between ordering of elements in the structure of these languages might affect the way people used working memory. The researchers looked at participants' ability to recall the first and last items in the lists that they were given in the memory tasks. They found that people who spoke left-branching languages were better at recalling what came first in a list, just as people who spoke right-branching languages were better at recalling what came last.[8] This suggests that working memory is affected by the way in which your language is organized. It means that different communities will remember things differently. Language differences don't just imply different surface structures or word meanings, but extend to more general and fundamental mechanisms of how we process, store, and retrieve information.

We've seen that language has the power to reach into our minds and alter our perceptions, our acts of categorization, our decisions and processes of reasoning, and our habits of memory.[9] If language can imperceptibly constrain or channel our thoughts in these ways, it raises a counterintuitive challenge to our sense of free will. Do our trains of thought run on tracks laid by language, such that each different language takes our thoughts to a different place? Language scientists have long posed and explored these questions, from Johann von Herder in the eighteenth century and Wilhelm von Humboldt in the nineteenth, to Franz Boas and Edward Sapir in the twentieth century and many more over recent decades.[10] Perhaps the best-known author to pose this question is Benjamin Lee Whorf, whom we met in the previous chapter, arguing that people's ways of talking about their surroundings may have affected their behavior in ways that resulted in fires.[11] If you think this means Whorf was taking language to be the sole determinant of behavior or even a straitjacket for thought, you would not be alone. But Whorf never said these things and did not think them.[12]

Here is what Whorf was suggesting. When deciding how to behave, a person might naturally use language in thinking. In so doing, she may effectively discard, or fail to notice, important information that happens not to feature in a linguistic rendering of the state of affairs at hand. It is not that people are incapable of thinking about reality in alternative ways and not that we can't think without language. It is that we are creatures of habit.

If language is our most practiced resource for socially situated behavior, it should be no surprise that language instills deep cognitive habits: habits of attention and disattention, habits of reasoning or failing to reason.

People are not mechanically coerced by language to think and act in certain ways. You *can* be influenced by language, as we've seen. But you are more likely to be influenced by language in these Whorfian ways if you uncritically accept the version of events that language happens to present—in other words, if you are not paying attention. If you are aware and critical of what language is doing to you and for you as you process it—for example, if you are reading a version of the news that you do not agree with—then you are not simply going to be putty in the hands of language. Similarly, if you know or suspect that scrap lead contains paraffin paper, simply hearing the words *scrap lead* is less likely to make you overlook that.

One might say that a language predisposes us to think certain things, but perhaps its main effect is in causing us *not* to think certain things. It is well established that we fail to notice much of what goes on around us.[13] Research on human decision making shows that while we routinely disregard a portion of available information, this in fact makes good sense.[14] Part of the logic of decision making is to minimize the costs involved. It is the same from small things, like choosing which brand of cereal to buy, to big things like finding a life partner. Once you have locked on to a decision-making problem, your next step is to find ways to narrow the search for an appropriate solution and lock off, or stop the search, by making the decision that yields the best balance: desired benefit for lowest cost. And you should make the decision quickly in order to get on with making the next incoming decision.

Take a simple decision: what to order at a restaurant. One strategy is to study the entire menu and weigh every option, comparing them on some list of criteria and selecting the best. But such thoroughness could be cognitively and socially costly, a waste of time and energy. A good alternative is the strategy known as satisficing.[15] Satisficing means not wasting your time studying all the options. Just settle on the first solution that is *good enough for current purposes* and stop the search. So if you see the mushroom risotto and you like the idea, it may not pay to keep reading the menu in the hope of finding something better.

How do we determine what qualifies as good enough? This is what *concepts* are for. Concepts—which define categories, as we saw in the previous chapter—are tools in decision making because they give us criteria for recognizing instances of what we are looking for and of what we are not looking for. Concepts are sieves.[16] We use them for making decisions and, in turn, for taking actions. Whorf's idea was simply that language is likely to play a central role in decision making.

At the root of this idea are two facts. First, the most ready-at-hand concepts that we reach for in reasoning are likely to be the ones encoded in the languages we speak.[17] Second, the languages we speak are known to differ radically in the kinds of concepts they encode. This suggests that different languages provide their speakers with different bases for decision making and, subsequently, different patterns of behavior.

*

It is one thing to suppose that language shapes our behavior, but can language shape reality? In one sense, the answer is, of course, no. Language cannot change the laws of nature. But in practice, a large part of what we call "reality" is quite subjective.[18] For humans with human ears, ultrasonic noises are out of range (although we can infer their existence using other means, from high-tech instruments such as spectrograms to low-tech measures such as watching what dogs do). The body defines an individual's horizons, both limiting and licensing our possible perceptions and actions. If you have the body of a bat, a pitch-dark cave will seem like a good place to be. With the body of an earthworm, you will feel at home in a stretch of turf. If these are not different worlds, they are certainly different worldviews.

Along similar lines, each language is a kind of body for thinking and acting. Philosopher of mind Gilbert Ryle suggested that thought is something that takes place in public, in people's observable behavior.[19] When we perceive or understand our world, we are engaging with it, interpreting it, and reacting to it. The reasoning involved draws on concepts and categories in a range of ways, and, as is clear to anyone who looks, many, if not most, of our concepts and categories are supplied by the languages we speak.

As Edward Sapir wrote, "The language habits of our community predispose certain choices of interpretation."[20] According to this view, the study of different languages, especially of those that are most different from so-called Standard Average European,[21] has the potential to supply us with new and different ways of actively interpreting the world. Whorf avidly promoted the study of lesser-known languages, such as those of Native

America, because each language provides an opportunity to broaden our understanding in one more way. Nobody is "free to describe nature with absolute impartiality," Whorf argued. But the person who would come closest "would be a linguist familiar with very many widely different linguistic systems."[22] Today's language explorers are fulfilling this ambition.

Whorf's ideas have been developed and extended since the late twentieth century and since, despite various objections and misconstruals.[23] The case has been made both for and against the idea that our language affects our thinking in distinct domains of reality, including color, space, and time.[24] Some sample findings: How we see and categorize color distinctions can be affected by cross-language differences in color words.[25] How we feel about inanimate objects such as bridges can be affected by whether the word for the object is grammatically feminine (as for "bridge" in German) or masculine (as in Spanish).[26] The way we reason about location can be affected by the frame of reference that is dominant in a language (cardinal directions in some languages versus left/right in others).[27]

Research on linguistic relativity, penetrating as it is, has covered only a thin slice of the possible scope of this topic because of its narrow interpretation of the three defining concepts: reality, thought, and language.[28] *Reality* has been taken to mean the realm of objective, nonsocial facts: "concepts of 'time,' 'space,' and 'matter.'"[29] *Thought* or *mind* has been taken to refer to forms of categorization, reasoning, and memory about reality, that is, general cognition as opposed to social cognition. And *language* has mostly been taken to refer to words and what they denote: that is, the referential function of language. But the referential function of language is just one among several.[30] The linguist Roman Jakobson defined six basic types of function that a piece of linguistic behavior can have—not just the referential function but also the functions he termed *emotive* (expressing feelings), *poetic* (focusing on structure or form in language), *conative* (influencing the hearer), *phatic* (opening up a channel between people), and *metalingual* (using language to talk about language).[31] Any swatch of language can usually be seen to perform several, if not all, of these functions at once. Jakobson's framework is grounded in the fundamental elements of a communicative act: context, sender, message, addressee, channel, and code.[32] While the referential function orients to the context, picking out or presenting objects and events for attention, the phatic function, for example, orients to the channel, opening up or maintaining a connection between interlocutors.

So linguistic relativity isn't just about how differences among languages affect the way language refers to things in the world. Consider the effects that differences between languages might have on the phatic function of language. In its phatic function, language opens up a channel between the sender and receiver of a message. When I say, *Hi*, this doesn't refer to any object or event, it opens up a channel of communication. Consider a form of linguistic relativity in the phatic function implied by differences in the sensory modality that a language relies on. Opening up a channel for communication between people is a very different matter in a spoken language than it is for deaf people using a sign language. Signers need others to be looking at them, while for speakers, it may be enough just to be heard.[33] The differences have implications both for how we think and how we behave.[34]

When people interact using sign language, they secure each other's attention "using a set of conventional behaviors, including tapping the addressee, waving a hand in the addressee's line of vision, pounding a surface, or even stomping one's foot."[35] When the channel of communication becomes a locus of contention—as happens when an interaction turns into a confrontation—again modality-specific effects are heightened. In a quarrel in sign language, a person may attempt to forcibly keep the channel open by physically turning someone's face (and hence that person's eye gaze) toward him if the other has looked away. Or he may force the channel shut by closing his eyes or even by holding an interlocutor's arms or wrists to prevent that person from signing.[36] These ways of manipulating the channel through which language is transmitted are determined by the nature of the language.[37]

Why has the referential function been treated as the privileged or main function of language? One answer is scholarly tradition. Lines of research such as psycholinguistics happen to have been heavily focused on reference, and these happen to be where currently dominant work on linguistic relativity is carried out. But we may also ask why tradition is like this in the first place. One possibility is that our scholarly work is influenced by our natural cognitive habits of linguistic awareness. It is arguably easier to isolate and focus our shared attention on the referential function of language than on other functions, leading us naturally to gravitate toward focusing on that function in our research, as well as in how we talk about language more generally.[38]

Linguistic diversity is causally related to cultural and cognitive diversity in numerous ways. We have reviewed some effects on thought from language differences in this chapter. There is still a lot to learn about the consequences of the true diversity of human languages. We do not know if effects such as verbal overshadowing are the same for all members of our language-using species, partly because we are still mapping the real extent of semantic and grammatical variance across the seven thousand or so languages spoken in the world today.

*

Imagine a language with a vocabulary for faces so perfect that you could recognize a stranger from a verbal description alone. An attacker's face would no longer "defy complete linguistic description," with the result that words in that language would not overshadow people's memory for faces and we could expect lower rates of wrongful conviction in that community based on witness misidentification. Linguistic fieldwork may yet uncover such a language, with a fine vocabulary for faces, but in the meantime, we know that English is not it.[39]

Not all the known effects of language on thought are as consequential as the witness misidentifications that can destroy people's lives. And not all linguistic effects are as innocuous as many neo-Whorfian findings seem to be: a subtle perturbation that color vocabulary can create in one eye but not the other[40] or a subconscious sexual stereotyping of inanimate objects such as keys or bridges in association with the grammatical gender of words.[41] If a speaker of one language is more likely to come home from the hardware store with the wrong shade of paint, then that might sound harmless, but not if it leads to a domestic argument. Nor is it harmless if a worker is more likely to cause a factory fire—or to misjudge her own potential culpability—or if a witness is more likely to put a man in prison for a crime he didn't commit. So the possibility is not trivial that the effects of language on thought and social reality can influence behavior and affect our lives.[42]

People have long been captivated by the idea that people with different languages are "not equivalent as observers."[43] But equally, people with different languages are not equivalent as agents. The mind, including the parts of it that are built through language, is a purpose-made tool kit for social action, just as a body is a tool kit for physical action. And because languages are so differently structured, each one is like the body plan of a different species, affording its users different ranges of possibilities within certain common constraints.

What does the linguistic relativity debate tell us about what language is good for? When scholars talk about linguistic relativity, they often highlight the idea that people are at the mercy of their languages, that our thoughts and actions are nudged, directed, and channeled by the languages we happen to have inherited. The more we learn about the diverse ways in which languages portray and construct reality, the more control we can gain over language's influence on us. A language, then, does not imprison you; it equips you. Seen in this way, a language is not a straitjacket; it is an action suit.

To understand what this means, we need to move our focus away from the relation between a person and the things they talk about. To better understand the role of language as a coordination device, we now turn our attention to the interpersonal relationship that any usage of language entails.

6 Communicative Need

If a lion could talk, we could not understand him.

—Ludwig Wittgenstein (1953)

One morning in the rainforested uplands of Kri territory in central Laos, I was traveling between village hamlets as I sought to learn more about the Kri language during my first field expedition to the area. All my energy was focused on building a vocabulary of the language. I had my notebook at the ready every minute. Two village men, Baai and Kham, were heading in the same direction as I was, and so they gave me a ride in their longboat. Kri territory is nestled just to the west of the Annamite Cordillera, the mountain chain whose ridge serves as the Laos-Vietnam border, near where Vietnam is at its narrowest. There are more plant, mammal, reptile, and bird species in this protected area than anywhere else in mainland Southeast Asia. The undulating riverine environment features chains of river pools, expanses of still water that create breaks in the forest canopy. Traveling along these pools quietly in a canoe is a time to see wildlife, such as bands of macaques coming down to drink at the edge the river, or to hear the calls of gibbons from the distant hilltops.

That morning, we sat in file, pushing along through a still and spacious river pool with no perceptible flow. The only sound was the light cutting of oars into the mirror-like water and the trickle of runoff. Suddenly, an enormous bird emerged from the jungle overstory to our right, arcing high over the open expanse of river and heading north. At the front of the boat, Baai pointed up. He turned to look at Kham and called out *vung vaawq!* This is the Kri word for the crested argus (*Rheinardia ocellata*), a spectacular peafowl-like pheasant of the forest. And as quick as that, the great bird was gone. That was all. Everyone was silent, and on we went.

Later that evening, I puzzled over that moment as I checked my notes. From photographs, I figured out which bird Baai had referred to. But why, in that moment, had Baai turned to look at Kham and say the bird's name? Just think about what this little example of language use consists of. A man sees something interesting, turns to his companion, and says the word for the thing out loud. If languages are problem-solving systems, what problem was Baai solving by calling out the word for the crested argus that day?[1]

A long-standing scientific debate points to some possible answers.[2] Anthropologists have puzzled over the kinds of data we reviewed in chapter 3 on global patterns in the number and kind of words that speakers of different languages have for things in their natural environment. We can now consider possible explanations. Why is it that "only a small subset of the species diversity in any one local habitat is ever recognized linguistically by local human populations"?[3] The cognitive anthropologist Brent Berlin has pointed to two possible explanations. One is the *intellectualist* view: languages make the distinctions they make because human beings are inherently interested in acknowledging—by naming—the distinctions that are perceptually most prominent in nature.[4] Words directly reflect this perceptual prominence. Berlin states that

> in the categorization of plants and animals by peoples living in traditional societies, there exists a specifiable and partially predictable set of plant and animal taxa that represent the smallest fundamental biological discontinuities easily recognized in any particular habitat. This large but finite set of taxa is special in each system in that its members stand out as beacons on the landscape of biological reality.[5]

Beacons on the landscape of reality. According to this view, when Baai turned to Kham and said *vung vaawq*, it was an intellectual act, a sheer expression of mental interest in distinguishing bird species and an act that was possible because the Kri language has a word for this bird.

Another view is *utilitarian*. According to this view, the naming of a plant or animal in a language will be guided by the "practical consequences of knowing or not knowing [that] plant or animal" in the relevant cultural context.[6] An obvious problem with this claim is that languages often have words for plants and animals that are of no obvious utility to speakers, whether this utility be concerned with the need to pursue, avoid, or otherwise be invested in the ability to identify a life form.[7] This is the case with the Kri word for the crested argus. Kri speakers do not hunt, breed, catch, or otherwise use these birds, or any other birds for that matter. Does this mean the word *vung vaawq* cannot be explained in utilitarian terms? We need to distinguish between the usefulness of a particular bird and the usefulness of the word for that bird. After all, we are trying to understand why the word exists, and not why the crested argus exists. So the question is not what the practical consequences are of knowing or not knowing a plant or animal. The question is: What are the practical consequences of knowing or not knowing *the word for* it?

It is clearly reasonable to assume that if something is useful to a group of people, those people will likely have a word to refer to it. This is because they will need a label for solving recurrent problems of social coordination around the thing. For example, there is a variety of Cyperacea reed (related to papyrus) that is useful to many Lao-speaking villagers for making floor mats, so it is useful for them to have a word for the plant (in Lao, the word is *phùù*). Note that the utility of the thing is logically quite distinct from the utility of *a word for* the thing. The word is needed in order to coordinate activity (e.g., in saying things like "Shall we go to the swamp tomorrow and collect some Cyperacea reeds?").

There are words for plants that appear to be of no direct utility to people who know the word—that is, where there are no consequences of knowing or not knowing those plants.[8] But there is what we might call *indirect* utility. Here is an example of the indirect utility of knowing a particular tree species and being able to distinguish it from others. The word *lkêêm* is Kri for the tree *Pterocarya tonkinensis* or Tonkin wingnut. Why do Kri speakers have a word for this tree? The only way to tell is to look at what Kri speakers are doing when they use the word in real life.

In one of my field recordings of conversation in Kri-speaking homes, two Kri-speaking men are talking about where they plan to plant crops in the next year: "I'm going to clear the vegetation up here and make a fence on the side of that other *lkêêm* tree there."[9] In mentioning this species of tree by name, the man takes it for granted that the other man knows which tree he means. This presupposes that the tree species is perceptually distinct enough to serve as a landmark. But nothing here suggests that the tree itself is of any direct use to the men in this conversation—for example, as a source of food, building material, or shelter. Nor is this reference motivated by intellectual interest. This example supports Berlin's view that the perceptual salience of the referent is important, but it suggests that the role of this salience is not to satisfy curiosity but to provide a basis for solving Schelling-style coordination problems. What matters is that the two men can mutually identify a specific tree for the purpose of coordinating their understanding of the location being spoken about. The reference to the tree as a landmark is opportunistic. It works only because both speakers share a rich common understanding of the local environment: they are able to distinguish tree species, they can reliably label them, and they are familiar with specific trees in the area. For Kri speakers, one payoff of recognizing and remembering tree species and their names is that their known positions can be exploited in getting people to coordinate around locations.

Another example is the phenomenon of calendar plants. In Tafea Province of southern Vanuatu, a hardy coastal shrub known as sea daisy (*Melanthera biflora*) is called *intop asiej* in the Aneityum language. The sea daisy goes into flower at the same time that sea turtles are fat and good to hunt.[10] The flowers have no causal connection to the lives of turtles; they just happen to be reliably correlated in the annual cycle of life. So if one person says, *Look, the sea daisy are flowering,* to an outsider, this might appear to be a random observation of no consequence. But to an insider who shares knowledge of the local environment it can mean, *We could go turtle hunting.* The observation of the flowering daisies would be understood as a reason for action.

When people share rich knowledge and associations of the natural ecology, they are like Schelling's parachutists, trying to meet in the same place, taking cues from landmarks they have common access to. Language brings these landmarks into shared attention for a shared purpose. A statement that a certain plant is flowering could have an intended meaning well separated from what its simple, literal meaning would suggest. The Vanuatu sea daisy example suggests that a person's reason to know a word for a certain plant might have nothing to do with their interest in that plant per se, but rather be solely in the service of their interest in hunting turtles.

Another example, taking us now beyond the domain of life forms, is the emu constellation in Australian Aboriginal astronomy, a huge, thin section of dark clouds in the Milky Way running from the Coalsack Nebula (the emu's head) longwise through the constellations of Scorpius and Sagittarius.[11] Through the year, people track the position of the emu in the night sky. When the emu is in a certain position in relation to the horizon, people know that the season for collecting emu eggs has come. They can use that constellation's position in the night sky as a device for social coordination. Let's return to the crested argus. That day on the river, when Baai turned to Kham and said the name of the bird, one possibility is that he was taking a simple opportunity for social bonding through sharing experience. In that boat, both men individually had the same visual experience of seeing the bird, but when Baai looked at Kham and called its name, it was a public act that took two parallel experiences and converted them into a *shared* experience. This is what one-year-old children do when they point to things that interest them. Often all they want is for others to look too and to share with them in the experience.[12] Pointing something out serves a bonding function between people by aligning their attention on a common focus, as when the capuchins of Costa Rica's dry forests forge coalitions by ganging up on patches of dirt.

We should also note that Baai's act of saying the bird's name may also have been a display of expertise. Maybe he was bragging: *I know what that bird is called.* Could it be that the only reason the Kri language even has a word for that bird is so that speakers can display that they know it? After all, Kri speakers know well over a hundred bird species names and yet have virtually no direct interactions with birds or any practical uses for them. They don't raise or eat birds apart from chickens. According to the commonsense referential view of language, we have words to convey information about the world and to update others about things they haven't experienced themselves. But in this case, the function of the word arguably has more to do with matters of social coordination and social bonding.[13]

The crested argus, the Emu Constellation, the Tonkin wingnut, the sea daisy: all of these things are not just perceptually prominent to individuals; they are *mutually* prominent in commonly shared knowledge about the environment among people who have words for these things. If we have the same perceptual systems, then perceptual prominence can be *shared* prominence.[14] People can exploit that mutual knowledge—of both the environment and words in the language—in order to coordinate their behavior.

In Thomas Schelling's famous work on social coordination, which we encountered in chapter 1, this mutual prominence is indispensable if coordination problems are to be solved. The idea that a word is primarily a device for coordination is fundamentally different from the idea that a word is for conveying information. Recall our two puzzles about the vocabulary that languages have for distinctions in nature: (1) why words capture such a small slice of reality and (2) why the world's languages are so consistent in what they do capture. These puzzles can't be explained if we see language as a system solely for transmitting information about our environment. Instead, let us see language as a system that people use for coordinating their action and attention. What kind of a system would be ideal for this function?

One idea is that the ideal communicative system would combine "perfectly informative (lossless) communication with perfect simplicity (no cognitive cost)," that is, telepathy or mind reading.[15] But nothing remotely like literal mind reading is necessary if your purpose is to coordinate with someone. We don't need perfect; we just need good enough. And so the question of what language is good for is really the question of what it's good *enough* for. If language were for lossless communication, it would not be much good for that. But if it were for directing attention and achieving social coordination, then it would be just right. For language to achieve social coordination, it only needs to provide a shared map with a landmark that is recognizable by both parties and prominent enough for both people to coordinate around the same thing, and tolerably well. Language could not faithfully transfer a complete idea or experience if it tried. There is no reason to think that when I use a word, my goal is for you to have exactly the same idea in your mind as I have in my mind. What I want is for you to respond in a certain way. Using language requires joint action. Even if I want to mercilessly manipulate you, if I am to do it through language, I must do it by successfully coordinating with you. The information that is transferred in language is a means to achieve this coordination. Whatever works to achieve that is good enough.

Let's consider the example of kinship: how we coordinate our social activities around family relationships. Every human society engages in child rearing and has norms around the relationships that this entails. In turn, every language has words for kin relations such as *daughter, brother, cousin,* and *aunt.* But the systems of kinship terminology in different languages vary widely. As a simple example, take the English word *aunt.* Suppose I tell you *My aunt taught me that.* If you understood what I said, you will know that I am talking about a sister of one of my parents, but you won't know whether she is the sister of my mother or my father. And you won't know whether she is the older or the younger sister.[16] By contrast, in the Kri language, there are four different words that could be translated into English as *aunt*: *mu'u'q* (your mother's younger sister), *naaj* (your mother's older sister), *qoo* (your father's younger sister), and *jaa* (your father's older sister).[17] The difference between these systems has implications for the cognition required when using English as opposed to Kri. Cognitive scientist Charles Kemp and colleagues explain:

> Language must be informative: It must convey the speaker's intended message to the listener with reasonable accuracy. Ideally, language should also be simple: It should require only minimal cognitive resources. These two desiderata necessarily compete against each other. A highly informative communicative system would be very fine-grained, detailed, and explicit—and would as a result be complex, not simple. A very simple system, in contrast, would necessarily leave implicit or unspecified many aspects of the speaker's intended meaning—and would therefore not be very informative. A system supports efficient communication to the extent that it achieves an optimal trade-off between these two competing considerations.[18]

The trade-off is between *communicative cost* and *cognitive cost*.[19] From a Kri speaker's point of view, when I say *aunt* in English, there is a communicative cost: information is lost.[20] Which aunt do I mean? If I wanted to convey more specific information about the kin relation when speaking English, I'd have to spell it out: *My dad's older sister taught me that.* Among English speakers, the distinctions between dad's side/mom's side and older/younger are usually not made unless they are somehow relevant. By contrast, the Kri system has a lower communicative cost than the English system because it makes more information available in one go. The distinction among kinds of aunt is always made. The downside is that the Kri system arguably presents a greater cognitive cost. Kri speakers are required to maintain a more complex system of kinship relations in mind.

The trade-off between the two costs generates an *optimal frontier*.[21] Each language system positions its speakers at a point along this frontier. The diagram in figure 6.1 displays the principle.

At the bottom left corner of figure 6.1, we would have true mind reading:[22] complete retrieval of the concept in another person's mind with zero effort to the sender. At the top right, we would have the opposite: all effort expended but with zero information retrieved. Kemp and colleagues

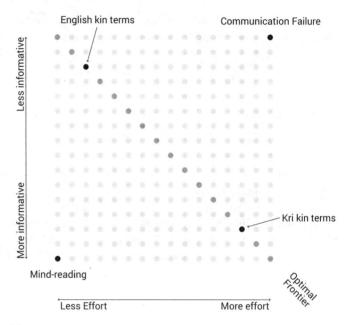

Figure 6.1

The trade-off between how simple and how informative a linguistic system is. Languages occupy an optimal frontier along a line that plays the two parameters off against each other. Many theoretical possibilities are unattested (for example, the extreme case of telepathy). After Kemp, Xu, and Regier, "Semantic Typology and Efficient Communication," 113.

predict that human languages should only have semantic systems that "lie along or near the optimal frontier of this region: the curve defined by systems that are as informative as possible for their level of simplicity, and as simple as possible for their level of informativeness."[23] (Again we see a form of constrained variation across languages. Languages are found to manifest only a small fraction of the full range of theoretically possible patterns—in this case, only the points along the optimal frontier shown in figure 6.1.) What determines the position that a language occupies on this frontier? One answer is "the communicative needs of language users."[24]

Many scholars have suggested that languages are designed to serve the needs and interests of the communities who speak them. In 1911, the anthropologist Franz Boas observed some striking differences between the vocabularies of European and Native American languages. For example, some languages have a greater number of words distinguishing types of snow and ice than others. Boas argued that these differences "must to a certain extent depend upon the chief interests of a people."[25] Similarly, Edward Sapir (Boas's student) wrote that the vocabulary of a language is "a complex inventory of all the ideas, interests, and occupations that take up the attention of the community."[26] This raises a further question: How does a group's interest in something translate into their talking about it more often and making finer distinctions when referring to it? The key to understanding this is that we are not talking about *individuals'* interest and attention but the *social coordination of* interest and attention. Interest alone isn't enough. That interest must be shared. People must coordinate around it.

Let's return to Kri and English words for "aunt." Kri has finer distinctions in this kin relation than English. What things do these words help people coordinate around? Kri kinship structures and norms are highly complex, and we won't go into their many complexities here.[27] What's important is that you cannot get by in life as a member of Kri-speaking society if you don't monitor the specific kinship distinctions that are encoded in the language. The distinction between *jaa* (your father's older sister) and *qoo* (your father's younger sister) has consequences for what you expect from the person and what she expects from you. In English-speaking society, there are no norms suggesting that we should treat the younger siblings of our parents differently from how we treat their older siblings. We don't label them differently. We don't talk to them differently. But for Kri speakers, the different categories of aunt imply different behaviors. The Kri language has a complex system for referring to persons, such that people are distinguished in highly sensitive ways by how we refer to them or address them. It is like French—in which the English word *you* can be translated as either *tu* or *vous*, depending on the degree of closeness or informality between the people talking—but instead of having a simple two-way distinction, there is a much more complex set of rules.

In Kri, the rules mean, say, that you would talk to, and talk about, two kinds of aunt quite differently. For example, you may use the personal name of your father's older sister when referring to her (as we might do in English, saying *Aunty Sam*). But you may not speak the name of someone who has married into your family. So if your father's brother's wife is named Sam, you must avoid saying her name. Instead, you refer to her by her first-born child's name. There are also differences in the pronouns that you are allowed to use in conversation with her in Kri. With your father's older sister, you can use *teeq/cak* (I/you), but with your father's brother's wife, you must use an alternative, polite set of pronouns. Not only do Kri speakers have to track these distinctions, but when someone gets things wrong—especially when children are making errors as they learn the norms of society—words for kin relations emerge in teaching moments. *You can't speak to her like that. she's not your **jaa**!* The effect is basically the same as when we say *Don't sit up there; it's a table, not a chair!* It tells the child that a disruption to the social norms has occurred, and it also tells her something about her language. So when people use these terms for aunt in Kri conversation, they are not so much transferring information as they are coordinating around landmarks on a collective cultural map.

*

The role of language is not primarily "to transfer ideas from one mind to another mind," as is often said.[28] That way of talking treats ideas as packages, to be shipped here and there, delivered and opened, filed away and stored. This is a metaphor in how we talk about how we talk. English speakers are so thoroughly practiced in framing language as a conduit for information that we hardly notice that it is a metaphor: *I can't seem to get these ideas into words. Your concepts come across beautifully. You can find more on that idea in the library.* But as linguist Michael Reddy warned:

> There are no ideas whatsoever in any libraries. All that is stored in any of these places are odd little patterns of marks or bumps or magnetised particles capable of creating odd patterns of noise. Now, if a human being comes along who is capable of using these marks or sounds as instructions, then this human being may assemble within his head some patterns of thought or feeling or perception which resemble those of intelligent humans no longer living. But this is a difficult task, for these ones no longer living saw a different world from ours, and used slightly different language instructions.[29]

Language is a tool for the *instruction of imagination*, as linguist Daniel Dor puts it.[30] Language does not provide direct access between minds because there is always an experiential gap. We all know the experiential gap—the one that means other people can never fully understand what we ourselves experience. They can never know all the details of things we describe to them. Language gives us a workaround for effectively bridging that gap. But as the previous few chapters have shown, only the smallest slice of natural reality is captured in language, in the world's vocabularies for plants and trees, for parts of the human body, for actions of cutting and breaking, for smells, for colors, and more.[31] We have also seen how the vagaries of language can channel and distract our attention, affect our processing, and overwrite our memories. What remains, then, is the barest sketch of reality amid a shower of noise.

We know that both for science and everyday experience, language isn't very good for capturing and conveying the details of reality. Here is the reason. Language isn't *for* capturing and conveying the details of reality. The sketches that language provides are cartoon-like in both the simplistic, caricatured rendering that they give of reality and their capacity for portraying situations with a strong interpretative bias. And this is fit for language's purpose. As a tool, language is not for informing but for persuading. This is why it is bad for scientists but good for lawyers.

When you put things into words, you are creating landmarks in the map of reality as pointers you want to coordinate around. The choice is a matter of framing. As we are about to find out, framing is not just an optional extra in language. Framing is where the partial and constrained nature of language's relationship with reality becomes weaponized.

7 Framing and Inversion

Man muss immer umkehren (One must always invert).

—Carl Jacobi (1820)

During his epic quest for true glory in the Way of the Sword, the great rōnin Miyamoto Musashi was summoned by the shōgun's Council of Elders. He was to become a teacher to the shōgun and found his own school of swordsmanship. People regarded this as one of the highest honors for a would-be samurai. But Musashi was uneasy. When he arrived for his appointment at the shōgun castle's Wadakura Gate, his mind was full of doubt. He feared that accepting an office like this, however noble it may be, would constrain him in his pursuit of the Way. As it turned out, on the day, the offer was withdrawn and Musashi, relieved, was free to go.

> In the courtyard, he did turn around for one last look at the imposing gate, one question filling his mind: Did glory lie inside or outside the gate?[1]

This parable is from "The Gateway to Glory," a chapter of the book *Musashi*, by Eiji Yoshikawa. The chapter's title alludes to the principle of figure-ground reversal. We call it the shogun's gate, not the world's gate. Yet every gate is a gate to the world if we choose to think of it that way. We can always invert or reverse our habitual perspective, but it can take effort.

Inversions and reversals are familiar from the abstract imagery of Gestalt psychology,[2] the nineteenth-century movement that introduced figure-ground reversal to the public consciousness. The famous image in figure 7.1 can be seen in two ways: it is either something black (a trophy) against a white background or something white (two faces) against a black background:

Figure 7.1
Trophy or faces?

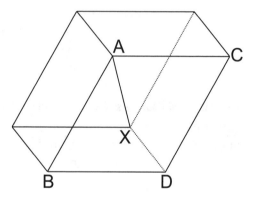

Figure 7.2
Necker cube. After L. A. Necker, "LXI. Observations on Some Remarkable Optical Phænomena Seen in Switzerland; and on an Optical Phænomenon Which Occurs on Viewing a Figure of a Crystal or Geometrical Solid," *The London, Edinburgh, and Dublin Philosophical Magazine and Journal of Science* 1, no. 5 (1832): 336, https://doi .org/10.1080/14786443208647909).

Similarly, the Necker cube (figure 7.2) can be seen in two ways (but we can't see it as both at the same time). We either see the line from X running back to A, with A the farthest point from us (with the face ABCD at the back of the figure, facing up to our left), or pointing forward to A, with point A now closest to us.[3]

These visual examples fascinate and engage us because the two construals are equally accessible. We can readily flip back and forth: now the trophy, now the faces. But with many other reversible images—like Musashi's gateway—one construal dominates. Reversal is hard. If a certain construal is habitual, normal, and always labeled, it's harder for us to entertain the alternatives. The inversion in the Musashi story works because it allows this wise character to surprise us with a new insight—something we weren't seeing. It illustrates the hero's capacity to look at things differently from the rest of us.

These examples introduce the concept of *framing*. How I see an image is a private matter. But how I *label* it is an imposition on others. If I hang figure 7.1 on the wall with a title plate that says "Faces," I'm inviting or instructing people as to how they should view the image. Think about this when you are next in an art gallery. Just because the image is labeled "Faces" doesn't mean that the trophy can't be seen. It does mean that somebody with authority—the artist, in this case—has claimed one of the available construals as the correct one, and this will create a bias toward that construal. When you give a title to an artwork, you publicly set the terms for interpretation. You draw the map that you want us to coordinate around, committing to one of a number of possible views, and you are effectively instructing others to take just that one view of the thing and to commit to that view over others. This is framing. We met this phenomenon earlier under another name. Frege called it *mode of presentation. The Morning Star, the Evening Star*, and *Venus* are alternative ways of framing the same entity.

I want to emphasize that linguistic framing is a way of influencing people. It is one of the things that language is especially good for. Framing is not just a different way of viewing a scene, as when in the privacy of my mind I can flip my vision of a Necker cube. Framing is a public act of influence, whether intentional or not. With framing, we use language to direct another person to see things in one way as opposed to the other ways they themselves might have seen it. It invokes one reference point over others that might have been possible. When you label figure 7.1 as "Faces," you are using words in a public way to make a claim as to what the image is. You are simultaneously directing people to see the image as faces *and not* to see it as something else—in this case, a trophy. Framing can be used intentionally to distract from other available frames. But even when you have no interest in misleading others, the fact remains that as with the Necker cube, at any moment you have to pick one way of seeing things.

What follows from a choice to frame things in one way and not another? One thing is that it can reveal our moral evaluation of a situation. If I say

Kim is thrifty, I'm saying two things: (1) she doesn't spend much money and (2) that's a good thing. An alternative framing is *Kim is stingy*. This would also describe a person who doesn't spend much money but frames it as a bad thing.[4] Even in describing a cup as *half full* versus *half empty*—the archetype example of arbitrary framing—there is arguably a difference in the situation being described. In a study of how people's reference point affects the way they describe situations, people were given the following scenario:[5]

> Imagine a 4-ounce measuring cup in front of you that is completely filled with water up to the 4-ounce line. You then leave the room briefly and come back to find that the water is now at the 2-ounce line. What is the most natural way to describe the cup now?

People had to select one of two options: (1) *The cup is half full* and (2) *The cup is half empty*. Given the scenario just described, around 70 percent of people said that the cup was *half empty*. But people in another group, who were asked to imagine that the cup started out *empty*, gave a very different response. Only around 20 percent said the two-ounce full cup was half empty. Even though the two groups were describing the same objective reality—a four-ounce cup with two ounces of water in it—the larger context was different. So people's different linguistic framings are not simply arbitrary choices but may be nudged in various ways.

The special power of framing is to direct our attention to certain things in a scene and therefore away from other things. It is hard to imagine a more important device for manipulating people than attention direction. All I have to do is look and point my finger in a certain direction, and you will be unable to resist looking to see what's there. When you do that, you're necessarily *not looking anywhere else*. That's when I pick your pocket. As magicians, marketing gurus, and school teachers have long known, controlling people's attention is key to influencing them.

Remember the experiment from chapter 4 where the position of a simple pointing arrow could get people either to use an active or a passive sentence to describe a simple event involving two fish. People saw the same scene, but the pointing arrow determined what people saw the scene as being *about* (*The black fish ate the white one* versus *The white fish got eaten*). By directing your attention to one of the fish at the key moment, I define your point of reference for linguistic framing:

Speaker's focus of attention (cause) → Speaker's linguistic framing (effect)

This can be inverted, such that a particular framing directs someone's attention to a chosen reference point:

Speaker's linguistic framing (cause) → Listener's focus of attention (effect)

Consider this example:[6] *I'm not his daughter. He's my father.* Two descriptions of the situation apply: (1) *He's my father*, (2) *I'm his daughter*. Indeed, if the first is true, then the second must also be (assuming the speaker is a "she"). But we can understand what the speaker is doing when she insists on one version. She wants the father defined in relation to her, not the other way around. She wants to claim that people will (or should) know who *she* is before they know who the father is.

Alternative framings are not a superficial matter of emphasis or style. Framing affects how we understand situations and reason about them. Recall the study of responsibility and blame for starting a restaurant fire, discussed in chapter 4. When the character was framed in subject position (*She toppled the candle* versus *The candle toppled*), this affected the degree to which people would judge her responsible and accountable for what happened in the scene. In this and other ways, people's decision-making strategies can be strongly affected by the way in which information is framed through language.

Suppose you have to choose between two programs to combat a disease outbreak that is expected to kill 600 people:[7]

If program A is adopted, 200 people will be saved.

If program B is adopted, there is one-third probability that 600 people will be saved and two-thirds probability that no people will be saved.

Which one do you choose? One difference between the two programs is that the outcome of program A is certain (200 people will be saved), while program B involves risk. That said, on balance, program B has the prospect of equal value and could even save everyone. In an experiment testing people's response in this task by psychologists Amos Tversky and Daniel Kahneman, the respondents were found to be firmly risk averse. Nearly three-quarters chose program A, opting for certainty (while tolerating a significant known cost).

But certainty versus risk is not the only factor. Look at the language of program A. Its outcome is framed in terms of how many people will be *saved*. An alternative framing would involve a simple change of wording:

from "200 (out of 600) people will be saved" to the equivalent "400 (out of 600) people will *die*." In Frege's terms, these two statements have the same reference but decidedly different senses. And unlike the seemingly arbitrary choice between *Evening Star* and *Morning Star* for Venus, the difference really does make a difference.

In the next part of the experiment, people were given the same problem but in a different frame, now presented in terms of how many would die rather than how many would be saved:

If program C is adopted, 400 people will die.

If program D is adopted, there is one-third probability that nobody will die and two-thirds probability that 600 people will die.

When people saw the problem framed like this, their decision making changed dramatically: the effect reversed. This time, more than three-quarters of participants in the experiment chose program D, preferring not to opt for "certain death of 400 people," despite the fact that this is exactly what people opted for when it was framed as certainly saving 200 people (program A).

This remarkably strong effect is due entirely to a choice of words. The two problems are worded differently but they are informationally identical.[8] This effect has been demonstrated many times since, supporting the following insight, in Tversky and Kahneman's words:

> Alternative descriptions of a decision problem often give rise to different preferences.[9]

Remember this when you hear somebody saying that he or she doesn't think language can influence thought or action.

You might be thinking that because you aren't usually in a position to decide on alternative government programs during a pandemic, this doesn't apply to you. Well, you do vote in your local and national elections. What effect might framing have on your beliefs and values as a voter? As in controlled psychological experiments on decision making, the framing of questions posed to the public in order to gauge political opinion can skew people's responses significantly. Imagine that a hate group is planning to hold a political rally. Would you favor it or oppose it? A political science study compared people's response to this question when it was prefaced by distinct framings that drew attention to different considerations.[10] When the question was prefaced with *Given the importance of free speech*, 85 percent of people said they would allow the hate group rally. But when the question was prefaced with

Given the risk of violence, only 45 percent of people said they would allow the rally.[11]

Here are two important elements of how framing works.[12] The first is that framing in itself won't make you believe things you don't already believe. But our beliefs are many and varied and may sometimes be contradictory. I might believe that free speech is good and that violence is bad, but when presented with the hate speech rally scenario, these two beliefs may come into competition. Second, for our beliefs to play a role in our decision making, they need to be accessible to us when it matters. Here is where framing works its magic. It is a tool for directing people's attention toward certain of their beliefs, making them prominent and relevant at a key moment—for example, just when they are going to cast a vote, purchase a product, or choose a course of action. And never forget the key corollary of any act of directing attention toward something. It directs attention away from everything else.

*

Framing often introduces analogies and metaphors that can function as "tools of thought."[13] An example is how you think about electricity. What is it, and how does it work? When people talk about electricity, they sometimes portray it as a moving crowd of individuals. Others describe it as being like flowing water. In an experiment, people were asked to solve a set of problems involving an electrical circuit with different combinations of batteries and resistors. Batteries and resistors have different properties, and understanding them demands different kinds of reasoning. People performed differently depending on which of these two analogies they were using. The experiment showed "that subjects using the water model (given that they understood the way water behaves) differentiated batteries more correctly than resistors, and that subjects who used the moving crowd model were more accurate for resistors than for batteries." As the authors put it, "Generative analogies can serve as inferential frameworks."[14]

Analogies are obviously useful in cases like talking about electricity. We use electricity all the time but can't see it. Figurative language gives us concrete ways to think about intangible things. Our conversations are full of metaphors, and these metaphors apply extraordinarily broadly. An example of the kind of pervasive metaphor found in ordinary discourse is the metaphor "argument is war" in everyday English:[15] Your claims are *indefensible.* He *attacked* every weak point in my argument. His criticisms were *right on target*. I *demolished* his argument. If you use that *strategy*, he'll *wipe you out*. He *shot down* all of my arguments. According to linguist George Lakoff and philosopher Mark Johnson, through metaphors like these, language can structure our behavior in fundamental ways.[16]

We are constantly framing things not just in terms of what we choose to include or omit, or which seemingly equivalent word we choose, but also in terms of when to reach for a metaphor at all. Metaphors and analogies are important forms of categorization, and arguably indispensable for coordinating around certain ideas. As Douglas Hofstadter and Emmanuel Sandar put it, "Without the ceaseless pulsating heartbeat of our 'categorization engine,' we would understand nothing around us, could not reason in any form whatever, could not communicate with anyone else, and would have no basis on which to take any action."[17] Now notice that while we must categorize in order to process reality in a manageable way, there is no single way to categorize. We always have options for how to present reality to ourselves and to others. Language provides those options. This is especially clear in the case of alternative metaphors.

Computer scientist Alan Turing was one of the twentieth century's greatest minds. What was the nature of his genius? Metaphors provide alternative ways of thinking about how his exceptional ideas came about. The following passage illustrates the metaphor of the *light bulb*:[18]

> i. Alan Turing is best known for his work on the Enigma code-breaking machine during World War II, which helped the British government gather intelligence and eventually win the war.
>
> ii. Another of Turing's contributions is an idea that contributed to the modern computer.
>
> iii. In 1936, a bright idea for an algorithm-based computing machine struck him. It was as if the idea was a light bulb that had suddenly turned on in his mind.
>
> iv. His idea was called a "Turing machine", and he argued that it could hypothetically answer any mathematical question presented in the form of an algorithm. Later on, he helped design an Automatic Computing Engine (ACE) that built on this early idea. The ACE concept was a precursor to the computers that eventually became the machine you're looking at right now.

An alternative is the *seed* metaphor. This is shown by replacing paragraph iii in the previous passage with this one (with the changes underlined):

> iii. In 1936, the seed of an idea for an algorithm-based computing machine took root. It was as if the idea was a growing seed that had finally borne fruit in his mind.

Table 7.1

Metaphorical Mappings of the Light Bulb Metaphor versus the Seed Metaphor for Good Ideas[19]

	Light Bulb Metaphor	Seed Metaphor
Idea quality	Brilliant; outstanding; exceptional	Fruitful; useful yet typical
Idea creation	Flipping a switch; creation out of nowhere	Nurturing; creation through effort
Idea creator	Individual is effortlessly enlightened with an idea	Individual expends effort to cultivate an idea
Timing	Fast; all of a sudden	Slow; developing over time

Source: Kristen C. Elmore and Myra Luna-Lucero, "Light Bulbs or Seeds? How Metaphors for Ideas Influence Judgments about Genius," *Social Psychological and Personality Science* 8, no. 2 (2017): 200–208, https://doi.org/10.1177/1948550616667611.

The two metaphors don't just invoke different images in the mind. Like all other metaphors, they have implications for how we think. The two metaphors for scientific ideas imply differences in the quality of the idea, how it came about, the person whose idea it was. Some of these are shown in table 7.1.

In the experiment, some people read the light bulb version of the passage about Turing, others read the seed version, and a third group read a neutral version of the text, without any metaphor. (In this third version, paragraph iii read: *In 1936, he had an idea for an algorithm-based computing machine.*) People then had to read the following statements and say how much they agreed or disagreed with each one:

a. Turing's idea about computers was a breakthrough.

b. Turing's idea about computers changed the world.

c. Many other people had similar ideas to Turing's. (Reverse coded)

d. Turing is one of the world's great thinkers.

People who read the passage with the light bulb metaphor agreed more strongly with the four statements than those who read the passage with the seed metaphor.

These kinds of effects have clear implications for public discourse and policy. Consider the most important and urgent problem facing us today: climate change. Here are the opening lines of three alternative articles that frame climate change in three distinct ways (with key words underlined):[20]

1. The <u>War</u> against Climate Change. When will Americans start to combat excessive energy use and <u>kill</u> the problems related to air pollution and the destruction of natural resources? The entire country should be <u>recruited</u> to <u>fight</u> this deadly <u>battle</u>. The United States is joining the <u>campaign</u> to reduce its carbon footprint in the next few decades.

2. The <u>Race</u> against Climate Change. When will Americans <u>go after</u> excessive energy use and <u>surge ahead</u> on problems related to air pollution and the destruction of natural resources? The entire country needs to <u>step up to the line</u> and <u>get in front</u> of this challenging problem. The United States is joining the <u>race</u> to reduce its carbon footprint in the next few decades.

3. The <u>Issue</u> of Climate Change. When will Americans start to <u>address</u> excessive energy use and resolve problems related to air pollution and the destruction of natural resources? The entire country needs to direct their <u>efforts</u> to address this important issue. The United States is joining the <u>effort</u> to reduce its carbon footprint in the next few decades.

In an experiment, people read one of these versions and were asked to give ratings relating to three general questions: (1) How urgent is the problem of climate change? (2) What degree of risk does the problem present? and (3) To what degree would you be willing to change your behavior in response to the problem? People who read the war metaphor gave higher ratings for all three of these questions than people who read the race or neutral metaphors. Again, the results show that the choice of words in framing a situation is no superficial matter.[21]

Let's look at one more study of the effect of metaphor on how people think about a societal problem. Consider the following scenario:[22]

> Crime is a virus ravaging the city of Addison. Five years ago Addison was in good shape, with no obvious vulnerabilities. Unfortunately, in the past five years the city's defense systems have weakened, and the city has succumbed to crime. Today, there are more than 55,000 criminal incidents a year—up by more than 10,000 per year. There is a worry that if the city does not regain its strength soon, even more serious problems may start to develop.

Now imagine you are asked the following questions:

1. In your opinion, what does Addison need to do to reduce crime?

2. Please underline the part of the report that was most influential in your decision.

The text and questions are from a study on the effects of metaphor on reasoning.[23] People in the experiment gave two kinds of response to the first question.[24] Some suggested a *reform* strategy, proposing that the underlying causes of the problem should be diagnosed and treated, allowing the population to then become inoculated and protected. Others suggested an *enforce* strategy, involving capture of criminals, enforcement of laws, and punishment. Of the people who read the scenario just given above, just under half (46 percent) proposed the reform strategy.

Another group was shown a different text from that given above, with one word changed (underlined):

> Crime is a <u>beast</u> ravaging the city of Addison. Five years ago Addison was in good shape, with no obvious vulnerabilities. Unfortunately, in the past five years the city's defense systems have weakened, and the city has succumbed to crime. Today, there are more than 55,000 criminal incidents a year—up by more than 10,000 per year. There is a worry that if the city does not regain its strength soon, even more serious problems may start to develop.

This version of the text replaces the *crime is a virus* with another metaphor: *crime is a beast*. The result? Participants' responses changed in the direction of the *enforce* strategy. When the text framed crime as a *beast*, nearly three-quarters (71 percent) of those in the experiment suggested the enforce strategy.

Think about what this means. The study shows that "even the subtlest instantiation of a metaphor (via a single word) can have a powerful influence over how people attempt to solve social problems like crime and how they gather information to make 'well-informed' decisions."[25] How often are *you* being affected so strongly by the framing of what you read when you form your opinions as a citizen and voter?

How we should respond to crime is a question of huge consequence for society, for communities, families, and individuals. The way we talk about crime is already shot through with metaphor, as a look at the newspaper on any day will show: "Increases in the prevalence of crime are described as crime *waves*, *surges* or *sprees*. A spreading crime problem is a crime *epidemic*, *plaguing* a city or *infecting* a community. Crimes themselves are *attacks* in which criminals *prey on unsuspecting victims*. And criminal investigations are *hunts* where criminals are *tracked* and *caught*."[26] Metaphor is all-pervasive, and yet people seem to be barely aware that metaphors affect our thinking. When people answered the second question in the "crime is a beast/virus" study—where they had to underline the section in the text that influenced their decision—almost nobody pointed to the metaphor-triggering word as an influence on their answer. Most simply cited the statistics provided in the text.[27] Not only does metaphorical language affect our thinking; it does so without us knowing.

With knowledge of what these experimental studies reveal of the influence of metaphor on thought, a natural application would be to strategically apply that knowledge to influence others. The value of framing is well known to practitioners of marketing and communications, who are paid to influence people with words. But consider that every single time you talk about a situation, whether it's in a policy meeting or at the breakfast table, your choice of words actively imposes just one of the possible framings that are available. Whether you like it or not and whether you are conscious of it or not, your choices of words are always priming people to think in certain ways and not others.

And this of course means that we aren't just priming others, but we are priming ourselves to keep thinking that way too. There is a tyranny of perspective, which is largely invisible to us. Not only must you take a perspective whenever you talk about something; you must direct attention away from other perspectives, putting them, at least momentarily, out of view.

The cases we have considered so far—the Necker cube, Tomlin's fish, *I'm not his daughter, he's my father*—have something in common. A person is focused on a clear idea and must choose among limited ways of framing that idea with words. But most of life is more complex than this. Reality is seldom as simple as the line drawings, video clips, and carefully worded vignettes that people are asked to consider in controlled psychology experiments. When faced with a complex situation in real life, we often have trouble figuring out what is going on at all. Framing isn't just useful for influencing other people. It is necessary for our own sense making. Framing is a tool that creates an interpretation of reality, which allows us to evaluate it, reason about it, and coordinate around it.[28]

Indeed, it is often only when we describe a situation in words that we feel we know what is happening at all. Human action must always be understood *under a description,* as the philosopher Elizabeth Anscombe argued.[29] Finding a description—often taken to be *the* description—is central to human sense making in social life. In his research on social gossip among Tzotzil speakers in Zinacantán in the central Chiapas highlands of Mexico, anthropologist John Haviland wrote that a person "may observe behavior and not know even *what he has seen* until he hears it described."[30] In this way, language takes us "beyond ordinary observables" by providing a sense-making map for us to coordinate around. As sociologist Erving Goffman remarked, "There are occasions when we must wait until things are almost over before discovering what has been occurring and occasions of our own activity when we can considerably put off deciding what to claim we have been doing."[31] The philosopher Karl Popper stated that even everyday observation is "theory-impregnated."[32] Framing through language gives us theories that are always there but that—precisely because they are always there—we rarely, if ever, see. Language for humans is like water for fish.

*

When we choose certain words to frame a situation, we are not just making a claim about what that situation is; we are proposing to others that they coordinate with us around that framing and not around other conceivable ones. This links the individual cognitive effects of language choices to our collective actions and their social or political outcomes. Every act of framing is like one of Schelling's maps. It makes claims about what territory needs to be traversed, and it foregrounds certain landmarks to be used for coordinating the journey. When you are handed a map made of language, remember that it is not the territory. Someone drew it. Someone chose what to include and what to omit. Someone is directing your attention to certain details and away from all manner of others. Only by being mindful of this can we decide whether we are happy to accept that map and the terms that it sets on us. Yes, language is collaborative and cooperative, even when it is competitive. But there is always someone who decides what game is being played.

III Made by Language

8 Russell's Conjugation and Wittgenstein's Ruler

Political language is designed to make lies sound truthful and murder respectable.

—George Orwell (1946)

Latin 101 begins with the first conjugation: *amō, amās, amat*: I love, you love, she/he loves. The form of the verb changes depending on who is the subject of the sentence, but its meaning is the same. In a wry twist on the concept of conjugation, the philosopher Bertrand Russell drew attention to our tendency to word things rather differently depending on who is the subject of the sentence. Here is his "irregular verb" pattern:

I am firm, you are obstinate, he is a pig-headed fool.

This is the *Russell conjugation*.[1] Jokes aside, there is obvious wisdom here. If I'm talking about myself, I may be naturally motivated to cast the situation in a good light.[2] And as the same reality is observed at greater levels of remove from myself, then I am less likely to display that empathy or positivity.[3] The three forms in Russell's example—*firm, obstinate, pig-headed*—refer to roughly the same property of being unlikely to change one's mind, but they differ in the evaluation or emotive stance that the speaker takes. (And recall the examples *thrifty/stingy* and *half-full/half-empty*.) US pollster Frank Luntz found that "many if not most people form their opinions based solely on whatever Russell conjugation is presented to them and *not* on the underlying facts. That is, the very same person will oppose a 'death tax' while having supported an 'estate tax' seconds earlier even though these taxes are two descriptions of the exact same underlying object."[4] We have seen numerous examples of these kinds of reframing already.

The Russell conjugation is a well-known tool for superficial forms of self-presentation such as corporate euphemisms:[5] My company has cloudy near-term visibility, hers hasn't planned ahead; I am facing headwinds, she has failed to anticipate forces; I am right-sizing, she is firing staff. But the Russell conjugation is also exploited for more nefarious purposes. Here is one that applies to President George W. Bush during his time in office in the 2000s:

> I detain illegal combatants, you interrogate war prisoners, he breaches the Geneva Conventions.

The most obvious feature of the Russell conjugation is that it portrays the self more favorably than others. This is something that language is good for: strategic framing in order to manipulate attention and frames of reference. This function can be exploited for influencing others, affecting how people evaluate situations, for shaping people's reputations. But what makes the Russell conjugation so important is the information it reveals *about its author*. Suppose that you read the following statements:

Person A: Bush detained illegal combatants.

Person B: Bush breached the Geneva Conventions.

If you already have a basic knowledge of the actions of the Bush administration in relation to the 2003–2004 events at Abu Ghraib prison complex west of Baghdad, Iraq, then these two statements tell us more about person A and person B than they tell us about George W. Bush. The revealing nature of perspective runs deep. It links the Russell conjugation to an adjacent concept, *Wittgenstein's ruler.*[6]

Consider the following statement:

> An isosceles triangle has two sides of equal length.

What information does this statement contain? The answer to this question depends on who makes the statement and in what context. At one level, the statement simply contains information about a kind of triangle. But a statement is always made by a person, to a person, in a context. And this gives it a second level of meaning. Suppose that the statement is made in a conversation between a third-grade school teacher and an eight-year-old pupil. If the teacher is the one who says *An isosceles triangle has two sides of equal length*, the pupil learns something new. The context fixes certain things in place: that the teacher is a knowledge authority about school subjects and that the schoolroom context is primarily a place for passing on new information. When the pupil has this context as an anchor for interpreting the statement, the statement gives her new information about triangles. Now imagine that it's the pupil who is speaking to the teacher. When the pupil says *An isosceles triangle has two sides of equal length*, the teacher won't be learning anything new about triangles. The new information is about the pupil. From the statement, the teacher learns that the pupil knows the definition of an isosceles triangle.

The philosopher Ludwig Wittgenstein observed this principle in his 1953 work, *Philosophical Investigations*:[7]

> The language-game of reporting can be given such a turn that a report is meant to inform the hearer not about its subject matter but about the person making the report. It is so when, for instance, a teacher examines a pupil. (You can measure to test the ruler.)

Risk analyst Nassim Taleb has emphasized that when we are provided with information, we should be interested not just in the content of that information but also—and perhaps more—in what the information can tell us about the person providing it.[8] Wittgenstein's ruler is the corollary of the Russell conjugation. While the Russell conjugation can be thought of as a guide for choosing the most strategic expression when speaking, the Wittgenstein ruler is a guide for interpreting the choices that others make.

We can use the principle even in our most mundane conversations, to gauge people's opinions, smoke out certain views, and test suspicions. Anthropologist John Haviland notes the habits of a "prudent gossip" in his research with Tzotzil speakers in Zinacantán, central upland Mexico:

> A woman in Nabenchauk whom I had frequent occasion to visit always grilled me about the doings of my neighbours—people whose affairs she knew well enough herself—simply to discover what my reactions were and how much I knew. . . . [A] particular old man who knew the histories of all concerned often feigned ignorance. He could thereby hear someone else's gossip and observe someone else's opinions.[9]

The principle of reversing the measurer and the measured is the insight behind the invention of the global positioning system (GPS). On October 4, 1957, the pint-sized satellite Sputnik I was launched by the Soviet Union from a site in present-day Kazakhstan.[10] The satellite orbited the earth at a speed of nearly 30,000 kilometers per hour for three weeks, all the while emitting radio pulses that were readily detectable on Earth. Physicists William Guier and George Weiffenbach, working in the Applied Physics Laboratory at Johns Hopkins University in Maryland, were monitoring the radio transmissions. They realized that with the data from those transmissions, they could pinpoint the exact location of the satellite at any time, thanks to the known properties of the Doppler effect: the frequency of a wave changes over time if an observer and a wave source are moving relative to each other. (This effect is what makes a police car's siren suddenly drop in pitch as the car speeds past.) Guier and Weiffenbach used the radio waves as a measure. Knowing their own location on Earth, they could establish the location of the satellite. At the time, the laboratory was also involved in the Polaris submarine–launched missile program, which was struggling with the submarine's challenge of determining its own exact location at any time. The lab's deputy director, Frank McClure, suggested that Guier and Weiffenbach's breakthrough could be inverted: they could use the table to measure the ruler. If they already knew the location of the satellite, then they could use the same radio-wave measures to determine their own location on Earth. This formed the basis of the Navy Navigation Satellite System, developed in the early 1960s, and is the idea behind the GPS system in your smartphone today.[11]

We use Wittgenstein's ruler in a wide range of situations. Often we ask for a description of something solely in order to probe the person giving the description. The Rorschach test—the famous inkblot test developed in the early twentieth century by Swiss psychiatrist Hermann Rorschach—has precisely this property.[12] Figure 8.1 shows Card I from Rorschach's ten-card array.

Compare these two responses to the card in psychiatric interviews:

Ms. Anderson (aged 40): My first reaction is a butterfly. It's got the wings of a butterfly. But maybe it's more of a moth. Yes, it's also a moth, appendages here, a mouth here, tail, and body shape. They have a fuzzy little mouth.[13]

Figure 8.1
Card I from Rorschach's inkblot test.

Ms. Fisher (aged 39): At first glance it looks like an evil cat's face. Without the jagged edges and stuff. A face, the ears here, the eyes, the mouth. It's evil because of all the jagged edges. Or it's been in a fight, tattered skin, its fur is tattered. . . . The dark spots are like blood.[14]

Card III is shown in figure 8.2.

Ms. Anderson (aged 40): Two dancers, Oriental I think. The feet, the posture, the shape of the head; it could be men as well as women, but it has an Oriental feeling. . . . They could be bowing to each other after the dance, as well as dancing.[15]

Mr. Baker (aged 27): Looks like two women's torsos reaching down, with a man's torso underneath them, reaching down into some kind of cauldron. They're two women, like washing or cooking something. The upper torso is like women, because they have breasts. The lower part—they're wearing high-heeled shoes, but there's a penis shape here.

Based on these and other inkblot responses, psychiatrist Irving Weiner explains that Ms. Anderson is *high lambda* in personality (associated with guardedness and avoidance)[16] while Mr. Baker and Ms. Fisher are both *low lambda* (associated with openness and involvement).[17] The descriptions do not tell psychiatrists anything about the inkblots. They tell them about the person giving the description. People vary widely in what they see.

In media discourse, the inkblot phenomenon is all too familiar. On January 18, 2019, outside the Lincoln Memorial in Washington, DC, a nose-to-nose encounter between Nicholas Sandmann, a teenaged Trump supporter

Figure 8.2
Card III from Rorschach's inkblot test.

from Kentucky's Covington Catholic High School for boys, and Nathan Phillips, an elderly Omaha demonstrator, was video-recorded and posted online.[18] Based on first images, many shared the view that the teenager and his peers were mobbing and mocking the elderly man. But when further footage emerged, it showed that the situation was more nuanced.[19] Some commentators retracted their initial evaluations, but others reiterated their first interpretation (that the kids were racist monsters), while yet others jumped to the complete opposite view (the kids were innocent victims). As writer Julie Zimmerman put it, "The story is a Rorschach test—tell me how you first reacted, and I can probably tell where you live, who you voted for in 2016, and your general take on a list of other issues."[20]

It is confirmation bias in action. We see what we want or expect to see, and this in turn reveals who we are. As we will see in this chapter, much of media and political discourse is like this. And the skewing of descriptions through differences of perspective is not just a pitfall to be avoided or monitored for. It is a tool of power in the hands of anyone with a mass audience. Framing creates alternative maps that can systematically direct people's attention to certain facts or ideas and away from others.

This idea is at the core of one of the best-known critiques of twentieth-century mass media. In their 1988 book, *Manufacturing Consent*, media commentators Edward Herman and Noam Chomsky developed what they call a *propaganda model* of mass communication. They argue that the mass media serve "to mobilize support for the special interests that dominate the state and private activity."[21]

Herman and Chomsky single out the "choices, emphases, and omissions" in media practice, focusing squarely on language—the words we choose to say and not to say. In the simplest kind of example, Herman and Chomsky ask, In the Vietnam conflict, was the United States a *victim* or an *aggressor*?[22] It might seem that this isn't a case of framing at all, as the two descriptions are not equivalent, at least not as in Tversky and Kahneman's framing experiment (*2/6 people will live = 4/6 people will die*). It's true that a victim is not (necessarily) an aggressor and the choice of words is not a simple matter of perspective reversal. But in complex situations, as with most of the sociopolitical issues that public opinion is concerned with, differences in focus of attention can be associated with contrasting, if not entirely opposite, views.

Which view you choose will not be random. One reason for your choice of framing is plain self-interest. As per the Russell conjugation, we often prefer to think of our own actions more positively than the actions of others. A powerful motivation relates to the law. Relabeling your actions may be a way to lessen or remove a risk of prosecution. Let's return to the example of George W. Bush. In the wake of 9/11 and the Second Iraq War, Bush captured and detained a large number of men in the conflict areas. He wanted to torture them for information, but the 1996 War Crimes Act made it a US federal crime to breach the Geneva Conventions, a set of humanitarian laws applying in armed conflict. Bush nevertheless was able to make this legal inconvenience go away. How? By changing the label. They were not prisoners of war. They were *illegal combatants*. Through a simple and superficial reframing of the situation, Bush's inhumane treatment of these prisoners, in breach of the Geneva Conventions, became harder to punish under international law.[23]

Another case is the 1765 transfer of tax duties that took place between Britain and China. The agreement was actually compelled by force, in a pattern that was repeated by the British through the nineteenth century.[24] But the British chose to refer to this resolution as a *treaty*, using a word that frames the agreement as a peaceful one. Later "'treaties" with China were similarly "negotiated" through brute military force.

Another approach is to keep using an old word but give it a new meaning. In Australia, *full employment* has been a formal government policy target since World War II.[25] From 1945, the Australian government established enduring policy around Prime Minister John Curtin's postwar vision of full employment. The term *full employment* meant what it sounds like: everybody should have a job. Full employment in this sense was a government policy target from 1945 until the mid-1970s. But then the global oil crisis resulted in a host of complications, including inflation, slowed growth, and rising unemployment. When Australian unemployment peaked at more than 10 percent in the 1980s, the Reserve Bank of Australia, whose job it was to "maintain full employment," dealt with the matter by changing the definition of the term: "Full employment would mean the level of unemployment that kept a lid on inflation (i.e., on wages and prices)".[26] The Reserve Bank has since been able to "continue to meet its original mandate (to maintain full employment) on paper, while adapting to the new economic reality." As a result, full employment is no longer what it sounds like.

In the examples of "illegal combatant," "treaty," and "full employment," people manipulate language in anticipating matters of accountability.[27] Sometimes our manipulations of language deal with other kinds of effects. In March 2020, when the World Health Organization formally declared that the COVID-19 outbreak was a *pandemic*, its use of that word reflected an official view that the disease was now prevalent throughout the world. In fact, it had already clearly fit the technical definition of a pandemic for some weeks. But in late February 2020, WHO officials intentionally delayed their declaration of a pandemic because "they wanted countries to pursue containment and mitigation simultaneously." According to the *Washington Post*, declaring a pandemic would have been "tantamount to throwing in the towel on containing the virus and signalling to governments that they should focus instead on mitigating its effects."[28] WHO officials understood that their declaration—a kind of speech act, turning on a specific choice of words—would have specific real-world consequences. A choice of words gave them, for a brief window in time, some control.

These examples illustrate what we can call *motivated framing*. I use this term by analogy with *motivated reasoning*, a term from cognitive psychology. Human reasoning is seldom dispassionate. It is usually biased. Linguistic framing is like this. It reflects people's underlying biases and motivations: what we already think is true, or what we would prefer to be true. But not only do our choices in framing *reflect* our often-biased perspectives on things. With motivated framing, they are often calculated—whether consciously or not—to *induce* the same biases in others.

In media and political discourse, alternative motivated framings compete for acceptance as accounts of current events. At issue are both the facts and our evaluation of them.

On October 1, 2018, at a press conference at the White House, ABC news reporter Cecilia Vega was called on by President Donald Trump. She hesitated for a moment. The brief moment of silence triggered the following exchange:[29]

Trump: She's shocked that I picked her. She's in a state of shock.

Vega: I'm not, thank you, Mr. President.

Trump: That's okay. I know you're not thinking, you never do.

Vega: I'm sorry?

Trump: No, go ahead.

CBS News reported the incident as follows: "As tensions between the Trump administration and the press continue, the president sparred with ABC correspondent Cecilia Vega in the Rose Garden today." CNN reporter Daniel Dale remarked on the wording of this: "One of my Trump-era media pet peeves is when Trump belittles or insults someone and it's described with words like 'sparred' or 'feud' even though the other person didn't do anything."[30]

We see the same in reports of clashes of a literal kind. On March 30, 2018, a Palestinian campaign of protest against conditions inside the Gaza Strip was launched near the Gaza-Israel border.[31] While demonstrations were going on near the border, a large group of young Palestinians entered the no-go zone at the border's edge. They began throwing rocks and Molotov cocktails and rolling burning tires in the direction of Israeli military. Israeli forces responded with live fire, killing 15 and wounding more than 750 demonstrators. The *New York Times* ran this headline: "Israeli Military Kills at Least 8 in Confrontations on Gaza Border." Media analyst Nima Shirazi reacted to the use of the word *confrontation*: "As usual, words like 'confrontations' and 'clashes' present a false parity of power, of 'both sides' engaging in comparable violence."[32]

In an extended analysis of media language used in relation to the Second Intifada (the 2000–2005 Palestinian uprising against Israel), communications scholar Daniel Dor documents the ways in which "the media 'construct' the news rather than simply 'report' it," in line with the general function of human language as a framing device.[33] With media, politics is a constant shaping force, where the modes of news construction "are intimately related to the media's relationships with the establishment, their perception of their own role in times of crisis, and the culture's general view of reality."[34] Dor emphasizes the discrepancy between field reporters' accounts of reality and the way in which these accounts are framed by the time they reach newspaper readers, presented as a specific narrative by editors, shaped by an array of powerful factors in framing, including the physical size and positioning of a media story, visual/graphical elements, and the correspondence between the facts reported in the text and the story's headline (for example, through specific word choices or rhetorical language in the headline).[35]

Commentators like Dale, Shirazi, and Dor are confident about their judgments as to the objective nature of the situations being described, as well as to what the words in question mean. For them, the media reports are Wittgenstein rulers. The reports tell us more about the reporters than about the events they report. But with language there is always leeway. In the Gaza border example, the *New York Times*'s headline wasn't false. It is true that there were confrontations. Shirazi's point is that reporters are responsible for conveying the facts in a fair way. Using the word *confrontation*, while technically applicable, is unfair and misleading because of the strongly asymmetrical nature of the exchange being described. Molotov cocktails and car tires are no match for live rifle ammunition. So to call this a confrontation arguably goes against journalistic ideals of accuracy and objectivity in reporting.

Domestic violence is—very sadly—a rich source of examples. An unaccountably large number of news reports of domestic incidents of assault and murder are reported in ways that are technically not false yet irresponsibly misleading.

A February 2020 Fox Sports Australia headline reads: "Ex-National Rugby League Player Rowan Baxter Dies alongside His Three Kids, Estranged Wife in Brisbane Car Fire Tragedy." Pause a moment and picture the scene. Now let me tell you the detail that the headline leaves out: Baxter set the fire that killed everyone in the car. He poured gasoline on Hannah Clarke and their three young children and lit them up. This missing information is painfully, obviously relevant to the story. Yet the headline was not false. Baxter did "die alongside" his three kids and estranged wife. But the headline omits information that is so vital to understanding the event that the omission arguably breaks the most basic journalistic principles of conveying the truth. The headline plainly omits information that readers need to know if they are going to gain a fair understanding of the situation.

A headline from the UK *Times* on May 9, 2019, states: "Schoolboys Died in Cliff Fall with Father after He Lost Faith in God."[36] Picture the situation, based just on this description. What do you see?

Now let's revise that mental image in light of another headline describing the same incident, this time from the BBC: "Man Stabbed Wife before Killing Sons."[37]

Neither of these descriptions is false, but they are clearly not just equally valid ways of describing the scene. The facts that the *Times* omits from its headline are as horrifying as they are central to the story. According to the coroner's court, the man in this story killed his wife, Laura, with a knife. He stabbed her sixty times. She had defensive wounds on her hands and arms. He then drugged their two young sons, Joaquin and Claudio, aged seven and ten, took them to a clifftop and either pushed them off or dragged them over the cliff with him, killing them. Now think back to the *Times* headline: "Schoolboys Died in Cliff Fall with Father after He Lost Faith in God." The boys died. Yes. But they were murdered. A woman—their mother—also died. Also murdered. A father died, yes. But he was also the killer. The *Times*'s framing leaves all of this out. As a language-made map, this is a distinctly defective representation of the terrain being shown, omitting the most objectively important features: no roads, no river, no bridge. Just dirt.

Jane Gilmore's Fixed It project seeks to correct these linguistic framings of events of assault and murder on women and children in domestic contexts.[38] Of the story in figure 8.3, Gilmore wrote:

> Lots of people have had crises of faith, they don't murder women and children. When they do, their relationship with god is not an excuse or a reason to feel sympathy for a killer. Mr Figueira de Faria killed his wife Laura and their two children, Claudio and Joaquin. He is not the victim or the object of sympathy here, he's the killer.[39]

For the powerless, the battle against framing is never ending. And for those with power, motivated framing is one of the most important tools around. When a conservative Florida state government directed workers

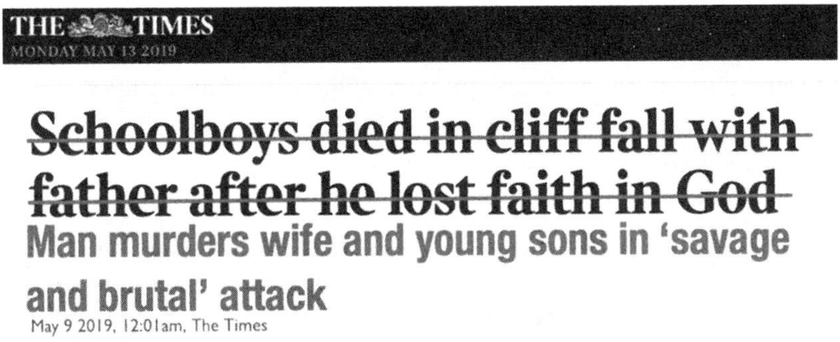
THE TIMES
MONDAY MAY 13 2019

~~Schoolboys died in cliff fall with father after he lost faith in God~~
Man murders wife and young sons in 'savage and brutal' attack
May 9 2019, 12:01am, The Times

Figure 8.3
Fixed it: Jane Gilmore's correction of the *Times*'s May 9, 2019, headline. http://janegilmore.com/fixedit-everything-in-this-headline-is-just-wrong/.

not to use terms including *climate change, global warming,* or *sustainability* in their communications,[40] the motivation was clearly political. When government agencies do this, it's an accountable transgression, but in the private sector, companies can freely determine the language used, in transparent forms of motivated framing. In July 2019, stock exchange indexer FTSE Russell announced a change in its designation of UK energy companies.[41] Companies engaging in solar and wind energy had been listed under the words *alternative energy.* Under the new designation, they would now be known as *renewable energy* companies, while oil and gas producers would be defined negatively in contrast to this, as *nonrenewable energy* companies. The change in terminology from *alternative* to *renewable* provides a distinctly different frame for the technologies, a reversal reminiscent of our earlier example: *I'm not his daughter, he's my father.* The change meant that solar and wind energy would no longer be defined via oil and gas (as an "alternative" to them). It would now be the other way around. Oil and gas would now be the thing that wind and solar are not ("renewable"). The change was to portray oil and gas in a distinctly negative way.

For some, this new framing seemed like a good thing, an appropriate reflection of an evolving understanding of energy in the era of climate change in which nonrenewables have no future. Others criticized the change as mere political correctness: they wanted it reversed. The change in language may have seemed cosmetic for some, "but was quite a bit more significant to the treasury departments of oil and gas producers."[42] especially given that more and more fund managers are divesting from nonrenewables. In late September 2019, only a few months after the change in labels, there was another change. *Renewable* energy companies would go back to the old name, *alternative* energy. Oil and gas companies would now appear under another new heading: *Oil, gas, and coal.* As Bloomberg opinion columnist Liam Denning remarks, this framing—which now saw them grouped together with coal— only introduced new problems for oil and gas:

> The industry has spent years (and millions) emphasizing the increasing role of natural gas as a bridge fuel to a lower carbon future at the expense of coal. Now oil and gas producers will be explicitly lumped in with coal in the new group's name. Coal is the easiest target for climate-change regulation. More importantly, it has suffered a decade of bankruptcies and declining financial strength that offers something like a foretaste of what could ultimately befall the oil industry.[43]

As names go, being called "non-renewable" looks better than suffering that sort of association.

The case shows that linguistic framing is far from superficial. To people with skin in the game—in this case, people with billions of dollars at stake in the energy industry—these matters of wording are potentially existential in nature.

Matters of wording often become lightning rods for charged political discourse. In a May 2020 media interview on the effects of COVID-19 on the US economy,[44] Kevin Hassett, a senior economic adviser to the White House, wanted to emphasize that business should resume after a period of lockdown due to the pandemic.[45] He made the following comment: "Our capital stock hasn't been destroyed. Our human capital stock is ready to get back to work."

Human capital stock. The phrase got a strong reaction for its disregard for the humanity of the workforce—particularly where going back to work would mean a serious risk of infection. Wittgenstein's ruler again. The words are a measure of the person speaking, as this tweet suggests:[46]

> He referred to American workers as "human capital stock!" Are you f*cking kidding me? It's bad enough that the Trump administration is calling for us to sacrifice our lives for the Dow Jones. Now we are spoken of as sub-human to boot?!

On Easter Sunday 2019, a coordinated set of bombing attacks hit three churches and three luxury hotels in the Sri Lankan capital, Colombo. More than 250 people were killed and 500 injured. A Sri Lankan militant jihadist group was held responsible. The symbolism of the attacks was clear, timed to occur on the most important day of the Christian calendar. And it was just a week after the horrific attack on a Christchurch, New Zealand, mosque that killed 51 people and injured 49.

US Democrat Hillary Clinton tweeted the following response:[47]

> On this holy weekend for many faiths, we must stand united against hatred and violence. I'm praying for everyone affected by today's horrific attacks on Easter worshippers and travelers in Sri Lanka.

Barack Obama's tweet was similar:

> The attacks on tourists and Easter worshippers in Sri Lanka are an attack on humanity. On a day devoted to love, redemption, and renewal, we pray for the victims and stand with the people of Sri Lanka.

And here is a comment from US Democrat Julián Castro:

> On a day of redemption and hope, the evil of these attacks on Easter worshippers and tourists in Sri Lanka is deeply saddening.

Easter worshippers. All three tweets used the phrase to describe the people who were killed. The phrasing frames the victims in terms of the activity they were engaged in: worshipping on Christianity's most sacred day. There are of course many imaginable other alternative framings to describe or identify who was killed. But they are evidently not equal. As it happened, US conservative commentators took exception to the term *Easter worshipper.* Why? Because they saw it not as merely an alternative to other possibilities but as a deliberate avoidance of those other possibilities.

National Review writer Alexandra DeSantis tweeted, "We're actually called Christians not 'Easter worshippers' wouldn't hurt to maybe just say that." Breitbart News wrote that Clinton and Obama "could not bring themselves to identify the victims of the attacks as 'Christians.'" And a *Washington Times* opinion piece called the phrase "anti-Christian."[48]

But think about this. The *Washington Times* op-ed implies that if there is an available label for something and you choose not to use that label, you are *anti* whatever is denoted by that label.[49] The problem is that you can't win at this game. Every time you label something, you aren't just choosing to frame it in a certain way; you are always choosing *not* to frame it in literally *every other conceivable way.* If I see a dog and ask, *Whose pet is this?* am I anti-dog for not using the word *dog?* If I say *My vehicle is parked over there,* am I anti-car for not specifying that it's a car? If I say *my mother's brother* instead of *my uncle,* am I against uncles?[50] These examples seem silly, but they are logically not unlike more charged cases. If I say Black Lives Matter, am I saying white lives don't? If I say we should invest in seeking a cure for COVID-19, am I saying that we should not seek cures for cancer and malaria?

Still, there are times when we can and surely should be held accountable for the things we don't say. In the *Easter worshippers* and *died alongside his estranged wife and kids* examples, critics took issue with the omission of a specific detail. But not just any detail. The unspoken detail was held to be so important and so relevant that not mentioning it was treated as an accountable act. Such an omission is held either to be deliberately misleading or at best a sign of a writer's ignorance or malice.

Now consider the inverse kind of case—not the omission of something relevant but the *mention* of something *irrelevant*. In January 2019 in the Melbourne suburb of Springvale, seven people were hospitalized after a serious two-car collision. The *Australian* newspaper reported:

> Seven have been hospitalised after a car carrying six youths of African appearance collided with another car in Melbourne.

Reporter Christine Ahern tweeted:

> Horror crash in Springvale. 6 youths of African appearance in white car aged 16–20yo all in hospital. Driver of black car in his 40s also in hospital.

Youths of African appearance. Not every car accident report mentions the physical appearance of the people involved, as writer Benjamin Millar comments, "Certain appearances of certain youth are considered worthy of noting."[51] In a report on the incident by the *Herald Sun* newspaper— which also stated that that the six youths were of African appearance— the physical appearance of the driver of the other car was not mentioned. The report also stated that the car the youths were driving in *was not a stolen car*. Why do these news reports mention the youths' racial appearance and not the other driver's? Why remark that the youths' car had not been stolen yet say nothing about the status of the other car? To understand why, you should know that the incident happened in the context of a heavily politicized controversy in Australian media at the time about an alleged problem with "African gangs" in Melbourne and Sydney. Conservative politician Peter Dutton, then federal home affairs minister, said, "We need to call it for what it is. Of course, this is African gang violence . . . people are scared to go out to restaurants of a night-time because they're followed home by these gangs."[52] Conservative politicians were railing against a "major law and order problem in Victoria." But media sociologist John Budarick noted the selective nature of the framing. Why, he asked, haven't the media blamed these incidents on "Melbourne gangs"? "Or, while we're at it, why not call them 'male gangs' or, as has sometimes been used in an attempt to include non-black offenders, 'youth gangs'?"[53] The media assume a certain common ground among their readers, landmarks that people can coordinate around in their discourse about current affairs. For better or worse, the "African gang" idea was in the common ground of media readership at the time.

Compare the case to one in which the mention of race is more obviously relevant. In a May 2020 incident in the Ramble, a forested area in the middle of Manhattan's Central Park, Amy Cooper had her dog off the leash. Birdwatcher Christian Cooper (no relation) asked her to put the dog on its leash, in line with the rules for park users. The exchange became tense, and Christian started recording the interaction on his phone. Amy, now on camera, states that she will call the police "and tell them there's an African American man threatening my life." And this is exactly what she does. Here are some of the news headlines reporting the story when it first happened:

> A white woman has apologized after calling police on a black man and saying "there's an African American man threatening my life."[54]

> White woman apologises for calling police on black bird watcher.[55]

The mentions of race are integral to understanding the story, first given that the racialized framing of the situation is the story itself. Amy Cooper told the 911 operator that her life was being threatened *by an African American man*. Not by a man. Not by a birdwatcher. Not by a person. While this in itself makes race relevant to the story, that relevance is also heightened in the context of ongoing media attention to a spate of cases in which white people have called 911 to report black people for mundane, harmless behavior.[56]

*

We have seen how people can engage in framing by using variations on the Russell conjugation. When we describe the world in different ways, we stake different claims to how the world is. We do this by both including and omitting specific words and by formally redefining words if necessary, as in the case of *full employment*. And in many cases, words can be redefined in less formal ways, potentially resulting in a permanent change of meaning over time.

Words in all languages naturally change their meanings. They often broaden so as to include things that were not previously included in the category. An example is the English word *tea*. This once referred to a drink made from a hot water infusion of the leaves of the tea plant (*Camellia sinensis*). While that remains the prototype today, *tea* can include herbal teas made from leaves or flowers of many other species of plant.[57] This tendency for words to broaden in scope may be natural, but it can have adverse consequences. Consider the broadening in meaning of terms used in psychology related to harm and pathology: for example, *abuse, bullying, trauma, mental disorder, addiction,* and *prejudice.* Psychologist Nick Haslam found that these words have expanded in scope over the period of a few decades to include a broader range of phenomena. For example, *bullying* used to refer specifically to repeated, intentional, aggressive acts carried out toward a child by someone stronger and more powerful (such as an older or bigger child). Now it also encompasses one-off actions in grown-up settings such as workplaces and where adverse effects are unintended. Haslam concludes that the trends reflect an "increasing sensitivity to harm" in public discourse, where this broadening of categories brings a possible risk of "pathologizing everyday experience."[58] We close this chapter with an extended case study of perhaps the archetypal example of language change marching in step with an increasing sensitivity to harm: the word *violence.*

Like *tea, violence* has a prototype. We can agree that hitting, stabbing, or shooting a person are acts of violence. But like any other word, *violence* invokes a large gray area, a set of cases where some people might use the term and others might say it doesn't apply. Murder by shooting has a number of features that make it a prototypical act of violence.[59] It is carried out by a person. That person has intention and control. The act causes direct physical harm to a person's body. If any of these features is absent in a situation, we might be less likely to apply the word *violence,* or at least we may acknowledge that the situation is less prototypical. Say you are driving along and a person dashes out from behind a barrier at the side of the street. You hit her before you even see she's there. This is bad, and it causes physical harm, but you had no intention of hitting her and no control over the event. This is not what we usually mean by *violence.* But recent trends in how the word is used in public discourse are broadening the scope recognizably. Those trends may have their roots in scholarly analyses of the concept.

In the 1960s, sociologist Johan Galtung—a founder of the discipline of peace and conflict studies—made a case for redefining the meaning of the word *violence* in an article titled "Violence, Peace, and Peace Research." Galtung starts by defining *peace* as the *absence of violence.* This in turn requires a definition of *violence.* If *violence* is usually understood as *personal violence*—direct bodily harm against a person by another person's intentional action—then "highly unacceptable social orders would still be compatible with peace," said Galtung.[60] So for the sake of his definition of *peace,* he proposed broadening the definition of *violence*. He argued that in order to have an absence of violence of the kind he wanted, then the category of *violence* must include what he called *structural violence*, a systematically and persistently unequal distribution of power and resources in society that could be seen as a cause of, or condition for, widespread suffering.[61] Galtung's extended concept of violence was a means to "an extended concept of peace," or what he called social justice.[62] Positive peace would be possible only when structural violence was absent.

At around the same time, philosopher Newton Garver developed a similarly broadened conception of *violence*, which included property damage and governmental restriction of citizens' freedoms.[63] The philosopher J. J. Degenaar cites Garver among others in examples from academic discourse showing extended uses of *violence* in the 1960s and 1970s:[64]

> Part of the "good order of society" is the routine oppression and racism committed against millions of Americans every day. That is where the real violence is.[65]

> Any institution which systematically robs certain people of rightful options generally available to others does violence to those people.[66]

> Structural violence shows itself when resources and powers are unequally shared and are the property of a restricted number who use them not for the good of all but for their own profit and for the domination of the less favoured.[67]

There is no question that structural inequalities are unjust. The question is what may be gained or lost by referring to any social injustice as *violence*. One risk is that if every social wrong were classed as violence, then nonviolent crimes and violent crimes could be treated alike.[68] It might even be taken to justify physical violence as a response to a much broader range of actions: "Structural violence invites physical violence, a view that some revolutionaries hold forth as a justification for the use of physical violence in liberation movements."[69] One need not endorse Frantz Fanon's idea that violence is a cleansing force[70] or Malcolm X's slogan, By Any Means Necessary,[71] but from the point of view of structurally oppressed peoples, the logic is understandable. On this broadened conception of violence, what range of actions would warrant a physically violent response?

In a July 2017 *New York Times* opinion article, psychologist Lisa Feldman Barrett argued that speech can be violence.[72] She noted that hateful speech can affect the brain with physiological stress and argued that if such speech is sustained, it can create "a culture of constant, casual brutality." It is therefore, literally, violence.[73] But this is "'a conflation of physical harm and violence," according to psychologist Jonathan Haidt and legal scholar Greg Lukianoff,[74] who resist this widening of the word *violence* for at least two reasons. First, they argue that it pathologizes experience: it risks making people unnecessarily anxious, adding to a sense that they are being harmed by things that are said around them.[75] Instead, Haidt and Lukianoff argue that stressors—at least, when not chronic—can make us stronger, not weaker. Second, they argue that broadening the category of *violence* makes people "more willing to justify physical harm."[76]

Clearly, speech can cause physical harm, as Feldman Barrett argued, but does it follow that speech is violence? And would it then follow that if you say something I perceive as harmful, I am justified in reacting physically, for example, by hitting you?[77] Some people now argue that the answer is yes (despite, for example, the awful potential implications of this for justifying acts of domestic violence). In February 2017, the University of California at Berkeley student-run newspaper, *Daily Californian*, ran an opinion column with several contributors arguing in favor of the use of violence in protests, building on the premise that unwanted or harmful speech is violence. And this doesn't just apply to the expression of offensive or hurtful ideas. One contributor wrote that "asking people to maintain peaceful dialogue with those who legitimately do not think their lives matter" is "a violent act."[78]

Under the broadened meaning, not only is asking for dialogue a violent act, so is even making an insufficiently strong statement of support. On June 3, 2020, in the wake of the murder of George Floyd and the worldwide Black Lives Matter protests, the Chicago-based Poetry Foundation released the following statement:[79]

> The Poetry Foundation and Poetry magazine stand in solidarity with the Black community, and denounce injustice and systemic racism. As an organization we recognize that there is much work to be done, and we are committed to engaging in this work to eradicate institutional racism. We acknowledge that real change takes time and dedication, and we are committed to making this a priority. We believe in the strength and power of poetry to uplift in times of despair, and to empower and amplify the voices of this time, this moment.

Three days later, an open letter of complaint about this statement was published, written by thirty poets and with more than a thousand signatures. The letter said the foundation's statement was "worse than the bare minimum" and included this statement:[80] "The watery vagaries of this statement are, ultimately, a violence." A few days later, the Poetry Foundation announced that its president and board chair had stepped down.[81]

These are just part of a broader pattern of change that the word *violence* is undergoing. In a 2018 article about bias in algorithm-based artificial intelligence decisions, data ethics researcher Anna Lauren Hoffman writes about *data violence*.[82] Her examples include a case in which Google's photo recognition software labeled photos of African Americans as gorillas[83] and in which Facebook auto-suspended Native Americans for using their real names:[84]

> "Violence" might seem like a dramatic way to talk about these accidents of engineering and the processes of gathering data and using algorithms to interpret it. Yet just like physical violence in the real world, this kind of "data violence" . . . occurs as the result of choices that implicitly and explicitly lead to harmful or even fatal outcomes.[85]

And in a final example, philosopher Kristie Dotson argues that *epistemic violence* occurs when a person is denied an audience "willing and capable of hearing" what she or he is saying. She states, for example, that if you do not heed a warning that a person gives you, this would be an act of "violence" against that person.[86]

The evidence is clear that the meaning of the word *violence* in public discourse has significantly broadened. It no longer needs to include the prototype features of physical harm or intention by the agent. In line with the notion of structural violence introduced in political commentary in the 1960s, the term is now being applied to just about any perceived injustice or harm to a social minority group.

The recent career of the word *violence* in public discourse is a particularly charged example of how a word's shift in meaning can have consequences. Whether those consequences are wanted or unwanted, they should be understood, for such shifts can change our moral and legal landscape, with real-life implications. The more charged a word becomes, the more powerful its role is in the Russell conjugation and the Wittgenstein ruler. We would not be surprised to hear someone to say *My words are strong* but *His words are violent.* Or if I say *Silence is violence*, this may tell you more about me than it tells you about silence. The more political a word becomes, the more its role as a landmark for social coordination becomes potentially world changing. New landmarks provide new reasons for action: new tools for justification, persuasion, and coercion.

Language can be used to engineer logics for social action and to create or bolster social power. This is most clearly seen in legal classification by words, as suggested earlier in the case of the detainees who were termed "illegal combatants." Formally categorizing someone as a terrorist will have obvious consequences. In April 2014, a royal decree in Saudi Arabia declared all political dissent, including atheism, to be terrorism.[87] In May 2020, the Royal Canadian Mounted Police brought terrorism charges against a seventeen-year old charged with murder and manslaughter motivated by incel ideology.[88] And in May 2020, President Donald Trump announced, "The United States of America will be designating ANTIFA as a Terrorist Organization." These language moves give a legal green light to treat these people, rightly or wrongly, in the same way as people who make political statements by bombing passenger trains or flying planes into buildings. While the moves may naturally be resisted by some who would suffer the consequences of being classed as a terrorist, in some cases people may fight *for* the classification. When Bobby Sands and nine other officers of the Provisional Irish Republican Army held a weeks-long hunger strike at Maze Prison outside Belfast in 1981, their key demand was that they be accorded *Special Category Status*, that is, that they be classified as political prisoners of war and not criminals. The ten men chose to die rather than forgo this demand.

Words like *violence* and *terrorist* can have major real-world consequences insofar as legal systems can coordinate around them in applying the force of law. This is why they shift in step with changes in our moral and political landscapes. They are, simultaneously, both mercurial maps of an ever-changing world and instructions for effecting (or resisting) that change. Language is good for creating these maps and instructions. but there are no guarantees that this power will be used for good.

*

Through the framing effects of word choice, language is good for staking claims over how reality should be seen, which parts of it we should be attending to and which parts we should ignore, and how we should respond to it. Not all framings are equal. But the question of which framing is the most relevant or appropriate cannot be settled with reference to objective or independent rules.[89] Controversy over a phrase like *Easter worshippers* is like a patch of dirt to a posse of Costa Rican capuchins at a loose end. It is something that a social group can opportunistically coordinate around in order to forge, display, or strengthen their coalition. The same is true of any politicized argument about motivated framing. If you measure the term *Easter worshippers* as "anti-Christian," then Wittgenstein's ruler measures *you* as the kind of person who would say that. And if we both measure it in that same way, we are calibrated to each other, like Schelling's parachutists with a shared map of the terrain in which we have just landed. For the function of social signalling and calibration, the important thing is not whether the map represents the terrain in an accurate, complete, or balanced fashion. What matters is that the map is shared and that it allows the parachutists to successfully coordinate their actions.

Words set our coordinates and give us citable reasons for action. They provide us with inventories of diverse framings of the parts of reality that interest us. While this diversity may confound or overwhelm the truth-seeking scientist, it enables the action-defending lawyer to pick and choose as befits the goals of the moment, especially when it comes to constructing rationalizations and justifications. When we want the world to be a certain way, we tend not to seek evidence that may challenge this. We look for reasons why things should stay the way we want. This explains why public discourse, rather than being a market for ideas, is mostly a market for justifications.[90]

So far, we have concentrated on the power of words. We now turn to what is surely the greatest tool for constructing shared maps for social coordination in culture and society: *the story.*

9   Stories and What They Do to Us

Somebody gets into trouble, gets out of it again. People love that story. They never get sick of it.

—Kurt Vonnegut

In fewer than ten words, author Kurt Vonnegut cuts to the core of what a story is: "Somebody gets in trouble, gets out of it again."[1] Stories are not only the specialist craft of novelists and scriptwriters.[2] A four-year-old child can readily tell a story in Vonnegut's mold:[3]

Once there was a wolf, he lived far off from his mom, and then the dad arrived, then they returned to the Mom. Now it is over.

This bare-bones tale includes the key elements of narrative found in every piece of advice you'll read on fiction writing.[4] It establishes a setting, with a central protagonist (*Once there was a wolf*). It introduces the trouble that the protagonist is in (*he lived far off from his mom*). The protagonist is extricated from the trouble (*then the dad arrived, then they returned to the mom*). Then there is resolution (*now it is over*).

You can find these elements in the kind of spontaneous recountings of experience that we all engage in every day, however mundane our experiences may seem and wherever in the world we find ourselves.

Here is an example from West Africa. It was told in the course of a conversation among three men—Odo, Koku, and Ruben—in the village of Mempeasem in the mountains of the central Volta Region of Ghana, east of Lake Volta.[5] In this conversation, on a day like any other, the men are taking a break from village work and chatting about encounters with dangerous animals. They are speaking Siwu, a language of the Kwa family of languages spoken in Ghana, Ivory Coast, and Togo. Koku has just been telling the others about people eating python meat, a practice that is frowned on in the area. Odo then comes in with a story about an encounter with a snake:[6]

> One day in the graveyard area I was going to farm, the palm bunches were ripe. It coiled, like this. It put its head in the stalks where the ripe palmfruit bunch is. I passed, and I stood on its left side. As soon as I saw it like this I turned away my head and I passed and moved away. So I passed, and turned around with my right hand towards the palm tree, slowly. I hit it with the flat part. I don't use the sharp edge of the cutlass to kill a snake. The flat part. I struck out into the palm-tree "bam!" The way it coiled, it struggled struggled struggled and untied. It hung down. And finally I hit it and killed it.

In no longer than a minute, and with no rehearsal, Koku builds a story with setting, protagonist, opponent and predicament, plan, and eventual resolution. All the elements.

Here is another example, this time from an informal interview in Harlem, New York City, in the mid-1960s:[7]

Interviewer: What was the most important fight that you remember, one that sticks in your mind?

Interviewee: Well, one I think was with a girl. Like I was a kid, you know. And she was the baddest girl, the baddest girl in the neighborhood. If you didn't bring her candy to school, she would punch you in the mouth. And you had to kiss her when she'd tell you. This girl was only about 12 years old, man, but she was a killer. She didn't take no junk. She whupped all her brothers. And I came to school one day and I didn't have no money. My ma wouldn't give me no money. I played hookies [skipped school] one day, she put something on me [she hit me hard]. I played hookies, man, so I said, you know, I'm not gonna play hookies no more 'cause I don't wanna get a whupping. So I go to school and this girl says, "Where's the candy?" I said, "I don't have it." She says, powww! So I says to myself, "There's gonna be times my mother won't give me money because we're a poor family. And I can't take this all, you know, every time she don't give me any money." So I say, "Well, I just gotta fight this girl. She gonna hafta whup me. I hope she don't whup me." And I hit the girl: powww! And I put something on it. I win the fight. That was one of the most important.

In this off-the-cuff story, again we see the key, compelling elements of narrative: setting, protagonist, opponent/predicament, plan/battle, transformation, and resolution. With no training or forethought, people tell stories with all of these elements on a daily basis in the flow of conversation. We don't learn the formula at school. We aren't taught it at home. But we know it well. In the stories told in everyday conversation, day in and day out, this template comes to us over and over again. It is a template for building and accessing much richer frames for social coordination than mere acts of word choice can create.

Stories are built out of language. Every element comes from words: settings, characters, actions, feelings, and what they all mean.[8] Even when we are working with gestures, images, and voices—which of course we do all the time in story—we frame them with language.[9] Stories draw on all of the cognitive mechanisms for priming, framing, and channeling of attention that any use of words implies. And as we shall find out in this chapter, stories have further powerful features to ramp up the power of language as a tool for lawyers: a tool of persuasion, justification, and social coordination.

At the core of any story are its characters. Most central, of course, is the protagonist. The wolf who has lost its mother. The villager who kills a snake. The kid who confronts a bully. We follow their struggle, we root for them, we will them to overcome obstacles, to defeat their foes. In literature from Asia to Africa to the Americas, from large-scale to small-scale societies, from written to oral traditions, from folk tales to Hollywood features, main characters have a lot in common.[10]

Protagonists in folk tales from across the world are usually young, reproductive aged,[11] and action oriented, taking steps to resolve their challenges and accomplish their goals.[12] Heroes and heroines find themselves on adventures, far from home, encountering new and dangerous challenges. And story protagonists—especially heroines—are often described as physically attractive.[13]

Almost as a rule, heroes and heroines suffer misfortune early in a story. Stories are defined by the presence of some form of predicament, and fiction is free to run wild with this theme. Take the stories of Roald Dahl. In *James and the Giant Peach*, the protagonist's loving parents are eaten by an angry rhinoceros on the streets of London and James is forced to live with his aunts Spiker and Sponge, who enslave and abuse him. In *Fantastic Mr Fox*, the hero has his tail shot off and is trapped underground by three murderous men—the farmers Boggis, Bunce, and Bean—who try to kill Mr. Fox and his family, first with guns and then with digging machines. In *The BFG*, the orphan Sophie is stolen from her bed in the middle of the night by a giant from another land, where she comes within an inch of being eaten alive by nine fifty-foot giants with names like Childchewer, Maidmasher, and Butcher Boy. And in *Matilda*, a child prodigy is ignored and belittled by her family, while at school her hammer-throwing headmistress, Miss Trunchbull, locks her in the chokey, something like an upright coffin with giant nails and glass shards pointing in at every angle. The misfortunes of Dahl's protagonists and the evil of their opponents are over the top, but in a way that's typical of human-made fictional worlds.

Why do main characters suffer such adversity? Because adversity creates a deep need in a person. And that need becomes the central driver behind the arc of any compelling story. As observers, we are especially tuned in to the goals and needs of our heroes and heroines, and this often works on more than one level. In a typical Hollywood screenplay, the main character will have two simultaneous goals. One is quite concrete and specific. The other is much deeper, more personal, and of greater consequence.

On the surface, these characters try to reach some defined, immediate objective. They might be trying to solve a crime, kill a beast, secure an artifact, or escape a monster. But they will always have an underlying and more important goal. Their surface actions must address their deeper need. In *The Silence of the Lambs*, Clarice is a detective trying to catch the serial killer, Buffalo Bill, and she is working with former forensic psychiatrist and convicted cannibal serial killer, Hannibal Lecter, to that end. By taking this surface course of action, she addresses a deeper weakness and need: Clarice is "inexperienced, suffering from haunting childhood memories, and a woman in a man's world"; she is driven by the need to "overcome the ghosts of her past and gain respect as a professional." [14] In *Zootopia*, rookie cop Judy Hopps is trying to solve the mystery of why otters, jaguars, and other predators are being kidnapped across the city. Below the surface, this mission is in the service of her deeper, personal goal: to show that she is not just a stupid dumb bunny, as her childhood bully—a fox named Gideon Gray—once called her, and to overcome her deep-seated fear and prejudice against those who are different from her.

A story's hero is the person who can—in the words of mythologist Joseph Campbell—"battle past his personal and local historical limitations," so that he may "return then to us, transfigured, and teach the lesson he has learned of life renewed,"[15] This transfiguring is where every story is resolved. Heroes and heroines are transformed by their efforts to confront the predicaments that drive stories. For the main character, there is self-revelation, leading to a new equilibrium, a satisfying resolution for the reader or viewer. In *James and the Giant Peach*, James doesn't just escape his abusive aunts; he proves his mettle by taking charge of a fantastic adventure with a team of fellow travelers, eventually settling in peace in Manhattan's Central Park. In *Zootopia*, Judy Hopps doesn't just solve the crime and catch the villain; she proves herself and moves beyond her own prejudices, kicking off a new career as a bunny cop with a fox as her partner.

Taken together, the common features of stories and their characters— relatable protagonists who suffer misfortune and embark on adventures to confront their predicaments and eventually emerge transformed—constitute the universal "sympathetic plot."[16] Why does this package of story features work so well and so reliably?

One answer is that good stories do things to us. They act on us in ways that make us unable to look away.[17] Language makes this possible. It gives a storyteller the tools for manipulating people's attention, reeling them in, making them want to know more.[18]

If you have ever been swept away by an engrossing novel or a captivating movie, you will know the phenomenon of *narrative transportation*.[19] When we are truly transported by a story, we don't just forget our real-world surroundings. At least two other things happen. One is that we become personally invested in the desires and needs of other (imagined) people. We feel real empathy, concern, connection, and affiliation with the main characters. The other is that we get a wonderful, warm, physical feeling, a kind of high that we wish wouldn't stop.

When we find a story especially captivating, this is in part thanks to a combination of social neurochemicals released by our brains.[20] Three self-made chemicals in particular have been singled out in the neuroscience of story: the neurotransmitter dopamine and the two neuropeptides, endorphin and oxytocin.[21] These chemicals play complex roles in human physiology and behavior. They heighten our sense of interpersonal commitment, social affiliation, and belonging. And they make us feel good.

Dopamine is a hormone and neurotransmitter that increases our motivation and focus on an anticipated outcome. It is associated with anticipation of rewards. This helps to explain the relationship between dopamine and stories. A compelling narrative makes us root for the hero or heroine until the end. We pursue and savor the reward of the climax and resolution that a good story should provide.[22]

Oxytocin is a peptide hormone produced in the hypothalamus, an evolutionarily old part of the brain.[23] The hormone plays a role in the process of childbirth, associated with uterine contractions and the milk-ejection or let-down reflex for nursing. It is also associated with mother-child bonding immediately after birth and with maternal behavior and social bonds more generally.[24] Oxytocin is often called the trust hormone, but it doesn't simply increase trust with anyone who happens to be around. It tends to strengthen social bonds with in-group people, that is, people with whom we identify.[25] "When the brain synthesizes oxytocin, people are more trustworthy, generous, charitable, and compassionate."[26] Oxytocin "promotes prosocial, empathic behavior, helps us to identify with central characters who are in every story."[27]

Endorphins are produced in the pituitary gland, an offshoot of the hypothalamus in the base of the brain.[28] The word *endorphin* comes from *endogenous morphine*. Endorphins are pain-killing morphines that our own bodies create for us. They are released when we suffer pain—both physical and emotional—as well as when we engage in typically social physical activities including dancing, singing, laughing, and group sport.[29] Endorphins inhibit pain and give us a feeling of well-being or even euphoria. They are what make us feel good after an aerobics class, a dance party, or an orgasm.

These aren't the only self-made drugs that are stimulated by stories. Cortisol is a hormone produced in the adrenal gland, associated with moments of stress. It heightens our attention (said to account for flashbulb memories) and is useful in moments of threat, but is unhealthy if produced for long or sustained periods. It doesn't play as strong a role in our experience of story in the sense we are exploring in this chapter, though it does help account for our visceral experience of certain turns of events that shock and jolt us in stories and stick in our minds.

I can remember to this day the punch that hit me as a high school student reading Orwell's *1984* when Winston and Julia discover they are being watched by Big Brother in the one place they thought they were safe. *"You are the dead," said an iron voice behind them.* Those words have stuck in my mind—verbatim—for decades, thanks to a burst of cortisol from deep in my brain.

An effective story can do many things to us in the space of just a few lines. Here is the story of Linda Ault, a young woman who lived with her parents in South Africa in the 1960s:[30]

> Linda failed to return home from a dance Friday night. On Saturday she admitted she had spent the night with an Air Force lieutenant. The Aults decided on a punishment that would wake Linda up. They ordered her to shoot the dog she had owned about two years. On Sunday, the Aults and Linda took the dog into the desert near their home. They had the girl dig a shallow grave. Then Mrs. Ault grasped the dog between her hands and Mr. Ault gave his daughter a pistol and told her to shoot the dog. Instead, the girl put the pistol to her right temple and shot herself. The police said there were no charges that could be filed against the parents except possibly cruelty to animals.

There's nothing fun about this story. But it grabs you and holds on to you. It transports you. For some reason, we seek out even these horror stories, for all that they offer us.

How does a tragedy like this compare to the lighter side of narrative? Say you watch a stand-up comedy routine and laugh like mad for twenty minutes. It makes you feel good. Why? Researchers looking at the relation between the emotions and the immune system discovered that after people enjoy watching a comedy routine, they show raised salivary concentrations of immunoglobulin A—an antibody that plays a role in the immune functions of mucous membranes.[31] The experience of following a comedy show affects us in a physical way.

Are the effects of comedy different from the effects of other forms of storytelling? In an experiment designed to test this question,[32] people were shown one of five programs (of around twenty minutes): (1) stand-up comedy (from *A Night at the Improv*), (2) situation comedy (*Married with Children*), (3) drama (*LA Law*), (4) instruction (cooking show *The Frugal Gourmet*), or (5) tragedy (excerpt from the movie *Terms of Endearment*). Just before they watched the program, participants put a blood pressure cuff on their arm and had to inflate it as tight as possible, stopping only at the point that they became "decidedly uncomfortable." This provided a measure of people's starting-level pain threshold. After each participant had finished watching his or her program, the researchers took the same pain threshold measure again. They compared the two measures to see whether people's pain threshold had changed as a result of watching the program. What they found was surprising. Stand-up comedy and tragedy—opposite extremes on the pleasure-pain spectrum in terms of our subjective experience—caused people to become more tolerant of physical pain. This effect didn't happen with the drama and instruction programs.

The comedy and tragedy programs could hardly be more different from each other. The stand-up comedy was from the program *A Night at the Improv*. The excerpts, dealing mostly with dating and sexual encounters, were judged to be "extremely funny for young adults."[33] The tragedy was an excerpt from the movie *Terms of Endearment*. The segment "concentrated on events precipitating and accompanying the death of a mother of three young children. The mother's final good-bye to her children was highlighted. The events in this sequence were deemed extremely grievous and heart-wrenching." The researchers wrote: "The elevation of the threshold for physical discomfort after exposure to tragedy was not only unexpected, but proved surprisingly strong. In this investigation, the effect produced by exposure to tragedy was equivalent to that produced by exposure to comedy."[34]

Why do comedy and tragedy have similar physical effects on us? In the experiment just described, participants' experience watching the two genres was entirely different in kind. People laughed while watching stand-up and cried when watching the tragedy (and did neither when watching the legal drama or the cooking show). But the experiences showed a similar intensity of "sympathetic" feeling toward the main character, a core element of any story.[35]

A later study went deeper into the question of why people enjoy tragedy at all.[36] The starting point was the observation that watching a tragic story reduces our sensitivity to physical pain, which they assumed can be explained by the release of the same neurochemicals that are triggered to offset the experience of real physical pain as opposed to the emotional pain that a tragedy can induce. The researchers "wanted to test the hypothesis that the mental pain inflicted by watching a tragic film would stimulate the endorphin system in the way physical pain is known to do."[37] In the experiment, people watched *Stuart: A Life Backwards*, a movie that tells the true story of Stuart Shorter's life of "turmoil and extreme suffering." The film's "decidedly downward arc" depicts Stuart's status as a "mentally ill violent criminal, and alcoholic, and a survivor of child abuse." It ends with Stuart killed by a train at age thirty-three.

Before and after watching the movie, viewers were asked to describe how they felt. Not surprisingly, given the movie's content, "average positive affect scores went down and, by twice the margin, negative affect went up as a result of the experience." But people can't report their endorphin levels, and directly measuring those levels would be invasive to say the least. (It could be done by inserting a needle between the vertebrae in the spine and taking a sample of cerebrospinal fluid.) Instead, the experimenters took an indirect measure, akin to the blood pressure cuff test in the earlier study. The measure is called a wall-sit test or a ski-test.

Before watching the film, participants in the experiment had to hold a sitting posture against the wall without the support of a chair. Holding this posture is easy at first, but after about a minute, it begins to burn. Participants were asked to hold the position for as long as possible. They averaged seventy-seven seconds. Then, after they had watched the tragedy of *Stuart*, they were asked to do the exercise again. On average, they were able to hold the wall-sit position for six seconds longer than before. When the same experiment was run with different material shown—natural history documentaries—there was no increase in the length of time that people were able to do the wall-sit test after the viewing. This showed that "pain-killing effects created by *Stuart* must have been triggered by the specific content of the film."[38] The experience of following a tragic story "does indeed seem to be providing an endorphin kick for its audience."[39]

The kick that a story gives us isn't just an individual-centered bodily experience. People who watched the movie (which they did in groups) were asked if they felt a connection to the people around them. The people whose pain tolerance increased after watching the movie also reported being more "connected to those around them." Language-induced endorphins don't just dim our pain and make us feel good individually. They make us feel more connected to the group we are with. Endorphins are released when people dance, laugh, sing, or exercise together, especially if they show close physical coordination.[40] An example is rowing. A study found that while rowers' pain thresholds go up at the end of an elite team rowing session—a *rowers' high*—they go up *more* if the rowers row in groups rather than alone.[41] Not only are endorphins implicated in reducing pain when under stress, but they are part of the feeling of belonging to a social group.[42]

A last piece of the puzzle of why a grippingly tragic story can give us an endorphin kick concerns the matter of reward. In the wall-sit experiment, people were asked to give ratings on various survey items after they had seen the movie *Stuart*. Only one of these ratings showed any correlation to the wall-sit pain threshold data. It was this: *Given the opportunity, I would watch this film again.* "The link between people's desire to repeat the experience of watching *Stuart* and their endorphin release arguably points to the feelgood factor with which endorphins 'reward us.'"[43] This is why after seeing a tragic movie, you may not say that you enjoyed it as such, but at some level, you would say that the experience was rewarding. You would recommend it. "The painful experience of watching tragedy stimulates the endorphin system, which then gives one a sense of euphoria that mingles with the intense pain to create the paradoxical phenomenon that we think of as the pleasure of tragedy."[44] The physical effect of a decrease in the feeling of pain as a result of following a story is a pretty extraordinary effect of something that is essentially built out of words.[45]

Does all of this mean that the effects stories have on us are purely chemical ones? At some level, yes: they operate on us with brute force. As cold makes us shiver and heat makes us sweat, compelling stories engage us and make us feel socially connected. If only you—as story narrator, screenwriter, public speaker, propagandist, or marketer—could craft just the right words, I would be putty in your hands. Right? Not quite. As much as some corporate marketing websites would like you to believe it, people don't simply yield like machines to the things we say. It's true—and amazing, when you think about it—that words can make our bodies release certain influential chemicals into our systems. I could say something shocking or offensive, and that would certainly set off a little blast in your brain. But that doesn't mean we respond robotically to people's words or to the chemicals that those words might trigger. Words don't simply control us. We have minds, and our minds stand between words and our brain's chemical dispensaries. We interpret. We evaluate. We think.

Our experience of storytelling will depend on how we frame the story to ourselves. We can say whether it makes us feel good or bad, whether we enjoyed it, whether and to what degree we identify with the characters, how transported we felt by the story, and, of course, what the story ultimately means to us. And we can explain our responses. Neurochemicals are only a part of the picture. They "have a lot to do with how we feel as we sit in the auditorium, but little to do with how we relate to the story on the screen."[46] Stories are important not just for how they make us feel but for what they make us think, what we can learn from them, what we can use them for.

*

Why have all human groups developed the practice of using language to tell stories? And with so many similarities in structure? In evolutionary terms, it is a question of adaptive value.[47] Who benefits from stories? There are three possible answers.[48]

One possibility is that stories benefit the teller. A skilled storyteller might increase his social standing by advertising his prowess as a wordsmith and entertainer. Or if a story is a good way to manipulate others' behavior, then this would also confer benefits on those who tell stories well. But it cannot be that stories benefit only their tellers. If that were true, nobody would be motivated to listen.[49] The second possibility is that stories benefit audiences. A story gives us access to someone else's experience. We can learn lessons without having to pay the costs that others may have paid in real life. It makes sense to pay attention to stories if it means we might gain useful information about potential opportunities and things to avoid, and gain insight into others' interpretations of the world. But conversely, what benefit would tellers get from merely giving away their knowledge for free? The truth is surely that storytelling is good for both speakers and listeners. This would account for why people are motivated both to tell stories to others and to pay attention to stories that others tell.

But there is a third answer to the question of who benefits from stories. It is that stories benefit *the teller and the listener together*. We see this when we change our unit of analysis from the individual to the social group. As we are about to see, the most powerful function of stories is social bonding.

10   Social Glue

Not, then, men and their moments. Rather moments and their men.

—Erving Goffman (1967)

In his 1936 book *The Hero with a Thousand Faces*, mythologist Joseph Campbell combed through mythological tales from different cultures, religions, and times in search of a common human core to the myth. He discovered the recurring structure that he called the *hero's journey*:

> A hero ventures forth from the world of common day into a region of supernatural wonder: fabulous forces are there encountered and a decisive victory is won: the hero comes back from this mysterious adventure with the power to bestow boons on his fellow man.[1]

Why does this story keep being told? It's not mere coincidence or accident. The story thrives because it performs a function in social life. In Campbell's words, the role of the hero is to "guide and save" society.[2] How does it do this? By creating and circulating landmarks that people can coordinate around.

When screenwriting guru John Truby defines the concept of story, he is careful to insist that there is no story without a speaker and a listener. Here is his definition of *story*:

> A speaker tells a listener what someone did to get what he wanted and why.

A speaker tells a listener. Crucial to the story are not only the narrated events but also the event of *telling* the story itself. When we think we are affected by a story, we are really being affected by the person telling it.

In the previous chapter, we focused on the kinds of stories that people encounter in the rarefied contexts of literature and film. At a macrolevel, these big stories both reflect and illuminate their cultural and historical contexts. And at a microlevel, they play on our individual preferences and thought processes, on the ways in which we as individuals are affected by the elements of story. But something must link societal trends and individual minds. That thing is social interaction—people talking to each other in real life.

We consume the great stories of literature and film at a pretty slow rate in life. How many movies or shows do you see per week? How many books do you read? For most people, it wouldn't be more than a few. But these aren't the only places we encounter stories. In other parts of life, we are flooded with them. I am talking about the everyday stories, the mundane stories, the little stories that pepper our conversations throughout the day. These little stories play a central role in creating and maintaining our social worlds.

Let's look at an example of the most mundane type of story we could imagine. This is from the beginning of a phone conversation between two friends, Jo and Li, in the suburban United States:[3]

Jo: How're you doing?

Li: Okay. How are you?

Jo: Oh all right.

Li: Your mother met Michael last night.

Jo: Oh really?

Li: Yeah.

Jo: Oh.

Li: Yeah, she was taking Shiloh [her dog] out, just as we were coming back from dinner.

Jo: Oh, I didn't see.

Li: And we had to park in front of your house. So Shiloh tried to get in the car. [Jo and Li both laugh] It was really funny; he was taking your mom all the way down the hill.

Jo: [Laughing]

Li: So he tried to jump in the car.

Jo: Oh boy.

Li: 'Cause I was just getting out.

Jo: So did you introduce her?

Li: Of course.

Jo: Yeah.

Li: So you know she said he—as he tried to yank her up and down the block. You know it was kind of a funny way to say hello.

Jo. Yeah

Li. So how are you?

This story seems like nothing. It is barely a story. But little stories like this arguably do more than any grand myths to guide and save society. In this chapter, I'm going to explain what I mean by this.

Li's story does at least three things. First, it updates and manages information about social networks. Second, it creates an opportunity for Jo and Li to publicly share agreement on how they view the world. Third, it creates a chance to table, and potentially resolve, possible or actual transgressions of social norms, thereby also advertising or reinforcing those norms.

The purpose of Li's little story at the beginning of the call is ostensibly to convey a simple piece of new information: Jo's mother has met Li's boyfriend, Michael. This is the kind of information that dominates our conversations: information about our social networks.[4] Here, Jo learns something that updates her knowledge of the current state of social relationships among the people in her life. She can now link two nodes—her mother and Li's boyfriend—changing their status from strangers to acquaintances. And not only does Jo now know that her mother has met Li's boyfriend, Michael, but the knowledge is now part of Li and Jo's common ground. This is *gossip*, in the technical sense: "the exchange of social information," as evolutionary biologist Robin Dunbar defines it.[5] For Dunbar, gossip is everything. Not only is it "the core of human social relationships," but gossip "makes human society as we know it possible."

This taps into at least three mechanisms of language. First, when we exchange social information, we are exploiting one of the key jobs that language performs: informing people about things they haven't seen for themselves. This is something that other animals, which lack language, can't do. (There are some obvious but highly limited exceptions, such as the dance that bees use to tell each other where food can be found.) In this way, gossip spreads information about social goings-on. But second, if I give you a piece of social information, I don't only update you on some situation or event. I also update you on *my view of* that situation or event. As we saw in previous chapters, I can't give you a neutral report of any event or situation, let alone a social one. I have to frame it somehow. Is it good news? Is it a scandal? Or what? It's the combination of the Russell conjugation and Wittgenstein's ruler. The way I choose to frame the information also tells you something about myself and my vantage point. In her phone call with Jo, Li chose to say *Your mother met Michael last night*. She could have said *Michael met your mother last night*, making the statement about Michael. There are many other ways she could have framed the scene. Then there is the third mechanism by which a piece of gossip has its effect: as something for the speaker and listener to coordinate around. As an interface for social bonding and for propagation of social norms, the story is an opportunity for people to share *agreement* by adopting the same stance toward what is being discussed.

These functions of exchanging social information are especially clear in talk that qualifies as gossip in the everyday sense, that is, where people exchange salacious or otherwise intimate stories about people in their social networks. The anthropologist John Haviland studied gossip sessions among Zinacantecos in the central Chiapas Highlands of Mexico. He points out the rich social and cultural value of gossip, beyond the specifics of any given story:

> We learn what constitutes sufficient excuse to break off a courtship; we learn how Zinacantecos express anger; we learn how it is possible to justify running away from one's husband, one's wife, a religious cargo, and so forth. Gossip always draws our attention immediately to the important facts, and it never fails to draw appropriate conclusions: deciding who is to blame, who acted badly, when things begin to turn sour, etc.[6]

As apprentice members of society, children rely on these public discussions of social values to come to grips with the norms they will soon be accountable to. Through gossip, they learn what is normal, what is exceptional, what is good and bad, and what are acceptable reactions to transgressions.

Gossip also allows people to publicly advertise their position relative to other people in their social network and to manage or influence the reputations of themselves and others. Because language can be used to frame things in any number of ways, when Tzotzil speakers tell each other about private goings-on in the villages of Zinacantan, different people may present competing versions of the truth.

An example concerns a dispute between two men, Xun and Lol, centering on Xun's wife.[7] Haviland collected two versions of the story, which agreed on certain basic facts: Xun had been drinking heavily; Xun's wife left and went to stay in the home of her younger sister, who is married to Lol; Xun wanted his wife back and so took the case to the local municipal town hall; Lol was briefly detained but then freed; Xun's wife left him; she then stayed in Lol's home thereafter. The end.

But the two versions of events that Haviland recorded are as different as chalk and cheese. In the version told by a friend of Lol, Xun is a hopeless and abusive drunk, and Lol is a good person who saved Xun's wife from a life of harm. In the version told by a friend of Xun, Xun had a run of bad luck, his wife was dissatisfied and so ran away to Lol's house and convinced him to try to kill her husband, Xun. After trying to kill Xun, Lol was caught and jailed at the town hall but used his influence and was quickly released. These radically different portrayals of the same events clearly aim to give entirely different accounts of who is at fault, who is good and who is bad, which actions were justified and which were not.

It is no coincidence that people's friends and allies talk about them in a good light. This is a simple extension of the Russell conjugation: *My friend saves lives; his friend steals wives.* Naturally, if someone is my ally, I will portray that person in good light. And the reverse is equally true. If I portray someone in good light, then that person is—or should become—my ally. How I talk about someone doesn't just reveal or reflect the kind of relationship I have with him or her; it creates and maintains that relationship. Language has the power to prime people and frame situations in highly varied ways. Perhaps our greatest use of that power is in engineering social relationships and their politics.

For someone telling someone else a story, it is more important to capture the desired social implications for the people involved—that is, how the story reflects or has an impact on relationships among the various parties involved, including the teller, the hearer, and the people in the story—than it is to ensure that the facts of the matter are accurate. This much is obvious in the case of textbook gossip, with its tendency for exaggeration. In the two Zinacantecan gossip stories about Xun's wife, the tellings of the story are less concerned with conveying the facts and more concerned—if not entirely concerned—with advertising and influencing social stances and relationships. This is clear enough in the case of gossip, but deep down, it is true of almost everything we say.

Language's role in signaling affiliation between individuals in a social group taps into an evolutionarily deep function of communication across the animal world. Take bottlenose dolphins. Many male pairs form lifelong partnerships, mostly to cooperate in guarding individual females while they are sexually receptive.[8] These coalition mates swim in formation to shield females from the attention of other males. While any two dolphins in the same social group may swim or feed together, what is special about coalition mates is the highly synchronous way they swim or feed together.[9] By swimming in synchrony, the dolphins show each other—and others in the group—that they are especially in tune.

Humans use language in exactly this way. This is particularly clear when it comes to stories. When we use language for building affiliation, we're doing something similar to what Costa Rican capuchins do when joining forces to direct aggression. But for us, it's usually not aggression we're expressing. When one person shares a story and the other listens, the two people are not unlike capuchins in overlord formation. Two individuals direct their stance toward a shared target as a way of joining forces. When people publicly coordinate around a single idea, showing that they are jointly focused on it and taking the same stance toward it, they show that they are closely affiliated.

Laughter works like this too. When people laugh together in a conversation, it shows not only that they each individually find the same thing funny, but that this brings them together. In conversation, Jo and Li laugh together at the image of Shiloh the dog trying to get into Li's car while Jo's mother has him on a leash. Even in this almost trivial example, we see the essential mechanism by which language is a form of social glue. It's the same with the competing stories of Xun's wife. The person who portrays Xun in a good light is advertising—and committing to—his own social position: *I'm on Xun's side.*[10] The recipient of that story has an opportunity to take the same position and thereby affiliate with the speaker. This would signal that they are with the speaker in Team Xun and, by extension, in the context of the competing accounts of the events, against Team Lol. Polarization is born, and storytelling is the source.

Language can signal social relationships in yet simpler ways. Take the case of greetings. Greetings are found across the animal world and in every human group. What are greetings for? One thing they do is kick start an interaction. A: *How're you doing?* B: *Okay. How are you?* Here we have a prepackaged way to get the turn-taking mechanism of conversation ticking along. And we have a signal of mutual validation. Greetings can remove a sense of uncertainty or even threat as people come together.

Human greetings can be complex and elaborate.[11] But even in their simplest form, they fulfill the basic functions of letting people display a stance toward each other and signal how closely aligned they are in their existing social network. This is true even for the exchange of mere monosyllables.

Imagine you are a college student, and you have been invited to a gathering at another student's apartment to watch a live broadcast of presidential election results. You arrive at the apartment and ring the doorbell. The door opens, and you lock eyes with your host. What does she say? *Hi,* of course. But there are many ways to say that little word. Sociologist Danielle Pillet-Shore took video recordings of scenarios like this and amassed more than three hundred examples of informal greetings among English speakers in the United States.[12] Let's look at two of her examples.

The election results party is at Paula's apartment. When Paula greets her good friend Amanda at the door, she does it with the word *Hey*. But not just any *Hey*. It's *Heeeeeeey!* stretching out for longer than a full second. That's four times as long as it takes to pronounce the average syllable in English.[13] A visual trace of this is shown in figure 10.1, where the line records the long journey that Paula's *Heeeeeeey* takes as she welcomes Amanda at the door.

The second example occurs during the same occasion, this time when Paula opens the door for Derik, whom she has never met before. Again, it's

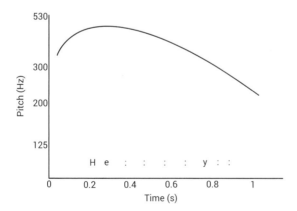

Figure 10.1

Pitch trace of Paula's greeting to her close friend Amanda. Adapted from Danielle Pillet-Shore, "Greeting: Displaying Stance Through Prosodic Recipient Design," *Research on Language and Social Interaction* 45, no. 4 (2012): 375–98, https://doi.org/10.1080/08351813.2012.724994.

the same simple greeting, but now in the form of a clipped *Hi-ee*. This time, her monosyllabic greeting goes for just a third as long as her greeting with Amanda (see figure 10.2).

Paula's greetings to the two people are variations on essentially the same little word. Why, when she greets her close friend Amanda, does she stretch the word out so long? It may be that the difference in length simply signals the difference in how close the relationships are, an effect of the extra effort she puts in when greeting Amanda. But there is an interesting side effect of Paula's super-long greeting with her close friend. It has to do with what happens when the guest greets her back. First, look at the exchange between Paula and Derik. Paula's *Hi-ee* is over so fast that when Derik says *Hi* back, the greetings have been produced one after the other, as illustrated in figure 10.3.

Now look at Paula's greeting to Amanda. When Paula's *Hey* is stretched out to three times the length, Amanda's returned greeting *Hello* is entirely in overlap with Paula (see figure 10.4). The effect is that people who are

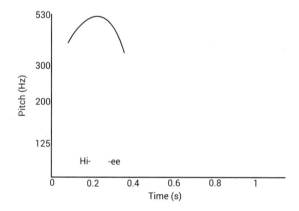

Figure 10.2
Pitch trace of Paula's greeting to Derik when she is meeting him for the first time. Adapted from Pillet-Shore, "Greeting."

Figure 10.3
Relative timing of Paula's greeting and Derik's response, showing no overlap.

Figure 10.4
Relative timing of Paula's greeting and Amanda's response, showing complete overlap.

close friends may produce greetings in complete overlap, as if they had a single voice, a direct sign of their fusion in social terms.

When you think about it, these greeting words mean almost nothing. They don't refer to anything. They don't convey any new information. But little words like these are important. They are finely tuned to our social relationships. As guests arrive at Paula's place, she is not free to greet people in any old way. She has to select just the right form to suit her relationship to each guest. If Paula were to greet her close friend Amanda with the clipped *Hi-ee* shown in figure 10.2, it would come across as weirdly distant. Amanda might wonder if their relationship had chilled. Or if Paula welcomed Derik with the exuberant *Heeeeeey!* shown in figure 10.1, he might find this to be awkwardly overfamiliar. He might wonder, *Is Amanda mistaking me for someone else?*

This social-signaling function of different versions of a simple bit of language arguably works just like the dolphins' different ways of swimming together and the capuchins' overlord antics. These signals have real social consequences. When swimming in sync makes you coalition mates, that isn't just a label. It is a public commitment. It means that later, you can rely on each other in times of need, more so than with those who swim in a less synchronized way. In a similar way, if we had no prior knowledge of Paula's relationships to Amanda and Derik and simply observed the way she pronounced that one syllable when greeting them at the door, we would have a reliable measure of the kinds of relationship they have. We could easily predict who of the two guests Paula could more likely rely on in a time of need.

To see what I mean, consider another kind of case in which the social relationships marked by how we talk—in this case, the way our accent signals our group membership—is linked to our sense of social obligation to other people. Imagine it is the early 1970s in a world without mobile phones, autodial, and caller recognition. People who need to make a call while they are out would have to find a pay phone and would need coins to operate it. You are at home in the evening and your phone rings. A man's voice says: "Hello, Ralph's Garage? This is George Williams. Listen, I'm stuck out here on the parkway and I'm wondering if you'd be able to come out here and take a look at my car?" You aren't Ralph's Garage and you don't know any George Williams. "Sorry," you say. "You have the wrong number." The voice continues: "This isn't Ralph's Garage?! Listen, I'm terribly sorry to have disturbed you, but listen, I'm stuck out here on the parkway and that was the last dime I had! I have bills in my pocket but no more change to make another phone call. Now I'm really stuck out here. What am I going to do now?" You could offer to call the garage for him. While you are thinking about it, the caller continues: "Listen, do you think you could do me the favor of calling the garage and letting them know where I am? I'll give you the number. They know me over there." At this point you could help the caller by dialing the number, or you could decline. What do you do?

A 1971 study ran the scenario just described, with actors playing out the role of the caller.[14] (They also had actors on another phone, waiting to take people's calls to "Ralph's Garage.") They phoned more than a thousand unsuspecting people in their New York homes and found that around two-thirds of people who received these calls would agree to make the call to Ralph's Garage on the caller's behalf. But there was a twist. The actors playing the role of George Williams spoke with markedly different accents. Half of the callers spoke with an accent that was recognizably African American. The other half spoke with an accent that was recognizably white. When the accent identified the caller as black, that person received help less often on average than if the caller sounded white. The same words in a different accent resulted in a different response from the hearer. This reveals yet another level at which language can work its influence over people.

Language can be used to lie, but it can also be a reliable signal. Quite independent of what you say, the accent you say it with reveals things about who you are—where you grew up, your socioeconomic status, which side of the tracks you are from. Your accent is a tag, telling people which social category you're in. Not unlike the stories we tell and the greetings we give, this kind of tag defines your social relationship with others. It says who you are more likely to be affiliated with. And unlike the choice of how to pronounce the word *Hi* when you greet someone at the door, your accent is less under your flexible control. It is harder to fake.[15]

How do these various linguistic signs of social affiliation scale up to the level of "human society as we know it," as Robin Dunbar put it? How can they "guide and save society" in all its complexity? The examples we've considered illustrate the role of language in signaling how we are related to other people, interpersonally or in terms of generic social categories. These signs have consequences for how others may treat us and whether we can rely on those others for help. Human relationships are embedded within complex networks, which vary from person to person. Some people have many relationships, others only a few. Some ties are strong, others weak. But there is a common underlying structure for how we all organize our social relationships. The structure consists of concentric rings, moving outward (see figure 10.5).[16]

In the center is the small group of people who are closest to us. This *support clique* contains a half a dozen or so people. We are in constant contact with these people, and they are the ones we would turn to—and who would turn to us—when disaster strikes. Next is a *sympathy group*, of around 20 people, a bit farther out. Then a *band* of about 35 people, and a core *social group* of around 150 people. This group of 150 is the well-known limit of social group size such that we know all the individuals in the group and can track their relationships to each other.[17]

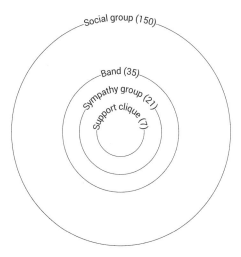

Figure 10.5
Levels of relationship intensity and the approximate sizes of each group.

Here is where the social affiliation mechanisms of language—from gossip to greetings to accents—come in. To maintain a multilevel system of relationships, we need clear ways of signaling to each other and to others who is in which level of relationship to us at any one time. Having a falling out or becoming distant are ways of describing what happens when someone moves from an inner level to an outer level in this structure. How do people know who is in which of these various levels?

If we were gelada monkeys in the Ethiopian highlands, we would signal our social proximity through physical grooming. We would scratch and pick away at each other's skin for hours of the day. This intimate activity is a form of communion. It not only provides pleasure for those involved (an endorphin high, in fact), but it is a genuine signal of the social commitment that individuals have to each other. Because time is finite, if I have spent hours grooming you, I have necessarily not spent time grooming others. In this way, an individual can send an honest signal of commitment and build a piece of social structure—a coalition—within the larger community. The society-creating function of the physical mechanism of grooming is performed in human social life by the informational mechanism of words.[18] While a dolphin may distinguish how close his social relationships are with certain others by how synchronously he swims alongside them, a human can use the information that language encodes for this kind of function.

Research on telephone conversations in English identifies some of the ways in which people with close personal relationships use language to signal their closeness. In conversations with people in our inner circles—close relatives or friends—we tend to track each others' events and activities, asking for and providing updates.[19] We tend to discuss our personal problems and show interest in the other's problems.[20]

A study of phone calls between a mother and daughter in semirural England in the 1980s found a recurrent set of themes in conversation among intimates such as close friends and relatives: "what they have had or are going to have for lunch, each other's minor ailments, meeting or speaking to a mutual acquaintance during the week, suitable presents for upcoming birthdays, the weather, what is in flower in the garden, the week's or day's events (such as that they have been to church that evening) and what other members of the family have been doing."[21]

Here are a few example statements made in these mother–daughter phone conversations:[22]

"The line's clear tonight."

"We had torrential rain today."

"Ooh, I've got a large black beetle looking at me here."

These lines are what we might call small talk, but they are not vacuous. They convey an important secondary meaning. You can't just say these kinds of things to anyone. If you are on the phone to a doctor's office, an insurance salesperson, or the CEO of the company you work at, these statements could be distinctly out of place or they would signal an effort to make the call unusually informal. In conversations among intimates, statements like these are not so much about exchanging information (although they do that). Instead, they function rather like the capuchins' patch of dirt: they provide an opportunity for two individuals to coordinate around something as a way of signaling the kind of relationship that they have.[23]

But talk among people who are close is more nuanced than simply reaching for random things to discuss. There are certain topics and certain kinds of information that only people in close relationships can readily share. And in fact they have a responsibility to share such information if the relationship is a truly close one. A clear example is information about health and personal problems. People who know each other well should ensure that they spend part of their talk time updating each other on personal news, and this also means inquiring on such matters since the last time they talked.[24] Here are some typical examples from recorded phone calls in research on people's talk about their troubles:[25]

"How's your foot?"

"How's your arthritis? You still taking shots?"

"How is your back, anyway?"

Questions like these can lead to extended discussions of such personal matters between people in close relationships. Consider this exchange in a phone call between two American friends, Emma and Lottie:[26]

Emma: I have to take two tub baths with tar in it every day.

Lottie: Yeah?

Emma: And I have to have ointment put on four times a day and I'm under violet ray for a few seconds and I got a shot in the butt of vitamin A.

Lottie: Jesus.

Emma: Lottie, honest to God, you know, I just broke out terribly when I left home. And I just—just my legs were covered.

When Lottie and Emma exchange information of this sort, it shows they are socially close. And given that closeness, we can predict that the next time they talk, Lottie will ask for an update on Emma's condition. In monitoring and exchanging this intimate information, Lottie and Emma don't just find language good for accessing situations and events they haven't directly witnessed; they find it good for maintaining the closeness of their relationship. To uphold the intimate nature of their relationship, they take care to coordinate around just these sorts of matters.[27]

Lottie and Emma's relationship is such that they are entitled to ask each other about those kinds of intimate and personal matters, of a kind that they wouldn't have a right to ask others. When I say "right," I mean that they wouldn't be sanctioned for asking or telling about such personal matters. But they *would* be sanctioned if they were to discuss the same kinds of things with complete strangers. And this is not only a right; it is also a *duty*. If Emma or Lottie were to avoid or otherwise not ask about, or offer, personal updates of this kind with each other, then this could equally be out of place and might be regarded as avoidance or distancing in the context of their usually close relationship.

If we are privy to certain information from a person, this indicates that we have special access to him or her. In the conversation we discussed at the start of this chapter, Jo learns that her mom has now met Li's boyfriend. Now suppose that Jo calls her mom and mentions that she knows about the meeting: "Oh I heard you met Li's boyfriend, Michael, the other day." This would give the mom direct evidence of Jo's position in the network around which personal information circulates and of her access to information through Li. This is a richer mechanism than just the sound of how Li might greet Jo at the door (*Heeeeey!* and not *Hi-ee*). The unique function of language as a form of social glue comes from the way the exchange of certain information is carefully controlled and monitored.

Suppose that you have just received a major piece of personal news. You are expecting a child. You've been diagnosed with a terminal illness. Your spouse is filing for divorce. You've landed a dream job overseas. Who do you tell? Who do you tell *first*? It matters deeply to people that life-changing news be delivered to people in the right order. Those who are close to you should be informed first. Suppose you find out you are pregnant, but before you tell your partner, you tell your family, your friends, your professor, and your dentist. This isn't likely to go down well with your partner. People have a strong sense of their right to be told certain information at a certain time, and in a certain order, relative to others.

The same sense of rights to receive information and responsibilities to share it applies even to the most mundane aspects of our conversations, from talking about the flowers in your garden to a beetle in front of you. We notice when these things are absent. You might not consciously think, *Why doesn't she update me on her garden any more when we talk?* but it might be manifest as a feeling that the relationship has become somehow distant.

An important aspect of the exchange of information of a personal nature, about ourselves or about others, is its role in the management of *reputation*. Reputation is central to the possibility of cooperation and other altruistic behavior in human society. If I am going to help you or form a coalition with you, I need to know that you are not a free rider—the sort of person who accepts help but will not pay it back. When information about people circulates in our communities, this provides some insurance against that possibility. A lot of what our conversations are about—the gossip component—is exchanging information about people's qualities, including our own.

Consider this line from the mother–daughter calls discussed above:

> We've been to church; we've been to the candlelight service tonight.

This is partly a report of an everyday event, a mundane updating of something that has happened during the speaker's day, not unlike, "We've had torrential rain today." But it also says something about the speaker—who she is and how she wants to be seen. She is the kind of person who goes to church. Of course, the daughter knows this, but to report it is to confirm it and reiterate it. If the mother had skipped going to church or hadn't said anything about church, this might invite inferences. By making this statement, the mother removes any doubt.

When our statements are about other people—as in a classic gossip session—then by sharing information, we are doing more than just adding a little glue to our relationship; we are building a person's public persona. Here's another line from one of the mother–daughter calls:

> Gordon's just come home. He's been at a party all night.

Whatever this says about Gordon, it contributes to a reputation that he goes to all-night parties. It might also be useful insofar as it helps to make predictions about Gordon's likely qualities and future decisions and actions. A reputation is not just one person's opinion about someone but a view of someone's personal qualities that is *agreed on* by a group of their peers. Reputation is a special feature of human society. Other primates have a great interest in the individuals in their group and the relationships among them, but their knowledge of those individuals and relationships is limited to direct observation. Not so with humans. Psychologist Nicholas Emler writes:

> Humans alone among the social vertebrates can know one another substantially by repute. People can inform themselves about events and exchanges at which they were not physically present from people who were, and so their knowledge of another individual can build on the experiences reported by third parties.[28]

Our social identities have to be signaled in various ways, and while our actions are obviously central in determining what people think of us, it is really words that matter in creating, circulating, and maintaining a reputation. There are two reasons for this.

The first is that a person's reputation is not based on people's individual beliefs (even if those beliefs converge) but on what people *agree on* about that person.[29] Reputation becomes a landmark for people to coordinate around. Such coordination and collective agreement is achieved only through language.

The second reason is that when we agree on what a person is like—trustworthy, deceitful, a mensch, a jerk—we rely on words. Whatever the reality of the events and situations we're talking about, it is *linguistic framings* of those events and situations that we coordinate around. Without a verbal rendition of people's actions and qualities, people would not know what they were agreeing to. And this must be done through the fog of priming, framing, and the partial and skewed coverage of reality that words offer, not to mention the heightened engagement that comes with stories.

Recall the two versions of the Zinacantec story of Xun's wife. There are facts to the story. If a telling of that story contains falsehoods, then there is clear reason to reject it (though of course falsehoods may spread anyway). For example, only one version included the claim that Lol tried to kill Xun. But even within the bounds of established fact, the story has no definitive version.[30] What matters—for reputation, at least—is which version of the story people agree on. Which version will they allow to stand as being the right one? This is the version they will coordinate around. Think back to the example of *thrifty* versus *stingy*. Let's say we agree that Kim is someone who doesn't like spending too much money. The alternative linguistic framings, *Kim is thrifty* versus *Kim is stingy*, are not so much different claims about reality as they are different proposals for an idea we should coordinate around. They are different claims to what we agree to treat as being the reality. And in turn, they are proposals for what Kim becomes accountable for.

*

Stories, gossip, news, reputation. These are all built out of words. They are bits of social glue that update us with information about our social networks. They bond us through joint commitment to shared values and opinions. They give us shared landmarks to coordinate around. Through the flow of information among social associates, we keep track of who is close and who is distant, who are friends and who are enemies, who owes what to whom, who has helped whom, and who has been wronged, lied to, or betrayed. In doing so we create the understandings of interpersonal networks and commitments that constitute our social reality, from our most intimate relationships to the most generic identities that are building blocks of our societies.

Stories—whether in gossip sessions or traditional myths—do more than simply connect us socially. They contain ideas that define and shape our shared knowledge and worldviews. Maps made of language don't just help us meet other people in the same place. They help us make sense of the world that we share.

11　Sense Making

In science and life a great deal depends on proper evaluation, tested by predictability, which depends in turn on the similarity of structure between territory-map or fact-language. Thus, we have to know scientific facts, as well as the intricacies and difficulties of language and its structure.

—Alfred Korzybski (1941)

When I first traveled to the hilltops of central Laos to study the Kri language, I was getting to know members of an entire community. Early in my time living in the village of Mrkaa, I wanted to pay a courtesy visit to as many of the village households as I could. The Kri practice of early-evening tea drinking around home fires gave me the chance to meet people and practice the language that I was learning more formally through the day. Early one evening, I approached the home of Mr. Siangthong and called out: *Saaw krnooq tôô ki dêêh?* (May I enter?). He replied: *Tôô* (You may!).

Kri homes are built up high on pylons. To enter a Kri house, you first have to climb a (usually quite rickety) ladder to get up to floor level. Once you are on the verandah, there are two doorways into the house, one at each end of the front wall. The floor plan of a Kri house is essentially a square, and the different sides of this square have social meaning for Kri speakers.[1] On a left/right axis, as you enter the house, one doorway opens into the "inner" half of the house. That doorway is used by family members, women, children, sons-in-law and daughters-in-law. The other doorway is on the "outer" half of the house. It is used by guests, senior people, strangers, people who are not close family. Which doorway will you use? Once you have entered the main room of the house—the living room, if you will—you take a seat on the floor. How far toward the back wall you will sit depends on how high your status is in terms of age or rank in the community. Older people, or those with a higher rank, will be seated farther toward the back of the room (the "high" side). Being split along two dimensions—inner/outer and high/low—the floor space of the Kri house becomes a map of people's social statuses. People are seated according to how they socially relate to each other. At least that is the theory.

I was oblivious to all of this. On that evening, when I entered Siangthong's house I happened to come in through the inner doorway and take a seat against the lower wall just inside. Without knowing it, I was committing something of a faux pas. As an honored guest and stranger, my rightful place was in the outer/upper corner of the room. Instead, I was sitting in exactly the wrong spot: the inner/lower corner, a place reserved for the lowest of the low, the son-in-law. That's when Siangthong called out in a joking voice: *Vòòk nik tôô matààm* (Grandpa Nick is a son-in-law!). People thought this was hilarious, as any in-law joke should be. I was promptly escorted to my rightful place. And for a while, the joke was recounted over and over in the village.

That was the moment I first became aware of the social significance of the Kri house's floor plan. What would normally go unspoken had to be articulated thanks to my transgression. Siangthong explained to me the social meaning of the house's spatial layout. He drew my attention to what I had seen every day but had not *seen* since my arrival in Mrkaa. After that, I saw it every time I looked. Whenever I went into someone's house, I would see that people were obeying these rules, everyone seated in their proper place.

This was an experience of *sense making*. Before that evening, I was oblivious to the orderly nature of a piece of social reality that had been in front of me all along. I don't know how many times I had made the same misstep, blissfully unaware. People were too polite to point it out, at least not while I was present.

What does it mean to make sense of something? When my host joked that I was a son-in-law because of where I sat, I learned a number of things at once. I learned something about the layout of the house. I learned something about the values that people attach to various places where a person might sit. I learned something about Kri sons-in-law and something about my own status in the Kri community. All this knowledge was transmitted through the heightened experience of being the butt of a joke—not traumatic but just heightened enough to be jolted into my memory. After that day, I never made the mistake again.

The process of sense making starts with disruption. Something going against the flow. Against expectations. People react with surprise and sanction. And this in turn requires an explanation. Think of how we deal with children's wayward behavior. It's not just in Kri houses that there are right and wrong places to sit. If a seven-year-old climbs onto my kitchen table and sits there, this breaks a well-established local norm, and the disruption would give me license to call her out. I might say *That's a table, not a chair*.[2] Now notice how the statement does multiple things at once. First, it communicates the fact that there is a problem, a deviation from the norm. Sitting on the table is out of order. Second, it says something specific about what chairs are for *and* something about what *tables* are *not* for. The remark points to several bits of social convention: how we should behave, what certain objects are rightfully for, and what certain words in our language mean.[3] Children are apprentices of sense making, and language is their master key.

Things make sense when we know what we should regard as normal and what we should be surprised at. Indeed, the very possibility of people remarking on something is a measure of how surprising or exceptional (literally, *remarkable*) it is. In conversation, by default we expect people to talk about things that are exceptional or unexpected to us. Have a look at the following two hypothetical narratives with two variants, a and b. Which option would you more likely hear in a natural conversation?[4]

I was walking quietly in the street when a total stranger stops before me, looks at me, and

a. asks me the time.

b. slaps me in the face.

I was just looking on the Internet at the town of Saint-Chéron. Guess what the population is:

a. 3,856 inhabitants

b. 4,444 inhabitants

People agree that the b options—denoting (seemingly) unlikely situations—are more likely to occur in natural conversation.[5] Unexpected events make stories interesting. This is even registered in the brain activity that accompanies surprise. Consider this:

I like my coffee with cream and socks.

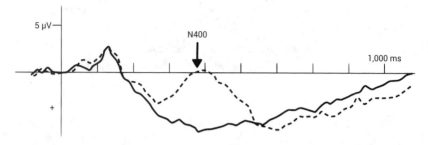

Figure 11.1
The standard N400 effect in sentential context. Adapted from Ellen F. Lau, Colin Phillips, and David Poeppel, "A Cortical Network for Semantics: (De)Constructing the N400," *Nature Reviews Neuroscience* 9, no. 12 (2008): 921, https://doi.org/10.1038/nrn2532.

As you processed that sentence, you were not expecting the word *socks*. It triggered in your brain an electrical signature of surprise called the N400 effect.[6] At about 400 milliseconds (four-tenths of a second) after an unexpected input, there is a change in the brain's electrical activity that can be measured on the scalp.

The solid line on figure 11.1 shows people's average response to hearing the sentence *I like my coffee with cream and sugar.*[7] The dotted line shows the response to *I like my coffee with cream and socks.* You can see that the N400 effect peaks at 400 milliseconds after onset of the word *socks*.

This is not the only physiological effect of surprise. Our skin conductance increases. Our heart rate changes. Our blood vessels constrict.[8] When things go against our expectations, we respond physically.[9] Even minor transgressions of expectation affect us directly, and this helps to explain why we pay attention to them and why, in turn, they have the mutual prominence needed to serve as landmarks in coordination games.

The stories we tell in daily conversations almost always center on disruptions from the normal flow of life. But they aren't usually the epic disruptions we see in novels and movies. Just about any little departure will do. Recall Li's recounting of Shiloh the dog:

Li: So, Shiloh tried to get in the car. It was really funny; he was taking your mom all the way down the hill.

Jo: [Laughing]

Li: So he tried to jump in the car.

Jo: Oh boy.

Li: 'Cause I was just getting out.

A dog trying to get into someone's car may be the smallest kink in the fabric of normality you can imagine, but it still qualifies. It's just remarkable enough to be *reportable*. And in reporting it, you reinforce that it's out of the ordinary. It's another little brick in the wall of social expectations.

Here's another example—the story of an incident with almost no merit other than it unexpectedly connects two unrelated contexts:[10]

> We had a section on figure drawing. And we had a model. It was really weird. We had her come, it was about two weeks ago, and then we did some figure drawing. Yeah. Everyone was like "Oh my God we can't believe it" we y'know midwest college, y'know, "we feel like we're in **art** school now". . . . And it was really weird, because um, then, like, just last week, we went downtown one night to see a movie. And when we were sitting in McDonald's, like downtown, waiting for our movie. And we saw her in McDonald's, and it was like "That's our **model**" [laughing] "in **clothes**" [laughing] and we were like "Oh wow" it was really weird.

If something is out of the ordinary, or otherwise seems unlikely, this gives us license to talk about it. The effect goes in the other direction too, thanks to Wittgenstein's ruler. The very fact that people are telling a story about something shows that they regard it as out of the ordinary. This is how we learn about social norms. It is how we learn about other people. When people show us what *they* find remarkable and why, they show us who they are.

If you're telling me something, it should be news. It wouldn't be a conversation if I just kept saying the same things. One of the strongest principles that has been discovered about language use by philosophers and psychologists of language is the cooperative maxim in communication: *Be relevant*.[11] In part, this means: Don't tell people things that they already know. At each point, what you say should be informative.[12]

Even one-year-old children are tuned into this. Psychologists Tibor Tauzin and György Gergely saw a link between the newness of every move in conversation and the human capacity for "mind reading."[13] The mind-reading capacity develops in humans from a young age. In fact, children who do not develop this capacity are likely to have difficulty learning language at all. In Tauzin and Gergely's experiments with one-year-olds,[14] the infants watched a cartoon with two blobs interacting and making simple sounds in an alternating pattern. One group of infants saw "conversations" in which the on-screen blobs made new signals at each turn, mirroring the norm in human conversation. For another group, the blobs exchanged repeated identical signals, not unlike the alternating call exchanges of many animal species. Two marmosets, for example, will exchange the same call (a whistle-like phrase known as a phee call), in alternation, over and over.[15] Imagine people talking like this:[16]

A: Hello, how are you?

B: Good, how are you?

A: Good, how are you?

B: Good, how are you?

A: Good, how are you?

B: Good, how are you?

A: Good, how are you?

B: Good, how are you?

When the infants in Tauzin and Gergely's experiment observed a computer-animated version of this—where two agents go back and forth making the exact same sound over and over—the infants did not infer that any relevant information was being exchanged.[17] But when the figures on the screen exchanged new and unpredictable signals with each turn, infants would infer that one agent was giving the other agent new information, for some practical purpose. For example, they understood that one partner was telling the other one where a misplaced object could be found.

Imagine a movie about the most ordinary and uneventful day in your life. Would people pay to watch it? No offense, but it seems unlikely. It's true that a good story often starts on an ordinary day, but it only really begins when that ordinariness is disrupted.[18] In novels and movies, this disruption and the ensuing trouble are often epic, harrowing, and life transforming. Most of us seldom, if ever, go through transformations of the kind we see in screenplays. And this is exactly what gives fictional stories one of their important sense-making functions: once transported, we get to live someone else's experience, without the real-life consequences. A good story is a flight simulator for the mind.[19]

This kind of simulation—written by one person, run by another—exploits the fundamental and unique trick of language: the fact that words can inform you about events you cannot witness for yourself. When I tell you, say, what happened on my subway ride this morning, my words are instructions for your imagination, to use linguist Daniel Dor's phrase.[20] This can be useful for obvious practical reasons. I can tell that it's raining at our destination, and you will know to carry an umbrella and raincoat. But in the case of fiction, what can you do with the contents of a novel or screenplay? An answer is found in the kinds of thing that fictional stories tend to be about.

The problems that fictional stories depict aren't just any disruption of norms. They tend to involve personal ordeals, of much greater intensity and scale than we experience in real life.

Take homicide. How likely are you to be murdered? In reality, an example annual estimate—for adults under age fifty in the United States in 1990—is 15 murders per 100,000 members of the population.[21] That's a high murder rate in the global context, but it is low in absolute terms: well below a fiftieth of 1 percent of people are murdered. In novels, the rate is orders of magnitude greater than this. A study of nearly 750 twentieth-century American novels found a murder rate of *11 percent*. That is, one out of ten people is murdered in those fictional worlds. It's a thousand times more likely that a person will be murdered in a novel than in real life. Why? Because that's what readers want. Novels are written for the audiences who will pay for them. The question is: Why do we want to read accounts of killing?

Cognitive scientist Olivier Morin and colleagues sought to explain not only why we like to read about murder and mayhem but also why we enjoy the kind of harrowing and emotional fiction that tragedy presents:[22]

Fictional narrative primarily simulates "ordeals": situations where a person's reaction might dramatically improve or decrease her fitness, such as deadly aggressions, or decisions on long-term matrimonial commitments. Experience does not prepare us well for these rare, high-stakes occasions, in contrast with situations that are just as fitness-relevant but more frequent (e.g., exposure to pathogens).

Other researchers have converged on the story-as-simulator idea, arguing that stories allow us to vicariously live through experiences we might not want to undergo ourselves. By following stories about the dramatic and the dangerous, we train, develop, and hone our social, emotional, and cognitive skills. Here are some of the conclusions that story researchers have arrived at:

- "Our propensity to create and enjoy narrative fictions was selected and maintained due to the training that we get from mentally simulating situations relevant to our survival and reproduction."[23]
- Fiction might "recruit and train our capacity to imagine other people's thoughts."[24]
- The simulation that fiction provides allows us "to anticipate mentally events that could occur in the future, and imagine possible reactions to them."[25]
- Fiction allows us to prepare "for real-world encounters with negative emotions and/or hostile others."[26]

These claims about stories are true because of a property unique to language: words can tell us about places other than the here and now. They present us with situations we haven't experienced and may never experience. One reason we read fiction, said literary critic Harold Bloom, is "because we cannot know enough people."[27] If stories are simulations, language itself is the raw material that makes such simulation possible. As the linguist Nick Evans points out, different languages are different resources for constructing our life-experience simulations. Building on Bloom's idea, Evans writes, "We study other languages because we cannot live enough lives."[28]

In the context of our own families, stories help us learn from the lives of the previous generation, who would wish to give us the benefits of experience without exposing us to the dangers.[29] A US study of teenagers' knowledge of their parents' lives showed that they draw on the informal stories and anecdotes that their parents pass on: "Adolescents and emerging adults can readily recount intergenerational stories from parents" and "many of these stories serve to build relationships with the parent, provide insights about parents, provide insights about self, and transmit life lessons."[30] The family is a core place where "cultural knowledge, collective memory, and narrative identity" are passed on:

> By hearing stories about different types of experiences, such as those that challenge the self (i.e., transgressions, rule breaking or moral violations), that affirm the self (i.e., proud moments), and that are self-defining, young people have opportunities to learn lessons about life, information about their parent, and information about their own identity as a family member.[31]

Most intergenerational stories in the family come from the parents' own youth. The stories are told for entertainment, teaching, and building the parent-child relationship. These stories convey values and illustrate or explain the identity of the teller.

Another way we learn through language is from explanation. Society is built on the passing on of knowledge about our inventions, ideas, tools, and techniques. It might seem that we can transmit know-how without using words—for example, by simply letting people watch how we do something—but even then we use words to define what we're showing, to frame it by specifying its purpose, to draw attention to what we want people to notice, to point to what's happening, where, and why. A friend might explain how a new app works. I might teach my daughter how to use an abacus. You might show me the difference between a major and a minor chord on the guitar. Language will always be involved.[32]

Simple acts of explaining or informing can have purely practical goals. I tell you how to use this app so you can use it later on your own. I show you this chord so you can play that song you're learning. But often, practical advice is embedded in fiction-style narrative. This makes the advice more engaging and easier to understand and remember. For example, stories about natural phenomena can help us make sense of our environment, and can also pass on important practical wisdom. Here is a folk tale from Japan:[33]

> An old man tended his rice fields high up on a mountain. One day, he saw the sea recede and the great wave coming for the shore. He did not know what to do, but he knew that something had to be done immediately to warn his friends, family and the villagers down below on the shore. In an instant, the answer came to him. He set fire to his house and rice fields. Instantly the flames engulfed his wooden house and fields, sending out thick plumes of black smoke.
>
> "Look!" The village people cried out. "There is a fire on the mountain! We must go and help!"
>
> All of the village people climbed up the mountain to help the farmer put out his fire, just in time to escape the giant tsunami wave that was headed their way and would destroy their village.

Coastal peoples around the world have similar tsunami tales. The stories recount world-altering events in a group's collective past as well as lifesaving information for later generations. People who know the Japanese folk tale know to run to higher ground if the sea recedes. The Moken people of the west coast of Thailand near the Thailand/Myanmar border say that "one day the navel of the sea would suck all water and spit it all back in the form of waves. Many people would die."[34] Put this way, the story has a fantastical element, but it still accurately describes a feature of tsunami events: the sea receding far into the distance before returning to wash over the land in the most terrifying and destructive way.

Folk tales like this are said to have saved lives during the tsunami of late 2005 that hit Thailand, Indonesia, Sri Lanka, and the Nicobar and Andaman Islands.[35] Similar stories are heard in Aboriginal Australia, Sri Lanka, the Northwest Pacific region of North America, and New Zealand.[36] This Maori tale was recorded in New Zealand more than a century ago:[37]

> "What is all this?" he asked. "These are the fish I have caught," replied Titipa. "This is the result of my power as a toohunga [priest; expert in traditional lore;

person skilled in specific activity; healer]." "But didn't I tell you I should expect the pick of the catch?" cried Te Pou. "If you want fish, catch them yourself," retorted Titipa. "You don't get the pick of my haul." "Indeed," said Te Pou, and he walked along the beach and inspected the fish that were drying in the sun. "We shall see whose catch this is presently." Walking to the water's edge and stretching out his arms towards the sea, he repeated mighty spells before the people. Everyone wondered what would happen, but it was not long before Te Pou came running up the beach. "Get back!" he cried. "Get back to the high ground, or you will be drowned," and running past his people he climbed the high cliff, where he took his stand, and repeated more spells. The people, thoroughly terrified, followed helter-skelter, and left Titipa alone upon the beach. Soon the sea grew dark and troubled and angry, and presently a great wave, which gathered strength as it came, swept towards the shore. It advanced over the sandy beach, sweeping Titipa and all his fish before it, till with the noise of thunder it struck the cliff on which the people stood. "That is one," said Te Pou. "That is for the first fish. There will be two more." The great wave receded, sucking with it innumerable boulders and the helpless, struggling Titipa. Then another wave, greater than the previous one, came with tremendous force and, sweeping the shore, struck the cliff with a thunderous roar. This was followed by a third which, when it receded, left the beach scoured and bare. Titipa and all his fish had disappeared. "I have finished," said Te Pou. "That is all. There will be no more trouble."

Many Australian Aboriginal groups have myths and legends about great floods. Port Phillip Bay (known as *Naarm* in Kulin, an indigenous language of the area) is a 2,000 square kilometer basin with an average depth of only 8 meters, near the Australian city of Melbourne. The sea entrance at the south of the bay is only 3 kilometers across (see figure 11.2).

About a thousand years ago, the bay's narrow, shallow entry was blocked by sediment, and the bay dried out completely for a period. Local communities would have gotten used to moving across the basin's expanse of dry land. But in time, the blockage was dislodged and the sea filled the bay again. We can only imagine the biblical nature of this event, a sudden deluge of a wall of seawater into and across an expanse of land bigger than the area of Greater London.

Members of the Woiworrung group of indigenous people provided this account in the 1930s, centuries after the event itself:

"Plenty long ago . . . men could cross, dry-foot, from our side of the bay [in the east] to Geelong [in the west]." They described a hurricane—trees bending to and fro—then the earth sank, and the sea rushed in through the Heads, till the void places became broad and deep, as they are today.[38]

Figure 11.2
Map of Port Phillip Bay showing its present form and rough bathymetry (form of the sea floor): areas of depth to 20 meters and below 20 meters. After Patrick D. Nunn and Nicholas J. Reid, "Aboriginal Memories of Inundation of the Australian Coast Dating from More than 7000 Years Ago," *Australian Geographer* 47, no. 1 (2016): 19, https://doi.org/10.1080/00049182.2015.1077539.

Many other stories like this are transmitted in Aboriginal communities around the country (see Figure 11.3).[39]

These flood stories capture the imagination. Like the tsunami stories, they combine great drama with causal explanation. Knowledge like the story of the Port Phillip Bay flood adds to people's understanding of their environment. And again like the tsunami stories, these stories may transmit knowledge that could help avoid potential dangers. This individually possessed knowledge is also collective knowledge. The knowledge provides

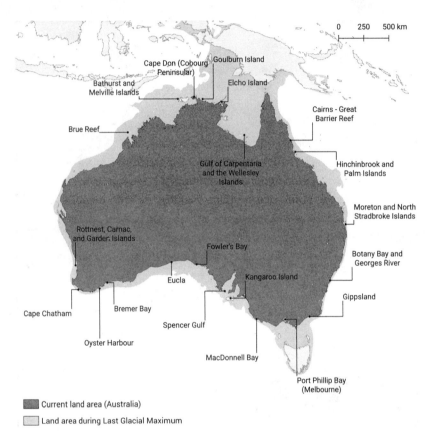

Figure 11.3

Map of Australia showing coastal locations from which Aboriginal stories about coastal inundation are described (after Nunn and Reid 2015). Also shown is the extent of continental shelf exposed during the low sea-level stage of the Last Glacial Maximum (about 20,000 years ago).

landmarks for people to coordinate around in social life. We could imagine, for example, the flood story being cited as a warning to someone not to take a certain walking route, for fear of danger.

The Australian flood stories are grounded in real events. They align with independent paleogeographic evidence about historical changes in sea levels and associated flooding. But there are of course many cultural origin stories that do not concur with known scientific evidence or that may seem more far-fetched, metaphors at best.[40] Here are two stories that I have heard about the deep history of the people I work with in upland Laos.

The Kri have no alphabet or other system for writing their language. Why not?

> Once upon a time, the Kri had a way of writing their language down. But they had no paper. Instead, they wrote on buffalo hides. One day, dogs ate the hides and the writing was lost forever. That is why, today, Kri speakers have no way of writing their language.

The Kri have a set of cultural prohibitions that are regarded as stricter than any of the many ethnic groups in their area. For example, traditionally, they don't eat any red meat at all, only fish. Why is this?

> Once upon a time, a tiger went to the water to find something to eat. It found a clam which opened up and said "Come here Tiger, put your tongue in here and eat me up." Suddenly, the clam shut its shell tight on the tiger's tongue. The tiger walked to a nearby Kri village to ask for help. The villagers just laughed and said "It serves you right!", and sent the tiger on its way. The tiger went to another village, of a different ethnic group, where villagers helped it to release the clam. The tiger returned to the Kri village. "You didn't help me. In return for that, from now on you have to follow these strict taboos. If you don't, I will attack you and eat you."[41]

This story is offered to explain why, from then on, Kri villagers have had to abide by stricter cultural prohibitions than other groups in the area.[42]

It doesn't matter if these stories aren't true. It doesn't even matter if people don't really believe them. What matters is that people coordinate around them—that the stories are told and heeded. The sharing of stories through language can be a goal in itself. They are landmarks for shared attention and for shared identity. The stories work because we agree to treat them as *ours*; they identify us and explain things about *us*.

What kinds of topics do we tend to coordinate around? It turns out that origin stories and natural disaster stories are not the most frequent. Mostly, it's gossip. In his survey of what Tzotzil speakers in Zinacantan talk about, anthropologist John Haviland reported that 78 percent of conversations were about social topics.[43] In her study of firelight conversations among southern African Ju/'hoansi people, anthropologist Polly Wiessner reported that 60 percent were purely social content.[44]

It seems straightforward enough to claim that one conversation is about a social topic (think of Li updating Jo about the incident of Michael meeting Jo's mother) while another is not (think of me explaining how to use an abacus). But as soon as you try to define more precisely what a certain utterance is "about," you will find it impossible. People have tried. In Polly Wiessner's study of conversation among Ju/'hoan (!Kung) Bushmen of northwest Botswana, she divides all the conversation she observed into distinct categories. Some bits of conversation are categorized as "complaint," others as about "land rights," others under "economics," and others "interethnic."[45] But it is easy to imagine an utterance that relates to all four of these things at once. *I've got nothing to sell at market thanks to those outsiders hunting on our lands!* Because of the massive flexibility of language, any sentence will be "about" many things at once.

When a measure is ambiguous, by the reversal principle of Wittgenstein's ruler we learn more about the person doing the measuring than the thing being measured. Consider psychologist Henry T. Moore's measures of the topics of conversation on the streets of New York in the 1920s. In 1922, Moore spent several weeks wandering slowly up and down Broadway in Manhattan in the evenings, pencil and paper in hand, eavesdropping on conversations.[46] He collected 174 fragments of conversation, which he then distinguished into topics. He saw differences between men and women. Women, he said, talk about *men, home,* and *fashion.* These are "the natural drive for sixty-seven per cent of woman's thoughts," while in men, these accounted for only 10 percent. By contrast, "sixty-two per cent of man's drive seems to originate in *money, business,* and *amusement,* motives which get altogether only seven per cent of woman's spontaneous consideration."[47]

But have a look at Moore's examples. Here is a sample woman's remark on her "predominant topic" of men:

He was in town for a visit of three days.

And this one is from "men's predominant topic" of money and business:

He'd lease it to you for a year.

Hang on a minute. The subject of both sentences is "he"—a man—yet according to Moore, only the woman's remark is "about men." Why aren't they both about men? Or for that matter, why aren't they both about "time" (*three days, a year*)? You see the problem: There is no way to single out one thing that these statements are about. Moore's study is telling not for what it says about the subjects Moore eavesdropped on, but about the eavesdropper and his biases. Moore's conclusion was that "there are very considerable and ineradicable differences in the original capacities of the two sexes for certain types of enthusiasm and this difference must of necessity set an ultimate limit to woman's success in assimilating male spheres of interest regardless of the apparent equality of capacity often indicated by mental tests."[48] Is Moore analyzing the data, or are the data analyzing Moore?

*

When we say that language plays an important role in sense making, this refers only partly to the process of making sense in an individual's mind. Most importantly, it establishes *shared* points of reference for sense making among members of a community, or at the very least, people who have some relationship to each other. Seen this way, the things we say—whether or not they convey true information—are attempts to publicly establish those points of reference. This is what language is good for. Of course, we often use language for informing people of things. And there will often also—or alternatively—be more strategic motivations. But whatever your reasons, simply by using some words and not others, you are always making a claim to set the agenda for what we should coordinate around.

Conclusion

Language is the main instrument of man's refusal to accept the world as it is.
—George Steiner (1975)

Reality matters because our survival depends on it. To navigate reality, as individuals, we first reduce its complexity through the interface of sensory perception. But to *coordinate around* reality, in concert with other people, our species' forte is to add another interface, a further level of transformation: the interface known as language. We present reality to each other in language-delineated pieces. As the mathematician Friedrich Waismann said, language is the knife we use to cut out facts. And like any knife, as I hope this book has shown, language is both destroyer and creator. We do not coordinate around reality but around versions of reality hewn by words. The result is awkward for the scientist but convenient for the lawyer.

A problem is that we naturally take our word-given versions of the world to be reliable. And when we feel that we understand something clearly, this has a "thought-terminating" effect, as the philosopher C. Thi Nguyen puts it: "A sense of confusion is a signal that we need to think more. But when things feel clear to us, we are satisfied."[1] This creates a kind of cognitive vulnerability that allows people to be manipulated by any system of thought that is "seductively clear." As specific examples of such systems, Nguyen discusses conspiracy theories and bureaucracies. What I have tried to convey in this book is that language itself is one such seductively clear system. In fact, it is *the* seductively clear system, with its thousands of problem-solving, information-discarding, thought-terminating conventional categories. It provides the tools and materials for building every other kind of social system, from the microlevel of our social relationships to the macro-level of our highest social and political institutions. In this way, a language is not only a source of attention-directing frames and moorings for social coordination, it is a great collection of off-switches for the mind.[2]

Such is the power of language. And so, in a world that desperately requires wisdom at all points, we have a duty to know and understand how language works, both on others and on ourselves. We have a responsibility to be mindful of how our linguistic choices manipulate people's attention, terminate their thinking, and implicate them in joint commitments. And when we hear the things that others say, we need to be mindful of their goals and motivations, which underlie their choices of certain words and not others. If their words invite us to coordinate around some linguistic construal of reality, we must ask: Why this map and why those landmarks? What are this person's reasons for saying *that*, and for saying it *like that*? How else could it have been said? In the mercurial cartography of language, we need to remember there is a real terrain beyond the maps.[3]

If your goal is to exploit and manipulate people with words, you might prefer that your audience not ask these critical questions about language. This is especially true of the politically powerful. If you can set the terms for social coordination, you can bend the meanings of words or reverse them entirely. Under fascism and its illiberal cousins, words take on "corrupted, opposite meanings," as philosopher Jason Stanley writes: "Corrupt politicians run anti-corruption campaigns; freedom of speech claims are used to suppress speech."[4] In the words of chess grandmaster and activist Garry Kasparov:

> If you're a thief, accuse your enemies of thievery. If corrupt, accuse your rivals of corruption. If a coward, accuse others of cowardice. Evidence is irrelevant; the goal is to dilute the truth.[5]

When dictators label others with words that apply to themselves, these aren't acts of "mere projection," says Kasparov. "They are a tactic to lower the moral bar for all," ultimately conveying "that there is no good or evil, no truth, just power."

Could mere words create or destroy the moral fabric of society? Yes and no. Words can't directly control people's vision of the world.[6] Usually people already know what they believe, or want to believe, about a situation.[7] The corrupting linguistic actions Kasparov describes cannot directly change a piece of physical reality. But remember Wittgenstein's ruler. A measuring rule can tell us the length of a table, just as the table can tell us something about the measuring rule. Only some people have the power to decide which units of measure we shall use, or indeed to redefine the units of measure entirely (or, furthermore, whether a measure is to be taken at all). Then, a new kind of statement about the table may be allowed to stand, potentially as a new reason for action (just as a "prisoner of war" may be redefined as an "illegal combatant", to that person's detriment). Meanwhile, the objective properties of the table stay the same.

Words should never be our trusted measure of reality because words won't stay still. We have a duty to heed reality, always at a step removed from the thinkable verbal descriptions of it. Reality must be our ultimate mooring.

Even if we acknowledge that people are not going to be convinced by any old bit of language that is put in front of them,[8] there is still a risk from letting anything be said, in any old way. The risk is that a certain framing or narrative—say, one that conveys a false, misleading, or harmful proposition—will become normalized. It will be seen and heard more frequently. It will become unremarkable, in the literal sense that people will no longer remark on it. When something that was once a noticeable breach is no longer surprising or sanctionable, it can fly under the radar of social accountability, our collective mechanism for keeping people in check. And language matters here because social accountability would be impossible without it. Just as language is the device we use for constructing the social order, it is the device we use for drawing attention to transgressions. Language sets the bounds of the Overton window, the range of ideas considered acceptable within the norms of a community.[9] When an idea is normalized in this sense, it doesn't mean that a statement expressing the idea is more likely to be believed. It means that the statement is more likely to be allowed to stand—to be accepted. And this in turn may affect the likelihood that people will publicly voice their true beliefs, whether that means they are now quiet when once they would have spoken or that they will now speak when they once would not.[10]

This matters because when we consent to coordinate around the maps that are handed to us, we are agreeing to a set of accepted *reasons for action*. Why did you punch her? Because her words harmed me. Why did you burn buildings at a nonviolent demonstration? Because property damage is not violence. Why did you put your workers in harm's way? Because they are our capital stock. When we agree that certain framings can stand, we agree to live in the world created by the actions that those framings would defend.

This isn't limited to political discourse and historical social movements. Young children on the playground know the power of framing in the moral politics of life. Two seven-year-olds are building a structure with blocks, the structure falls, one child gives a scream, and an adult admonishes them: *Guys, too loud.* Then:[11]

Child A: She poked it.

Child B: I tapped it.

It's Russell's conjugation in the wild. We may never know whether *poke* or *tap* was the right word for what happened. Indeed, how *could* we know? Most of our words are vague enough to allow leeway and overlap, even when we have a precise measure of the facts. What matters is which word is allowed to stand, for that is the word that will determine the consequences. But whatever the stakes—from children at play to ideologically charged disputes over *riot* versus *protest* or *terrorist* versus *freedom fighter*—ultimately our choices of words are bids to set the terms that suit us best, not necessarily the terms that get us closest to the truth.

The power to frame arguments persuasively is—like the lawyer herself—not intrinsically good or bad. But when that power is exerted, its effects are real, and we must take responsibility for them. As we learned from the story of John Gluck, at the opening of this book, it is possible to examine one's own linguistic choices and become more mindful of them, of what they are doing, what story they are telling, what consequences they would allow, and who we would be by choosing them.[12] Gluck's story shows that we are not simply subject to the seduction of language. We have agency.

Recall that at a turning point in his life, Gluck consciously revised his language to reflect his new-found values and priorities. He would no longer say that his monkeys had been "housed" in his research facilities. Rather, they were *held in empty stainless-steel mesh boxes that restricted their movement and offered little opportunity for the monkeys to do what monkeys naturally do.* The newborns weren't "removed" from their mothers; they were *torn from their arms shrieking and terrified.* When Gluck changed himself, he changed his words. When he changed the norms we wished to defend, he changed the way he chose to portray reality. And this is key. Among the many things it is good for, language is a device for choosing among different ways of portraying one and the same reality. We create our worlds by the language we use.

Because language is both powerful and flawed—just like our faculty of reason—we have a responsibility to use it mindfully and ethically. This means being accurate and fair in the words we choose given the goals we want to pursue. It also means striving to know what it means to be accurate and fair, for it will mean different things on different occasions. And when I refer to our responsibility in using language, I don't just mean in the things we say, but in how we interpret, understand, and act on the things that *other* people say. When we find ourselves accepting assertions we can't confirm, or even false or wrongful assertions, some might argue that it's not our fault if we are simply seduced by them, given how powerful language is and given people's tendency to accept statements on trust.[13] But this is surely the wrong direction to take.

Bad behavior—from something as seemingly innocuous as boosting a conspiracy-theory meme on social media to something as heinous as committing a war crime—is sometimes said to be the fault of bad barrels, not bad apples. When psychologist Philip Zimbardo testified in a US court in defense of Ivan Frederick, one of the military police responsible for abuses of detainees in Abu Ghraib Prison, Baghdad, in 2003, he argued that Frederick and colleagues were victims of a corrupting situation. They were merely swept up into doing what they did (in part, it was claimed, because of the language used in communications from command concerning how the detainees were to be treated).[14] But Zimbardo's route is the coward's route. Yes, bad barrels exist. But one of the hallmarks of the human spirit is that people are capable of *not* becoming rotten.[15] After all, Ivan Frederick and his colleagues would not have been in court were it not for the actions of a man who—like John Gluck—was able to stand up against the abuses he witnessed. Military police sergeant Joseph Darby saw something wrong at Abu Ghraib and decided to act. In January 2004, at age twenty-four, Darby was the whistle-blower who exposed the crimes.[16]

The analogy with language is the following. We tend to talk in the same ways as others in our community, but in going along with majority ways of framing things, especially within the confines of our subcultures, we may find ourselves parroting and circulating inapposite, inaccurate, uncharitable, or even pernicious takes. Are we then simply innocent victims of context? Or should we be accountable for how we talk? Without some framework for constraining the answer to this question we risk falling victim to uncharitable and unforgiving interpretations of people's everyday language choices.

This is one of our most pressing challenges: to identify criteria by which we can determine—and agree on—the best ways to describe the things that concern us, given that there are always alternatives. It's a duty to ourselves and to others, and to our communities, to strive to get our language exactly right. Of course, there will be disagreement. This is public discourse. But we can and should make progress. It requires us to be serious about our shared understandings of what words mean. Thanks to our incorrigible confirmation bias, we are usually too quick to assume that others use and interpret words in the same ways that we do.[17]

If truth is what we must seek, then we have both opportunities and responsibilities.[18] We have opportunities to discover facts, which by virtue of being true are likely to be useful, certainly more useful than falsehoods. And we have responsibilities not to pollute the infosphere with falsehood and bluster. This requires a form of cognitive and linguistic literacy: an awareness of how language works on the mind and in social interaction. And it requires intellectual discipline. When we unthinkingly boost the signal of some misinformation, even just by "liking" a post we haven't verified, the effect is like burning fossil fuels in our cars. As individuals, when we produce emissions, we feel that our singular contribution to the problem does not make a difference in the larger context. But of course it would make a difference if only we acted collectively. In the same way, says legal scholar Ilya Somin, "Widespread public ignorance is a type of pollution that infects the political system."[19] Somin's solution is to change our political system on the assumption that public ignorance is here to stay. But we could instead—or also—seek to remedy our lack of mindfulness of how language works and our overwillingness to use language uncritically, in circulating certain framings and not others, and thereby in shaping the value of our informational currency.[20]

We are all ignorant to varying degrees, but we don't let this stop us from forming opinions and voicing them. This brings significant risks, as the philosopher William Clifford warned in his 1877 *Ethics of Belief*: "It is wrong always, everywhere, and for anyone, to believe anything upon insufficient evidence." In Clifford's example, a ship's owner believes his vessel is seaworthy but chooses not to check for evidence that may disconfirm the belief. Naturally, the owner had an incentive to remain unaware:

he collected a handsome insurance payout when the ship sank, drowning its passengers and crew. As Clifford stressed, this was all wrong. Not only does our responsibility to treat statements critically have consequences for individuals, it is in the interests of upholding a shared culture of respect for evidence and reason, and respect for reality. "The danger to society is not merely that it should believe wrong things, though that is great enough; but that it should become credulous, and lose the habit of testing things and inquiring into them."[21]

*

A classical ideal of truth and knowledge is the concept of a market for ideas: as thinking individuals, we encounter competing ideas, we evaluate them for their best fit to reality, and then let the best and brightest facts form the basis of our beliefs. That would be the scientist's way, in theory at least. But in practice, most of the time we are in a *market for justifications*.[22] We shop for words not because they contain ideas, but because they contain stories about ideas. Often we are not seeking statements as facts to help us figure out what we should believe. Usually we already know what we believe. What we seek are statements to justify those beliefs—the lawyer's way. Language might be good for this function but we can use it to do better. By treating language with greater respect, we can achieve more than simple self-defense.

The way forward is to pursue collective truth seeking—an impossible enterprise without language—and make it the value that defines human well-being through a shared grounding in reason and respect for reality. For that, we need a collective respect for language itself. This respect must in part be a sense of humility at the myriad ways in which we are played by language, through the distractions, the framings, the overshadowing, the switching off of thinking, the stripping down of experience to the tiny slice of reality that language only manages to allude to. But this respect must also be a sense of awe at language's power, at its capacity to provide shared maps and moorings, to enable social coordination, to create rights and duties, and to bring sense to our social minds, our societies and cultures, and our selves.

Notes

Preface and Acknowledgments

1. M. R. Pointer and G. G. Attridge, "The Number of Discernible Colours," *Color Research and Application* 23, no. 1 (1998): 52–54, https://doi.org/10.1002/(SICI)1520-6378(199802)23:1<52::AID-COL8>3.0.CO;2-2.

2. See Stephen C. Levinson and Asifa Majid, "Differential Ineffability and the Senses," *Mind and Language* 29, no. 4 (2014): 407–427, https://doi.org/10.1111/mila.12057.

Introduction

1. John P. Gluck, *Voracious Science and Vulnerable Animals: A Primate Scientist's Ethical Journey* (Chicago: University of Chicago Press, 2016).

2. Some related thoughts from predecessors: Wittgenstein: "The limits of my language mean the limits of my world"; Bach: "Argue for your limitations, and sure enough they're yours"; Scharling: "We see things not as they are but as we are." Ludwig Wittgenstein, *Tractatus Logico-Philosophicus*, trans. C. K. Ogden (London: Kegan Paul, 1922); Richard Bach, *Jonathan Livingston Seagull* (New York: Macmillan, 1970); Henrik Scharling, *Nicolai's Marriage: A Picture of Danish Family Life* (London: Richard Bentley and Son, 1876).

3. See Gerd Gigerenzer, *Gut Feelings: Short Cuts to Better Decision Making* (London: Penguin, 2007); Daniel Kahneman, *Thinking, Fast and Slow* (London: Penguin, 2011); Julia Galef, *The Scout Mindset* (New York: Portfolio, 2021).

4. This, of course, does not entail that it's good to convince people of false things!

5. With apologies to members of those two important professions, I am using the terms "scientist" and "lawyer" as caricatures for two different ways of thinking about what language is good for. The term *inner lawyer* is from Jonathan Haidt, *The Righteous Mind: Why Good People Are Divided by Politics and Religion* (New York: Pantheon Books, 2012). Also, the point I am making here owes a debt to Mercier and Sperber's

arguments about rationality. I'm emphasizing the role that language plays in those arguments. Hugo Mercier and Dan Sperber, *The Enigma of Reason* (Cambridge, MA: Harvard University Press, 2017). A similar distinction to lawyer/scientist is soldier/ scout, made by Julia Galef in *The Scout Mindset* (New York: Portfolio, 2021): the "soldier" is concerned with defending their position against possible attacks, while the "scout" is concerned with discovering what's true.

6. See in particular J. A. Jolly, "Lemur Social Behavior and Primate Intelligence," *Science* 153, no. 3735 (1966): 501–506, https://doi.org/10.1126/science.153.3735.501; Nicholas K Humphrey, "The Social Function of Intellect," in *Growing Points in Ethology*, ed. P. Bateson and Robert A Hinde (Cambridge: Cambridge University Press, 1976), 303–321; Richard W. Byrne and Andrew Whiten, eds., *Machiavellian Intelligence: Social Expertise and the Evolution of Intellect in Monkeys, Apes, and Humans* (Oxford: Clarendon Press; Oxford University Press, 1988); Andrew Whiten and Richard W. Byrne, eds., *Machiavellian Intelligence II: Extensions and Evaluations* (Cambridge: Cambridge University Press, 1997).

7. "Humans who participate collectively in magico-religious ritual performances do so precisely in order to instill belief in fictional 'other worlds.' Representations of such fictions are more than epiphenomenal; they are central in securing cognitive acknowledgement of an allegiance to the contractual intangibles underpinning cooperation in human social groups. Given the characteristically collaborative, cooperative nature of the rituals designed to generate such illusions, the 'deceptions' which emerge may be dubbed 'collective deceptions,' corresponding to Durkheim's classic notion of "collective representations.'" Chris Knight, Robin Dunbar, and Camilla Power, "An Evolutionary Approach to Human Culture," in *The Evolution of Culture: A Historical and Scientific Overview*, ed. Robin Dunbar, Chris Knight, and Camilla Power (New Brunswick, NJ: Rutgers University Press, 1999), 6. See also Spencer Mermelstein, Michael Barlev, and Tamsin German, "She Told Me about a Singing Cactus: Counterintuitive Concepts Are More Accurately Attributed to Their Speakers than Ordinary Concepts," preprint, PsyArXiv (June 7, 2019), https://doi.org/10.31234 /osf.io/6cp8e.

8. https://www.unqualified-reservations.org/2008/05/ol4-dr-johnsons-hypothesis/.

9. In Hume's words: "Whether your scepticism be as absolute and sincere as you pretend, we shall learn by and by, when the company breaks up: we shall then see, whether you go out at the door or the window; and whether you really doubt if your body has gravity, or can be injured by its fall." David Hume, *Dialogues Concerning Natural Religion*, ed. Dorothy Coleman (Cambridge: Cambridge University Press, 2007), 8.

10. Of course, language has a private existence as well: we can think and reason using words, in the privacy of our minds. But the internal uses of language are secondary. The words we use would not exist were it not for a history of public, social

interactions using those words in the communities that speak the languages of the world. This runs counter to a view expressed by Noam Chomsky and followers who have asserted that language is primarily a private phenomenon and only secondarily a public one. For further discussions of this point, see N. J. Enfield, *Natural Causes of Language: Frames, Biases, and Cultural Transmission* (Berlin: Language Science Press, 2014) and *The Utility of Meaning: What Words Mean and Why* (Oxford: Oxford University Press, 2015).

11. Physicist Steven Wolfram writes, "When viewed in computational terms most of the great historical triumphs of theoretical science turn out to be remarkably similar in their basic character. For at some level almost all of them are based on finding ways to reduce the amount of computational work that has to be done in order to predict how some particular system will behave." Stephen Wolfram, *A New Kind of Science* (Champaign, IL: Wolfram Media, 2002), 737.

12. On the concept of choice architecture, see Donald A. Norman, *The Design of Everyday Things* (New York: Basic Books, 1988), Richard H. Thaler and Cass R. Sunstein, *Nudge: Improving Decisions about Health, Wealth, and Happiness* (New Haven, CT: Yale University Press, 2008).

Chapter 1

1. Susan Perry, "Male–Male Social Relationships in Wild White-Faced Capuchins, *Cebus capucinus,*" *Behavior* 135, no. 2 (1998): 139–172; Susan Perry, *Manipulative Monkeys: The Capuchins of Lomas Barbudal* (Cambridge, MA: Harvard University Press, 2008).

2. Perry, "Male–Male Social Relationships," 142.

3. Technically, the "scream" is called an "intense vocal threat" See Julie J. Gros-Louis et al., "Vocal Repertoire of *Cebus capucinus*: Acoustic Structure, Context, and Usage," *International Journal of Primatology* 29, no. 3 (2008): 641–670, https://doi.org/10.1007/s10764-008-9263-8.

4. Susan Perry, "Case Study 4A: Coalitionary Aggression in White-Faced Capuchins," in *Animal Social Complexity*, ed. Frans B. M. de Waal and Peter L. Tyack (Cambridge, MA: Harvard University Press, 2003), 113, https://doi.org/10.4159/harvard.9780674419131.c8.

5. From economist Thomas Schelling's *Strategy of Conflict* (Cambridge, MA: Harvard University Press, 1960), 55.

6. Schelling, *Strategy of Conflict*, 55.

7. Schelling, 56.

8. I mean without direct communication between the parties who are coordinating. As Daniel Dor and others point out to me, some communication has taken place here.

In particular, the person who drew the map and who chose to place the bridge in the center has influenced the attention of the people looking at the map. See Herbert H. Clark, Robert Schreuder, and Samuel Buttrick, "Common Ground and the Understanding of Demonstrative Reference," *Journal of Verbal Learning and Verbal Behavior* 22, no. 2 (1983): 245–258, https://doi.org/10.1016/S0022-5371(83)90189-5.)

9. The term *mind reading* is not to be taken literally here. It is standard in certain fields of research interested in the human capacity for imagining, inferring, or attributing mental states to other people. These capacities are indispensable for using language. If children do not acquire these abilities, they cannot acquire language. Also, arguably, it is through the process of learning their first language that children acquire and fully develop their "theory of mind." Janet W. Astington. "The developmental interdependence of theory of mind and language," in *Roots of Human Sociality*, ed. N. J. Enfield and Stephen C. Levinson (Oxford: Berg, 2006), 179-206; Michael Tomasello, *Origins of Human Communication* (Cambridge, MA: MIT Press, 2008).

10. Omer Nevo et al., "Frugivores and the Evolution of Fruit Colour," *Biology Letters* 14, no. 9 (2018): 20180377, https://doi.org/10.1098/rsbl.2018.0377.

11. This wording is from Daniel Dor, *The Instruction of Imagination: Language as a Social Communication Technology* (Oxford; New York: Oxford University Press, 2015).

12. On their model of communication as a form of managing other life forms by exploiting their habits of assessment, see J. R. Krebs and R. Dawkins, "Animal Signals: Mind Reading and Manipulation," in *Behavioral Ecology: An Evolutionary Approach*, ed. J. R. Krebs and N. B. Davies, 2nd ed. (Oxford: Blackwell, 1984), 380–405.

13. Dor, *The Instruction of Imagination*, develops a model of language as a tool for "instructing the imagination." My view of language is closely akin to this.

14. I focus on this in my 2017 book, *How We Talk: The Inner Workings of Conversation* (New York: Basic Books, 2017). See references in that book to Emanuel A. Schegloff, "Sequencing in Conversational Openings," *American Anthropologist* 70, no. 6 (1968): 1075–1095, https://doi.org/10.1525/aa.1968.70.6.02a00030 and his *Sequence Organization in Interaction: A Primer in Conversation Analysis* (Cambridge: Cambridge University Press, 2007); Stephen C. Levinson, "On the Human 'Interaction Engine,'" in *Roots of Human Sociality: Culture, Cognition and Interaction*, ed. N. J. Enfield and Stephen C. Levinson (New YorK: Berg, 2006), 39–69; Jack Sidnell and Tanya Stivers, eds., *The Handbook of Conversation Analysis* (Oxford: Wiley-Blackwell, 2013), https://doi.org/10.1002/9781118325001.

15. I mean "social reality" in the specific sense of rights and duties (desire-independent reasons for action) built out of conventional agreement, following John R. Searle, *Speech Acts: An Essay in the Philosophy of Language* (Cambridge: Cambridge University Press, 1969). Of course, there are other senses in which animals have social realities.

16. Philip K. Dick, "How to Build a Universe That Doesn't Fall Apart Two Days Later" (1978), https://urbigenous.net/library/how_to_build.html.

17. See Dennis Proffitt and Drake Baer, *Perception: How Our Bodies Shape Our Minds* (New York: St. Martin's Press, 2020).

18. Donald D. Hoffman, Manish Singh, and Chetan Prakash, "The Interface Theory of Perception," *Psychonomic Bulletin and Review* 22, no. 6 (2015): 1480–1506, https://doi.org/10.3758/s13423-015-0890-8.

19. Hoffman, Singh, and Prakash, 1488; my emphasis.

20. Hoffman, Singh, and Prakash, 1488.

21. David Marr, *Vision: A Computational Investigation into the Human Representation and Processing of Visual Information* (Cambridge, MA: MIT Press, 1982), 340.

22. Marr, 34.

23. Hoffman, Singh, and Prakash, "The Interface Theory of Perception." Satisficing is shutting down a decision-making process as soon as a *good-enough* solution is found—regardless of the possibility that a better solution might be found. Suppose the restaurant has a huge menu, with hundreds of items. You could study the entire thing and weigh all the options in search of the best one of all. Or you might figure that this would take up too much time from your table conversation. So when you see something that's good enough, that's your solution, and you stop the search.

24. See here: https://www.lesswrong.com/posts/L32LHWzy9FzSDazEg/motivated-stopping-and-motivated-continuation.

25. M. R. Pointer and G. G. Attridge, "The Number of Discernible Colours, " *Color Research and Application* 23, no. 1 (1998): 52–54. https://doi.org/10.1002/(SICI)1520-6378(199802)23:1<52::AID-COL8>3.0.CO;2-2.

26. G. E. M. Anscombe, "On Brute Facts," *Analysis* 18, no. 3 (1958): 72, https://doi.org/10.1093/analys/18.3.69.

27. Wilfrid Sellars, *In the Space of Reasons: Selected Essays of Wilfrid Sellars*, ed. Kevin Scharp and Robert Brandom (Cambridge, MA: Harvard University Press, 2007), 42.

28. http://anthropos-lab.net/wp/wp-content/uploads/2011/12/Weber-Politics-as-a-Vocation.pdf.

29. John A. Lucy, "Linguistic Relativity," *Annual Review of Anthropology* 26, no. 1 (1997): 291, https://doi.org/10.1146/annurev.anthro.26.1.291.

30. These examples are from the philosopher John Searle, who says that the model for knowledge of this kind is the natural sciences, and "the basis for all knowledge of this kind is generally supposed to be simple empirical observations recording sense experiences." Searle, *Speech Acts*, 50.

31. This complicates the cheery optimism of physicist Sean Carroll's "poetic natural-ism", the idea that while "there are many ways of talking about the world," we can determine "the best way of talking" by consulting "our purposes in the moment". Sean Carroll. 2016. *The Big Picture: On the Origins of Life, Meaning and the Universe Itself.* London: OneWorld, 2016, 20.

32. In conversation with Lex Fridman, artificial intelligence podcast: https://youtu .be/EYIKy_FM9x0?t=3945.

33. Quoted in Paul McEvoy, *Niels Bohr: Reflections on Subject and Object*, vol. 1 (San Francisco: Microanalytix, 2001), 135; emphasis added.

34. David Bohm, *Wholeness and the Implicate Order* (London; New York: Routledge, 1980), 34.

35. David Deutsch, *The Fabric of Reality* (New York: Viking, 1997), 153. Deutsch imagines a hypothetical language that can neatly encode an impossible or at least anomalous physical situation and asks whether that language would resolve appar-ent conceptual anomalies. His response is that just because the language allows you to describe a paradoxical situation neatly doesn't mean you understand the situation or have captured the reality: "just as your theory would be summarily rejected, your language would be rejected too, for it is just another way of stating your theory" (Deutsch, 155).

36. Douglas R. Hofstadter and Emmanuel Sander, *Surfaces and Essences: Analogy as the Fuel and Fire of Thinking* (New York: Basic Books, 2013), 15 and passim.

37. Carroll, *The Big Picture*, 17–18.

38. Clearly people can come to a new understanding in the privacy of their mind, without communicating it. But if that understanding is to enter into common knowledge so that it may be built on cumulatively—as is crucial to scientific prog-ress, given that science is a collective enterprise—then it must be shared, or in the sense I mean here, *coordinated around*. And for that we must rely on language.

39. Edwin Hutchins and Christine M. Johnson, "Modeling the Emergence of Lan-guage as an Embodied Collective Cognitive Activity," *Topics in Cognitive Science* 1, no. 3 (2009): 523–546, https://doi.org/10.1111/j.1756-8765.2009.01033.x.

40. See Jakob von Uexküll, "The Theory of Meaning," *Semiotica* 42, no. 1 (1982): 25–82. Note that it is possible for language to be channeled through direct bodily connection between people, as in the language of the DeafBlind. Terra Edwards, "Bridging the Gap between DeafBlind Minds: Interactional and Social Foundations of Intention Attribution in the Seattle DeafBlind Community," *Frontiers in Psychol-ogy* 6 (2015), https://doi.org/10.3389/fpsyg.2015.01497.

41. Of course, for language to work, we need to make sensory impressions on people, through sound and/or vision, and in that sense, there is, technically speaking, a

kind of "direct manipulation." But it's not the kind of artifactual, causal manipulation embodied in examples like the spider web and the coffee cup. Uexküll, "The Theory of Meaning." Again note the DeafBlind language case.

42. Edwin Hutchins and Brian Hazlehurst, "How to Invent a Shared Lexicon: The Emergence of Shared Form-Meaning Mappings in Interaction," in *Social Intelligence and Interaction: Expressions and Implications of the Social Bias in Human Intelligence*, ed. Esther N. Goody (Cambridge: Cambridge University Press, 1995), 54, https://doi.org/10.1017/CBO9780511621710.005.

43. As Hutchins and Hazlehurst, 64, write, "By putting particular kinds of structure in each other's environments," individuals "all achieve a useful internal organization."

44. Hutchins and Hazlehurst, 66.

Chapter 2

1. As outlined by the philosopher Margaret Gilbert, "Rationality and Salience," *Philosophical Studies* 57, no. 1 (1989): 62–63, https://doi.org/10.1007/BF00355662.

2. Gilbert, 62–63.

3. David K. Lewis, *Convention: A Philosophical Study* (Oxford: Blackwell, 1969), 6.

4. Two percent of all US car collisions are head-on: https://en.wikipedia.org/wiki/Head-on_collision.

5. The case of the Madagascan fruits also shows alignment of incentives (of the plants and the seed-dispersers), but the other cases do not. The fly has no desire to be caught in the web. The coffee (which my coffee cup is designed for me to interface with) has no desire at all. These are interfaces, but they are not coordination problems.

6. Thomas Schelling, *The Strategy of Conflict* (Cambridge, MA: Harvard University Press, 1960), 16.

7. The first three are from Schelling, *The Strategy of Conflict*, the last two from Lewis, *Convention*. See longer lists of examples in Schelling, *The Strategy of Conflict*; Lewis, *Convention*; Gilbert, "Rationality and Salience."

8. This is often referred to as *salience*. If something is salient, it is most noticeable; it stands out. The word is from Latin *salient* (leaping), from the verb *salire* (to leap).

9. Psychologist Herbert H. Clark has long championed this view of language. See Herbert H. Clark, *Using Language* (Cambridge: Cambridge University Press, 1996).

10. This is partly because of the information encoded in the word *spoon* and partly because of people's capacity to take context into account. So, *spoon* could include a

teaspoon or a tablespoon, but if I've just poured tea and I'm holding a sugar bowl when I say *Pass me a spoon*, you'll figure it's a teaspoon I need.

11. See Charles Kemp, Yang Xu, and Terry Regier, "Semantic Typology and Efficient Communication," *Annual Review of Linguistics* 4, no. 1 (2018): 109–128, https://doi .org/10.1146/annurev-linguistics-011817-045406; Jon W. Carr et al., "Simplicity and Informativeness in Semantic Category Systems," *Cognition* 202 (2020): 104289, https:// doi.org/10.1016/j.cognition.2020.104289.

12. This is true of English and many other languages, though patterns and practices of personal naming vary widely in the world. See N. J. Enfield and Tanya Stivers, eds., *Person Reference in Interaction: Linguistic, Cultural and Social Perspectives* (Cambridge: Cambridge University Press, 2007), https://doi.org/10.1017/CBO9780511486746.

13. From a recorded phone conversation in American English: Gail Jefferson, "A Case of Precision Timing in Ordinary Conversation: Overlapped Tag-Positioned Address Terms in Closing Sequences," *Semiotica* 9, no. 1 (1973), https://doi.org/10.1515/semi .1973.9.1.47; also cited in Herbert H. Clark and Deanna Wilkes-Gibbs, "Referring as a Collaborative Process," *Cognition* 22, no. 1 (1986): 8, https://doi.org/10.1016/0010 -0277(86)90010-7.

14. To prefigure something we'll have more to say about later, I note here that Ann's words that lead Ben's mind to understand who is meant—Gina—function as coordinating tools at multiple levels. At one level, the coordination problem is simply about securing a common understanding of who is being spoken about. But then the question arises as to why this person is mentioned at all. What coordination problem does *that* solve? In this case, one thing that it does is supply information about the source of the assertion that Ann is making. Hugo Mercier, *Not Born Yesterday: The Science of Who We Trust and What We Believe* (Princeton, NJ: Princeton University Press, 2020), 89, https://doi.org/10.1515/9780691198842, has argued that expressions of evidence like this are "commitment signals" that address matters of reputation in the context of the unreliable nature of language. Here, Ann doesn't just assert that Ben was at the beach, but that she *heard* he was. In this case, the reason for mentioning Gina at all appears to be for nothing more than further refining this basis for evidence in relation to the thing she wants to talk about, which is that Ben was at the beach. So in this case, the name *Gina* would be the practiced solution to the problem of coordinating around that particular person, someone who is mutually known to Ann and Ben.

15. Clark and Wilkes-Gibbs, "Referring as a Collaborative Process." See Robert D. Hawkins, Michael C. Frank, and Noah D. Goodman, "Characterizing the Dynamics of Learning in Repeated Reference Games," *Cognitive Science* 44, no. 6 (2020), https://doi.org/10.1111/cogs.12845, for an update on this work.

16. I use the term *instruction* here following Daniel Dor, *The Instruction of Imagination: Language as a Social Communication Technology* (Oxford: Oxford University Press, 2015). See also Michael J. Reddy, "The Conduit Metaphor: A Case of Frame

Conflict in Our Language about Language," in *Metaphor and Thought*, ed. Andrew Ortony (Cambridge: Cambridge University Press, 1979), 284–324, https://doi.org/10.1017/CBO9781139173865.012.

17. From a study by cognitive scientists Alex Mesoudi and Andrew Whiten, "The Hierarchical Transformation of Event Knowledge in Human Cultural Transmission," *Journal of Cognition and Culture* 4, no. 1 (2004): 1–24, https://doi.org/10.1163/156853704323074732), using a method designed by F. C. Bartlett, *Remembering: A Study in Experimental and Social Psychology* (Cambridge: Cambridge University Press, 1932). I have changed the text here, replacing the British terms *trolley* and *queue* with the US terms *grocery cart* and *line*.

18. With regard to personal names, the philosopher John Searle suggested that one reason we have names at all is to avoid having to choose specific ways in which we should describe people, given that many descriptions are possible. If, rather than say *Gina*, you say *the tall redhead who lives across the street from Larry*, I may wonder why you're mentioning those details and not others. Sticking to simple names avoids creating that kind of interpretative turbulence, and it points to a general principle in language use to explain why we tend to opt for simpler, more conventional ways of saying what we want to say. It is a principle of avoiding inviting inference.

19. The term *recipient design* is often attributed to Harold Garfinkel, *Studies in Ethnomethodology* (Upper Saddle River, NJ: Prentice Hall, 1967). Harvey Sacks, *Lectures on Conversation*, ed. Gail Jefferson, vol. 2 (London: Blackwell, 1992), 438, 564, 568, in lectures delivered in 1971, states that one of the "major operating maxims" is "design your talk to another with an orientation to what you know they know." Harvey Sacks, Emanuel A. Schegloff, and Gail Jefferson, "A Simplest Systematics for the Organization of Turn-Taking for Conversation," *Language* 50, no. 4 (1974): 40: "By recipient design, we refer to a multitude of respects in which the talk by a party in a conversation is constructed or designed in ways which display an orientation and sensitivity to the particular other(s) who are the co-participants." See also Ellen A. Isaacs and Herbert H. Clark, "References in Conversation between Experts and Novices.," *Journal of Experimental Psychology: General* 116, no. 1 (1987): 26–37, https://doi.org/10.1037/0096-3445.116.1.26; Clark, *Using Language*; Dale J. Barr, "Establishing Conventional Communication Systems: Is Common Knowledge Necessary?" *Cognitive Science* 28, no. 6 (2004): 937–962, https://doi.org/10.1207/s15516709cog2806_3; and Boaz Keysar et al., "Taking Perspective in Conversation: The Role of Mutual Knowledge in Comprehension," *Psychological Science* 11, no. 1 (2000): 32–38, https://doi.org/10.1111/1467-9280.00211. Dale J. Barr and Boaz Keysar, "Making Sense of How We Make Sense: The Paradox of Egocentrism in Language Use," in *Figurative Language Comprehension: Social and Cultural Influences* (Mahwah, NJ: Erlbaum, 2004), 21–41. Sarah E. Newman-Norlund et al., "Recipient Design in Tacit Communication," *Cognition* 111, no. 1 (2009): 46–54, https://doi.org/10.1016/j.cognition.2008.12.004.

20. Clark and Wilkes-Gibbs, "Referring as a Collaborative Process," 33.

21. E. B. Hunt and M. R. Banaji, "The Whorfian Hypothesis Revisited: A Cognitive Science View of Linguistic and Cultural Effects on Thought," in *Indigenous Cognition: Functioning in Cultural Context*, ed. J. W. Berry, S. H. Irvine, and E. B. Hunt (Dordrecht: Springer Netherlands, 1988), 57–84, https://doi.org/10.1007/978-94-009-2778-0.

22. Hunt and Banaji, 69–70.

23. But with notable exceptions, for example, the work of Edwin Hutchins: Edwin Hutchins, *Cognition in the Wild* (Cambridge, MA: MIT Press, 1995); his "The Distributed Cognition Perspective on Human Interaction," in *Roots of Human Sociality*, ed. N. J. Enfield and Stephen C. Levinson (Oxford: Berg, 2006), 375–98, https://doi.org/10.4324/9781003135517-19; and Edwin Hutchins and Brian Hazlehurst, "How to Invent a Shared Lexicon," in *Social Intelligence and Interaction: Expressions and Implications of the Social Bias in Human Intelligence*, edited by Esther N. Goody, 53–67 (Cambridge: Cambridge University Press, 1995), https://doi.org/10.1017/CBO9780511621710.005.

24. Eleanor Rosch, "Principles of Categorization," in *Cognition and Categorization*, ed. Eleanor Rosch and B. B. Lloyd (Hillsdale, NJ: Erlbaum, 1978), 27–48, https://doi.org/10.1016/B978-1-4832-1446-7.50028-5.

25. Because they are publicly shared, the concepts contained in bits of language *must* play a role in solving interpersonal coordination problems. Why? Because there can only be words—publicly shared entities—if they have been transmitted through a community through usage. "If words exist, they have survived. If they have survived, they have been used. And if they have been used, it has been for a reason." Enfield, *The Utility of Meaning*, 179. What is that reason? The answer: social coordination. It's clear that we need concepts in order to explain and predict things that we have to confront in our worlds, but it's not clear why those concepts need to be encoded *in words* if not for the purpose of social coordination.

Chapter 3

1. In English I say, *Buy one, get one free*, while in Dutch it is, *twee halen één betalen* (take two, pay for one).

2. Alongside the sense/reference distinction in language, Frege introduced a third concept, which he called *idea*. In addition to a referent and the various senses that language may provide for denoting that referent, individual users of a language will also have a much richer mental representation of an object. My reference might be Barack Obama, whom I could denote as "44." The sense of this expression comes from a conventional way to speak of US presidents, namely, to refer to their number in historical order. The sense of this expression—meaning "44th President of the United States of America"—profiles only a fragment of my complete mental file of knowledge, beliefs, opinions and perceptions of Obama.

3. Dan I. Slobin, "The Role of Language in Language Acquisition," invited address, 50th Annual Meeting of the Eastern Psychological Association, Philadelphia, 1979,

6. See also Eve V. Clark, *First Language Acquisition* (Cambridge: Cambridge University Press, 2003), 17. Language is "far from being an exact representation of our experience"; it "does not offer us exact maps of the experiences we may wish to recount." Dor, *The Instruction of Imagination*, 2: Language allows speakers to "instruct their interlocutors in the process of imagining the intended experience—instead of directly experiencing it. The speaker provides the receiver with a code, a plan, a skeletal list of the basic co-ordinates of the experience—which the receiver is then expected to use as a scaffold for experiential imagination." Also consider Gilles Fauconnier's idea that words are essentially prompts to construct mental space and Randy LaPolla's argument that the primary job of words is to provide constraints on inference.

4. Levelt states that the German philologist and philosopher Heymann Steinthal (1823–1889) "took the first steps" in founding a psychology of language. Willem J. M. Levelt, ed., *A History of Psycholinguistics: The Pre-Chomskyan Era* (Oxford: Oxford University Press, 2012), 40.

5. George A. Miller and Philip N. Johnson-Laird, *Language and Perception* (Cambridge, MA: Belknap Press of Harvard University Press, 1976), 702.

6. This is not to say that these authors had no interest in observing the ways in which language is actually used. Miller and Johnson-Laird, 703, said, for example, that in everyday language use, to understand the sentence *Smith is sitting in the chair*, our job is not only to draw on the sense of these words in order to identify the state of affairs that they refer to, and thereby "verify the sentence," but also to ascribe an intended *function* of the sentence in the context. "It may identify Smith for you; it may identify a particular chair for you; it may tell you where Smith is; . . . it may function as a request or command" (e.g., "Warn him that it will collapse"). Yet these contextual functions have been at the margin of the study of language, for two reasons. One reason is that it is much easier to study how words link to objects than it is to study how people actually use words in conversation. See Enfield, *How We Talk: The Inner Workings of Conversation* (New York: Basic Books, 2017). A second reason may be that the research has been done within cultures that generally foreground an individual point of view. The question has centrally been: How is language processed in an individual's mind?

7. Gregory L. Murphy, *The Big Book of Concepts* (Cambridge, MA: MIT Press, 2002), 391.

8. Language is used "to talk about real objects, people, events, and states" (Murphy, 386–387).

9. See W. J. M. Levelt, *Speaking: From Intention to Articulation* (Cambridge, MA: MIT Press, 1989), among others.

10. Anne Cutler, *Native Listening: Language Experience and the Recognition of Spoken Words* (Cambridge, MA: MIT Press, 2012).

11. These are not the only points of focus in psycholinguistics. There is also research on the acquisition of language by infants, and this field is more naturally concerned with the social context of communication. Additionally, in more recent years, psycholinguists have begun to pay more attention to language in social interaction. Herbert H. Clark, *Using Language* (Cambridge: Cambridge University Press, 1996); Boaz Keysar et al., "Taking Perspective in Conversation: The Role of Mutual Knowledge in Comprehension," *Psychological Science* 11, no. 1 (2000): 32–38, https://doi.org/10.1111/1467-9280.00211; Dale Barr, "Establishing Conventional Communication Systems: Is Common Knowledge Necessary?" *Cognitive Science* 28, no. 6 (2004): 937–962. https://doi.org/10.1207/s15516709cog2806_3; Dale Barr and Boaz Keysar, "Making Sense of How We Make Sense: The Paradox of Egocentrism in Language Use," in *Figurative Language Comprehension: Social and Cultural Influences*, 21–41 (Mahwah, NJ: Erlbaum, 2004); Stephen C. Levinson, "Turn-Taking in Human Communication— Origins and Implications for Language Processing," *Trends in Cognitive Sciences* 20, no. 1 (2016): 6–14, https://doi.org/10.1016/j.tics.2015.10.010; Enfield, *How We Talk*. But the bulk of work in this field has focused on how words link to the world, and so that is where we are going to start.

12. N. J. Enfield, "Everyday Ritual in the Residential World," in *Ritual Communication*, ed. Gunter Senft and Ellen B. Basso (Oxford: Berg, 2009), 51–80; Charles H. P. Zuckerman and N. J. Enfield, "The Unbearable Heaviness of Being Kri: House Construction and Ethnolinguistic Transformation," *Journal of the Royal Anthropological Institute* (28, no. 1, 2022).

13. https://www.worldwildlife.org/ecoregions/im0136. The Northern Annamites Rain Forests area is one of the 867 terrestrial ecoregions recognized by the World Wide Fund for Nature (ecoregion code IM0136; ADB/UNEP 2004:68–69) and one of the Global 200 subset of ecoregions that are "outstanding examples of biodiversity" in the world (ADB/UNEP, 72). "This Treasure Trove of Biological Diversity Is Still Divulging Its True Riches." https://www.worldwildlife.org/ecoregions/im0136 ADB/UNEP, 2004. Greater Mekong Subregion Atlas of the Environment. Asian Development Bank (ADB), Manila, Phillipines, and United Nations Environment Programme (UNEP) Regional Resources Centre for Asia and the Pacific, Pathumthani, Thailand. Manila/Pathumthani: ADB/UNEP.

14. Information on numbers of generic taxa from Brent Berlin, *Ethnobiological Classification: Principles of Categorization of Plants and Animals in Traditional Societies* (Princeton, NJ: Princeton University Press, 1992), 98–100.

15. Julie Anne Waddy, *Classification of Plants and Animals from a Groote Eylandt Aboriginal Point of View* (Darwin: Australian National University, 1988).

16. Eugene Hunn, "The Utilitarian Factor in Folk Biological Classification," *American Anthropologist* 84, no. 4 (1982): 830–847, https://doi.org/10.1525/aa.1982.84.4.02a00070, cited in Berlin, *Ethnobiological Classification*.

17. Following data are from Berlin, *Ethnobiological Classification*, 96ff. Claude Levi-Strauss, *The Savage Mind* (Chicago: University of Chicago Press, 1966), 153–154, noticed that in reports of traditional peoples' knowledge of biology and names for species and varieties, that there was a tendency for people to have "in the order of several hundred" names.

18. Pierre Grenand, *Introduction a l'Étude de l'Univers Wayãpi* (Paris: Société d'Études Linguistiques et Anthropologiques de France, 1980).

19. Brent Berlin, "The Concept of Rank in Ethnobiological Classification: Some Evidence from Aguaruna Folk Botany," *American Ethnologist* 3, no. 3 (1976): 381–399.

20. R. S. Felger and M. B. Moser, *People of the Desert and Sea* (Tucson: University of Arizona Press, 1985).

21. T. E. Hays, "Mauna: Explorations in Ndumba Ethnobotany" (PhD diss., University of Washington, 1974).

22. See also Phillip Wolff, Douglas L. Medin, and Connie Pankratz, "Evolution and Devolution of Folkbiological Knowledge," *Cognition* 73, no. 2 (1999): 177–204, https://doi.org/10.1016/S0010-0277(99)00051-7.

23. And not only do urban dwellers know a small number of plants, they also work at a coarser level of distinction; for US college students, basic categories are at the level of "tree" and "fish," not "maple" and "trout." Eleanor Rosch et al., "Basic Objects in Natural Categories," *Cognitive Psychology* 8, no. 3 (1976): 382–439, https://doi.org/10.1016/0010-0285(76)90013-X.

24. Mark Newman et al., *A Checklist for the Vascular Plants of Lao PDR*, 2007, 4–5, https://portals.iucn.org/library/node/9074.

25. E. Beech et al., "GlobalTreeSearch: The First Complete Global Database of Tree Species and Country Distributions," *Journal of Sustainable Forestry* 36, no. 5 (2017): 454–489, https://doi.org/10.1080/10549811.2017.1310049. For all known species, see Maarten J. M. Christenhusz and James W. Byng, "The Number of Known Plants Species in the World and Its Annual Increase," *Phytotaxa* 261, no. 3 (2016): 201, https://doi.org/10.11646/phytotaxa.261.3.1. For Laos, see Newman et al., *Checklist*. See also the 2017 report released by researchers at the Royal Botanic Gardens, Kew, in the United Kingdom: https://stateoftheworldsplants.org/2017/.

26. R. McNeill Alexander, *Locomotion of Animals* (Glasgow; London: Blackie, 1982); G. Schöner, W. Y. Jiang, and J. A. S. Kelso, "A Synergetic Theory of Quadrupedal Gaits and Gait Transitions," *Journal of Theoretical Biology* 142, no. 3 (1990): 359–391, https://doi.org/10.1016/S0022-5193(05)80558-2.

27. Barbara C. Malt et al., "Talking about Walking: Biomechanics and the Language of Locomotion," *Psychological Science* 19, no. 3 (2008): 232–240, https://doi.org/10.1111/j.1467-9280.2008.02074.x.

28. We expect [Slow walk, fast walk] [slow run, fast run] but not [Slow walk] [fast walk, slow run] [fast run].

29. Malt et al., "Talking about Walking," 232: "Naming reflects the biomechanical discontinuity between walking and running and . . . shared elements of naming can arise from correlations among stimulus properties that are dynamic and fleeting. The results support the proposal that converging naming patterns reflect structure in the world, not only acts of construction by observers."

30. Niclas Burenhult (Jahai, Malaysia); Nick Enfield (Lao, Laos); Alice Gaby (Kuuk Thaayorre, Australia); Stephen Levinson (Yélî Dnye, Papua New Guinea); Asifa Majid (Punjabi, Pakistan/India); Sergio Meira (Tiriyó, Brazil/Surinam); Jennie Pyers (American Sign Language, United States); Angela Terrill (Lavukaleve, Solomon Islands); Claudia Wegener (Savosavo, Solomon Islands).

31. It might also be what a researcher would expect to find in other languages. Anthropologist Cecil Brown remarked in a 1976 paper on the human body that all languages will have words that label the human hand. Cecil H. Brown, "General Principles of Human Anatomical Partonomy and Speculations on the Growth of Partonomic Nomenclature," *American Ethnologist* 3, no. 3 (1976): 400–424, https://doi.org/10.1525/ae.1976.3.3.02a00020. Anna Wierzbicka made the same claim more recently: Anna Wierzbicka, "The Human Conceptualisation of Shape," plenary paper, International Conference on Cognitive Science, Sydney, July 2003.

32. Stephen C. Levinson, "Parts of the Body in Yélî Dnye, the Papuan Language of Rossel Island," *Language Sciences* 28, no. 2–3 (2006): 231, https://doi.org/10.1016/j.langsci.2005.11.007.

33. Brown, "General Principles," 409.

34. Elaine S. Andersen, "Lexical Universals of Bodypart Terminology," in *Universals of Human Language*, ed. Joseph H. Greenberg. (Stanford, CA: Stanford University Press, 1978), 335–368.

35. Andersen, 352, says that the categories finger and toe are always labeled by one of "four general patterns": (1) different terms for each (*finger* versus *toe*), (2) one term referring to either (*digit*), (3) different terms sharing a common root (*hand-digit* versus *foot-digit*), or (4) toe derived from finger (*finger* versus *foot-finger*). Nail is always labeled by one of "two general patterns": (1) one term referring to either (*nail*), (2) different terms sharing a common root (*finger-nail* versus *toe-nail*).

36. Asifa Majid et al., "The Semantic Categories of Cutting and Breaking Events: A Crosslinguistic Perspective," *Cognitive Linguistics* 18, no. 2 (2007), https://doi.org/10.1515/COG.2007.005.

37. "Predictability of the locus of separation in the affected object": Asifa Majid, James S. Boster, and Melissa Bowerman, "The Cross-Linguistic Categorization of

Everyday Events: A Study of Cutting and Breaking," *Cognition* 109, no. 2 (2008): 242, https://doi.org/10.1016/j.cognition.2008.08.009.

38. Majid, Boster, and Bowerman, 242.

39. Majid, Boster, and Bowerman, 242.

40. There is, of course, the possibility of having no terms at all for colors. This has been claimed, for example, for the Pirahã language of Brazil. Daniel L. Everett, "Cultural Constraints on Grammar and Cognition in Pirahã: Another Look at the Design Features of Human Language," *Current Anthropology* 46, no. 4 (2005): 621–646, https://doi.org/10.1086/431525.

41. Paul Kay and Luisa Maffi, "Color Appearance and the Emergence and Evolution of Basic Color Lexicons," *American Anthropologist* 101, no. 4 (1999): 743–760, https://doi.org/10.1525/aa.1999.101.4.743.

42. This section with data from languages at the various stages draws on Paul Kay et al., "Color Naming across Languages," in *Color Categories in Thought and Language,* ed. C. L. Hardin and Luisa Maffi (Cambridge: Cambridge University Press, 1997), 37ff., https://doi.org/10.1017/CBO9780511519819.002.

43. See Joshua T. Abbott, Thomas L. Griffiths, and Terry Regier, "Focal Colors across Languages Are Representative Members of Color Categories," *Proceedings of the National Academy of Sciences* 113, no. 40 (2016): 11178–11183, https://doi.org/10.1073 /pnas.1513298113. Some argue that focal colors are actually derived from naming conventions—for example, Debi Roberson, Ian Davies, and Jules Davidoff, "Color Categories Are Not Universal: Replications and New Evidence from a Stone-Age Culture," *Journal of Experimental Psychology: General* 129, no. 3 (2000): 369–398, https://doi.org /10.1037/0096-3445.129.3.369. Compare Don Burgess, Willett Kempton, and Robert E. Maclaury, "Tarahumara Color Modifiers: Category Structure Presaging Evolutionary Change," *American Ethnologist* 10, no. 1 (1983): 133–149, https://doi.org/10.1525/ae .1983.10.1.02a00080.

44. See Ian R. L. Davies and Greville G. Corbett, "A Cross-Cultural Study of Colour Grouping: Evidence for Weak Linguistic Relativity," *British Journal of Psychology* 88, no. 3 (1997): 493–517, https://doi.org/10.1111/j.2044-8295.1997.tb02653.x, for analysis of the criteria used to determine which color terms in a language are "basic."

45. These criteria for the "basicness" of a word are closely related to those used in determining a word's "codability" (see below).

46. https://www.duluxtradepaintexpert.co.uk/en/colours/collections.

47. M. R. Pointer and G. G. Attridge, "The Number of Discernible Colours," *Color Research and Application* 23, no. 1 (1998): 52–54, https://doi.org/10.1002/(SICI)152 0-6378(199802)23:1<52::AID-COL8>3.0.CO;2-2. Deane Brewster Judd and Günter Wyszecki, *Color in Business, Science, and Industry,* 3rd ed. (New York: Wiley, 1975), 388.

48. Quotes from Asifa Majid and Niclas Burenhult, "Odors Are Expressible in Language, as Long as You Speak the Right Language," *Cognition* 130, no. 2 (2014): 266, https://doi.org/10.1016/j.cognition.2013.11.004. Hans Henning *Der Geruch* (Leipzig: J. A. Barth, 1916), 66, saying, "Olfactory abstraction is impossible." Yaara Yeshurun and Noam Sobel, "An Odor Is Not Worth a Thousand Words: From Multidimensional Odors to Unidimensional Odor Objects," *Annual Review of Psychology* 61, no. 1 (2010): 226, https://doi.org/10.1146/annurev.psych.60.110707.163639: "Humans are astonishingly bad at odor identification and naming" (226).

49. Rara & Universals Archive, https://typo.uni-konstanz.de/rara/category/raritaeten kabinett/.

50. Ewelina Wnuk and colleagues (2020) provide a rich list of references. Ewelina Wnuk, Rujiwan Laophairoj, and Asifa Majid, "Smell Terms Are Not Rara: A Semantic Investigation of Odor Vocabulary in Thai," *Linguistics* 58, no. 4 (2020): 20, https://doi.org/10.1515/ling-2020-0009.

51. H. P. Aschmann, "Totonac Categories of Smell," *Tlalocan* 2 (1946): 187.

52. See references in Wnuk, Laophairoj, and Majid, "Smell Terms Are Not Rara."

53. Asifa Majid et al., "Olfactory Language and Abstraction across Cultures," *Philosophical Transactions of the Royal Society B: Biological Sciences* 373, no. 1752 (2018): 1–8, https://doi.org/10.1098/rstb.2017.0139.

54. They selected monomolecular odors so as to hone in on pure smells for labeling.

55. Majid et al., "Olfactory Language and Abstraction across Cultures," 4.

56. Majid and Burenhult, "Odors Are Expressible in Language," 269.

57. Majid et al., "Olfactory Language and Abstraction across Cultures," 3.

58. From Asifa Majid et al., "What Makes a Better Smeller?" *Perception* 46, no. 3–4 (2017): 407, https://doi.org/10.1177/0301006616688224: "The human visual system can distinguish millions of colors (e.g., Pointer and Attridge, 'Number of Discernible Colours') and the auditory system hundreds of thousands of tones (S. S. Stevens & Davis, 1938). In comparison, then, the olfactory sense seemed paltry. But this conclusion has recently been overturned by the work of Bushdid et al., 'Humans Can Discriminate More Than 1 Trillion Olfactory Stimuli,' *Science* 343, no. 6177 (2014): 1370–1372, https://doi.org/10.1126/science.1249168, who estimate people can distinguish trillions of odors. Although estimating the capacity of any perceptual system is fraught with pitfalls and is by no means uncontentious (cf., Gerkin & Castro, 2015; Kuehni, 2016; Masaoka, Berns, Fairchild, & Abed, 2013, Bushdid et al.'s study has served to galvanize the discussion about the limits of sensory systems, as well as showing the feats the human sense of smell can accomplish. As Yeshurun and Sobel, 'An Odor Is Not Worth a Thousand Words' (223), stated a few years earlier 'Humans are astonishingly good at odor detection and discrimination.'"

59. Bushdid et al., "Humans Can Discriminate More Than 1 Trillion Olfactory Stimuli," say: "On the basis of the results of psychophysical testing, we calculated that humans can discriminate at least 1 trillion olfactory stimuli. This is far more than previous estimates of distinguishable olfactory stimuli. It demonstrates that the human olfactory system, with its hundreds of different olfactory receptors, far outperforms the other senses in the number of physically different stimuli it can discriminate."

60. Donald D. Hoffman, *The Case against Reality: Why Evolution Hid the Truth from Our Eyes* (New York: Norton, 2019).

Chapter 4

1. This example is from G. B. Flores d'Arcais and R. Schreuder, "Semantic Activation during Object Naming," *Psychological Research* 49, no. 2 (1987): 153–159, https://doi .org/10.1007/BF00308681.

2. See Peter Indefrey, "The Spatial and Temporal Signatures of Word Production Components: A Critical Update," *Frontiers in Psychology* 2 (2011), https://doi.org/10.3389 /fpsyg.2011.00255. See also W. J. M. Levelt, *Speaking: From Intention to Articulation* (Cambridge, MA: MIT Press, 1989): "When speakers are shown pictures of objects and asked to name the objects as quickly as possible, it takes some 600 to 1,200 milliseconds from picture presentation to the initiation of the vocal response," 222). The variation from fast to slow depends on many factors, including how frequent the word is: "'Oldfield and Wingfield (1965) found a high correlation between naming latency and the frequency with which the object name occurs in language use. Speech onset for *basket*, for instance, took 640 milliseconds from picture onset; *syringe* took 1,080 milliseconds on the average" (Levelt, 230),

3. Walter Bowers Pillsbury, "A Study in Apperception," *American Journal of Psychology* 8, no. 3 (1897): 315–393, https://doi.org/10.2307/1411485. This study is described in Willem J. M. Levelt, *A History of Psycholinguistics: The Pre-Chomskyan Era* (Oxford: Oxford University Press, 2012), 140.

4. As Pillsbury, 374–375, put it, when people were primed with related words, they had "greater certainty that the word suggested should be the correct word, and thus strengthened the effect of the word suggested upon the separate letters so that the misprints were overlooked more frequently."

5. We focus in this chapter on *linguistic* priming effects. Extensive research on priming in psychology more broadly has drawn much attention, but problems with failure to replicate test results has cast doubt on the reliability of findings in many social priming studies. See Tom Chivers, "What's Next for Psychology's Embattled Field of Social Priming," Nature 576, no. 7786 (2019): 200–202, https://doi.org/10.1038 /d41586-019-03755-2.

6. Tomlin hypothesizes that "at the time of utterance formulation, the speaker codes the referent currently in FOCAL ATTENTION as the SYNTACTIC SUBJECT of the utterance," so framing as passive is a fruit of a particular state of focal attention, which we can read off. He puts the hypothesis very strongly: "This mechanism is localistically controlled, which means that neither global theme nor local saliency is adequate to determine the selection of linguistic form, though both may contribute to the assignment of focal attention during the discourse production process.—This rule is invariant and automatic. It is invariant in that it governs the discourse production behavior of all native speakers in exactly the same way. It is automatic in that it applies to each and every instance of sentence production without easy or noticeable conscious access by the speaker." Russell S. Tomlin, "Focal Attention, Voice, and Word Order: An Experimental, Cross-Linguistic Study," in *Word Order in Discourse*, ed. Pamela A. Downing and Michael Noonan (Amsterdam: John Benjamins, 1995), 527, https://doi .org/10.1075/tsl.30.

7. Some languages didn't show the same pattern strongly or clearly: Polish, Russian, Bulgarian, and Akan. Tomlin, 541, notes that Akan and Bulgarian have no grammatical resources that work like the active/passive alternation to do what English speakers did in the experiment. I note that this points to a kind of linguistic relativity; because of the nature of Akan grammar, the language doesn't force or allow the "automatic" assigning of a grammatical framing by means of an agent alternation as a result of attention at the time of encoding.

8. These experiments show that people can be manipulated into placing different components of a scene into subject position. Note that when there is no such experimental manipulation, certain forces may still naturally prime us to make certain choices. According to a psychological "animacy hierarchy," we are disposed to focus on animate things more than objects and more on ourselves than on other things. For example, it sounds more natural to say, "He was struck by lightning" than "Lightning struck him."

9. Friedrich Wulf, "Beitrage Zur Psychologie Der Gestalt; vi. Über Die Veranderung von Vomellungen (Gedachtnis Und Gestalt)," *Psychologische Forschung* 1 (1922): 333–733.

10. James J. Gibson, "The Reproduction of Visually Perceived Forms," *Journal of Experimental Psychology* 12, no. 1 (1929): 9.

11. L. Carmichael, H. P. Hogen, and A. A. Walter, "An Experimental Study of the Effect of Language on the Reproduction of Visually Perceived Form," *Journal of Experimental Psychology* 15, no. 1 (1932): 73–86, https://doi.org/10.1037/h0072671, 81: "Naming a form immediately before it is visually presented may in many cases change the manner in which it will be reproduced."

12. Elizabeth F. Loftus and John C. Palmer, "Reconstruction of Automobile Destruction: An Example of the Interaction between Language and Memory," *Journal of Verbal Learning and Verbal Behavior* 13, no. 5 (1974): 585–589, https://doi.org/10 .1016/S0022-5371(74)80011-3.

13. The Schooler and Englster-Schooler 1990 study—Jonathan W. Schooler and Tonya Y. Engstler-Schooler, "Verbal Overshadowing of Visual Memories: Some Things Are Better Left Unsaid," *Cognitive Psychology* 22, no. 1 [1990]: 36–71, https://doi.org /10.1016/0010-0285(90)90003-M—has been replicated: V. K. Alogna et al., "Registered Replication Report: Schooler and Engstler-Schooler (1990)," *Perspectives on Psychological Science* 9, no. 5 (2014): 556–578, https://doi.org/10.1177/1745691614545653.

14. Hugo Mercier suggests an interesting possibility: "I wonder whether it's language itself that's doing the work, or trust in the individual who's speaking. For instance, with the effects of 'bumped' vs. 'smashed,' the words change, but presumably the listener thought the speaker meant different things, and was influenced by this—nearly in the same way as if the speaker had explicitly mentioned that they believe the speed of the vehicles was different." Even so, language would be playing a causal role in the change in belief. Hugo Mercier, *Not Born Yesterday: The Science of Who We Trust and What We Believe* (Princeton: Princeton University Press, 2020).

15. Gary Lupyan, "From Chair to 'Chair': A Representational Shift Account of Object Labeling Effects on Memory," *Journal of Experimental Psychology: General* 137, no. 2 (2008): 348, https://doi.org/10.1037/0096-3445.137.2.348.

16. Lupyan, 349: "In this view, an object's name is more than just the output of the conceptual system (see Gleitman & Papafragou, 2005, for discussion) but rather can feed back to alter the representation of the labeled item."

17. Lupyan, 349: "From a very young age, words draw our attention to object categories. Nine-month-old infants, for example, pay more attention to labeled than to unlabeled objects (Balaban & Waxman, 1997), and contrasting words (e.g., duck and ball) can facilitate object individuation in infants (Xu, 2002). Later in development, calling things by the same name leads children to look for similarities among objects (Loewenstein & Gentner, 1998; Smith, Jones, & Landau, 1996; Waxman & Markow, 1995), whereas calling things by different names leads children to treat the objects as more distinct (Katz, 1963; Landau & Shipley, 2001). In addition, labels, acting as cues to categories, facilitate inductive inferences in children (Gelman & Markman, 1986), possibly by competing with perceptual similarity (Sloutsky & Fisher, 2004a), and promote taxonomic over thematic groupings (Markman & Hutchinson, 1984; Waxman & Hall, 1993)." See also Gary Lupyan, David H. Rakison, and James L. McClelland, "Language Is Not Just for Talking: Redundant Labels Facilitate Learning of Novel Categories," *Psychological Science* 18, no. 12 (2007): 1077–1083, https://doi.org/10.1111/j .1467-9280.2007.02028.x.

18. Schooler and Engstler-Schooler, "Verbal Overshadowing of Visual Memories."

19. Charity Brown and Toby J. Lloyd-Jones, "Verbal Overshadowing of Multiple Face and Car Recognition: Effects of Within- versus Across-Category Verbal Descriptions," *Applied Cognitive Psychology* 17, no. 2 (2003): 183–201, https://doi.org/10.1002/acp.861; Joseph M. Melcher and Jonathan W. Schooler, "The Misremembrance of Wines Past: Verbal and Perceptual Expertise Differentially Mediate Verbal Overshadowing of Taste

Memory," *Journal of Memory and Language* 35, no. 2 (1996): 231–245, https://doi.org /10.1006/jmla.1996.0013; Lee H. V. Wickham and Hayley Swift, "Articulatory Suppression Attenuates the Verbal Overshadowing Effect: A Role for Verbal Encoding in Face Identification," *Applied Cognitive Psychology* 20, no. 2 (2006): 157–169, https://doi.org /10.1002/acp.1176.

20. Schooler and Engstler-Schooler, "Verbal Overshadowing of Visual Memories," 66.

21. Lupyan, "From Chair to 'Chair,'" 366.

22. Lupyan, 366.

23. Roger Brown, "How Shall a Thing Be Called?" *Psychological Review* 65, no. 1 (1958): 14–21, https://doi.org/10.1037/h0041727.

24. Rosch et al., "Basic Objects in Natural Categories," 384. This obviously depends on what the purposes at hand are. There are plenty of circumstances in which *vehicle* is appropriate, just as there are plenty of circumstances in which *convertible sports car* is appropriate. The idea of basic-level categorization applies to a default setting for how specific we normally expect people to be.

25. See also Louise Nuttall, "Transitivity, Agency, Mind Style: What's the Lowest Common Denominator?" *Language and Literature: International Journal of Stylistics* 28, no. 2 (2019): 159–179, https://doi.org/10.1177/0963947019839851.

26. Chris Kennedy, "Systemic Grammar and Its Use in Literary Analysis," in *Language and Literature: An Introductory Reader in Stylistics*, ed. Ronald Carter, 3rd ed. (London: Routledge, 1991), 88–89, cited in Nuttall, "Transitivity, Agency, Mind Style," 160.

27. Kennedy, "Systemic Grammar and Its Use in Literary Analysis."

28. Nuttall, "Transitivity, Agency, Mind Style," 166.

29. Nuttall, 170.

30. Caitlin M. Fausey and Lera Boroditsky, "Subtle Linguistic Cues Influence Perceived Blame and Financial Liability," *Psychonomic Bulletin and Review* 17, no. 5 (2010): 644, https://doi.org/10.3758/PBR.17.5.644.

31. Technically, this is not an example of passive/active alternation, but for our purposes, it is the same in a crucial respect. Verbs like *burn* and *break* can sometimes have an agent as their subject (like an active sentence, as in *They burned it* or *They broke it*) and other times a "patient" as their subject (like a passive sentence; as in *It burned* or *It broke*). True passive versions of these sentences would be *It was burned (by them)* and *It was broken (by them)*.

32. https://www.innocenceproject.org/.

33. Ziv Epstein, Sydney Levine, David G. Rand, and Iyad Rahwan, "Who Gets Credit for AI-Generated Art?" *iScience* 23 (9) (2020): 101515, https://doi.org/10.1016/j.isci .2020.101515.

34. Marine Riou et al., "'Tell Me Exactly What's Happened': When Linguistic Choices Affect the Efficiency of Emergency Calls for Cardiac Arrest," *Resuscitation* 117 (2017): 58–65, https://doi.org/10.1016/j.resuscitation.2017.06.002.

35. Riou et al., 62.

36. John Heritage et al., "Reducing Patients' Unmet Concerns in Primary Care: The Difference One Word Can Make," *Journal of General Internal Medicine* 22, no. 10 (2007): 1429–1433, https://doi.org/10.1007/s11606-007-0279-0.

37. Rein Ove Sikveland and Elizabeth Stokoe, "Should Police Negotiators Ask to 'Talk' or 'Speak' to Persons in Crisis? Word Selection and Overcoming Resistance to Dialogue Proposals," *Research on Language and Social Interaction* 53, no. 3 (2020): 324–340, https://doi.org/10.1080/08351813.2020.1785770.

38. Sikveland and Stokoe, 338.

39. Benjamin Lee Whorf, *Language, Thought, and Reality* (Cambridge, MA: MIT Press, 1956), 135.

40. Whorf, 135.

41. Whorf, 136.

42. Whorf, 136–137.

43. Edward Sapir, cited in Whorf, 137.

44. Daniel Dor's (2015) theory of language as a tool for the instruction of imagination invokes the idea of an experiential gap between people: you can't experience what I experience. But with language, I can provide a bridge for that gap by giving you instructions for how to imagine what I've experienced. Dor, *The Instruction of Imagination: Language as a Social Communication Technology* (Oxford: Oxford University Press, 2015).

Chapter 5

1. Russell Tomlin, "Focal Attention, Voice, and Word Order: An Experimental, Cross-Linguistic Study," in *Word Order in Discourse*, edited by Pamela A. Downing and Michael Noonan (Amsterdam: John Benjamins, 1995), 517–554.

2. Linguistic relativity has long been an issue of heated debate. See John J. Gumperz and Stephen C. Levinson, *Rethinking Linguistic Relativity* (Cambridge: Cambridge University Press, 1996); John Lucy, "Linguistic Relativity," *Annual Review of Anthropology* 26, no. 1 (1997): 291–312, https://doi.org/10.1146/annurev.anthro.26.1.291; Stephen C, Levinson, *Space in Language and Cognition: Explorations in Cognitive Diversity* (Cambridge: Cambridge University Press, 2003); John H. McWhorter, *The Language Hoax: Why the World Looks the Same in Any Language* (Oxford: New York: Oxford University Press, 2014); Caleb Everett, *Linguistic Relativity: Evidence across Languages and Cognitive Domains* (Berlin: De Gruyter Mouton, 2013), https://doi.org/10.1515

/9783110308143; N. J. Enfield, "Linguistic Relativity from Reference to Agency," *Annual Review of Anthropology* 44, no. 1 (2015): 207–224, https://doi.org/10.1146 /annurev-anthro-102214-014053, and many other references in those sources. But it is odd that the debate is heated because people agree on most of the facts. Most scholars acknowledge that language can and does affect thought and behavior and that different languages can do so differently. The debate is around whether these effects should be regarded as central to our understanding of language or peripheral. Are the effects profound? Or are they trivial? The answer depends on the researcher's narrative about the human capacity for language. Some researchers are focused on the ways in which languages are diverse and culturally variable. Others are focused on language as a human universal. But obviously these two perspectives are not contradictory.

Lila Gleitman and Anna Papafragou, *New Perspectives on Language and Thought* (Oxford: Oxford University Press, 2012), 3: "In one sense, it is obvious that language use has powerful and specific effects on thought. After all, that's what it is for, or at least that is one of the things it is for: to transfer ideas from one mind to another mind. Imagine Eve telling Adam Apples taste great. This fragment of linguistic information, as we know, caused Adam to entertain a new thought with profound effects on his world knowledge, inferencing, and subsequent behavior. Much of human communication is an intentional attempt to modify others' thoughts and attitudes in just this way. This information transmission function is crucial for the structure and survival of cultures and societies in all their known forms."

Dedre Gentner and Susan Goldin-Meadow, eds., *Language in Mind: Advances in the Study of Language and Thought* (Cambridge, MA: MIT Press, 2003), 3: "For the last two decades, the hypothesis that language can influence thought—generally known as the Whorfian hypothesis—has been in serious disrepute. Admitting any sympathy for, or even curiosity about, this possibility was tantamount to declaring oneself to be either a simpleton or a lunatic. The view of most language researchers is well expressed by Pinker (1994, 65): 'Most of the experiments have tested banal "weak" versions of the Whorfian hypothesis, namely that words can have some effect on memory or categorization. Some of these experiments have actually worked, but that is hardly surprising.' Devitt and Sterelny (1987, 178) express this scepticism even more strongly: '[T]he argument for an important linguistic relativity evaporates under scrutiny. The only respect in which language clearly and obviously does influence thought turns out to be rather banal: language provides us with most of our concepts.' The latter quotation exemplifies the rather schizophrenic way in which the Whorfian question has been viewed. The language-and-thought question is dismissed as banal and unimportant, yet in the same breath it is stated (almost in passing) that language provides us with most of our concepts—a view far stronger than that of even the most pro-Whorf researchers."

3. Take the area of causality, a fundamental sense in which two events can be connected. The psychologist Albert Michotte studied the human perception of causality

with simple animations in which balls hit each other, like billiard balls do; people would perceive causality in some circumstances and not in others (e.g., when one ball is approaching another but the second ball starts moving before the first ball makes contact). He showed that there were certain thresholds and certain tendencies in attribution of causation. A. Michotte, *The Perception of Causality* (Oxford: Basic Books, 1963). In a 2002 study, psychologists Brian Scholl and Ken Nakayama showed that even this basic causal perception can be strongly affected by context. They speculate that "causal capture" occurs because we are wired (or at least our vision system is wired) not to view strong correlations as coincidences. Brian J. Scholl and Ken Nakayama, "Causal Capture: Contextual Effects on the Perception of Collision Events," *Psychological Science* 13, no. 6 (2002): 493–498, https://doi.org/10.1111/1467-9280.00487.

4. The question also arises: What causes this difference between the two languages in the first place? One answer appeals to cultural differences among the populations that speak these languages. N. J. Enfield, *Ethnosyntax: Explorations in Culture and Grammar* (Oxford: Oxford University Press, 2002); Daniel Everett, "Cultural Constraints on Grammar and Cognition in Pirahã: Another Look at the Design Features of Human Language," *Current Anthropology* 46, no. 4 (2005): 621–646, https://doi.org/10.1086/431525; Everett, *Linguistic Relativity*. Caitlin M. Fausey et al., "Constructing Agency: The Role of Language," *Frontiers in Psychology* 1 (2010): 1, https://doi.org/10.3389/fpsyg.2010.00162, speculate about cultural underpinnings of the effect (see their paper for the references): "Social context also plays an important role. Societies across the world instantiate different concepts of the self, with East Asian societies emphasizing interdependent ways of being and Western societies emphasizing more independent notions of self (e.g., Markus and Kitayama, 1991, 2004). Compared to people in interdependent societies, people in independent societies are more likely to select a single proximal cause for an event (e.g., Chiu et al., 2000; Choi et al., 2003), are less aware of distal consequences of events (e.g., Maddux and Yuki, 2006), are more susceptible to correspondence bias (e.g., Choi et al., 1999), and are more motivated by personal choice (e.g., Iyengar and Lepper, 1999). The role that individuals play in events may depend on notions of agency that are culture-specific (e.g., Morris et al., 2001). What it means to be an 'agent' does not appear to be a stable, universal property of events in the world. What people see and believe to be an agent is constructed in context." Fausey et al. propose that "patterns in everyday descriptions (e.g., whether someone says 'He shattered the crystal' or 'The crystal shattered') may serve as pervasive and powerful cues to agency."

5. See also Lewis Forder and Gary Lupyan, "Hearing Words Changes Color Perception: Facilitation of Color Discrimination by Verbal and Visual Cues," PsyArXiv preprint (August 29, 2017), https://doi.org/10.31234/osf.io/f83au.

6. See Asifa Majid et al., "What Makes a Better Smeller?" *Perception* 46, no. 3–4 (2017): 406–430, https://doi.org/10.1177/0301006616688224.

7. Federica Amici et al., "The Word Order of Languages Predicts Native Speakers' Working Memory," *Scientific Reports* 9, no. 1 (2019), https://doi.org/10.1038/s41598 -018-37654-9.

8. Amici et al.: "These results confirm our hypothesis and suggest that sensitivity to branching direction predicts the way in which humans remember and/or process sequences of stimuli."

9. Some commentators of language have used the metaphor that language is a prison for the mind. See the discussion in Raymond Tallis, *Not Saussure: A Critique of Post-Saussurean Literary Theory*, 2nd ed. (1988; reprint, Basingstoke: Macmillan, 1997), 48; Fredric Jameson, *The Prison-House of Language: A Critical Account of Structuralism and Russian Formalism* (Princeton: Princeton University Press, 1972); Peter D. Mathews, *Lacan the Charlatan* (*Cham, Switzerland: Palgrave*, 2020). Farhad Manjoo's op-ed column about pronouns makes mention of a "prison of the mind." Manjoo, "It's Time for 'They,'" New York Times, July 10, 2019, https://www.nytimes.com/2019/07/10 /opinion/pronoun-they-gender.html.

10. J. G. von Herder, *Herder: Philosophical Writings*, ed. Michael N. Forster (Cambridge: Cambridge University Press, 2002), in the eighteenth century, and Wilhelm von Humboldt, *On Language: The Diversity of Human Language-Structure and Its Influence on the Mental Development of Mankind* (1836; reprint, Cambridge: Cambridge University Press, 1988), in the nineteenth, to Franz Boas, "Introduction," in *Handbook of American Indian Languages*, ed. Franz Boas (1911; reprint, Lincoln: University of Nebraska Press, 1966), 1–79, and Edward Sapir, *Selected Writings* (Berkeley: University of California Press, 1949). See John Leavitt, *Linguistic Relativities: Language Diversity and Modern Thought* (Cambridge: Cambridge University Press, 2010); Everett, *Linguistic Relativity*.

11. Whorf's considerable accomplishments in Native American and Mesoamerican linguistics, including his 1930s fieldwork on the Aztec language and his contributions to the deciphering of Mayan hieroglyphs, are still referenced in the specialist literature of that area. In linguistics, Whorf made lasting contributions to the study of how meaning is encoded, both overtly and covertly, in grammatical systems. But Whorf is discussed most for his proposals concerning relations between language, thought, and reality. See Benjamin Lee Whorf, *Language, Thought, and Reality* (1956; reprint, Cambridge, MA: MIT Press, 2012).

12. Whorf's famous article about the fire insurance cases was short. In presenting it in "condensed and unqualified form," he had hoped readers "would use their thinking apparatus" and adjust accordingly. These quotes are from a letter to his editor cited in Penny Lee, *The Whorf Theory Complex: A Critical Reconstruction* (Amsterdam: Benjamins, 1996), 153. In response to his editor's suggestion that he may have overemphasized the role of language in channeling behavior, Whorf explained,

> I have thought of possibly adding a brief statement or a footnote saying that I don't wish to imply that language is the sole or even the leading factor in the types of behavior mentioned

such as the fire-causing carelessness through misunderstandings induced by language, but that this is simply a coordinate factor along with others. It didn't seem at first that this should be necessary if the reader uses ordinary common sense.

13. J. Grimes, "On the Failure to Detect Changes in Scenes across Saccades," in *Perception*, ed. K. Akins (New York: Oxford University Press, 1996), 89–110. Daniel T. Levin and Daniel J. Simons, "Failure to Detect Changes to Attended Objects in Motion Pictures," *Psychonomic Bulletin and Review* 4, no. 4 (1997): 501–506, https://doi.org/10.3758/BF03214339.

14. Gerd Gigerenzer, Ralph Hertwig, and Thorsten Pachur, eds., *Heuristics: The Foundations of Adaptive Behavior* (Oxford: Oxford University Press, 2011).

15. H. A. Simon, "Rational Choice and the Structure of the Environment," *Psychological Review* 63, no. 2 (1956): 129–138, https://doi.org/10.1037/h0042769; Herbert A. Simon, *Reason in Human Affairs* (Stanford, CA: Stanford University Press, 1983). Compare Gerd Gigerenzer, *Gut Feelings: Short Cuts to Better Decision Making* (London: Penguin, 2007); Kahneman, *Thinking, Fast and Slow* (New York: Penguin, 2011).

16. Paul Kockelman, *Agent, Person, Subject, Self: A Theory of Ontology, Interaction, and Infrastructure* (Oxford: Oxford University Press, 2013); N. J. Enfield, *Relationship Thinking: Agency, Enchrony, and Human Sociality* (Oxford: Oxford University Press, 2013), 58.

17. Of special interest for Whorf and many since was the encoding of concepts in grammatical as opposed to lexical forms, given that the former are maximally requisite, tacit, and practiced and thus maximally habitual.

18. Our primary measuring instruments are our bodies: James J. Gibson, *The Ecological Approach to Visual Perception* (Boston: Houghton Mifflin, 1979); Tim Ingold, *The Perception of the Environment: Essays on Livelihood, Dwelling and Skill* (London: Routledge, 2000). See also Donald Hoffman, *The Case against Reality: Why Evolution Hid the Truth from Our Eyes* (New York: Norton, 2019).

19. Gilbert Ryle, *The Perception of the Environment Essays on Livelihood, Dwelling and Skill* (London: Hutchinson, 1949), 45. Enfield, *Relationship Thinking*, 58.

20. Sapir, *Selected Writings*, 162. Sapir was Whorf's teacher at Yale.

21. This is Whorf's term. Whorf, *Language, Thought, and Reality*, 358.

22. Whorf, 274.

23. Roger W. Brown and Eric H. Lenneberg, "A Study in Language and Cognition," *Journal of Abnormal and Social Psychology* 49, no. 3 (1954): 454–462, https://doi.org/10.1037/h0057814. Paul Henle, ed., *Language, Thought, and Culture* (Ann Arbor: University of Michigan Press, 1958). Eleanor Rosch, "Linguistic Relativity," in *Thinking: Readings in Cognitive Science*, ed. P. N. Johnson-Laird and P. C. Wason (Cambridge: Cambridge University Press, 1977), 501–522. M. Silverstein, "Language Structure and Linguistic Ideology," in *The Elements: A Parasession on Linguistic Units and Levels*, ed.

P. Clyne, W. Hanks, and C. Hofbauer (Chicago: Chicago Linguistic Society, 1979), 193–247. Kenneth L. Hale, "Notes on World View and Semantic Categories: Some Warlpiri Examples," in *Features and Projections*, ed. Pieter Muysken and Henk van Riemsdijk (Dordrecht: Foris, 1986), 233–254. Anna Wierzbicka, "Baudouin De Courtenay and the Theory of Linguistic Relativity," in *Jan Niecisław Baudouin de Courtenay a lingwistyka światowa: materiały z konferencji międzynarodowej, Warszawa, 4–7 IX 1979*, ed. Janusz Rieger et al. (Wrocław: Zakład Narodowy im. Ossolińskich, 1989), 51–57. E. Schultz, *Dialogue at the Margins: Whorf, Bakhtin, and Linguistic Relativity* (Madison: University of Wisconsin Press, 1990); Jane H. Hill and Bruce Mannheim, "Language and World View," *Annual Review of Anthropology* 21, no. 1 (1992): 381–404, https://doi.org /10.1146/annurev.an.21.100192.002121; John A. Lucy, *Language Diversity and Thought: A Reformulation of the Linguistic Relativity Hypothesis* (Cambridge: Cambridge University Press, 1992); John A. Lucy, "The Scope of Linguistic Relativity," in *Rethinking Linguistic Relativity*, ed. John J. Gumperz and Stephen C. Levinson (Cambridge: Cambridge University Press, 1996), 37–69, https://www.jstor.org/stable/2743696; Gumperz and Levinson, *Rethinking Linguistic Relativity*; L. Michael, "Reformulating the Sapir-Whorf Hypothesis: Discourse, Interaction, and Distributed Cognition," in *Texas Linguistic Forum*, ed. I. Mey et al., vol. 45 (Austin: University of Texas Press, 2002), http://salsa .ling.utexas.edu/proceedings/2002/michael.pdf; Gentner and Goldin-Meadow, *Language in Mind*; Paul Kockelman, *Language, Culture, and Mind: Natural Constructions and Social Kinds* (Cambridge: Cambridge University Press, 2010); A. K. Webster, "In Favor of Sound: Linguistic Relativity and Navajo Poetry," in *Texas Linguistic Forum*, ed. M. Siewert, M. Ingram, and B. Anderson, vol. 57 (Austin: University of Texas Press, 2014), http://salsa.ling.utexas.edu/proceedings/2014/Webster.pdf. Among many others, Whorf, *Language, Thought, and Reality*, 2012, includes an extended bibliography. Since Whorf's time, some have taken his proposals to be no more than a suggestive framework, a conceptual guide for anthropological research or as a source of hypotheses for experimental testing. See Gumperz and Levinson, *Rethinking Linguistic Relativity*; Gentner and Goldin-Meadow, *Language in Mind*. Others have pressed too hard on the idea, dismissing it for its failure to take the weight. McWhorter, *The Language Hoax*. But it is not clear that Whorf's work was designed to bear that load. Nor are people always critiquing the thing that Whorf actually proposed. Cognitive anthropologist Stephen C. Levinson describes the problem: "It is as if the topic of 'Whorfianism' is a domain where anybody can let off steam, go on mental holiday, or pounce upon an ideological enemy." Stephen C. Levinson, "Language and Mind: Let's Get the Issues Straight," in *Language and Mind: Advances in the Study of Language and Thought*, ed. Dedre Gentner and Susan Goldin-Meadow (Cambridge, MA: MIT Press, 2003), 25. Whorf scholar Penny Lee counts the ways Whorf has been "misread, unread, and superficially treated." Lee, *The Whorf Theory Complex*, 14. See also Stephen C. Levinson, Foreword to *Language, Thought, and Reality*, by Benjamin Lee Whorf (Cambridge, MA: MIT Press, 2012), xiii.

24. Lucy, "Linguistic Relativity," 192. See also Lucy, *Language Diversity and Thought* and "The Scope of Linguistic Relativity"; Paul Bloom and Frank C. Keil, "Thinking

through Language," *Mind and Language* 16, no. 4 (2001): 352–353, https://doi.org/10 .1111/1468-0017.00175; Phillip Wolff and Kevin J. Holmes, "Linguistic Relativity: Linguistic Relativity," *Wiley Interdisciplinary Reviews: Cognitive Science* 2, no. 3 (2011): 254, https://doi.org/10.1002/wcs.104. Other taxonomies include Maria Francisca Reines and Jesse Prinz, "Reviving Whorf: The Return of Linguistic Relativity," *Philosophy Compass* 4, no. 6 (2009): 2017–1028, https://doi.org/10.1111/j.1747-9991.2009 .00260.x) on four types of linguistic relativity (radical, trivial, habitual, and ontological), and Gentner and Goldin-Meadow, *Language in Mind*, 9–10, on three types of language–thought relation (language as lens, language as tool kit, and language as category maker). Much of the extensive literature is reviewed by Leavitt, *Linguistic Relativities*, and Everett, *Linguistic Relativity*. See also the wide-ranging bibliography in Whorf, *Language, Thought, and Reality*.

25. Debi Roberson et al., "Color Categories: Evidence for the Cultural Relativity Hypothesis," *Cognitive Psychology* 50, no. 4 (2005): 378–411, https://doi.org/10.1016 /j.cogpsych.2004.10.001; J. Winawer et al., "Russian Blues Reveal Effects of Language on Color Discrimination," *Proceedings of the National Academy of Sciences* 104, no. 19 (2007): 7780–7785, https://doi.org/10.1073/pnas.0701644104; Debi Roberson and R. Hanley, "Relatively Speaking: An Account of the Relationship between Language and Thought in the Color Domain," in *Words and the Mind: How Words Capture Human Experience*, ed. Barbara C. Malt and Phillip Wolff (New York: Oxford University Press, 2010), 183–198.

26. L. Boroditsky, L. Schmidt, and W. Phillips, "Sex, Syntax, and Semantics," in *Language in Mind: Advances in the Study of Language and Thought*, ed. Dedre Gentner and Susan Goldin-Meadow (Cambridge, MA: MIT Press, 2003), 61–80.

27. John B. Haviland, "Anchoring, Iconicity, and Orientation in Guugu Yimithirr Pointing Gestures," *Journal of Linguistic Anthropology* 3, no. 1 (1993): 3–45, https:// doi.org/10.1525/jlin.1993.3.1.3; Levinson, *Space in Language and Cognition*; Asifa Majid et al., "Can Language Restructure Cognition? The Case for Space," *Trends in Cognitive Sciences* 8, no. 3 (2004): 108–114, https://doi.org/10.1016/j.tics.2004.01 .003; Daniel B. M. Haun et al., "Plasticity of Human Spatial Cognition: Spatial Language and Cognition Covary across Cultures," *Cognition* 119, no. 1 (2011): 70–80, https://doi.org/10.1016/j.cognition.2010.12.009.

28. See Enfield, "Linguistic Relativity from Reference to Agency."

29. Whorf, *Language, Thought, and Reality*, 178.

30. J. L. Austin, *How to Do Things with Words* (Cambridge, MA: Harvard University Press, 1962); M. Silverstein, "Shifters, Linguistic Categories, and Cultural Description," ed. K. Basso and H. Selby (Albuquerque: University of Mexico Press, 1976), 11–55; Silverstein, "Language Structure and Linguistic Ideology"; M. Silverstein, "The Limits of Awareness," Sociolinguistic Working Paper 84 (Austin, TX: Southwest Educational Development Lab, 1981); M. Silverstein, "Denotation and the Pragmatics of Language,"

in *The Cambridge Handbook of Linguistic Anthropology*, ed. N. J. Enfield, Paul Kockelman, and Jack Sidnell (Cambridge: Cambridge University Press, 2014), 128–157; J. Zinken, "The Metaphor of "Linguistic Relativity," *History and Philosophy of Psychology*. 10, no. 2 (2008): 1–10; Kockelman, *Language, Culture, and Mind.*

31. R. Jacobson, "Concluding Statement: Linguistics and Poetics.," in *Style in Language*, ed. Thomas A. Sebeok (Cambridge, MA: MIT Press, 1960).

32. C. E. Shannon, "A Mathematical Theory of Communication," *Bell System Technical Journal* 27, no. 3 (1948): 379–423, https://doi.org/10.1002/j.1538-7305.1948.tb 01338.x.

33. C. Baker, "Regulators and Turn-Taking in American Sign Language Discourse," in *On the Other Hand: New Perspectives on* American Sign Language, ed. L. Friedman (New York: Academic Press, 1977), 215–236; Ronnie B. Wilbur and Laura A. Petitto "Discourse structure in American sign language conversations (or, how to know a conversation when you see one)" Discourse Processes 6, no. 3 (1983): 225–228, https://doi.org/10.1080/01638538309544565; Amy M. Lieberman, "Attention-Getting Skills of Deaf Children Using American Sign Language in a Preschool Classroom," *Applied Psycholinguistics* 36, no. 4 (2015): 1–19, https://doi.org/10.1017/S0142716413000532.

34. "A deaf child must understand that it is not enough to be able to see his intended addressee; the addressee must be visually attending to the child as well. Thus, before any conversational turns can take place, a child must first evaluate the locus of attention of his addressee and then obtain the addressee's attention if it is directed elsewhere. Only when visual attention is established can a successful interaction take place. This ability to take into account another person's locus of attention arguably requires a level of visual perspective-taking skill that typically does not develop before the age of twenty-four months." Lieberman, "Attention-Getting Skills," 2.

35. Lieberman, 2.

36. Thanks to Trevor Johnston and Adam Schembri for helpful information about these aspects of sign language usage.

37. On this point, for an extended exploration of linguistic relativity in relation to the poetic function of language, see Paul Friedrich, "Social Context and Semantic Feature: The Russian Prononimal Usage," in *Directions in Sociolinguistics: The Ethnography of Communication*, ed. John J. Gumperz and Dell H. Hymes, 2nd ed. (London: Basil Blackwell, 1986), 270–300. See also Joel Sherzer, "A Discourse-Centered Approach to Language and Culture," *American Anthropologist* 89, no. 2 (1987): 295–309, https://doi.org/10.1525/aa.1987.89.2.02a00010; Webster, "In Favor of Sound"; Mark Dingemanse, "Ezra Pound among the Mawu," *Semblance and Signification. Iconicity in Language and Literature* 10 (2011): 39–54; Mark Dingemanse, "Making New Ideophones in Siwu: Creative Depiction in Conversation," *Pragmatics and Society* 5,

no. 3 (2014): 384–405, https://doi.org/10.1075/ps.5.3.04din. These examples suggest that linguistic relativity takes many more forms than Whorf's prototype, in which a word affects the way you reason and act in a practical situation (e.g., *empty* for fuel drums). The example from sign language conversation shows a form of relativity grounded in the phatic function of language and manifest in the domain of social attention and action rather than (solely) in perception, conceptual structure, or reasoning. Forms of linguistic relativity such as these are not included in the taxonomies given above. Those taxonomies focus on language's referential function and on the relatively private and nonsocial psychological domains of conceptual structure and reasoning.

38. Silverstein, "Denotation and the Pragmatics of Language"; Silverstein, "The Limits of Awareness." See also Kockelman, *Language, Culture, and Mind*; Everett, *Linguistic Relativity*; N. J. Enfield, Paul Kockelman, and Jack Sidnell, eds., *The Cambridge Handbook of Linguistic Anthropology* (Cambridge: Cambridge University Press, 2014).

39. Schooler and Engstler-Schooler, "Verbal Overshadowing of Visual Memories."

40. A. L. Gilbert et al., "Whorf Hypothesis Is Supported in the Right Visual Field But Not the Left," *Proceedings of the National Academy of Sciences* 103, no. 2 (2006): 489–494, https://doi.org/10.1073/pnas.0509868103.

41. Boroditsky, Schmidt, and Phillips, "Sex, Syntax, and Semantics."

42. See McWhorter's *The Language Hoax* for an attempt to make the case that "language dances only ever so lightly on thought" and that terminology "doesn't shape thought, it follows it." John McWhorter, *The Language Hoax: Why the World Looks the Same in Any Language* (Oxford: Oxford University Press, 2014).

43. Whorf, *Language, Thought, and Reality*, 2012, 283.

Chapter 6

1. Christian Lehmann, "Roots, Stems and Word Classes," *Studies in Language* 32, no. 3 (2008): 546–567, https://doi.org/10.1075/sl.32.3.04leh.

2. Subsequent paragraphs are revised from N. J. Enfield, *The Utility of Meaning: What Words Mean and Why* (Oxford: Oxford University Press, 2015).

3. Brent Berlin, *Ethnobiological Classification: Principles of Categorization of Plants and Animals in Traditional Societies* (Princeton, NJ: Princeton University Press, 1992), 80.

4. Berlin, 8

5. Berlin, 53.

6. Hunn, "The Utilitarian Factor in Folk Biological Classification" *American Anthropologist* 84, no. 4 (1982): 834–847. https://doi.org/10.1525/aa.1982.84.4.02a00070.

7. Berlin, *Ethnobiological Classification*, 80–90.

8. In Berlin's critique of the utilitarian hypothesis, he seems to imply that if a referent does not have direct utility, then a utilitarian account should predict that it will not therefore be labeled. But this does not follow. For one thing, it is an instance of the logical fallacy of affirming the consequent: "If a referent is useful, then the referent is labeled" does not entail that "if a referent is labeled, then the referent is useful." There can be other reasons it is labeled. One such reason, as argued here, is that *the word for* the referent is useful, regardless of whether the referent itself is.

9. From Enfield, *The Utility of Meaning*, paraphrased. The example is from a video-recorded conversation.

10. https://www.nybg.org/blogs/science-talk/2018/03/plants-as-calendars/,

11. Ray P. Norris, "Dawes Review 5: Australian Aboriginal Astronomy and Navigation," *Publications of the Astronomical Society of Australia* 33 (2016): 16–17, https://doi.org/10.1017/pasa.2016.25. Hugh Cairns and Yidumduma Bill Harney, *Dark Sparklers: Yidumduma's Wardaman Aboriginal Astronomy: Night Skies, Northern Australia* (Merimbula, N.S.W.: H. C. Cairns, 2004). https://www.abc.net.au/news/2017-04-05/aboriginal-astronomy-basis-of-dreamtime-stories-stargazing/8413492.

12. Michael Tomasello, "Why Don't Apes Point?," in *Roots of Human Sociality: Culture, Cognition, and Interaction*, ed. N. J. Enfield and Stephen C. Levinson (London: Berg, 2006), 506–24; Tomasello, *Origins of Human Communication*; Ulf Liszkowski et al., "Twelve-Month-Olds Point to Share Attention and Interest," *Developmental Science* 7, no. 3 (June 2004): 297–307, https://doi.org/10.1111/j.1467-7687.2004.00349.x; Ulf Liszkowski, "Infant Pointing at Twelve Months: Communicative Goals, Motives, and Social-Cognitive Abilities," in *Roots of Human Sociality: Culture, Cognition, and Interaction*, ed. N. J. Enfield and Stephen C. Levinson (London: Berg, 2006), 153–178.

13. It may be that calling out the bird's name was an act of ratification and calibration in that moment. Anticipating that he would be able to report the bird sighting to others back in the villages, Baai calls out the bird's name to secure agreement among those present that what he saw was in fact a crested argus. When Kham did not respond to his saying *vung vaawq*, for example, by trying to correct him and suggest that it's actually a different bird, he thereby tacitly accepted that Baai was correct.

14. This said, people need to develop a sensitivity to *noticing* certain forms of prominence; the very fact of having a name for something is actually a force in motivating people to pay attention to certain distinctions. The anthropologist Robert Levy distinguished between *hypocognition* (ideas that are "culturally invisible") and *hypercognition* (ideas that are "discriminated"); Robert I. Levy, *Tahitians: Mind and Experience in the Society Islands*. Chicago: University of Chicago Press (1973).

15. Kemp, Xu, and Regier, "Semantic Typology and Efficient Communication," 112–114. They add: "This situation amounts to mind reading, and is of course impossible.

However, it is still useful conceptually, for it suggests that mind reading is the ideal to which language aspires but can never actually reach." I would, however, not say that mind reading would be aspired to at all. See Mark Dingemanse's essay on this question: https://aeon.co/essays/why-language-remains-the-most-flexible-brain-to-bra in-interface.

16. Also note that for many English speakers, *aunt* may refer to someone who isn't even kin, but a family friend.

17. Kri didn't always have these terms. And Old English in fact had a system that looks like what Kri has today. Old English: *fædera* (paternal uncle); *faþu* (paternal aunt); *ēam* (uncle, esp. maternal); *mōdrige* (aunt, esp. maternal). Data from https://www.ling.upenn.edu/~kurisuto/germanic/oe_bosworthtoller_about.html and https://thehousecarpenter.wordpress.com/2015/08/07/a-brief-history-of-english-kinship-terminology/.

18. Kemp, Xu, and Regier, "Semantic Typology and Efficient Communication," 111.

19. Kemp, Xu, and Regier, "Semantic Typology and Efficient Communication."

20. Actually it is not certain that "information is lost" when I use words like *aunt, nephew,* or *brother,* which leave information unspecified, such as whether the siblings implied in these relationships are older or younger. I will know if my own brother is older or younger than me, but I can talk about a friend's brother without knowing (or minding) if he is older or younger than the friend. And with uncles, we might not even know if they are older or younger than our parent. And we don't need to. So, (1) no information is lost and (2) the language is implicated in a piece of knowledge I mightn't have. But if we are speaking Kri, then I *must* know whether the uncle is older or younger. This is key: having the category in your language means you need to monitor for it and know things you otherwise wouldn't necessarily need to know. This is true, for example, for communities that use absolute frames of reference (North, South, East, West) more frequently than relative frames of reference (to the left, to the right) when talking about location (see Stephen C. Levinson, *Space in Language and Cognition: Explorations in Cognitive Diversity.* Cambridge: Cambridge University Press, 2003). Also note the distinction between parallel cousins (cousins whose sibling-parents are same sex, for example, the children of two brothers) and cross cousins (cousins whose sibling-parents are of the opposite sex). English speakers may be able to answer the question of whether a given cousin is cross or parallel, but they would not be able to do so until the concept was explained (and labeled), would not attach any significance to it, and could not imagine any significance. So, it is not clear that information is really "lost" in a system that has a single word for "cousin."

21. Kemp, Xu, and Regier, "Semantic Typology and Efficient Communication," 113.

22. Mark Dingemanse has published useful critique of the idea that mind-reading would make language obsolete: https://aeon.co/essays/why-language-remains-the-most-flexible-brain-to-brain-interface.

23. Kemp, Xu, and Regier, "Semantic Typology and Efficient Communication," 114.

24. Bodo Winter, Marcus Perlman, and Asifa Majid. 2018. "Vision Dominates in Perceptual Language: English Sensory Vocabulary Is Optimized for Usage," *Cognition* 179 (2018): 213–220, https://doi.org/10.1016/j.cognition.2018.05.008.

25. Franz Boas, "Introduction," in *Handbook of American Indian Languages*, edited by Franz Boas (1911; reprint, Lincoln: University of Nebraska Press, 1966), 26. See also Laura Martin, "Eskimo Words for Snow: A Case Study in the Genesis and Decay of an Anthropological Example," *American Anthropologist* 88, no. 2 (1986): 418–423.

26. Edward Sapir, *Selected Writings* (Berkeley: University of California Press, 1949), 90–91.

27. See N. J. Enfield, "Asymmetries in the System of Person Reference in Kri, a Language of Upland Laos," in *Signs of Deference, Signs of Demeanour: Interlocutor Reference and Self-Other Relations across Southeast Asian Speech Communities*, edited by Dwi Noverini Djenar and Jack Sidnell (Singapore: NUS Press, 2022).

28. This quote is from Lila Gleitman and Anna Papafragou, "Language and Thought," *Cambridge Handbook of Thinking and Reasoning*, 2005, 3. See also this: With language, "we can reliably cause precise new combinations of ideas to arise in each other's minds." Steven Pinker, *The Language Instinct: The New Science of Language and Mind* (London: Allen Lane, Penguin Press, 1994).

29. Reddy, "The Conduit Metaphor," 309.

30. Dor, *The Instruction of Imagination.*

31. Relates to "ineffability." See Levinson and Majid, "Differential Ineffability and the Senses"; Daniel L. Everett, *Dark Matter of the Mind: The Culturally Articulated Unconscious* (Chicago: Chicago University Press, 2017).

Chapter 7

1. From the chapter titled "The Gateway to Glory" in Eiji Yoshikawa's novel *Musashi*.

2. https://en.wikipedia.org/wiki/Gestalt_psychology Image from here: https://public -media.interaction-design.org/images/ux-daily/562e4c0c6a018.jpg

3. In Necker's words, "The rhomboid AX is drawn so that the solid angle A should be seen the nearest to the spectator, and the solid angle X the furthest from him, and that the face ACBD should be the foremost, while the face XDC is behind. But in looking repeatedly at the same figure, you will perceive that at times the apparent position of the rhomboid is so changed that the solid angle X will appear the nearest, and the solid angle A the furthest; and that tile face ACDB will recede behind the face XDC, which will come forward; which effect gives to the whole solid a quite contrary apparent inclination." L. A. Necker, "LXI. *Observations on Some Remarkable*

Optical Phænomena Seen in Switzerland; and on an Optical Phænomenon Which Occurs on Viewing a Figure of a Crystal or Geometrical Solid," The London, Edinburgh, and Dublin Philosophical Magazine and Journal of Science 1, no. 5 (1832): 336, https://doi.org/10.1080/14786443208647909.

4. See George Lakoff, *Women, Fire, and Dangerous Things: What Categories Reveal about the Mind* (Chicago: Chicago University Press, 1987), 132, for an analysis of this. Lakoff gives another example showing the same point: "You didn't *spare* me a trip to New York; you *deprived* me of one." I should clarify that just because the words *thrifty* and *stingy* can be used to describe the same person does not mean that the only difference between the words is the speaker's view of the situation as good (*thrifty*) versus bad (*stingy*). The two words could also differ in the details of what they describe. For example, being *stingy* might specifically mean not wanting to spend money *on others*, while *thrifty* might have no such implication (and indeed, this difference might explain why we regard *stingy* as a morally bad quality). See other work by Lakoff on the power of linguistic framing in political discourse: George Lakoff, *Don't Think of an Elephant! Know Your Values and Frame the Debate* (White River Junction, VT: Chelsea Green, 2004).

5. Craig R. M. McKenzie and Jonathan D. Nelson, "What a Speaker's Choice of Frame Reveals: Reference Points, Frame Selection, and Framing Effects," *Psychonomic Bulletin and Review* 10, no. 3 (2003): 598, https://doi.org/10.3758/BF03196520. See other work by McKenzie and colleagues: Craig R. M. McKenzie, "Framing Effects in Inference Tasks—and Why They Are Normatively Defensible," *Memory and Cognition* 32, no. 6 (2004): 874–885, https://doi.org/10.3758/BF03196866; Shlomi Sher and Craig R. M. McKenzie, "Framing Effects and Rationality," in *The Probabilistic Mind: Prospects for Bayesian Cognitive Science*, ed. Nick Chater and Mike Oaksford (Oxford: Oxford University Press, 2008).

6. From D. Wilson, *Presupposition and Non-Truth-Conditional Semantics* (New York: Academic Press, 1975). See also McKenzie and Nelson, "What a Speaker's Choice of Frame Reveals," on the relation between framing and points of reference.

7. From an experiment by psychologists Amos Tversky and Daniel Kahneman. A. Tversky and D. Kahneman, "The Framing of Decisions and the Psychology of Choice," *Science* 211, no. 4481 (1981): 453, https://doi.org/10.1126/science.7455683.

8. "The only difference between them is that the outcomes are described in problem 1 by the number of lives saved and in problem 2 by the number of lives lost." Tversky and Kahneman, 453.

9. Amos Tversky and Daniel Kahneman, "Rational Choice and the Framing of Decisions," *Journal of Business* 59, no. 4 (1986): S251.

10. Sniderman and Theriault (2004), cited in Dennis Chong and James N. Druckman, "Framing Theory," *Annual Review of Political Science* 10, no. 1 (2007): 104, https://doi.org/10.1146/annurev.polisci.10.072805.103054.

11. Further studies are referred to in Chong and Druckman, 108.

12. See Chong and Druckman, 111.

13. D. Gentner and D. R. Gentner, "Flowing Waters or Teeming Crowds: Mental Models of Electricity," in *Mental Models*, ed. D. Gentner and A. L. Stevens (Hillsdale, NJ: Erlbaum, 1983), 124.

14. Gentner and Gentner, 125–127.

15. George Lakoff and Mark Johnson, *Metaphors We Live By* (Chicago: University of Chicago Press, 1980), 4.

16. "We don't just *talk* about arguments in terms of war. We can actually win or lose arguments. We see the person we are arguing with as an opponent. We attack his positions and we defend our own. We gain and lose ground. We plan and use strategies. If we find a position indefensible, we can abandon it and take a new line of attack. Many of the things we *do* in arguing are partially structured by the concept of war. Though there is no physical battle, there is a verbal battle, and the structure of an argument—attack, defense, counterattack, etc.—reflects this. It is in this sense that the ARGUMENT IS WAR metaphor is one that we live by in this culture; it structures the actions we perform in arguing." Lakoff and Johnson, 4.

17. Douglas R. Hofstadter and Emmanuel Sander, *Surfaces and Essences: Analogy as the Fuel and Fire of Thinking* (New York: Basic Books, 2013), 15.

18. Kristen C. Elmore and Myra Luna-Lucero, "Light Bulbs or Seeds? How Metaphors for Ideas Influence Judgments about Genius," *Social Psychological and Personality Science* 8, no. 2 (2017): 200–208, https://doi.org/10.1177/1948550616667611.

19. From Elmore and Luna-Lucero, 202.

20. From a study by psychologist Stephen Flusberg and colleagues: Stephen J. Flusberg, Teenie Matlock, and Paul H. Thibodeau, "Metaphors for the War (or Race) against Climate Change," *Environmental Communication* 11, no. 6 (2017): 769–783, https://doi.org/10.1080/17524032.2017.1289111.

21. An alternative is to instruct those responsible for communications not to use the term *climate change* at all, as the Florida state government did from 2011 when Rick Scott became governor: https://www.miamiherald.com/news/state/florida/article12983720.html

22. This and the two questions are from Paul H. Thibodeau and Lera Boroditsky, "Metaphors We Think With: The Role of Metaphor in Reasoning," *PLoS One* 6, no. 2 (2011): e16782, https://doi.org/10.1371/journal.pone.0016782.

23. Work by psychologists Paul Thibodeau and Lera Boroditsky: Paul H. Thibodeau and Lera Boroditsky, "Natural Language Metaphors Covertly Influence Reasoning,"

ed. Attila Szolnoki, *PLoS One* 8, no. 1 (2013): e52961, https://doi.org/10.1371/journal .pone.0052961.

24. Responses were categorized as "'diagnose/treat/inoculate" if they suggested investigating the underlying cause of the problem (e.g., "look for the root cause") or suggested a particular social reform to treat or inoculate the community (e.g., fix the economy, improve education, provide health care). Responses were categorized as "capture/enforce/punish" if they focused on the police force or other methods of law enforcement (e.g., calling in the National Guard) or modifying the criminal justice system (e.g., instituting harsher penalties, building more jails). For brevity, I will refer to the diagnose/treat/inoculate category as "reform" and the capture/ enforce/punish category as "enforce."

25. Thibodeau and Boroditsky, "Natural Language Metaphors," 1.

26. See also Aaron M. Scherer, Laura D. Scherer, and Angela Fagerlin, "Getting Ahead of Illness: Using Metaphors to Influence Medical Decision Making," *Medical Decision Making* 35, no. 1 (2015): 37–45, https://doi.org/10.1177/0272989X14522547; Arie W. Kruglanski et al., "What Should This Fight Be Called? Metaphors of Counterterrorism and Their Implications," *Psychological Science in the Public Interest* 8, no. 3 (2007): 97–133, https://doi.org/10.1111/j.1539-6053.2008.00035.x.

27. A general conclusion is that metaphor is a kind of framing. See the discussions reviewed in Paul H. Thibodeau, Rose K. Hendricks, and Lera Boroditsky, "How Linguistic Metaphor Scaffolds Reasoning," *Trends in Cognitive Sciences* 21, no. 11 (2017): 852–863, https://doi.org/10.1016/j.tics.2017.07.001; Thibodeau and Boroditsky, "Natural Language Metaphors."

28. Chong and Druckman, "Framing Theory," 106: "A frame in a communication 'organizes everyday reality' (Tuchman 1978, p. 193) by providing 'meaning to an unfolding strip of events' (Gamson & Modigliani 1987, p. 143; 1989)."

29. G. E. Anscombe, Intention (Cambridge, MA: Harvard University Press, 1957). See also Jack Sidnell, "Action in Interaction Is Conduct under a Description." Language in Society 46, no. 3 (2017): 313–337. https://doi.org/10.1017/S0047404517000173.

30. J. B. Haviland, *Gossip, Reputation and Knowledge in Zinacantan* (Chicago: University of Chicago Press, 1977), 56.

31. Erving Goffman, *Frame Analysis: An Essay on the Organization of Experience* (New York: Harper, 1974), 1. Goffman is careful to make this about what we *claim* to have been doing, not what we were *actually* doing, if that could be determined independent of language at all. This is because the very act of putting it into words is an act of committing to a claim.

32. Haviland, *Gossip, Reputation*, 56, citing Karl R. Popper, *Objective Knowledge: An Evolutionary Approach* (Oxford Clarendon Press, 1972), 72.

Chapter 8

1. From an appearance by Russell on the BBC's *Brains Trust* radio program. A subsequent competition in the *New Statesman* magazine of May–June 1948 elicited a good list more from the British public, including:

  • I am righteously indignant, you are annoyed, he is making a fuss over nothing.
  • I have reconsidered the matter, you have changed your mind, he has gone back on his word.
  • I am Oxford, You are Cambridge, He is London School of Economics

Mathematician Eric Weinstein discusses the concept here: https://www.edge.org/response-detail/27181.

2. This claim should not be understood to apply universally, across all contexts or cultures. There are settings in which the proper thing to do is cast *the other* in better light than the self: in certain contexts, compliments are good and bragging is bad. See A. Pomerantz, "Compliment Responses: Notes on the Co-Operation of Multiple Constraints," in *Studies in the Organization of Conversational Interaction*, ed. J. Schenkein (New York: Academic Press, 1978), 79–112; A. Pomerantz, "Agreeing and Disagreeing with Assessments: Some Features of Preferred/Dispreferred Turn Shapes," in *Structures of Social Action*, ed. J. M. Atkinson and J. Heritage (Cambridge: Cambridge University Press, 1984), 57–101; A. Pomerantz, *Asking and Telling in Conversation* (New York: Oxford University Press, 2021); Danielle Pillet-Shore, "When to Make the Sensory Social: Registering in Face-to-Face Openings," *Symbolic Interaction*, March 27, 2020, https://doi.org/10.1002/symb.481.

3. "The Freeloading Term": Ralph H. Johnson and J. Anthony Blair, *Logical Self-Defense* (New York: International Debate Education Association, 2006), 160.

4. https://www.edge.org/response-detail/27181. See Frank I. Luntz, *Words That Work: It's Not What You Say, It's What People Hear* (New York: Hyperion, 2008), 164–166.

5. Accounting professor Kate Suslava looked at 78,000 conference calls and analyzed corporate euphemisms: https://www.abc.net.au/news/2019-05-24/kate-suslava-management-euphemisms-and-corporate-speak/11114992.

6. Risk analyst Nassim Taleb coined this term, referring to Ludwig Wittgenstein, *Philosophical Investigations* (New York: Macmillan, 1953), sec. 94

7. Wittgenstein, sec. 94.

8. Taleb on Twitter: "Wittgenstein's ruler: nerds use the ruler to measure the table; Fat Tonies (and real scientists) use the table to measure the ruler."

9. John Haviland, *Gossip, Reputation and Knowledge in Zinacantan* (Chicago: University of Chicago Press, 1977), 66.

10. See W. H. Guier and G. C. Weiffenbach, "Genesis of Satellite Navigation," *Johns Hopkins APL Technical Digest* 19, no. 1 (1997): 178–181. See also the discussion in

Steven Johnson, *Where Good Ideas Come From: The Natural History of Innovation* (New York: Riverhead Books, 2010).

11. In another example of Wittgenstein's ruler, I once downloaded a smartphone application that lets you point your phone camera at a flower or plant and the app will tell you what it is. I pointed it at a few plants that I did not recognize, and the app told me some species names. But I wondered whether the app was accurate. Was it giving us reliable measures? To find out, I looked for plants that I could identify myself and pointed the app at those to test whether it gave back accurate results. In those cases, the information given in the word for the plant was not new—I already knew the species—but given that I did not yet know or trust the app, the new information was about the accuracy of the app—again, using the table to measure the ruler. Depending on my prior knowledge or belief about the world, a measuring instrument—whether it is a smartphone app, a ruler, or a person describing something to you—may tell you something about either the world or itself. Usually it does both.

12. Irving B. Weiner, *Principles of Rorschach Interpretation* (London: Routledge, 2003).

13. Weiner, *Principles of Rorschach Interpretation*, 256.

14. Weiner, 332.

15. Weiner, 256.

16. Weiner, 256.

17. Weiner, 266.

18. www.theatlantic.com/technology/archive/2019/01/viral-clash-students-and-native-americans-explained/580906/.

19. www.theatlantic.com/ideas/archive/2019/01/media-must-learn-covington-catholic-story/581035/.

20. www.theatlantic.com/ideas/archive/2019/01/julie-irwin-zimmerman-i-failed-covington-catholic-test/580897/.

21. Edward S. Herman and Noam Chomsky, *Manufacturing Consent: The Political Economy of the Mass Media* (New York: Pantheon Books, 2002), lix.

22. Herman and Chomsky, xxix.

23. Linsey McGoey, *The Unknowers: How Strategic Ignorance Rules the World* (London: Zed Books, 2019), 73. A similar case is Saudi Arabia's declaration that "atheists are terrorists" and are thereby subject to the same lack of legal protections as terrorists: https://www.independent.co.uk/news/world/middle-east/saudi-arabia-declares-all-atheists-are-terrorists-in-new-law-to-crack-down-on-political-dissidents-9228389.html.

24. McGoey, 178.

25. See "The Use and Abuse of Language—Why the Unemployment Rate Is Not What It Seems," by business and economics reporter Gareth Hutchins: https://www.abc.net.au/news/2020-07-12/unemployment-figures-hard-to-interpret-because-of-definition/12446608.

26. See "The Use and Abuse of Language."

27. In 2020, the University of Melbourne was found to have committed wage theft by classifying tutorials as *practice classes* "to avoid paying staff the full rate, therefore reducing wages by up to a third": https://www.abc.net.au/news/2020-08-05/university-of-melbourne-exposed-in-decade-long-wage-theft-case/12519588.

28. https://www.washingtonpost.com/world/2020/02/28/coronavirus-live-updates/.

29. https://www.elle.com/culture/career-politics/a23550588/president-trump-female-reporter-press-conference/.

30. Daniel Dale, Twitter, @ddale8, October 2, 2018, https://twitter.com/ddale8/status/1046864215611465733.

31. https://apnews.com/8f899b0a97b441f5835f3f77c2f6d8c6/6-Palestinians-killed-by-Israel-fire-on-Gaza-border.

32. Tweet by Nima Shirazi, @WideAsleepNima, March 31, 2018, https://twitter.com/wideasleepnima/status/979749449672089600. The tweet continues: "Only one side fired ALL the bullets, ALL the mortar shells, ALL the tear gas. Only one side has ALL the tanks, ALL the members, ALL the drones."

33. Daniel Dor, *Intifada Hits the Headlines: How the Israeli Press Misreported the Outbreak of the Second Palestinian Uprising* (Bloomington: Indiana University Press, 2004).

34. Dor, 5.

35. Dor, 7–8.

36. https://www.thetimes.co.uk/article/schoolboys-died-in-cliff-fall-with-father-after-he-lost-faith-in-god-t8bnkt8r2

37. https://www.bbc.com/news/uk-england-london-48199547.

38. See Jane Gilmore, *Fixed It: Violence and the Representation of Women in the Media* (Australia: Viking, 2019).

39. http://janegilmore.com/fixedit-everything-in-this-headline-is-just-wrong/.

40. This was an informal direction, not a legal rule.

41. "'Oil' and 'Gas' Become Dirty Words in FTSE Rebranding," July 5, 2019: https://www.ft.com/content/74c1e548-9ccd-11e9-b8ce-8b459ed04726.

42. Bloomberg opinion columnist Liam Denning: https://www.bloomberg.com /opinion/articles/2019-09-30/ftse-russell-energy-oil-gas-name-change-is-a-pyrrhic -victory.

43. www.bloomberg.com/opinion/articles/2019-06-19/arch-coal-peabody-powder -river-venture-holds-lessons-for-frackers.

44. CNN, State of the Union, May 24, 2020.

45. https://www.huffingtonpost.com.au/entry/kevin-hasset-economy-human -capital-stock_n_5ecb395fc5b61967c333b309?ri18n=true.

46. @3_in_austin May 24, 2020.

47. https://reason.com/2019/04/22/conservative-twitter-pounces-on-obama-clinton -for-expressing-sympathy-for-easter-worshippers-killed-in-sri-lankan-attacks/.

48. According to journalist Barbara Boland, such language is a politically motivated denial of a worldwide "persecution of Christians." https://cnsnews.com/news/article /barbara-boland/pew-study-christians-are-world-s-most-oppressed-religious-group; https://www.theamericanconservative.com/articles/easter-worshippers-and-the-lefts -allergy-to-language/. At the same time, others have pointed out that most victims of Islamist violence are Muslims.

49. A problem is that these principles are seldom applied consistently. In relation to the Sri Lankan bombings, Trump's reaction on Twitter didn't use the term "Easter worshippers" and did not mention Christians specifically. I'm not aware of any commentators referring to this as anti-Christian.

50. Actually, it's not hard to imagine an uncle having his feelings hurt by this. See Tanya Stivers, Alternative Recognitionals in Person Reference," in *Person Reference in Interaction*, ed. N. J. Enfield and Tanya Stivers (Cambridge: Cambridge University Press, 2007); https://doi.org/10.1017/CBO9780511486746.005 on the difference between *my mom's sister* versus *my aunt*.

51. https://www.crikey.com.au/2019/01/17/australian-journalism-african-appearance/.

52. https://www.aljazeera.com/programmes/101east/2019/01/australia-african -gangs-190109093042022.html.

53. https://www.abc.net.au/news/2018-08-01/media-outlets-racialising-african -gang-problem-melbourne/10060834.

54. Amir Vera and Laura Ly, "White Woman Who Called Police on a Black Man Bird-Watching in Central Park Has Been Fired," CNN.com, May 26, 2020, https:// edition.cnn.com/2020/05/26/us/central-park-video-dog-video-african-american -trnd/index.html.

55. *Sydney Morning Herald*, May 27, 2020.

56. https://www.latimes.com/opinion/story/2020-06-03/svitlana-flom-amy-cooper
-george-floyd-police-racism.

57. Words can, of course, also narrow in their reference. Modern English *deer* is
from Old English *dēor* (animal).

58. Nick Haslam, "Concept Creep: Psychology's Expanding Concepts of Harm and
Pathology," *Psychological Inquiry* 27, no. 1 (2016): 1, https://doi.org/10.1080/1047840X
.2016.1082418.

59. See J. J. Degenaar, "The Concept of Violence," *Politikon* 7, no. 1 (1980): 14–27,
https://doi.org/10.1080/02589348008704765.

60. Johan Galtung, "Violence, Peace, and Peace Research," *Journal of Peace Research* 6,
no. 3 (1969): 168, https://doi.org/10.1177/002234336900600301.

61. Galtung, 183, states that structural violence, in his sense, is "also referred to as
'social injustice.'"

62. Galtung, 183.

63. See, for example, Joseph Betz, "Violence: Garver's Definition and a Deweyan Correction," *Ethics* 87, no. 4 (1977): 339–351, https://doi.org/10.1086/292046. Newton
Garver, "What Violence Is," *Nation*, June 24, 1968, 817–22. The article has appeared
in numerous anthologies, including Richard A. Wasserstrom, *Today's Moral Problems*
(Riverside, NJ: Macmillan, 1975).

64. Galtung, "Violence, Peace, and Peace Research."

65. Lafayette, cited by Degenaar, "The Concept of Violence," 19.

66. Garver, cited by Degenaar, 20.

67. Davies, cited by Degenaar, 20.

68. The philosopher Joseph Betz argues that changing the meaning of this word had
unwanted consequences:

> If violence is violating a person or a person's rights, then every social wrong is a violent one,
> every crime against another a violent crime, every sin against one's neighbor an act of violence.
> If violence is whatever violates a person and his rights of body, dignity, or autonomy, then lying
> to or about another, embezzling, locking one out of his house, insulting, and gossiping are all
> violent acts. . . . But this enlargement of the extension of the term comes at considerable cost,
> for there is simply no extension left for the term "nonviolent social wrong" in Garver's account.
> If what he says is true, our legislatures, judges, and juries are incorrect in punishing what they
> believe are violent crimes more severely than nonviolent ones. (Betz, "Violence," 341)

69. Degenaar suggested that "the problem of the justification of political violence
should not be formulated in terms of legitimacy but in terms of morality":

> This means that the use of extreme force by the state can be legitimate, but if the laws them-
> selves are violent, i.e., unjust and therefore destructive of the freedom of the citizens, the

violence used by the state is unjustified. This, precisely, is the claim made by revolutionary movements who also use the dramatic metaphorical description of "structural violence." It is said that the state cannot justify its use of violence because the laws of the state violate moral rights. The revolutionary movement claims that it can justify its own violence because this violence is primarily counter-violence: it opposes the violence of an unjust system; it works towards a just system—in this sense the end justifies the means; and its own violence is constructive rather than destructive, progressive rather than entrenched in unjust laws. It is only constructive violence that can liberate man from structural violence that perpetuates itself. (Degenaar, "The Concept of Violence," 20–21).

70. Frantz Fanon, *The Wretched of the Earth* (New York: Grove, 1963), 94.

71. 1964: https://www.blackpast.org/african-american-history/speeches-african-americ an-history/1964-malcolm-x-s-speech-founding-rally-organization-afro-american-unity/.

72. *When is speech violence?* www.nytimes.com/2017/07/14/opinion/sunday/when-is -speech-violence.html?_r=1. See also this: https://daily.jstor.org/wittgenstein-whether -speech-violence/.

73. Similarly, the linguist George Lakoff argues, "Like violence, hate speech can also be a physical imposition on the freedom of others. That is because language has a psychological effect imposed physically—on the neural system, with long-term crippling effects." Lakoff says that because language "neurally activates thought," it can therefore change people's brains. But this is obviously true of any communicative act, not just "hate speech." Communication can't work if it doesn't "neurally activate thought." The question here seems to be whether there is "harm." Lakoff's view on this is particularly stark: "This internal harm can be even more severe than an attack with a fist. It imposes on the freedom to think and therefore act free of fear, threats, and distrust. It imposes on one's ability to think and act like a fully free citizen for a long time." Hence, Lakoff says, if something is hate speech, then it isn't free speech. But how shall we define hate speech? It's not defined by physical effects on the brain at all. Those things may be involved, but the usual definition brings in two factors that are ultimately subjective and appeal to social judgments. The first is whether a certain statement is literally harmful or merely unwelcome. Both may result in stressful neural effects, but typically only an observer's subjective judgment will decide. In this connection, Jonathan Haidt and Greg Lukianoff are concerned about the claim that speech is violence when it "is deemed by members of an identity group to be critical of the group, or speech that is otherwise upsetting to members of the group." https://www.theatlantic.com/education/archive/2017/07/why-its-a-bad-idea-to-tell -students-words-are-violence/533970/. The second is whether the perceived harm has been perpetrated in a downward direction in terms of the social power relations involved (i.e., the view that harmful words from the powerful about the powerless can be hate speech, but not the other way around). October 29, 2018: https://medium .com/@GeorgeLakoff/why-hate-speech-is-not-free-speech-428497fa616c

74. Haidt and Lukianoff: https://www.theatlantic.com/education/archive/2017/07 /why-its-a-bad-idea-to-tell-students-words-are-violence/533970/.

75. As an example, consider the remarks of Desmond Meagley, reporter and illustrator for Youth Radio, in the wake of violent protests against a scheduled public talk at the University of California at Berkeley: "I put my safety and my freedom on the line because letting Yiannopoulos speak was more terrifying to me than potential injury or arrest." https://www.dailycal.org/2017/02/07/condemning-protesters -condoning-hate-speech/.

76. Haidt and Lukianoff argue that Feldman Barrett is right on two key points. The first is that speech can cause stress, and stress—if chronic—can cause "physical damage." But, they argue, Barrett is mistaken in making the following inference: "If words can cause stress, and if prolonged stress can cause physical harm, then it seems that speech—at least certain types of speech—can be a form of violence." They say that the conclusion isn't that words can be violent but that words can cause physical harm. They suggest running the logic on other things. For example, giving students lots of homework can be a source of chronic stress. But can we—or should we—say that giving homework to students is violence? They write: "This is why the idea that speech is violence is so dangerous. It tells the members of a generation already beset by anxiety and depression that the world is a far more violent and threatening place than it really is. It tells them that words, ideas, and speakers can literally kill them. Even worse: At a time of rapidly rising political polarization in America, it helps a small subset of that generation justify political violence. A few days after the riot that shut down Yiannopoulos's talk at Berkeley, in which many people were punched, beaten, and pepper-sprayed by masked protesters, the main campus newspaper ran five op-ed essays by students and recent alumni under the series title, 'Violence as Self Defense.' One excerpt: 'Asking people to maintain peaceful dialogue with those who legitimately do not think their lives matter is a violent act.'"

77. https://quillette.com/2019/07/20/how-the-left-turned-words-into-violence-and -violence-into-justice/.

78. Nisa Dang, UC Berkeley alumna: https://www.dailycal.org/2017/02/07/check-pri vilege-speaking-protests/; https://www.dailycal.org/2017/02/07/violence-self-defense/.

79. https://www.poetryfoundation.org/foundation/press/153832/a-message-to-our -community-contributors. See here for more on the matter: https://www.nytimes .com/2020/06/09/books/poetry-foundation-black-lives-matter.html; https://www.npr .org/sections/live-updates-protests-for-racial-justice/2020/06/10/874324678/poetry -foundation-leaders-resign-after-criticism-of-their-response-to-protests.

80. https://docs.google.com/forms/d/e/1FAIpQLSf4u5Ns8Blz0gutuanOHF6I026XiO dE9lT36HQtg5pDKeT5uQ/viewform.

81. https://www.poetryfoundation.org/foundation/press/153859/announcement-of -leadership-changes.

82. https://medium.com/s/story/data-violence-and-how-bad-engineering-choices
-can-damage-society-39e44150e1d4.

83. https://www.usatoday.com/story/tech/2015/07/01/google-apologizes-after
-photos-identify-black-people-as-gorillas/29567465/.

84. https://www.theguardian.com/technology/2015/feb/16/facebook-real-name
-policy-suspends-native-americans.

85. https://medium.com/s/story/data-violence-and-how-bad-engineering-choices
-can-damage-society-39e44150e1d4.

86. Kristie Dotson, "Tracking Epistemic Violence, Tracking Practices of Silencing,"
Hypatia: A Journal of Feminist Philosophy 26, no. 2 (2011): 236–257, https://doi.org/10
.1111/j.1527-2001.2011.01177.x.

87. https://www.independent.co.uk/news/world/middle-east/saudi-arabia-declares
-all-atheists-are-terrorists-in-new-law-to-crack-down-on-political-dissidents-9228389
.html.

88. https://www.theglobeandmail.com/opinion/article-incel-related-violence-is
-terrorism-and-the-world-should-start/. See Bruce Hoffman, Jacob Ware, and Ezra
Shapiro, "Assessing the Threat of Incel Violence," *Studies in Conflict and Terrorism* 43,
no. 7 (2020): 565–587, https://doi.org/10.1080/1057610X.2020.1751459.

89. Note, though, that it's often *not* a matter for debate. Someone's dog could also
be called a pug, a pet, or an animal. In some cases, we can imagine one of these uses
being grounds for sanction (e.g., if someone says, "Please do not bring your animal
into this store") but in many other cases not.

90. This phrasing is from Hugo Mercier, *Not Born Yesterday: The Science of Who We
Trust and What We Believe* (Princeton, NJ: Princeton University Press, 2020).

Chapter 9

1. "Kurt Vonnegut on the Shapes of Stories," YouTube video, https://youtu.be/oP3c
1h8v2ZQ?t=82.

2. For example, one highly developed realm of storytelling is the Hollywood screenplay. In a classical Hollywood screenplay, there is a "minimum of seven steps in its
growth from beginning to end: 1. Weakness and need; 2. Desire; 3. Opponent; 4.
Plan; 5. Battle; 6. Self-revelation; 7. New equilibrium." See John Truby, *The Anatomy
of Story* (New York: Farrar, Straus and Giroux, 2007), 39–51. US box office revenue
alone averaged more than $10 billion per year over the previous decade. The reason
people keep coming back to movies? Story. Spectacle is nice, but movie makers agree
that spectacle is nothing without a compelling story. Close analysis of commercially

successful Hollywood screenplays reveals that they not only tend to follow simple formulas (character + predicament + attempted extrication); they also include further refinements, which indeed are shared with forms of literature, written and spoken, around the world over millennia. Once you know the formula, you see it in every Hollywood movie.

3. From Stig Broström, "Children Tell Stories," *European Early Childhood Education Research Journal* 10, no. 1 (2002): 85–97, https://doi.org/10.1080/1350293028520 8861.

4. Jonathan Gottschall, *The Storytelling Animal: How Stories Make Us Human* (Boston: Houghton Mifflin Harcourt, 2012), 52, offers the following formula defining the core elements of any story: *Story = Character + predicament + attempted extrication*.

5. This example was kindly provided to me by Mark Dingemanse, who recorded and translated the story.

6. This was recorded and translated by Mark Dingemanse. I have made some light edits for readability here. The Siwu original text, provided by Mark Dingemanse is as follows: iyiɔ ìwɛ̃ àbɔɔmɛ̀ ní ŋto lo kɛlɛ̀ sia—ìbɛrɛ itì ɔbe. ngbɔ ɔ́ mìminisó kùgɔ́ ngbe. ɔsu itì ɔsɛ̀ ɔ̃̀ù pia ì ɛ̀ɛ—akpe amɛ ŋ́gbegɔ́ ibɛrɛ itì ɔbe mmɔ̀. lo fè, lo ba laa yaū í kúbènà iso isɛ. gɔ́ ló nyà lo nyà—ngbɔ ló mɔɛ̃ itì lo su kugɔ́ ngbe nɛ nɛ ló ki lo fè nɛ. lofe nɛ lo sɛ̀ laa pɛ lo fīnīkī lo su kuɖeára lo sɔ̃ kubɛrɛ. pɔkɔsɔɔ. lo ɖeū ípɛ́bàbà, ūmɛ lèi sɛ lò sú kúpɛ́ ɔbe lo ɖoè ayɛ̀ɛ—ipɛ bàbà. wūi ǔ lo pia akpe amɛ kpàrà. kùgɔ́ ɔ́ mìmìnì i kat̄ó ngbɔ ɛ̀mɛ̀ ɔ́kpɛ̃̀—ɔkpɛ̃—ɔkpɛ̃ ɔkurisi. ɔ sāráā̃. nɛ ló tsuara ū ɔ̀ɖeɖe ɔ̀ɖoè nɛ.

7. William Labov, *Language in the Inner City: Studies in the Black English Vernacular* (Philadelphia: University of Pennsylvania Press, 1972), 358–359. In his research on vernacular language in southwest Harlem, linguist William Labov simply asked people whether they'd had dangerous experiences, and his respondents would deliver well-structured stories off the cuff.

8. Obviously stories are also built out of much more than just words—gestures, facial expressions, voices, images. But without the linguistic basis for building the ideas that drive a story, none of those things would carry the meaning they do in narrative.

9. See N. J. Enfield, *The Anatomy of Meaning: Speech, Gesture, and Composite Utterances* (Cambridge,: Cambridge University Press, 2009).

10. See this useful overview by Manvir Singh: https://aeon.co/essays/what-makes -the-sympathetic-plot-a-universal-story-type.

11. This is from a comparison of more than a thousand folk tales from Africa, East and Southeast Asia, indigenous Australia, indigenous Americas, the Pacific, Europe and the Middle East, by a team led by literary theorist Jonathan Gottschall. Jonathan Gottschall, "The Heroine with a Thousand Faces: Universal Trends in the Charac-terization of Female Folk Tale Protagonists," *Evolutionary Psychology* 3, no. 1 (2005):

93, https://doi.org/10.1177/147470490500300108. Most of the protagonists (three-quarters) are unmarried at the beginning of the story, and of those, two-thirds are married by the end.

12. Though with a major difference between men at 71 percent and women at 50 percent being described in this way. Gottschall, "The Heroine with a Thousand Faces." See also J. Gottschall et al., "World Literature's Missing Daughters," paper presented at the annual meeting of the North Eastern Modern Language Association, Pittsburgh, 2004. Gottschall, "The Heroine with a Thousand Faces." also found that around three-quarters of the main characters in folk tales are men.

13. Focusing on female protagonists, Gottschall's team found that if there was any mention of a female protagonist's appearance, "they were almost universally described as physically attractive'" (97 percent of all cases: Gottschall, "The Heroine with a Thousand Faces," 94). They summarized their discovery of a universal profile of a heroine in folk tales as follows: "The vast majority of female protagonists are unmarried women at peak reproductive age. When physical descriptions are provided, they are almost universally beautiful, and this beauty is often stressed repetitively. In comparison to her male counterpart, the female protagonist places greater emphasis on a potential mate's kindness and control of social and material resources, and less emphasis on physical attractiveness. She achieves her goals through different means than the male protagonist: she is less likely to actively pursue her goals and she is less likely to achieve them in ways requiring conspicuous courage or physical heroism. She is solicitous of her family's well being, devoting much energy to promote the welfare of her close kin."

14. Truby, *The Anatomy of Story*, 40.

15. Joseph Campbell, *The Hero with a Thousand Faces* (Princeton: Princeton University Press, 1949), 18.

16. British journalist Christopher Booker reviewed 450 stories, spanning movies, plays, novels, ancient epics, and fairy tales. He organized them into his book *The Seven Basic Plots* (London; New York: Continuum, 2004):

1. Overcoming the monster (*Dracula; Theseus and the Minotaur*)
2. Rags to riches (*Aladdin and the Enchanted Lamp; The Ugly Duckling*)
3. The quest (*Aeneid; The Lord of the Rings*)
4. Voyage and return (*Alice in Wonderland; Goldilocks and the Three Bears*)
5. Comedy/romance (*Emma; Some Like It Hot*)
6. Tragedy (*Faust; Romeo and Juliet*)
7. Rebirth (*Beauty and the Beast; The Frog Prince*)

On pp. 17–18 he outlines what they all have in common: setting; a character we can identify with; and something happening that presents a challenge to the main character, likely with opponents, and that will eventually transform their lives, after they have grappled with the conflict that their challenge presents. It all ends with resolution.

17. I draw here on Manvir Singh's useful summary: https://aeon.co/essays/what-makes -the-sympathetic-plot-a-universal-story-type

18. In visual arts such as movies and theater, much of a story can be conveyed not by language but by the depiction of actions and events. In some cases, such as silent or modern movies such as *A Quiet Place* and *All Is Lost*, it appears that a story may be told without any use of language at all. The same might even be said about cave paintings (though that would be under a generous definition of "story"). But I want to argue that all of these kinds of story would be impossible without drawing on the essentially linguistic infrastructure in which a speaker draws a listener's attention to a course of events for a communicative purpose.

19. See psychologist Richard Gerrig's 1993 book *Experiencing Narrative Worlds* (Boulder, CO: Westview Press, 1993). A 2014 meta-analysis counted 279 publications on the topic of narrative transportation: Tom van Laer et al., "The Extended Transportation-Imagery Model: A Meta-Analysis of the Antecedents and Consequences of Consumers' Narrative Transportation," *Journal of Consumer Research* 40, no. 5 (2014): 797–817, https://doi.org/10.1086/673383.

20. Raymond A. Mar, "The Neural Bases of Social Cognition and Story Comprehension," *Annual Review of Psychology* 62, no. 1 (2011): 103–134, https://doi.org/10.1146 /annurev-psych-120709-145406.

21. Eiluned Pearce et al., "Variation in the β-Endorphin, Oxytocin, and Dopamine Receptor Genes Is Associated with Different Dimensions of Human Sociality," *Proceedings of the National Academy of Sciences* 114, no. 20 (2017): 5300–5305, https:// doi.org/10.1073/pnas.1700712114. See: https://www.inc.com/jessica-stillman/here-s -what-great-storytelling-does-to-your-brain.html.

22. "Zak found that during the rising action people release cortisol, at the climax people release oxytocin if they feel empathy with the main character, and if there's a happy ending people release dopamine. Interest can be maintained by cycling through these story pieces and keeping the brain chemistry going," writes Weinshenk: https://www.blog.theteamw.com/2016/05/11/the-next-100-things-you-need-to -know-about-people-114-great-stories-release-brain-chemicals/ and https://www.meet cortex.com/blog/why-we-empathize-with-characters.

23. See Paul J Zak, "Why Inspiring Stories Make Us React: The Neuroscience of Narrative," *Cerebrum: The Dana Forum on Brain Science* 2 (2015): 1–13; Joseph Feher, "Hypothalamus and Pituitary Gland," in *Quantitative Human Physiology* (Amsterdam: Elsevier, 2017), 870–882, https://doi.org/10.1016/B978-0-12-800883-6.00085-9; Heon-Jin Lee et al., "Oxytocin: The Great Facilitator of Life," *Progress in Neurobiology*, April 10, 2009, https://doi.org/10.1016/j.pneurobio.2009.04.001.

24. Keith M. Kendrick, "The Neurobiology of Social Bonds," *Journal of Neuroendocrinology* 16, no. 12 (2004): 1007–1008, https://doi.org/10.1111/j.1365-2826.2004.01262.x.

25. Feng Sheng et al., "Oxytocin Modulates the Racial Bias in Neural Responses to Others' Suffering," *Biological Psychology* 92, no. 2 (2013): 380–386, https://doi.org/10.1016/j.biopsycho.2012.11.018; S. Shalvi and C. K. W. De Dreu, "Oxytocin Promotes Group-Serving Dishonesty," *Proceedings of the National Academy of Sciences* 111, no. 15 (2014): 5503–5507, https://doi.org/10.1073/pnas.1400724111.

26. https://greatergood.berkeley.edu/article/item/how_stories_change_brain.

27. Jorge A. Barraza and Paul J. Zak, "Empathy toward Strangers Triggers Oxytocin Release and Subsequent Generosity," *Annals of the New York Academy of Sciences* 1167, no. 1 (2009): 182–189, https://doi.org/10.1111/j.1749-6632.2009.04504.x.

28. G. B. Stefano et al., "Endogenous Morphine: Up-to-Date Review 2011," *Folia Biologica* 58, no. 2 (2012): 49–56.

29. Felix Budelmann et al., "Cognition, Endorphins, and the Literary Response to Tragedy," *Cambridge Quarterly* 46, no. 3 (2017): 229–250, https://doi.org/10.1093/camqtly/bfx016.

30. From Garver, "What Violence Is" (1970), cited in Degenaar, "The Concept of Violence," 18.

31. Kathleen M. Dillon, Brian Minchoff, and Katherine H. Baker, "Positive Emotional States and Enhancement of the Immune System," *International Journal of Psychiatry in Medicine* 15, no. 1 (1985–1986): 13–18, https://doi.org/10.2190/R7FD-URN9-PQ7F-A6J7.

32. Dolf Zillmann et al., "Does Humor Facilitate Coping with Physical Discomfort?" *Motivation and Emotion* 17, no. 1 (1993): 1–21, https://doi.org/10.1007/BF00995204.

33. Zillmann et al., 8–9.

34. Zillmann et al., 17.

35. Zillmann et al., 18–19.

36. R. I. M. Dunbar et al., "Emotional Arousal When Watching Drama Increases Pain Threshold and Social Bonding," *Royal Society Open Science* 3, no. 9 (2016): 160288, https://doi.org/10.1098/rsos.160288.

37. Budelmann et al., "Cognition, Endorphins, and the Literary Response to Tragedy," 231.

38. Budelmann et al., 236.

39. Budelmann et al., 236.

40. A. J. Machin and R. I. M Dunbar, "The Brain Opioid Theory of Social Attachment: A Review of the Evidence," *Behavior* 148, no. 9–10 (2011): 985–1025, https://doi.org/10.1163/000579511X596624.

41. Emma E. A. Cohen et al., "Rowers' High: Behavioral Synchrony Is Correlated with Elevated Pain Thresholds," *Biology Letters* 6, no. 1 (2010): 106–108, https://doi .org/10.1098/rsbl.2009.0670. See also Philip J. Sullivan, Kate Rickers, and Kimberley L. Gammage, "The Effect of Different Phases of Synchrony on Pain Threshold," *Group Dynamics: Theory, Research, and Practice* 18, no. 2 (2014): 122–128, https://doi .org/10.1037/gdn0000001.

42. Cf. Machin and Dunbar, "The Brain Opioid Theory," and Lauri Nummenmaa et al., "Adult Attachment Style Is Associated with Cerebral μ-Opioid Receptor Availability in Humans: Opioids and Attachment," *Human Brain Mapping* 36, no. 9 (2015): 3621–3628, https://doi.org/10.1002/hbm.22866. Endorphins have accordingly been shown to be elicited by a number of social activities, such as singing, making music, dancing, and laughing. See R. I. M. Dunbar et al., "Social Laughter Is Correlated with an Elevated Pain Threshold," *Proceedings of the Royal Society B: Biological Sciences* 279, no. 1731 (2012): 1161–1167, https://doi.org/10.1098/rspb.2011.1373. R. I. M. Dunbar et al., "Performance of Music Elevates Pain Threshold and Positive Affect: Implications for the Evolutionary Function of Music," *Evolutionary Psychology* 10, no. 4 (2012): 688–702, https://doi.org/10.1177/147470491201000403; Eiluned Pearce, Jacques Launay, and Robin I. M. Dunbar, "The Ice-Breaker Effect: Singing Mediates Fast Social Bonding," *Royal Society Open Science* 2, no. 10 (2015): 150221, https://doi.org/10.1098/rsos .150221; Daniel Weinstein et al., "Singing and Social Bonding: Changes in Connectivity and Pain Threshold as a Function of Group Size," *Evolution and Human Behavior* 37, no. 2 (2016): 152–158, https://doi.org/10.1016/j.evolhumbehav.2015.10.002. Budelmann et al., "Cognition, Endorphins, and the Literary Response to Tragedy."

43. Budelmann et al., "Cognition, Endorphins, and the Literary Response to Tragedy," 238.

44. Budelmann et al., 238.

45. I have emphasized that stories are made out of language, and this is most obviously true when we pick up a book, which may contain nothing but words. But stories can also feature visual elements such as the gestures, facial expressions, and enactments produced when narrating events in face-to-face interaction. And in movies, storytelling is heavily dependent—sometimes almost entirely dependent—on the visual construction of events. But even in the extreme case of a silent movie, any story is ultimately grounded in language. Or perhaps more accurately, there is ultimately no storytelling without language. This is because a story will be impossible without the cooperative infrastructure for information exchange that underlies the capacity for language itself. If a silent film or a piece of art tells a story, it is because we understand it to be an expression of some communicative intent, produced by one person to be interpreted by another.

46. Budelmann et al., "Cognition, Endorphins, and the Literary Response to Tragedy," 238.

47. Michelle Scalise Sugiyama, "On the Origins of Narrative: Storyteller Bias as a Fitness-Enhancing Strategy," *Human Nature* 7, no. 4 (1996): 403–425, https://doi.org/10.1007/BF02732901; Michelle Scalise Sugiyama, "Food, Foragers, and Folklore: The Role of Narrative in Human Subsistence," *Evolution and Human Behavior* 22, no. 4 2001): 221–240, https://doi.org/10.1016/S1090-5138(01)00063-0; Michelle Scalise Sugiyama, "Reverse-Engineering Narrative: Evidence of Special Design," in *The Literary Animal*, ed. J. Gottschall and D. S. Wilson (Evanston, IL: Northwestern University Press, 2005), 177–196; Michelle Scalise Sugiyama, "Oral Storytelling as Evidence of Pedagogy in Forager Societies," *Frontiers in Psychology* 8 (2017), https://doi.org/10.3389/fpsyg.2017.00471.

48. For a rich discussion, see Lucas M. Bietti, Ottilie Tilston, and Adrian Bangerter, "Storytelling as Adaptive Collective Sensemaking," *Topics in Cognitive Science* 11, no. 4 (2019): 710–732, https://doi.org/10.1111/tops.12358. "Three main accounts of the adaptive function of storytelling include (a) manipulating the behavior of the audience to enhance the fitness of the narrator, (b) transmitting survival-relevant information while avoiding the costs involved in the first-hand acquisition of that information, and (c) maintaining social bonds or group-level cooperation." "The specific adaptive value of storytelling lies in making sense of non-routine, uncertain, or novel situations, thereby enabling the collaborative development of previously acquired skills and knowledge, but also promoting social cohesion by strengthening intragroup identity and clarifying intergroup relations" (710). See also Daniel Smith et al., "Cooperation and the Evolution of Hunter-Gatherer Storytelling," *Nature Communications* 8, no. 1 (2017), https://doi.org/10.1038/s41467-017-02036-8.

49. Hugo Mercier, *The Science of Who We Trust and What We Believe* (Princeton: Princeton University Press, 2020) makes this proposal about language in general.

Chapter 10

1. Campbell, *The Hero with a Thousand Faces* (Princeton, NJ: Princeton University Press, 1949), 28.

2. Campbell, 362.

3. In the story, Michael is Li's boyfriend, and Shiloh is Jo's family dog.

4. Robin I. M. Dunbar, "Coevolution of Neocortical Size, Group Size, and Language in Humans," *Behavioral and Brain Sciences* 16 (1993): 681–735; R. I. M. Dunbar, "Gossip in Evolutionary Perspective," *Review of General Psychology* 8, no. 2 (2004): 100–110, https://doi.org/10.1037/1089-2680.8.2.100.

5. Dunbar, "Gossip," 103.

6. Haviland, *Gossip, Reputation and Knowledge in Zinacantan* (Chicago: University of Chicago Press, 1977), 56.

7. Haviland, 61–63.

8. Peter L. Tyack, "Dolphins Communicate about Individual-Specific Social Relationships," in *Animal Social Complexity: Intelligence, Culture, and Individualized Societies*, ed. Frans B. M. de Waal and Peter L. Tyack (Cambridge, MA: Harvard University Press, 2003), 343.

9. Randall S. Wells, "Dolphin Social Complexity: Lessons from Long-Term Study and Life-History," in *Animal Social Complexity: Intelligence, Culture, and Individualized Societies*, ed. Frans B. M. de Waal and Peter L. Tyack (Cambridge, MA: Harvard University Press, 2003), 49.

10. This doesn't mean that he believes the position; it's that he's committing to it publicly. We can and do engage in "preference falsification." Timur Kuran, *Private Truths, Public Lies: The Social Consequences of Preference Falsification* (Cambridge, MA: Harvard University Press, 1997).

11. See Ibrahim Ag Youssouf, Allen D. Grimshaw, and Charles S. Bird, "Greetings in the Desert," *American Ethnologist* 3, no. 4 (1976): 797–824, https://doi.org/10.1525/ae.1976.3.4.02a00140; Adam Kendon, *Conducting Interaction: Patterns of Behavior in Focused Encounters* (Cambridge: Cambridge University Press, 1990).

12. Danielle Pillet-Shore, "Greeting: Displaying Stance Through Prosodic Recipient Design," *Research on Language and Social Interaction* 45, no. 4 (2012): 375–398, https://doi.org/10.1080/08351813.2012.724994.

13. Alan Cruttenden, *Gimson's Pronunciation of English*, 8th ed. (London: Routledge, 2014), 54.

14. Samuel Gaertner and Leonard Bickman, "Effects of Race on the Elicitation of Helping Behavior: The Wrong Number Technique," *Journal of Personality and Social Psychology* 20, no. 2 (1971): 218–222, https://doi.org/10.1037/h0031681. See also Mary B. Harris and Hortensia Baudin, "The Language of Altruism: The Effects of Language, Dress, and Ethnic Group," *Journal of Social Psychology* 91, no. 1 (1973): 37–41, https://doi.org/10.1080/00224545.1973.9922643; Roy E. Feldman, "Response to Compatriot and Foreigner Who Seek Assistance," *Journal of Personality and Social Psychology* 10, no. 3 (1968): 202–214, https://doi.org/10.1037/h0026567.

15. On the role of language in tag-based cooperation, see Emma Cohen, "The Evolution of Tag-Based Cooperation in Humans: The Case for Accent," *Current Anthropology* 53, no. 5 (2012): 588–616.

16. This model has been developed by evolutionary psychologists R. A. Hill and Robin Dunbar: "Social Network Size in Humans," *Human Nature* 14 (2003): 68. Note that they also discuss groupings at higher levels than this.

17. While the idea of "Dunbar's number" is widely accepted, it has also been critiqued; See, for example, P. Lindenfors, A. Wartel, and J. Lind "'Dunbar's number' deconstructed," *Biology Letters* 17 (2021): 1–4, https://doi.org/10.1098/rsbl.2021.0158.

18. Dunbar, "Coevolution of Neocortical Size, Group Size, and Language in Humans"; Anita Pomerantz and Jenny Mandelbaum, "Conversation Analytic Approaches to the Relevance and Uses of Relationship Categories in Interaction," in *Handbook of Language and Social Interaction*, ed. Kristine L. Fitch and Robert E. Sanders (Mahwah, NJ: Erlbaum, 2005), 160; N. J. Enfield, *Relationship Thinking: Agency, Enchrony, and Human Sociality* (Oxford: Oxford University Press, 2013).

19. Paul Drew and K. Chilton, "Calling Just to Keep in Touch: Regular and Habitualised Telephone Calls as an Environment for Small Talk," in *Small Talk*, ed. J. Coupland (Harlow: Pearson Education, 2000), 137–162; Jody D. Morrison, "Enacting Involvement: Some Conversational Practices for Being in Relationship" (PhD diss., Temple University, 1997).

20. Gail Jefferson and J. R. E. Lee, "End of Grant Report to the British SSRC on the Analysis of Conversations in Which 'Troubles' and 'Anxieties' Are Expressed," ref. HR 4805/2, 1980.

21. Drew and Chilton, "Calling Just to Keep in Touch," 138.

22. From Drew and Chilton.

23. The anthropologist Bronislaw Malinowski termed this "phatic communion."

24. These data are from Anglo contexts. There is variation in details across cultural contexts.

25. From Gail Jefferson, *Talking about Troubles in Conversation* (New York: Oxford University Press, 2015), 33, on "troubles telling" in conversation.

26. Jefferson and Lee, "End of Grant Report," 24, cited in Pomerantz and Mandelbaum, "Conversation Analytic Approaches," 163.

27. Related to matters of intimate and sometimes unseemly information exchange is the kind of backstage talk that close associates often engage in, such as swear words and other obscenities, laughter, and suspension of the constraints that are usually suppressed by norms of politeness:

> Throughout our society there tends to be one informal or backstage language of behavior, and another language of behavior for occasions when a performance is being presented. The backstage language consists of reciprocal first-naming, co-operative decision-making, profanity, open sexual remarks, elaborate griping, smoking, rough informal dress, "sloppy" sitting and standing posture, use of dialect or sub-standard speech, mumbling and shouting, playful aggressivity and "kidding," inconsiderateness for the other in minor but potentially symbolic acts, minor physical self-involvements such as humming, whistling, chewing, nibbling, belching, and flatulence. The frontstage behavior language can be taken as the absence (and in some sense the opposite) of this. In general, then, backstage conduct is one which allows minor acts which might easily be taken as symbolic of intimacy and disrespect for others present and for the region, while front region conduct is one which disallows such potentially offensive behavior. (Erving Goffman, *The Presentation of Self in Everyday Life* [New York: Doubleday, 1959], 78)

28. Nicholas Emler, "A Social Psychology of Reputation," *European Review of Social Psychology* 1, no. 1 (1990): 171–193, https://doi.org/10.1080/14792779108401861. See also Boissevain (1974). Full quote (Emler, 191–192):

> Humans are categorically different, and what makes them so is the capacity for individuals to become informed about their societies without relying on their direct personal experience alone. And this capacity reflects the unique power of language as a means for exchanging information about matters other than the immediate present (Hockett, 1958). The consequences of language for social organization are extensive and profound but I want to concentrate here on just one of the peculiarities of human society, the way in which the individual members are known to one another. Humans alone among the social vertebrates can know one another substantially by repute. People can inform themselves about events and exchanges at which they were not physically present from people who were, and so their knowledge of another individual can build on the experiences reported by third parties. And in this respect what the members of human societies know about one another may be based on a far larger, and potentially more representative, sample of each other's actions than could be provided by direct contact alone.

29. Reputation is "a collective phenomenon and a product of social processes, and not as an impression in the head of any single individual" (Emler, 171). See also Dan Sperber and Nicolas Baumard, "Moral Reputation: An Evolutionary and Cognitive Perspective: Moral Reputation," *Mind and Language* 27, no. 5 (2012): 495–518, https://doi.org/10.1111/mila.12000; Gloria Origgi, *Reputation: What It Is and Why It Matters*, trans. Stephen Holmes and Noga Arikha (Princeton: Princeton University Press, 2018); Magnus Enquist and Olof Leimar, "The Evolution of Cooperation in Mobile Organisms," *Animal Behavior* 45, no. 4 (1993): 747–757, https://doi.org/10.1006/anbe.1993.1089; Cohen, "The Evolution of Tag-Based Cooperation in Humans."

30. As journalism scholar Michael Schudson puts it: "All stories can be read in more than one way." Schudson, *Watergate in American Memory: How We Remember, Forget, and Reconstruct the Past* (New York: Basic Books, 1992).

Chapter 11

1. See N. J. Enfield, *The Anatomy of Meaning: Speech, Gesture, and Composite Utterances* (Cambridge: Cambridge University Press, 2009). Zuckerman and Enfield, "The Unbearable Heaviness of Being Kri: House Construction and Ethnolinguistic Transformation," *Journal of the Royal Anthropological Institute* 28, no. 1 (2022).

2. Compare a scenario in which she does the normal thing and sits on a chair: I would hardly be able to remark *That's a chair, not a table*. It wouldn't make sense.

3. In the terminology of Frege, the reference of the word *chair* is any chair, but its *sense*—playing a crucial role in sense making—must include things like "for sitting on." Cases like this one help to establish that part of a word's sense in a community. See Anna Wierzbicka, *Lexicography and Conceptual Analysis* (Ann Arbor, MI: Karoma, 1985).

4. Adapted from a study by cognitive scientists Adrian Dimulescu and Jean-Louis Dessalles: "Understanding Narrative Interest: Some Evidence on the Role of

Unexpectedness," in *Proceedings of the 31st Annual Conference of the Cognitive Science Society*, ed. N. A. Taatgen and H. van Rijn (Amsterdam: Cognitive Science Society, 2009), 1734–1739, http://141.14.165.6/CogSci09/papers/367/paper367.pdf

5. Dimulescu and Dessalles ran an experiment using scenarios with options like these.

6. M. Kutas and S. Hillyard, "Reading Senseless Sentences: Brain Potentials Reflect Semantic Incongruity," *Science* 207, no. 4427 (1980): 203–205, https://doi.org/10.1126/science.7350657.

7. Ellen F. Lau, Colin Phillips, and David Poeppel, "A Cortical Network for Semantics: (De)Constructing the N400." *Nature Reviews Neuroscience* 9, no. 12 (2008): 921, https://doi.org/10.1038/nrn2532.

8. Lucas M. Bietti, Ottilie Tilston, and Adrian Bangerter, "Storytelling as Adaptive Collective Sensemaking," *Topics in Cognitive Science* 11, no. 4 (2019): 720, https://doi.org/10.1111/tops.12358.

9. Bietti, Tilston, and Bangerter, 720. "In these situations, the incongruity between preexisting schemas and events leads to subjective experience of surprise (Reisenzein, Horstmann, & Schützwohl, 2017) and a state of 'aversive arousal' (Proulx et al., 2012, p. 317) at the level of very basic physiological parameters (e.g., increased skin conductance and cardiac variability; vascular constriction). These physiological signatures of negative arousal produced by expectancy violations occur irrespective of how momentous or trivial the violation is or of its valence."

10. Neal R. Norrick, *Conversational Narrative: Storytelling in Everyday Talk* (Amsterdam: John Benjamins, 2000), 56.

11. H. Paul Grice, "Logic and Conversation.," in *Speech Acts*, ed. Peter Cole and Jerry L. Morgan (New York: Academic Press, 1975), 41–58; Dan Sperber and Dierdre Wilson, *Relevance: Communication and Cognition,* 2nd ed. (Oxford: Blackwell, 1995); Stephen C Levinson, *Presumptive Meanings: The Theory of Generalized Conversational Implicature* (Cambridge, MA: MIT Press, 2000).

12. How do we know what's relevant? It depends on the language game you are playing.

13. This doesn't mean that people can literally read minds. It is a standard term for our propensity to infer or attribute perceptions, beliefs, and knowledge to other people despite the fact that we have no access to their internal states.

14. Tibor Tauzin and György Gergely, "Communicative Mind-Reading in Preverbal Infants," *Scientific Reports* 8, no. 1 (2018), https://doi.org/10.1038/s41598-018-27804-4; Tibor Tauzin and György Gergely, "Variability of Signal Sequences in Turn-Taking Exchanges Induces Agency Attribution in 10.5-Mo-Olds," *Proceedings of the National Academy of Sciences* 16, no. 31 (2019): 15441–15446.

15. D. Y. Takahashi, D. Z Narayanan, and A. A. Ghazanfar, "Coupled Oscilator Dynamics of Vocal Turn-Taking in Monkeys," *Current Biology* 23 (2013): 2162–2168.

16. Actually there are ways of talking in certain communities where exchanges with a high degree of mutual repetition do occur, such as in indigenous groups of central Mexico. See Penelope Brown, Mark Sicoli, and Olivier Le Guen, "Cross-Speaker Repetition in Tzeltal, Yucatec, and Zapotec Conversation," paper presented at the International Conference on Conversation Analysis, Mannheim, Germany, 2010. But these occur in specific contexts and don't characterize the general nature of conversation.

17. The researchers based this conclusion on observations of the infants' "looking time." In infant psychology research, if infants look longer at something, this is taken to be a sign that it takes longer to process that thing cognitively, for example, if something unexpected or surprising is happening.

18. See journalist Leigh Sales's *Any Ordinary Day: Blindsides, Resilience and What Happens after the Worst Day of Your Life* (Sydney: Hamish Hamilton, 2019). Here's how the book begins:

> The day that turns a life upside down usually starts like any other. You open your eyes, swing your body out of bed, eat breakfast, get dressed and leave the house, your mind busy. As you close the front door behind you, rarely is there a tingle of unease that something is off. Later, when the story of what happened next comes to be told, it will start with the day's deceptive ordinariness, something that will now seem incredible. How could a blindside so momentous have struck on a day that began so unremarkably?

My point is that this is not so much about the events of that day itself, but rather what happens *when it comes to be told*. That is, the ordinariness of the beginning is crucial to *how we tell it*. It's what makes the exceptional exceptional.

19. Psychologists Raymond Mar and Keith Oatley write that fiction is "a kind of simulation that runs on minds" in their "The Function of Fiction Is the Abstraction and Simulation of Social Experience," *Perspectives on Psychological Science* 3, no. 3 (2008): 187, https://doi.org/10.1111/j.1745-6924.2008.00073.x. They also write that "authors of fiction literature and research psychologists are both interested in the same thing: understanding human behavior and its underlying cognitions and motivations. The product of an author's investigation into human nature is a story."

20. See Daniel Dor's *The Instruction of Imagination: Language as a Social Communication Technology* (Oxford: Oxford University Press, 2015).

21. This is the figure for the United States in 1990, for adults younger than age fifty. From Olivier Morin, Alberto Acerbi, and Oleg Sobchuk, "Why People Die in Novels: Testing the Ordeal Simulation Hypothesis," *Palgrave Communications* 5, no. 1 (2019): 62, https://doi.org/10.1057/s41599-019-0267-0.

22. Morin, Acerbi, and Sobchuk.

23. Morin, Acerbi, and Sobchuk, 1.

24. Morin, Acerbi, and Sobchuk, 2. See their discussion and references.

25. Brian Boyd. *On the Origin of Stories* (Cambridge, MA: Harvard University Press,2009).

26. Mathias Clasen, Jens Kjeldgaard-Christiansen, and John A. Johnson, "Horror, Personality, and Threat Simulation: A Survey on the Psychology of Scary Media," *Evolutionary Behavioral Sciences* 14, no. 3 (2020): 213–230, https://doi.org/10.1037/ebs0000152.

27. Harold Bloom, *How to Read and Why* (New York: Scribner, 2000).

28. Nicholas Evans, *Dying Words: Endangered Languages and What They Have to Tell Us* (New York: Wiley-Blackwell, 2009), 155, citing Bloom.

29. Natalie Merrill, Jordan A. Booker, and Robyn Fivush, "Functions of Parental Intergenerational Narratives Told by Young People," *Topics in Cognitive Science* 11, no. 4 (2019): 752–773, https://doi.org/10.1111/tops.12356. Nicole Alea et al., "The Social Function of Autobiographical Stories in the Personal and Virtual World: An Initial Investigation," *Topics in Cognitive Science* 11, no. 4 (2019): 794–810, https://doi.org/10.1111/tops.12370.

30. Merrill, Booker, and Fivush, "Functions of Parental Intergenerational Narratives."

31. Merrill, Booker, and Fivush, 753–754. See Natalie Merrill and Robyn Fivush, "Intergenerational Narratives and Identity across Development," *Developmental Review* 40 (2016): 72–92, https://doi.org/10.1016/j.dr.2016.03.001.

32. This does not mean that language can convey everything that nonlanguage can. See Wittgenstein among many others. Also: "There are secrets to our world that only practice can reveal, and no opinion or analysis will ever capture in full." Nassim Nicholas Taleb, *Antifragile: Things That Gain from Disorder* (New York: Random House, 2012).

33. https://www.storytimeyoga.com/japanese-tsunami-folk-tale-to-tell-in-this-time-of-tragedy/. Another version:

> One day, Ojiisan, standing on a hill overlooking his village, feels a strong earthquake. He knows that earthquakes can cause a tsunami. He sets fire to the village rice fields. Tada didn't know what to think. Did his grandfather go mad? Enraged, the villagers race up the hill to save the rice. Suddenly, the old man points to the sea and cries, "Look." As a huge wave engulfs their village, the people realize that Ojiisan burned the rice to save their lives.

From here: https://bit.ly/3aYZU89. See the movie *The Wave*: https://youtu.be/IvbfNfnX6So

34. https://rense.com/general62/pretsn.htm; http://www.bangkokpost.net/en/Outlook/17Jan2005_out79.php.

35. It was also reported that Andaman and Nicobar Islanders were saved by their knowledge passed on by folk tales: http://news.bbc.co.uk/2/hi/south_asia/4181855.stm. And the same in Indonesia: https://www.ifrc.org/en/news-and-media/news-stories/asia-pacific/indonesia/the-story-that-saved-the-lives-of-the-people-of-simeuleu

-indonesia/. See also R. L. Parry *Ghosts of the Tsunami* (New York: MCD/Farrar, Straus and Giroux, 2017).

36. See https://rense.com/general62/pretsn.htm; https://www.forbes.com/sites/david bressan/2018/03/23/ancient-stories-preserve-the-memory-of-tsunami-in-the -pacific-ocean/; and R. S. Ludwin et al., "Serpent Spirit-Power Stories along the Seattle Fault," *Seismological Research Letters* 76, no. 4 (2005): 426–431, https://doi.org/10.1785 /gssrl.76.4.426.

37. "The Rival Wizards," in A. Grace, *Folktales of the Maori*. (Wellington: Gordon & Gotch, 1907). From Darren N. King et al., "Māori Oral Histories and the Impact of Tsunamis in Aotearoa-New Zealand," *Natural Hazards and Earth System Sciences* 18, no. 3 (2018): 907–919, https://doi.org/10.5194/nhess-18-907-2018.

38. Cited in Patrick N. Nunn and Nicholas J. Reid, "Aboriginal Memories of Inunda-tion of the Australian Coast Dating from More than 7000 Years Ago," *Australian Geographer* 47, no. 1 (2016), 18, https://doi.org/10.1080/00049182.2015.1077539.

39. The 2015 study by geographer Nunn and linguist Reid details stories from around the entire coast of Australia.

40. For sample origin stories, see David Adams Leeming, *Creation Myths of the World: An Encyclopedia*, 2nd ed. (Santa Barbara, CA: ABC-CLIO, 2010).

41. My associate Dr Charles Zuckerman collected a recording of this story.

42. Enfield, *The Anatomy of Meaning*; Charles H. P. Zuckerman and N. J. Enfield, "Heavy Sound Light Sound: A Nam Noi Metalinguistic Trope," in *Studies in the Anthropology of Language in Mainland Southeast Asia*, ed. N. J. Enfield, Jack Sidnell, and Charles H. P. Zuckerman (Honolulu: University of Hawai'i Press, 2020), 85–92; Zuckerman and Enfield, "The Unbearable Heaviness of Being Kri."

43. Haviland, *Gossip, Reputation and Knowledge in Zinacantan* (Chicago: University of Chicago Press, 1977).

44. P. W. Wiessner, "Embers of Society: Firelight Talk among the Ju/'hoansi Bush-men," *Proceedings of the National Academy of Sciences of the United States of America* 111 (2014): 14027–14035, cited in Mahdi Dahmardeh and R. I. M. Dunbar, "What Shall We Talk about in Farsi? Content of Everyday Conversations in Iran," *Human Nature* 28, no. 4 (2017): 424, https://doi.org/10.1007/s12110-017-9300-4. See also R. I. M. Dunbar, Anna Marriott, and N. D. C. Duncan, "Human Conversational Behav-ior," *Human Nature* 8, no. 3 (1997): 231–246, https://doi.org/10.1007/BF02912493; Dunbar, "Gossip in Evolutionary Perspective"; Dahmardeh and Dunbar, "What Shall We Talk about in Farsi?" See also Matthias R. Mehl and James W. Pennebaker, "The Sounds of Social Life: A Psychometric Analysis of Students' Daily Social Envi-ronments and Natural Conversations.," *Journal of Personality and Social Psychology* 84, no. 4 (2003): 857–870, https://doi.org/10.1037/0022-3514.84.4.857.

45. Wiessner. "Embers of Society," 14029.

46. "The writer made a practice for several weeks of walking slowly up Broadway from Thirty-third Street to Fifty-fifth Street at about seven-thirty every evening. Every bit of audible conversation was jotted down." Henry T. Moore, "Further Data Concerning Sex Differences," *Journal of Abnormal Psychology and Social Psychology* 17, no. 2 (1922): 211–212, https://doi.org/10.1037/h0064645.

47. Moore, 212.

48. Moore, 214.

Conclusion

1. C. Thi Nguyen, "The Seductions of Clarity," *Royal Institute of Philosophy Supplement* 89 (2021): 227–255, https://doi.org/10.1017/S1358246121000035. The idea of "thought termination" is central to the fast and frugal heuristics described by authors from Herbert Simon to Daniel Kahneman to Gerd Gigerenzer. See Simon "Rational Choice and the Structure of the Environment"; Kahneman, *Thinking, Fast and Slow*; Gigerenzer *Gut Feelings*.

2. And do not forget that this concept must be multipled by seven thousand, the approximate number of languages—or great collections of attention-directing off-switches—spoken in the world today.

3. Language never gives us anything more than the barest outlines—however satisfying and functional those outlines may be—and so we must be mindful that our languages "must be considered *only as maps*," as mathematician Alfred Korzybski put it. "A map *is not* the territory it represents, but, if correct, it has a *similar structure* to the territory, which accounts for its usefulness." Alfred Korzybski, *Selections from Science and Sanity: An Introduction to Non-Aristotelian Systems and General Semantics* (Forest Hills, NY: Institute of General Semantics, 1933), 58. Also, just as "perception always intercedes between reality and ourselves" (Ann Marie Seward Barry, *Visual Intelligence: Perception, Image, and Manipulation in Visual Communication*. Albany: State University of New York, 1997, 16), language often intercedes between our perception and ourselves.

4. Jason Stanley (@jasonintrator), Twitter, August 25, 2020, https://twitter.com /jasonintrator/status/1298432340205670401.

5. Garry Kasparov (@Kasparov63), Twitter, May 18, 2020, https://twitter.com/kasp arov63/status/1262083583893803008.

6. Hugo Mercier, *Not Born Yesterday: The Science of Who We Trust and What We Believe* (Princeton, NJ: Princeton University Press, 2020). Also: "People will judge the situation for themselves and will not simply buy into whatever language is used by talking heads (whom they probably despise)." Philosopher Oliver Traldi (@olivertraldi), Twitter, May 30, 2020.

7. Sometimes people *will* buy into whatever language is used, but this would be in those somewhat rare cases in which they have no prior opinion on a matter and when they approach a story with no prior position on the source and with zero prejudice or mindfulness.

8. See Mercier, *Not Born Yesterday.*

9. Named after Joseph P. Overton, former vice president of the Mackinac Centre for Public Policy: https://www.mackinac.org/OvertonWindow.

10. See Timur Kuran, *Private Truths, Public Lies: The Social Consequences of Preference Falsification* (Cambridge, MA: Harvard University Press, 1997).

11. Research by the conversation analysts Jack Sidnell and Rebecca Barnes: Jack Sidnell and Rebecca Barnes, "Alternative, Subsequent Descriptions," in *Conversational Repair and Human Understanding,* ed. Geoffrey Raymond, Jack Sidnell, and Makoto Hayashi, Studies in Interactional Sociolinguistics (Cambridge: Cambridge University Press, 2013), 330–331, https://doi.org/10.1017/CBO9780511757464.011.

12. The Roman emperor and Stoic philosopher Marcus Aurelius wrote of the striking and useful effects of applying descriptions that "pierce right through" the shroud of our habitual descriptions: "How useful, when roasted meats and other foods are before you to see them in your mind as here the dead body of a fish, there the dead body of a bird or pig. Or again, to think of Falernian wine as the juice of a cluster of grapes, of a purple robe as sheep's wool dyed with the blood of a shellfish, and of sexual intercourse as internal rubbing accompanied by a spasmodic ejection of mucus. What useful perceptual images these are! They go to the heart of things and pierce right through them, so that you see things for what they are. You must do this throughout life; when things appear too enticing, strip them naked, destroy the myth which makes them proud." Marcus Aurelius, *The Meditations* (Indianapolis: Hackett, 1983), book 6, section 13. George Orwell made similar remarks on the methods by which euphemistic political writing can "defend the indefensible": "Defenseless villages are bombarded from the air, the inhabitants driven out into the countryside, the cattle machine-gunned, the huts set on fire with incendiary bullets: this is called *pacification*. Millions of peasants are robbed of their farms and sent trudging along the roads with no more than they can carry: this is called *transfer of population* or *rectification of frontiers*. People are imprisoned for years without trial, or shot in the back of the neck or sent to die of scurvy in Arctic lumber camps: this is called *elimination of unreliable elements*. Such phraseology is needed if one wants to name things without calling up mental pictures of them." George Orwell, "Politics and the English Language," *Horizon* 13, no. 76 (1946): 252–265.

13. See Mercier, *Not Born Yesterday,* for a dissenting voice, arguing that people are nowhere near as gullible as we are often made out to be.

14. "'Give me an image of the all-American boy, and it's this young man,' said Zimbardo. 'He is a wonderful young man who did these horrible things.' But Major

Michael Holley, prosecuting, told the court that Frederick was an adult who could tell right from wrong." https://www.theguardian.com/world/2004/oct/22/usa.iraq.

15. This is not to say that it comes easily. In the trial of Nazi war criminal Adolf Eichmann for crimes against humanity, Eichmann was held individually responsible for his actions in a context in which "the whole of respectable society had in one way or another succumbed to Hitler," as political theorist Hannah Arendt wrote. The trial for crimes committed in the context of a state project demanded that defendants be "capable of telling right from wrong even when all they have to guide them is their own judgment, which, moreover, happens to be completely at odds with what they must regard as the unanimous opinion of all those around them." Hannah Arendt. *Eichmann in Jerusalem: A Report on the Banality of Evil* (New York: Penguin Books, 1965), 294–295.

16. Another example of the human capacity to reject the wrongful behavior of people in one's group is Ron Ridenhour, who exposed the March 1968 massacre of civilians by US troops at My Lai in Vietnam.

17. Neil Greenspan, "Taxicab Geometry as a Vehicle for the Journey Toward Enlightenment," *Humanistic Mathematics Network Journal* 1, no. 27 (2004): article 5: "Experience with those who lack patience for fine distinctions in language has led me to the formulation of what can be referred to as The Bold Ontological Hypothesis: Most of the time, most people do not know (precisely) what they are talking about. The only way to know what you are talking about is to exert the extra effort it takes to know *exactly what* you are talking about."

18. This paragraph and the three paragraphs that follow it are adapted from a review published in the *Times Literary Supplement* in 2020: https://www.the-tls.co.uk/articles/fit-facts-around-prejudices-review/.

19. Ilya Somin, *Democracy and Political Ignorance: Why Smaller Government Is Smarter* (Stanford, CA: Stanford University Press, 2013), 6.

20. In his argument for the political power of linguistic framing (George Lakoff, *Don't Think of an Elephant!*, 2004), Lakoff states that it is "a vain hope" to expect that people are rational enough to reach the right conclusion if only they have access to the facts (p. 73). In this sense, Lakoff's 2004 work on framing is a handbook for lawyers, not scientists.

21. Clifford, 1877.

22. Mercier, *Not Born Yesterday*, 206.

Bibliography

Abbott, Joshua T., Thomas L. Griffiths, and Terry Regier. "Focal Colors across Languages Are Representative Members of Color Categories." *Proceedings of the National Academy of Sciences* 113, no. 40 (2016): 11178–11183. https://doi.org/10.1073/pnas .1513298113.

ADB/UNEP, *Greater Mekong Subregion Atlas of the Environment.* Asian Development Bank (ADB), Manila, Phillipines, and United Nations Environment Programme (UNEP) Regional Resources Centre for Asia and the Pacific, Pathumthani, Thailand. Manila; Pathumthani: ADB/UNEP, 2004.

Alea, Nicole, Susan Bluck, Emily L. Mroz, and Zanique Edwards. "The Social Function of Autobiographical Stories in the Personal and Virtual World: An Initial Investigation." *Topics in Cognitive Science* 11, no. 4 (2019): 794–810. https://doi.org/10 .1111/tops.12370.

Alexander, R. McNeill. *Locomotion of Animals.* Dordrecht: Springer Netherlands, 1982.

Alogna, V. K., M. K. Attaya, P. Aucoin, Š. Bahník, S. Birch, A. R. Birt, B. H. Bornstein, et al. "Registered Replication Report: Schooler and Engstler-Schooler (1990)." *Perspectives on Psychological Science* 9, no. 5 (2014): 556–578. https://doi.org/10.1177 /1745691614545653.

Amici, Federica, Alex Sánchez-Amaro, Carla Sebastián-Enesco, Trix Cacchione, Matthias Allritz, Juan Salazar-Bonet, and Federico Rossano. "The Word Order of Languages Predicts Native Speakers' Working Memory." *Scientific Reports* 9, no. 1 (2019). https://doi.org/10.1038/s41598-018-37654-9.

Andersen, Elaine S. "Lexical Universals of Bodypart Terminology." In *Universals of Human Language*, edited by Joseph H. Greenberg, 335–368. Stanford, CA: Stanford University Press, 1978.

Anscombe, G. E. M. *Intention.* Cambridge, MA: Harvard University Press, 1957.

Anscombe, G. E. M. "On Brute Facts." *Analysis* 18, no. 3 (1958): 69–72. https://doi .org/10.1093/analys/18.3.69.

Arendt, Hannah. *Eichmann in Jerusalem: A Report on the Banality of Evil*, revised and enlarged edition. New York: Penguin Books, 1965.

Aschmann, H. P. "Totonac Categories of Smell." *Tlalocan* 2 (1946): 187–189.

Astington, Janet W. "The Developmental Interdependence of Theory of Mind and Language." In *Roots of Human Sociality*, edited by N. J. Enfield and Stephen C. Levinson, 179–206. Oxford, UK: Berg, 2006.

Aurelius, Marcus. *The Meditations*. Indianapolis: Hackett, 1983.

Austin, J. L. *How to Do Things with Words*. Cambridge, MA: Harvard University Press, 1962.

Bach, Richard. *Jonathan Livingston Seagull*. New York: Macmillan, 1970.

Baker, C. "Regulators and Turn-Taking in American Sign Language Discourse." In *On the Other Hand: New Perspectives on American Sign Language*, edited by L. Friedman, 215–236. New York: Academic Press, 1977.

Barr, Dale J. "Establishing Conventional Communication Systems: Is Common Knowledge Necessary?" *Cognitive Science* 28, no. 6 (2004): 937–962. https://doi.org/10.1207/s15516709cog2806_3.

Barr, Dale J., and Boaz Keysar. "Making Sense of How We Make Sense: The Paradox of Egocentrism in Language Use." In *Figurative Language Comprehension: Social and Cultural Influences*, 21–41. Mahwah, NJ: Erlbaum, 2004.

Barraza, Jorge A., and Paul J. Zak. "Empathy toward Strangers Triggers Oxytocin Release and Subsequent Generosity." *Annals of the New York Academy of Sciences* 1167, no. 1 (2009): 182–189. https://doi.org/10.1111/j.1749-6632.2009.04504.x.

Barry, Ann Marie Seward. *Visual Intelligence: Perception, Image, and Manipulation in Visual Communication*. Albany: State University of New York Press, 1997.

Bartlett, F. C. *Remembering: A Study in Experimental and Social Psychology*. Cambridge: Cambridge University Press, 1932.

Beech, E., M. Rivers, S. Oldfield, and P. P. Smith. "GlobalTreeSearch: The First Complete Global Database of Tree Species and Country Distributions." *Journal of Sustainable Forestry* 36, no. 5 (2017): 454–489. https://doi.org/10.1080/10549811.2017.1310049.

Berlin, Brent. "The Concept of Rank in Ethnobiological Classification: Some Evidence from Aguaruna Folk Botany." *American Ethnologist* 3, no. 3 (1976): 381–399.

Berlin, Brent. *Ethnobiological Classification: Principles of Categorization of Plants and Animals in Traditional Societies*. Princeton, NJ: Princeton University Press, 1992.

Betz, Joseph. "Violence: Garver's Definition and a Deweyan Correction." *Ethics* 87, no. 4 (1977): 339–351. https://doi.org/10.1086/292046.

Bierman, A. K., and James A. Gould, eds. *Philosophy for a New Generation*, 2nd ed. New York: Macmillan, 1973.

Bietti, Lucas M., Ottilie Tilston, and Adrian Bangerter. "Storytelling as Adaptive Collective Sensemaking." *Topics in Cognitive Science* 11, no. 4 (2019): 710–732. https://doi.org/10.1111/tops.12358.

Bloom, Paul, and Frank C. Keil. "Thinking through Language." *Mind and Language* 16, no. 4 (2001): 351–367. https://doi.org/10.1111/1468-0017.00175.

Boas, Franz. "Introduction." In *Handbook of American Indian Languages*, edited by Franz Boas, 1–79. 1911. Reprint, Lincoln: University of Nebraska Press, 1966.

Bock, J. Kathryn. "Meaning, Sound, and Syntax: Lexical Priming in Sentence Production." *Journal of Experimental Psychology: Learning, Memory, and Cognition* 12, no. 4 (1986): 575–586. https://doi.org/10.1037/0278-7393.12.4.575.

Boissevain, Jeremy. *Friends of Friends: Networks, Manipulators and Coalitions*. Oxford: Blackwell, 1974.

Booker, Christopher. *The Seven Basic Plots: Why We Tell Stories*. London: Continuum, 2004.

Boroditsky, L., L. Schmidt, and W. Phillips. "Sex, Syntax, and Semantics." In *Language in Mind: Advances in the Study of Language and Thought*, edited by Dedre Gentner and Susan Goldin-Meadow, 61–80. Cambridge, MA: MIT Press, 2003.

Broström, Stig. "Children Tell Stories." *European Early Childhood Education Research Journal* 10, no. 1 (2002): 85–97. https://doi.org/10.1080/13502930285208861.

Brown, Cecil H. "General Principles of Human Anatomical Partonomy and Speculations on the Growth of Partonomic Nomenclature." *American Ethnologist* 3, no. 3 (1976): 400–424. https://doi.org/10.1525/ae.1976.3.3.02a00020.

Brown, Charity, and Toby J. Lloyd-Jones. "Verbal Overshadowing of Multiple Face and Car Recognition: Effects of Within- versus Across-Category Verbal Descriptions." *Applied Cognitive Psychology* 17, no. 2 (2003): 183–201. https://doi.org/10.1002/acp.861.

Brown, Penelope, Mark Sicoli, and Olivier Le Guen. "Cross-Speaker Repetition in Tzeltal, Yucatec, and Zapotec Conversation." Paper presented at International Conference on Conversation Analysis, Mannheim, Germany, 2010.

Brown, Roger. "How Shall a Thing Be Called?" *Psychological Review* 65, no. 1 (1958): 14–21. https://doi.org/10.1037/h0041727.

Brown, Roger W., and Eric H. Lenneberg. "A Study in Language and Cognition." *Journal of Abnormal and Social Psychology* 49, no. 3 (1954): 454–462. https://doi.org/10.1037/h0057814.

Budelmann, Felix, Robin Dunbar, Sophie Duncan, Evert van Emde Boas, Laurie Maguire, Ben Teasdale, and Jacqueline Thompson. "Cognition, Endorphins, and the Literary

Response to Tragedy." *Cambridge Quarterly* 46, no. 3 (2017): 229–250. https://doi.org /10.1093/camqtly/bfx016.

Burgess, Don, Willett Kempton, and Robert E. Maclaury. "Tarahumara Color Modifiers: Category Structure Presaging Evolutionary Change." *American Ethnologist* 10, no. 1 (1983): 133–149. https://doi.org/10.1525/ae.1983.10.1.02a00080.

Bushdid, C., M. O. Magnasco, L. B. Vosshall, and A. Keller. "Humans Can Discriminate More Than 1 Trillion Olfactory Stimuli." *Science* 343, no. 6177 (2014): 1370–1372. https://doi.org/10.1126/science.1249168.

Byrne, Richard W., and Andrew Whiten, eds. *Machiavellian Intelligence: Social Expertise and the Evolution of Intellect in Monkeys, Apes, and Humans.* Oxford: Clarendon Press, 1988.

Cairns, Hugh, and Yidumduma Bill Harney. *Dark Sparklers: Yidumduma's Wardaman Aboriginal Astronomy: Night Skies, Northern Australia.* Merimbula, N.S.W.: H. C. Cairns, 2004.

Campbell, Joseph. *The Hero with a Thousand Faces.* Princeton: Princeton University Press, 1949.

Carmichael, L., H. P. Hogen, and A. A. Walter. "An Experimental Study of the Effect of Language on the Reproduction of Visually Perceived Form." *Journal of Experimental Psychology* 15, no. 1 (1932): 73–86. https://doi.org/10.1037/h0072671.

Carr, Jon W., Kenny Smith, Jennifer Culbertson, and Simon Kirby. "Simplicity and Informativeness in Semantic Category Systems." *Cognition* 202 (2020): 104289. https://doi.org/10.1016/j.cognition.2020.104289.

Chivers, Tom. "What's Next for Psychology's Embattled Field of Social Priming." *Nature* 576 (7786) (2019): 200–202. https://doi.org/10.1038/d41586-019-03755-2.

Chong, Dennis, and James N. Druckman. "Framing Theory." *Annual Review of Political Science* 10, no. 1 (2007): 103–126. https://doi.org/10.1146/annurev.polisci.10 .072805.103054.

Christenhusz, Maarten J. M., and James W. Byng. "The Number of Known Plants Species in the World and Its Annual Increase." *Phytotaxa* 261, no. 3 (2016): 201. https://doi.org/10.11646/phytotaxa.261.3.1.

Clark, Eve V. *First Language Acquisition.* Cambridge: Cambridge University Press, 2003.

Clark, Eve V—. *First Language Acquisition*, 2nd ed. Cambridge: Cambridge University Press, 2009.

Clark, Herbert H. *Using Language.* Cambridge: Cambridge University Press, 1996.

Clark, Herbert H., Robert Schreuder, and Samuel Buttrick. "Common Ground at the Understanding of Demonstrative Reference." *Journal of Verbal Learning and Verbal Behavior* 22, no. 2 (1983): 245–258. https://doi.org/10.1016/S0022-5371(83)90189-5.

Clark, Herbert H., and Deanna Wilkes-Gibbs. "Referring as a Collaborative Process." *Cognition* 22, no. 1 (1986): 1–39. https://doi.org/10.1016/0010-0277(86)90010-7.

Clasen, Mathias, Jens Kjeldgaard-Christiansen, and John A. Johnson. "Horror, Personality, and Threat Simulation: A Survey on the Psychology of Scary Media." *Evolutionary Behavioral Sciences* 14, no. 3 (2020): 213–230. https://doi.org/10.1037/ebs0000152.

Cohen, Emma. "The Evolution of Tag-Based Cooperation in Humans: The Case for Accent." *Current Anthropology* 53, no. 5 (2012): 588–616.

Cohen, Emma E. A., Robin Ejsmond-Frey, Nicola Knight, and R. I. M. Dunbar. "Rowers' High: Behavioral Synchrony Is Correlated with Elevated Pain Thresholds." *Biology Letters* 6, no. 1 (2010): 106–108. https://doi.org/10.1098/rsbl.2009.0670.

Cruttenden, Alan. *Gimson's Pronunciation of English*, 8th ed. London: Routledge, 2014.

Cutler, Anne. *Native Listening: Language Experience and the Recognition of Spoken Words*. Cambridge, MA: MIT Press, 2012.

Dahmardeh, Mahdi, and R. I. M. Dunbar. "What Shall We Talk about in Farsi? Content of Everyday Conversations in Iran." *Human Nature* 28, no. 4 (2017): 423–433. https://doi.org/10.1007/s12110-017-9300-4.

Davies, Ian R. L., and Greville G. Corbett. "A Cross-Cultural Study of Colour Grouping: Evidence for Weak Linguistic Relativity." *British Journal of Psychology* 88, no. 3 (1997): 493–517. https://doi.org/10.1111/j.2044-8295.1997.tb02653.x.

Degenaar, J. J. "The Concept of Violence." *Politikon* 7, no. 1 (1980): 14–27. https://doi.org/10.1080/02589348008704765.

Deutsch, David. *The Fabric of Reality*. New York: Viking, 1997.

Devylder, Simon, Christoph Bracks, Misuzu Shimotori, and Poppy Siahaan. "Carving the Body at Its Joints: Does the Way We Speak about the Body Shape the Way We Think about It?" *Language and Cognition* 12, no. 4 (2020): 577–613. https://doi.org/10.1017/langcog.2020.13.

Dick, Philip K. "How to Build a Universe That Doesn't Fall Apart Two Days Later." 1978. https://urbigenous.net/library/how_to_build.html.

Dillon, Kathleen M., Brian Minchoff, and Katherine H. Baker. "Positive Emotional States and Enhancement of the Immune System." *International Journal of Psychiatry in Medicine* 15, no. 1 (1985–1986): 13–18. https://doi.org/10.2190/R7FD-URN9-PQ7F-A6J7.

Dimulescu, Adrian, and Jean-Louis Dessalles. "Understanding Narrative Interest: Some Evidence on the Role of Unexpectedness." In *Proceedings of the 31st Annual Conference of the Cognitive Science Society*, edited by N. A. Taatgen and H. van Rijn, 1734–1739. Amsterdam: Cognitive Science Society, 2009.

Dingemanse, Mark. "Ezra Pound among the Mawu." *Semblance and Signification. Iconicity in Language and Literature* 10 (2011): 39–54.

Dingemanse, Mark. "Making New Ideophones in Siwu: Creative Depiction in Conversation." *Pragmatics and Society* 5, no. 3 (2014): 384–405. https://doi.org/10.1075/ps.5.3.04din.

Dor, Daniel. *The Instruction of Imagination: Language as a Social Communication Technology.* Oxford: Oxford University Press, 2015.

Dor, Daniel. *Intifada Hits the Headlines: How the Israeli Press Misreported the Outbreak of the Second Palestinian Uprising.* Bloomington: Indiana University Press, 2004.

Dotson, Kristie. "Tracking Epistemic Violence, Tracking Practices of Silencing." *Hypatia: A Journal of Feminist Philosophy* 26, no. 2 (2011): 236–257. https://doi.org/10.1111/j.1527-2001.2011.01177.x.

Downing, Pamela A., and Michael Noonan, eds. *Word Order in Discourse.* Amsterdam: John Benjamins, 1995. https://doi.org/10.1075/tsl.30.

Drew, Paul, and K. Chilton. "Calling Just to Keep in Touch: Regular and Habitualised Telephone Calls as an Environment for Small Talk." In *Small Talk,* edited by J. Coupland, 137–162. Harlow: Pearson Education, 2000.

Dunbar, Robin I. M. "Coevolution of Neocortical Size, Group Size, and Language in Humans." *Behavioral and Brain Sciences* 16 (1993): 681–735.

Dunbar, R. I. M. "Gossip in Evolutionary Perspective." *Review of General Psychology* 8, no. 2 (2004): 100–110. https://doi.org/10.1037/1089-2680.8.2.100.

Dunbar, R. I. M., Rebecca Baron, Anna Frangou, Eiluned Pearce, Edwin J. C. van Leeuwen, Julie Stow, Giselle Partridge et al. "Social Laughter Is Correlated with an Elevated Pain Threshold." *Proceedings of the Royal Society B: Biological Sciences* 279, no. 1731 (2012): 1161–1167. https://doi.org/10.1098/rspb.2011.1373.

Dunbar, R. I. M., Kostas Kaskatis, Ian MacDonald, and Vinnie Barra. "Performance of Music Elevates Pain Threshold and Positive Affect: Implications for the Evolutionary Function of Music." *Evolutionary Psychology* 10, no. 4 (2012): 688–702. https://doi.org/10.1177/147470491201000403.

Dunbar, R. I. M., Anna Marriott, and N. D. C. Duncan. "Human Conversational Behavior." *Human Nature* 8, no. 3 (1997): 231–246. https://doi.org/10.1007/BF02912493.

Dunbar, R. I. M., Ben Teasdale, Jackie Thompson, Felix Budelmann, Sophie Duncan, Evert van Emde Boas, and Laurie Maguire. "Emotional Arousal When Watching Drama Increases Pain Threshold and Social Bonding." *Royal Society Open Science* 3, no. 9 (2016): 160288. https://doi.org/10.1098/rsos.160288.

Edwards, Terra. "Bridging the Gap between DeafBlind Minds: Interactional and Social Foundations of Intention Attribution in the Seattle DeafBlind Community." *Frontiers in Psychology* 6 (2015). https://doi.org/10.3389/fpsyg.2015.01497.

Elmore, Kristen C., and Myra Luna-Lucero. "Light Bulbs or Seeds? How Metaphors for Ideas Influence Judgments about Genius." *Social Psychological and Personality Science* 8, no. 2 (2017): 200–208. https://doi.org/10.1177/1948550616667611.

Emler, Nicholas. "A Social Psychology of Reputation." *European Review of Social Psychology* 1, no. 1 (1990): 171–193. https://doi.org/10.1080/14792779108401861.

Enfield, N. J. *The Anatomy of Meaning: Speech, Gesture, and Composite Utterances.* Cambridge: Cambridge University Press, 2009.

Enfield, N. J. *Ethnosyntax: Explorations in Culture and Grammar.* Oxford: Oxford University Press, 2002.

Enfield, N. J. "Everyday Ritual in the Residential World." In *Ritual Communication,* edited by Gunter Senft and Ellen B. Basso, 51–80. Oxford: Berg, 2009.

Enfield, N. J. *How We Talk: The Inner Workings of Conversation.* New York: Basic Books, 2017.

Enfield, N. J. "Linguistic Relativity from Reference to Agency." *Annual Review of Anthropology* 44, no. 1 (2015): 207–224. https://doi.org/10.1146/annurev-anthro-102214 -014053.

Enfield, N. J. *Natural Causes of Language: Frames, Biases, and Cultural Transmission.* Berlin: Language Science Press, 2014.

Enfield, N. J. *Relationship Thinking: Agency, Enchrony, and Human Sociality.* Oxford: Oxford University Press, 2013.

Enfield, N. J. *The Utility of Meaning: What Words Mean and Why.* Oxford: Oxford University Press, 2015.

Enfield, N. J. "Asymmetries in the System of Person Reference in Kri, a Language of Upland Laos." In *Signs of Deference, Signs of Demeanour: Interlocutor Reference and Self-Other Relations across Southeast Asian Speech Communities,* edited by Dwi Noverini Djenar and Jack Sidnell. Singapore: NUS Press, 2022.

Enfield, N. J., Paul Kockelman, and Jack Sidnell, eds. *The Cambridge Handbook of Linguistic Anthropology.* Cambridge: Cambridge University Press, 2014.

Enfield, N. J., and Tanya Stivers, eds. *Person Reference in Interaction: Linguistic, Cultural and Social Perspectives.* Cambridge: Cambridge University Press, 2007. https://doi.org /10.1017/CBO9780511486746.

Enquist, Magnus, and Olof Leimar. "The Evolution of Cooperation in Mobile Organisms." *Animal Behavior* 45, no. 4 (1993): 747–757. https://doi.org/10.1006/anbe.1993 .1089.

Epstein, Ziv, Sydney Levine, David G. Rand, and Iyad Rahwan. "Who Gets Credit for AI-Generated Art?" *iScience* 23 (9) (2020): 101515, https://doi.org/10.1016/j.isci.2020 .101515.

Evans, Nicholas. *Dying Words: Endangered Languages and What They Have to Tell Us.* Oxford: Wiley-Blackwell, 2009.

Everett, Caleb. *Linguistic Relativity: Evidence across Languages and Cognitive Domains.* Berlin: De Gruyter Mouton, 2013. https://doi.org/10.1515/9783110308143.

Everett, Daniel L. "Cultural Constraints on Grammar and Cognition in Pirahã: Another Look at the Design Features of Human Language." *Current Anthropology* 46, no. 4 (2005): 621–646. https://doi.org/10.1086/431525.

Everett, Daniel L. *Dark Matter of the Mind: The Culturally Articulated Unconscious.* Chicago: Chicago University Press, 2017.

Fanon, Frantz. *The Wretched of the Earth.* New York: Grove, 1963.

Fausey, Caitlin M., and Lera Boroditsky. "Subtle Linguistic Cues Influence Perceived Blame and Financial Liability." *Psychonomic Bulletin and Review* 17, no. 5 (2010): 644–650. https://doi.org/10.3758/PBR.17.5.644.

Feher, Joseph. "Hypothalamus and Pituitary Gland." In *Quantitative Human Physiology*, 870–882. Amsterdam: Elsevier, 2017. https://doi.org/10.1016/B978-0-12-800883 -6.00085-9.

Feldman, Roy E. "Response to Compatriot and Foreigner Who Seek Assistance." *Journal of Personality and Social Psychology* 10, no. 3 (1968): 202–214. https://doi.org/10 .1037/h0026567.

Felger, R. S., and M. B. Moser. *People of the Desert and Sea.* Tucson: University of Arizona Press, 1985.

Flores d'Arcais, G. B., and R. Schreuder. "Semantic Activation during Object Naming." *Psychological Research* 49, no. 2 (1987): 153–159. https://doi.org/10.1007/BF 00308681.

Flusberg, Stephen J., Teenie Matlock, and Paul H. Thibodeau. "Metaphors for the War (or Race) against Climate Change." *Environmental Communication* 11, no. 6 (2017): 769–783. https://doi.org/10.1080/17524032.2017.1289111.

Forder, Lewis, and Gary Lupyan. "Hearing Words Changes Color Perception: Facilitation of Color Discrimination by Verbal and Visual Cues." PsyArXiv, August 29, 2017. https://doi.org/10.31234/osf.io/f83au.

Friedrich, Paul. "Social Context and Semantic Feature: The Russian Prononimal Usage." In *Directions in Sociolinguistics: The Ethnography of Communication*, 2nd ed., edited by John J. Gumperz and Dell H. Hymes, 270–300. London: Basil Blackwell, 1986.

Gaertner, Samuel, and Leonard Bickman. "Effects of Race on the Elicitation of Helping Behavior: The Wrong Number Technique." *Journal of Personality and Social Psychology* 20, no. 2 (1971): 218–222. https://doi.org/10.1037/h0031681.

Galtung, Johan. "Violence, Peace, and Peace Research." *Journal of Peace Research* 6, no. 3 (1969): 167–191. https://doi.org/10.1177/002234336900600301.

Gamson, W. A., and A. Modigliani, eds. "The Changing Culture of Affirmative Action." In *Research in Political Sociology*, 3:137–777. Greenwich, CT: JAI, 1987.

Garfinkel, Harold. *Studies in Ethnomethodology*. Upper Saddle River, NJ: Prentice Hall, 1967.

Garver, Newton. "What Violence Is." *Nation*, June 24, 1968, 817–822.

Gentner, D., and D. R. Gentner. "Flowing Waters or Teeming Crowds: Mental Models of Electricity." In *Mental Models*, edited by D. Gentner and A. L. Stevens, 99–129. Hillsdale, NJ: Erlbaum, 1983.

Gentner, Dedre, and Susan Goldin-Meadow, eds. *Language in Mind: Advances in the Study of Language and Thought*. Cambridge, MA: MIT Press, 2003.

Gerkin, Richard C., & Castro, Jason B. "The Number of Olfactory Stimuli That Humans Can Discriminate Is Still Unknown." *Elife* 4 (2015): 1–15. https://doi.org/10.7554/eLife.08127.001.

Gerrig, Richard J. *Experiencing Narrative Worlds: On the Psychological Activities of Reading*. Boulder, CO: Westview Press, 1993.

Gibson, James J. *The Ecological Approach to Visual Perception*. Boston: Houghton Mifflin, 1979.

Gibson, James J. "The Reproduction of Visually Perceived Forms." *Journal of Experimental Psychology* 12, no. 1 (1929): 1.

Gigerenzer, Gerd. *Gut Feelings: Short Cuts to Better Decision Making*. London: Penguin, 2007.

Gigerenzer, Gerd, Ralph Hertwig, and Thorsten Pachur, eds. *Heuristics: The Foundations of Adaptive Behavior*. Oxford: Oxford University Press, 2011.

Gilbert, A. L., T. Regier, P. Kay, and R. B. Ivry. "Whorf Hypothesis Is Supported in the Right Visual Field But Not the Left." *Proceedings of the National Academy of Sciences* 103, no. 2 (2006): 489–494. https://doi.org/10.1073/pnas.0509868103.

Gilbert, Margaret. "Rationality and Salience." *Philosophical Studies* 57, no. 1 (1989): 61–77. https://doi.org/10.1007/BF00355662.

Gilmore, Jane. *Fixed It: Violence and the Representation of Women in the Media*. Sydney: Viking, 2019.

Gleitman, Lila, and Anna Papafragou. "Language and Thought." In *Cambridge Handbook of Thinking and Reasoning*, edited by Keith J. Jolyoak and Robert G. Morrison, 633–661. Cambridge: Cambridge University Press, 2005.

Gleitman, Lila, and Anna Papafragou. *New Perspectives on Language and Thought*. Oxford: Oxford University Press, 2012. https://doi.org/10.1093/oxfordhb/9780199734689.013.0028.

Gluck, John P. *Voracious Science and Vulnerable Animals: A Primate Scientist's Ethical Journey*. Chicago: University of Chicago Press, 2016.

Goffman, Erving. *Frame Analysis: An Essay on the Organization of Experience*. New York: Harper, 1974.

Goffman, Erving. *The Presentation of Self in Everyday Life*. New York: Doubleday, 1959.

Gottschall, Jonathan. "The Heroine with a Thousand Faces: Universal Trends in the Characterization of Female Folk Tale Protagonists." *Evolutionary Psychology* 3, no. 1 (2005). https://doi.org/10.1177/147470490500300108.

Gottschall, Jonathan. *The Storytelling Animal: How Stories Make Us Human*. Boston: Houghton Mifflin Harcourt, 2012.

Gottschall, J., C. Callanan, N. Casamento, N. Gladd, K. Manganini, T. Milan-Robertson, P. O'Connell, et al. "World Literature's Missing Daughters." Paper presented at the annual meeting of the Northeast Modern Language Association, Pittsburgh, PA, 2004.

Grace, A. *Folktakes of the Maori*. Wellington: Gordon & Gotch, 1907.

Greenspan, Neil. "Taxicab Geometry as a Vehicle for the Journey toward Enlightenment." *Humanistic Mathematics Network Journal* 1, no. 27 (2004): article 5.

Grenand, Pierre. *Introduction a l'Étude de l'Univers Wayãpi*. Paris: Société d'Études Linguistiques et Anthropologiques de France, 1980.

Grice, H. Paul. "Logic and Conversation." In *Speech Acts*, edited by Peter Cole and Jerry L. Morgan, 41–58. New York: Academic Press, 1975.

Grimes, J. "On the Failure to Detect Changes in Scenes across Saccades." In *Perception*, edited by K. Akins, 2:89–110. New York: Oxford University Press, 1996.

Gros-Louis, Julie J., Susan E. Perry, Claudia Fichtel, Eva Wikberg, Hannah Gilkenson, Susan Wofsy, and Alex Fuentes. "Vocal Repertoire of *Cebus capucinus*: Acoustic Structure, Context, and Usage." *International Journal of Primatology* 29, no. 3 (2008): 641–670. https://doi.org/10.1007/s10764-008-9263-8.

Guier, W. H., and G. C. Weiffenbach. "Genesis of Satellite Navigation." *Johns Hopkins APL Technical Digest* 19, no. 1 (1997): 178–181.

Gumperz, John J., and Stephen C. Levinson. *Rethinking Linguistic Relativity*. Cambridge: Cambridge University Press, 1996.

Haidt, Jonathan. *The Righteous Mind: Why Good People Are Divided by Politics and Religion*. New York: Pantheon Books, 2012.

Hale, Kenneth L. "Notes on World View and Semantic Categories: Some Warlpiri Examples." In *Features and Projections*, edited by Pieter Muysken and Henk van Riemsdijk, 233–254. Dordrecht: Foris, 1986.

Harris, Mary B., and Hortensia Baudin. "The Language of Altruism: The Effects of Language, Dress, and Ethnic Group." *Journal of Social Psychology* 91, no. 1 (1973): 37–41. https://doi.org/10.1080/00224545.1973.9922643.

Haslam, Nick. "Concept Creep: Psychology's Expanding Concepts of Harm and Pathology." *Psychological Inquiry* 27, no. 1 (2016): 1–17. https://doi.org/10.1080/1047840X.2016.1082418.

Haun, Daniel B. M., Christian J. Rapold, Gabriele Janzen, and Stephen C. Levinson. "Plasticity of Human Spatial Cognition: Spatial Language and Cognition Covary across Cultures." *Cognition* 119, no. 1 (2011): 70–80. https://doi.org/10.1016/j.cognition.2010.12.009.

Haviland, John B. "Anchoring, Iconicity, and Orientation in Guugu Yimithirr Pointing Gestures." *Journal of Linguistic Anthropology* 3, no. 1 (1993): 3–45. https://doi.org/10.1525/jlin.1993.3.1.3.

Haviland, John B. *Gossip, Reputation and Knowledge in Zinacantan*. Chicago: University of Chicago Press, 1977.

Hawkins, Robert D., Michael C. Frank, and Noah D. Goodman. "Characterizing the Dynamics of Learning in Repeated Reference Games." *Cognitive Science* 44, no. 6 (2020). https://doi.org/10.1111/cogs.12845.

Hays, T. E. "Mauna: Explorations in Ndumba Ethnobotany." PhD diss., University of Washington, 1974.

Heath, Stephen, Colin MacCabe, and Denise Riley. "Raymond Tallis, Not Saussure: A Critique of Post-Saussurean Literary Theory (1988)." In *The Language, Discourse, Society Reader*, edited by Stephen Heath, Colin MacCabe, and Denise Riley, 157–173. London: Palgrave Macmillan, 2004. https://doi.org/10.1057/9780230213340_11.

Henle, Paul, ed. *Language, Thought, and Culture*. Ann Arbor: University of Michigan Press, 1958.

Henning, Hans. *Der Geruch*. Leipzig: J. A. Barth, 1919.

Herder, J. G. von. *Herder: Philosophical Writings*. Edited by Michael N. Forster. Cambridge: Cambridge University Press, 2002.

Heritage, John, Jeffrey D. Robinson, Marc N. Elliott, Megan Beckett, and Michael Wilkes. "Reducing Patients' Unmet Concerns in Primary Care: The Difference One Word Can Make." *Journal of General Internal Medicine* 22, no. 10 (2007): 1429–1433. https://doi.org/10.1007/s11606-007-0279-0.

Herman, Edward S., and Noam Chomsky. *Manufacturing Consent: The Political Economy of the Mass Media*. New York: Pantheon Books, 2002.

Hill, Jane H., and Bruce Mannheim. "Language and World View." *Annual Review of Anthropology* 21, no. 1 (1992): 381–404. https://doi.org/10.1146/annurev.an.21.100192.002121.

Hill, R. A., and Robin I. M. Dunbar. "Social Network Size in Humans." *Human Nature* 14 (2003): 53–72.

Hockett, Charles F. "The Origin of Speech." *Scientific American* 203 (1960): 89–96.

Hoffman, Bruce, Jacob Ware, and Ezra Shapiro. "Assessing the Threat of Incel Violence." *Studies in Conflict and Terrorism* 43, no. 7 (2020): 565–587. https://doi.org/10.1080/1057610X.2020.1751459.

Hoffman, Donald D. *The Case against Reality: Why Evolution Hid the Truth from Our Eyes*. New York: Norton, 2019.

Hoffman, Donald D., Manish Singh, and Chetan Prakash. "The Interface Theory of Perception." *Psychonomic Bulletin and Review* 22, no. 6 (2015): 1480–1506. https://doi.org/10.3758/s13423-015-0890-8.

Hofstadter, Douglas R., and Emmanuel Sander. *Surfaces and Essences: Analogy as the Fuel and Fire of Thinking*. New York: Basic Books, 2013.

Humboldt, Wilhelm von. *On Language: The Diversity of Human Language-Structure and Its Influence on the Mental Development of Mankind*. 1836. Reprint. Cambridge: Cambridge University Press, 1988.

Hume, David. *Dialogues Concerning Natural Religion*. Edited by Dorothy Coleman. Cambridge: Cambridge University Press, 2007.

Humphrey, Nicholas K. "The Social Function of Intellect." In *Growing Points in Ethology*, edited by P. Bateson and Robert A. Hinde, 303–321. Cambridge: Cambridge University Press, 1976.

Hunn, Eugene. "The Utilitarian Factor in Folk Biological Classification." *American Anthropologist* 84, no. 4 (1982): 830–847. https://doi.org/10.1525/aa.1982.84.4.02a00070.

Hunt, E. B., and M. R. Banaji. "The Whorfian Hypothesis Revisited: A Cognitive Science View of Linguistic and Cultural Effects on Thought." In *Indigenous Cognition: Functioning in Cultural Context*, edited by J. W. Berry, S. H. Irvine, and E. B. Hunt, 57–84. Dordrecht: Springer Netherlands, 1988.

Hutchins, Edwin. *Cognition in the Wild*. Cambridge, MA: MIT Press, 1995.

Hutchins, Edwin. "The Distributed Cognition Perspective on Human Interaction." In *Roots of Human Sociality*, edited by N. J. Enfield and Stephen C. Levinson, 375–398. Oxford: Berg, 2006. https://doi.org/10.4324/9781003135517-19.

Hutchins, Edwin, and Brian Hazlehurst. "How to Invent a Shared Lexicon: The Emergence of Shared Form: Meaning Mappings in Interaction." In *Social Intelligence and Interaction: Expressions and Implications of the Social Bias in Human Intelligence*, edited by Esther N. Goody, 53–67. Cambridge: Cambridge University Press, 1995. https://doi.org/10.1017/CBO9780511621710.005.

Hutchins, Edwin, and Christine M. Johnson. "Modeling the Emergence of Language as an Embodied Collective Cognitive Activity." *Topics in Cognitive Science* 1, no. 3 (2009): 523–46. https://doi.org/10.1111/j.1756-8765.2009.01033.x.

Hymes, Dell H. *Language in Culture and Society: A Reader in Linguistics and Anthropology*. New York: Harper, 1964.

Indefrey, Peter. "The Spatial and Temporal Signatures of Word Production Components: A Critical Update." *Frontiers in Psychology* 2 (2011). https://doi.org/10.3389/fpsyg.2011.00255.

Ingold, Tim. *The Perception of the Environment: Essays on Livelihood, Dwelling and Skill*. London; New York: Routledge, 2000.

Isaacs, Ellen A., and Herbert H. Clark. "References in Conversation between Experts and Novices." *Journal of Experimental Psychology: General* 116, no. 1 (1987): 26–37. https://doi.org/10.1037/0096-3445.116.1.26.

Jacobson, R. "Concluding Statement: Linguistics and Poetics." In *Style in Language*, edited by Thomas A. Sebeok. Cambridge, MA: MIT Press, 1960.

Jameson, Fredric. *The Prison-House of Language: A Critical Account of Structuralism and Russian Formalism*. Princeton, NJ: Princeton University Press, 1972.

Jefferson, Gail. "A Case of Precision Timing in Ordinary Conversation: Overlapped Tag-Positioned Address Terms in Closing Sequences." *Semiotica* 9, no. 1 (1973). https://doi.org/10.1515/semi.1973.9.1.47.

Jefferson, Gail. *Talking about Troubles in Conversation*. New York: Oxford University Press, 2015.

Jefferson, Gail, and J. R. E. Lee. "End of Grant Report to the British SSRC on the Analysis of Conversations in Which 'Troubles' and 'Anxieties' Are Expressed." Ref. HR 4805/2, 1980. Cited in Jefferson, Gail. *Talking about Troubles in Conversation*. New York: Oxford University Press, 2015.

Johnson, Ralph H., and J. Anthony Blair. *Logical Self-Defense*. New York: International Debate Education Association, 2006.

Johnson, Steven. *Where Good Ideas Come From: The Natural History of Innovation*. New York: Riverhead Books, 2010.

Jolly, A. "Lemur Social Behavior and Primate Intelligence." *Science* 153, no. 3735 (1966): 501–506. https://doi.org/10.1126/science.153.3735.501.

Judd, Deane Brewster, and Günter Wyszecki. *Color in Business, Science, and Industry*, 3rd ed. New York: Wiley, 1975.

Kahneman, Daniel. *Thinking, Fast and Slow*. New York: Penguin, 2011.

Kaplan, Michael, Sam L. Campbell, John M. Martin, David G. Wulp, and C. Edward Lipinski. "A Restraining Device for Psychophysiological Experimentation with Dogs." *Journal of the Experimental Analysis of Behavior* 5, no. 2 (1962): 209–211. https://doi.org/10.1901/jeab.1962.5-209.

Kay, Paul, Brent Berlin, Luisa Maffi, and William Merrifield. "Color Naming across Languages." In *Color Categories in Thought and Language*, edited by C. L. Hardin and Luisa Maffi, 21–56. Cambridge: Cambridge University Press, 1997. https://doi.org/10.1017/CBO9780511519819.002.

Kay, Paul, and Luisa Maffi. "Color Appearance and the Emergence and Evolution of Basic Color Lexicons." *American Anthropologist* 101, no. 4 (1999): 743–760. https://doi.org/10.1525/aa.1999.101.4.743.

Kemp, Charles, Yang Xu, and Terry Regier. "Semantic Typology and Efficient Communication." *Annual Review of Linguistics* 4, no. 1 (2018): 109–128. https://doi.org/10.1146/annurev-linguistics-011817-045406.

Kendon, Adam. *Conducting Interaction: Patterns of Behavior in Focused Encounters*. Cambridge: Cambridge University Press, 1990.

Kendrick, Keith M. "The Neurobiology of Social Bonds." *Journal of Neuroendocrinology* 16, no. 12 (2004): 1007–1008. https://doi.org/10.1111/j.1365-2826.2004.01262.x.

Kennedy, Chris. "Systemic Grammar and Its Use in Literary Analysis." In *Language and Literature: An Introductory Reader in Stylistics*, 3rd ed., edited by Ronald Carter, 82–99. London: Routledge, 1991.

Keysar, Boaz, Dale J. Barr, Jennifer A. Balin, and Jason S. Brauner. "Taking Perspective in Conversation: The Role of Mutual Knowledge in Comprehension." *Psychological Science* 11, no. 1 (2000): 32–38. https://doi.org/10.1111/1467-9280.00211.

King, Darren N., Wendy S. Shaw, Peter N. Meihana, and James R. Goff. "Māori Oral Histories and the Impact of Tsunamis in Aotearoa-New Zealand." *Natural Hazards and Earth System Sciences* 18, no. 3 (2018): 907–919. https://doi.org/10.5194/nhess-18-907-2018.

Knight, Chris, Robin Dunbar, and Camilla Power. "An Evolutionary Approach to Human Culture." In *The Evolution of Culture: A Historical and Scientific Overview*, edited by Robin Dunbar, Chris Knight, and Camilla Power, 1–11. New Brunswick , NJ: Rutgers University Press, 1999.

Kockelman, Paul. *Agent, Person, Subject, Self: A Theory of Ontology, Interaction, and Infrastructure*. Oxford: Oxford University Press, 2013.

Kockelman, Paul. *Language, Culture, and Mind: Natural Constructions and Social Kinds.* Cambridge: Cambridge University Press, 2010.

Korzybski, Alfred. *Selections from Science and Sanity: An Introduction to Non-Aristotelian Systems and General Semantics.* Forest Hills, NY: Institute of General Semantics, 1933.

Krebs, J. R., and R Dawkins. "Animal Signals: Mind Reading and Manipulation." In *Behavioral Ecology: An Evolutionary Approach,* 2nd ed., edited by J. R. Krebs and N. B. Davies, 380–405. Oxford: Blackwell Scientific, 1984.

Kruglanski, Arie W., Martha Crenshaw, Jerrold M. Post, and Jeff Victoroff. "What Should This Fight Be Called? Metaphors of Counterterrorism and Their Implications." *Psychological Science in the Public Interest* 8, no. 3 (2007): 97–133. https://doi .org/10.1111/j.1539-6053.2008.00035.x.

Kuehni, R. G. "How Many Object Colors Can We Distinguish?" *Color Research & Application* 41 (2016): 439–444. https://doi.org/ 10.1002/col.21980

Kuran, Timur. *Private Truths, Public Lies: The Social Consequences of Preference Falsification.* Cambridge, MA: Harvard University Press, 1997.

Kutas, M., and S. Hillyard. "Reading Senseless Sentences: Brain Potentials Reflect Semantic Incongruity." *Science* 207, no. 4427 (1980): 203–205. https://doi.org/10 .1126/science.7350657.

Labov, William. *Language in the Inner City: Studies in the Black English Vernacular.* Philadelphia: University of Pennsylvania Press, 1972.

Laer, Tom van, Ko de Ruyter, Luca M. Visconti, and Martin Wetzels. "The Extended Transportation-Imagery Model: A Meta-Analysis of the Antecedents and Consequences of Consumers' Narrative Transportation." *Journal of Consumer Research* 40, no. 5 (2014): 797–817. https://doi.org/10.1086/673383.

Lakoff, George. *Women, Fire, and Dangerous Things: What Categories Reveal about the Mind.* Chicago: University of Chicago Press, 1987.

Lakoff, George, and Mark Johnson. *Metaphors We Live By.* Chicago: University of Chicago Press, 1980.

Lakoff, George. *Don't Think of an Elephant! Know Your Values and Frame the Debate.* Vermont: Chelsea Green, 2004.

Lau, Ellen F., Colin Phillips, and David Poeppel. "A Cortical Network for Semantics: (De)Constructing the N400." *Nature Reviews Neuroscience* 9, no. 12 (2008): 920–933. https://doi.org/10.1038/nrn2532.

Leavitt, John. *Linguistic Relativities: Language Diversity and Modern Thought.* Cambridge: Cambridge University Press, 2010.

Lee, Heon-Jin, Abbe H. Macbeth, Jerome Pagani, and W. Scott Young. "Oxytocin: The Great Facilitator of Life." *Progress in Neurobiology*, April 10, 2009. https://doi.org /10.1016/j.pneurobio.2009.04.001.

Lee, Penny. *The Whorf Theory Complex: A Critical Reconstruction*. Amsterdam: John Benjamins, 1996.

Lee, Steven. "Poverty and Violence." *Social Theory and Practice* 22, no. 1 (1996): 67–82. https://doi.org/10.5840/soctheorpract199622119.

Leeming, David Adams. *Creation Myths of the World: An Encyclopedia*, 2nd ed. Santa Barbara, CA: ABC-CLIO, 2010.

Lehmann, Christian. "Roots, Stems and Word Classes." *Studies in Language* 32, no. 3 (2008): 546–567. https://doi.org/10.1075/sl.32.3.04leh.

Levelt, Willem J. M. *Speaking: From Intention to Articulation*. Cambridge, MA: MIT Press, 1989.

Levelt, Willem J. M. *A History of Psycholinguistics: The Pre-Chomskyan Era*. Oxford: Oxford University Press, 2012.

Levin, Daniel T., and Daniel J. Simons. "Failure to Detect Changes to Attended Objects in Motion Pictures." *Psychonomic Bulletin and Review* 4, no. 4 (1997): 501–506. https://doi.org/10.3758/BF03214339.

Levinson, Stephen C. "Foreword." In *Language, Thought, and Reality*, edited by Benjamin Lee Whorf, vii–xxiii. Cambridge, MA: MIT Press, 2012.

Levinson, Stephen C. "Language and Mind: Let's Get the Issues Straight." In *Language and Mind: Advances in the Study of Language and Thought*, edited by Dedre Gentner and Susan Goldin-Meadow, 25–46. Cambridge, MA: MIT Press, 2003.

Levinson, Stephen C. "On the Human 'Interaction Engine.'" In *Roots of Human Sociality: Culture, Cognition and Interaction*, edited by N. J. Enfield and Stephen C. Levinson, 39–69. New York: Berg, 2006.

Levinson, Stephen C. "Parts of the Body in Yélî Dnye, the Papuan Language of Rossel Island." *Language Sciences* 28, no. 2–3 (2006): 221–240. https://doi.org/10.1016/j.langsci .2005.11.007.

Levinson, Stephen C. *Presumptive Meanings: The Theory of Generalized Conversational Implicature*. Cambridge, MA.: MIT Press, 2000.

Levinson, Stephen C. *Space in Language and Cognition: Explorations in Cognitive Diversity*. Cambridge: Cambridge University Press, 2003.

Levinson, Stephen C. "Turn-Taking in Human Communication—Origins and Implications for Language Processing." *Trends in Cognitive Sciences* 20, no. 1 (2016): 6–14. https://doi.org/10.1016/j.tics.2015.10.010.

Levinson, Stephen C., and Asifa Majid. "Differential Ineffability and the Senses." *Mind and Language* 29, no. 4 (2014): 407–427. https://doi.org/10.1111/mila.12057.

Lévi-Strauss, Claude. *The Savage Mind*. Chicago: University of Chicago Press, 1966.

Levy, Robert I. *Tahitians: Mind and Experience in the Society Islands*. Chicago: University of Chicago Press (1973).

Lewis, David K. *Convention: A Philosophical Study*. Oxford: Blackwell, 1969.

Lieberman, Amy M. "Attention-Getting Skills of Deaf Children Using American Sign Language in a Preschool Classroom." *Applied Psycholinguistics* 36 (2014): 1–19. https://doi.org/10.1017/S0142716413000532.

Lindenfors, Patrik, Andreas Wartel, and Johan Lind. "'Dunbar's Number' Deconstructed." *Biology Letters* 17 (2021): 1–4. https://doi.org/10.1098/rsbl.2021.0158.

Liszkowski, Ulf. "Infant Pointing at Twelve Months: Communicative Goals, Motives, and Social-Cognitive Abilities." In *Roots of Human Sociality: Culture, Cognition, and Interaction*, edited by N. J. Enfield and Stephen C. Levinson, 153–178. London: Berg, 2006.

Liszkowski, Ulf, Malinda Carpenter, Anne Henning, Tricia Striano, and Michael Tomasello. "Twelve-Month-Olds Point to Share Attention and Interest." *Developmental Science* 7, no. 3 (2004): 297–307. https://doi.org/10.1111/j.1467-7687.2004.00349.x.

Livholts, Mona. "The Loathsome, the Rough Type and the Monster: The Violence and Wounding of Media Texts on Rape." In *Sex, Violence and the Body*, edited by Viv Burr and Jeff Hearn, 194–211. London: Palgrave Macmillan, 2008.

Lloyd Parry, Richard. *Ghosts of the Tsunami: Death and Life in Japan's Disaster Zone*. New York: MCD/Farrar, Straus and Giroux, 2017.

Loftus, Elizabeth F., and John C. Palmer. "Reconstruction of Automobile Destruction: An Example of the Interaction between Language and Memory." *Journal of Verbal Learning and Verbal Behavior* 13, no. 5 (1974): 585–589. https://doi.org/10.1016/S0022-5371(74)80011-3.

Lucy, John A. *Language Diversity and Thought: A Reformulation of the Linguistic Relativity Hypothesis*. Cambridge: Cambridge University Press, 1992.

Lucy, John A. "Linguistic Relativity." *Annual Review of Anthropology* 26, no. 1 (1997): 291–312. https://doi.org/10.1146/annurev.anthro.26.1.291.

Lucy, John A. "The Scope of Linguistic Relativity." In *Rethinking Linguistic Relativity*, edited by John J. Gumperz and Stephen C. Levinson, 37–69. Cambridge: Cambridge University Press, 1996. https://www.jstor.org/stable/2743696.

Ludwin, R. S., C. P. Thrush, K. James, D. Buerge, C. Jonientz-Trisler, J. Rasmussen, K. Troost, and A. de los Angeles. "Serpent Spirit-Power Stories along the Seattle Fault."

Seismological Research Letters 76, no. 4 (2005): 426–431. https://doi.org/10.1785/gssrl
.76.4.426.

Luk, Ellison, and Maïa Ponsonnet. "Discourse and Pragmatic Functions of the Dala-bon 'Ergative' Case-Marker." *Australian Journal of Linguistics* 39, no. 3 (2019): 287–328. https://doi.org/10.1080/07268602.2019.1623758.

Luntz, Frank I. *Words That Work: It's Not What You Say, It's What People Hear.* New York: Hyperion, 2008.

Lupyan, Gary. "From Chair to 'Chair': A Representational Shift Account of Object Labeling Effects on Memory." *Journal of Experimental Psychology: General* 137, no. 2 (2008): 348–369. https://doi.org/10.1037/0096-3445.137.2.348.

Lupyan, Gary, David H. Rakison, and James L. McClelland. "Language Is Not Just for Talking: Redundant Labels Facilitate Learning of Novel Categories." *Psychological Science* 18, no. 12 (2007): 1077–1083. https://doi.org/10.1111/j.1467-9280.2007.02028.x.

Machin, A. J., and R. I. M. Dunbar. "The Brain Opioid Theory of Social Attachment: A Review of the Evidence." *Behavior* 148, no. 9–10 (2011): 985–1025. https://doi.org/10.1163/000579511X596624.

Majid, Asifa. "Words for Parts of the Body." In *Words and the Mind: How Words Capture Human Experience*, edited by Barbara Malt and Phillip Wolff, 58–71. Oxford: Oxford University Press, 2010.

Majid, Asifa, Melissa Bowerman, Sotaro Kita, Daniel B.M. Haun, and Stephen C. Levinson. "Can Language Restructure Cognition? The Case for Space." *Trends in Cognitive Sciences* 8, no. 3 (2004): 108–114. https://doi.org/10.1016/j.tics.2004.01.003.

Majid, Asifa, Melissa Bowerman, Miriam van Staden, and James S. Boster. "The Semantic Categories of Cutting and Breaking Events: A Crosslinguistic Perspective." *Cognitive Linguistics* 18, no. 2 (2007). https://doi.org/10.1515/COG.2007.005.

Majid, Asifa, and Niclas Burenhult. "Odors Are Expressible in Language, as Long as You Speak the Right Language." *Cognition* 130, no. 2 (2014): 266–270. https://doi.org/10.1016/j.cognition.2013.11.004.

Majid, Asifa, Niclas Burenhult, Marcus Stensmyr, Josje de Valk, and Bill S. Hansson. "Olfactory Language and Abstraction across Cultures." *Philosophical Transactions of the Royal Society B: Biological Sciences* 373, no. 1752 (2018): 1–8. https://doi.org/10.1098/rstb.2017.0139.

Majid, Asifa, Laura Speed, Ilja Croijmans, and Artin Arshamian. "What Makes a Better Smeller?" *Perception* 46, no. 3–4 (2017): 406–430. https://doi.org/10.1177/0301006616688224.

Majid, Asifa, and Miriam van Staden. "Can Nomenclature for the Body Be Explained by Embodiment Theories?" *Topics in Cognitive Science* 7, no. 4 (2015): 570–594. https://doi.org/10.1111/tops.12159.

Malt, Barbara C., Silvia Gennari, Mutsumi Imai, Eef Ameel, Naoaki Tsuda, and Asifa Majid. "Talking about Walking: Biomechanics and the Language of Locomotion." *Psychological Science* 19, no. 3 (2008): 232–240. https://doi.org/10.1111/j.1467-9280 .2008.02074.x.

Mar, Raymond A. "The Neural Bases of Social Cognition and Story Comprehension." *Annual Review of Psychology* 62, no. 1 (2011): 103–134. https://doi.org/10.1146 /annurev-psych-120709-145406.

Mar, Raymond A., and Keith Oatley. "The Function of Fiction Is the Abstraction and Simulation of Social Experience." *Perspectives on Psychological Science* 3, no. 3 (2008): 173–192. https://doi.org/10.1111/j.1745-6924.2008.00073.x.

Marr, David. *Vision: A Computational Investigation into the Human Representation and Processing of Visual Information*. Cambridge, MA: MIT Press, 1982.

Martin, Laura. "Eskimo Words for Snow: A Case Study in the Genesis and Decay of an Anthropological Example." *American Anthropologist* 88, no. 2 (1986): 418–423.

Masaoka, Kenichiro, Roy S. Berns, Mark D. Fairchild, and Farhad Moghareh Abed. "Number of Discernible Object Colors Is a Conundrum." *Journal of the Optical Society of America A* 30, no. 2 (2013): 264. https://doi.org/10.1364/JOSAA.30.000264.

Mathews, Peter D. *Lacan the Charlatan*. Cham, Switzerland: Palgrave, 2020.

McEvoy, Paul. *Niels Bohr: Reflections on Subject and Object*. San Francisco: Microanalytix, 2001.

McGoey, Linsey. *The Unknowers: How Strategic Ignorance Rules the World*. London: Zed Books, 2019.

McKenzie, Craig R. M. "Framing Effects in Inference Tasks—and Why They Are Normatively Defensible." *Memory and Cognition* 32, no. 6 (2004): 874–885. https://doi .org/10.3758/BF03196866.

McKenzie, Craig R. M., and Jonathan D. Nelson. "What a Speaker's Choice of Frame Reveals: Reference Points, Frame Selection, and Framing Effects." *Psychonomic Bulletin and Review* 10, no. 3 (2003): 596–602. https://doi.org/10.3758/BF031 96520.

McWhorter, John H. *The Language Hoax: Why the World Looks the Same in Any Language*. Oxford: Oxford University Press, 2014.

Mehl, Matthias R., and James W. Pennebaker. "The Sounds of Social Life: A Psychometric Analysis of Students' Daily Social Environments and Natural Conversations." *Journal of Personality and Social Psychology* 84, no. 4 (2003): 857–870. https://doi.org /10.1037/0022-3514.84.4.857.

Melcher, Joseph M., and Jonathan W. Schooler. "The Misremembrance of Wines Past: Verbal and Perceptual Expertise Differentially Mediate Verbal Overshadowing of Taste Memory." *Journal of Memory and Language* 35, no. 2 (1996): 231–245. https://doi.org/10.1006/jmla.1996.0013.

Mercier, Hugo. *Not Born Yesterday: The Science of Who We Trust and What We Believe.* Princeton: Princeton University Press, 2020.

Mercier, Hugo, and Dan Sperber. *The Enigma of Reason.* Cambridge, MA: Harvard University Press, 2019.

Mermelstein, Spencer, Michael Barlev, and Tamsin German. "She Told Me about a Singing Cactus: Counterintuitive Concepts Are More Accurately Attributed to Their Speakers than Ordinary Concepts." PsyArXiv, June 7, 2019. https://doi.org/10.31234/osf.io/6cp8e.

Merrill, Natalie, Jordan A. Booker, and Robyn Fivush. "Functions of Parental Intergenerational Narratives Told by Young People." *Topics in Cognitive Science* 11, no. 4 (2019): 752–773. https://doi.org/10.1111/tops.12356.

Merrill, Natalie, and Robyn Fivush. "Intergenerational Narratives and Identity across Development." *Developmental Review* 40 (2016): 72–92. https://doi.org/10.1016/j.dr.2016.03.001.

Mesoudi, Alex, and Andrew Whiten. "The Hierarchical Transformation of Event Knowledge in Human Cultural Transmission." *Journal of Cognition and Culture* 4, no. 1 (2004): 1–24. https://doi.org/10.1163/156853704323074732.

Michael, L. "Reformulating the Sapir-Whorf Hypothesis: Discourse, Interaction, and Distributed Cognition." In *Texas Linguistic Forum*, edited by Inger Mey, Ginger Pizer, Hsi-Yao Su, and Susan Szmania. Austin: University of Texas Press, 2002. http://salsa.ling.utexas.edu/proceedings/2002/michael.pdf.

Michotte, A. *The Perception of Causality.* Oxford: Basic Books, 1963.

Miller, George A., and Philip Nicholas Johnson-Laird. *Language and Perception.* Cambridge, MA: Belknap Press of Harvard University Press, 1976.

Moore, Henry T. "Further Data Concerning Sex Differences." *Journal of Abnormal Psychology and Social Psychology* 17, no. 2 (1922): 210–214. https://doi.org/10.1037/h0064645.

Morin, Olivier, Alberto Acerbi, and Oleg Sobchuk. "Why People Die in Novels: Testing the Ordeal Simulation Hypothesis." *Palgrave Communications* 5, no. 1 (2019): 62. https://doi.org/10.1057/s41599-019-0267-0.

Morrison, Jody D. "Enacting Involvement: Some Conversational Practices for Being in Relationship" (PhD diss., Temple University, 1997).

Murphy, Gregory L. *The Big Book of Concepts.* Cambridge, MA: MIT Press, 2002.

Necker, L.A. "LXI. *Observations on Some Remarkable Optical Phænomena Seen in Switzerland; and on an Optical Phænomenon Which Occurs on Viewing a Figure of a Crystal or*

Geometrical Solid." *The London, Edinburgh, and Dublin Philosophical Magazine and Journal of Science* 1, no. 5 (1832): 329–337. https://doi.org/10.1080/14786443208647909.

Nevo, Omer, Kim Valenta, Diary Razafimandimby, Amanda D. Melin, Manfred Ayasse, and Colin A. Chapman. "Frugivores and the Evolution of Fruit Color." *Biology Letters* 14, no. 9 (2018): 20180377. https://doi.org/10.1098/rsbl.2018.0377.

Newman, Mark, Sounthone Ketphanh, Bouakhaykhone Svengsuksa, Philip Thomas, Khamphone Sengdala, Vichith Lamxay, and Kate Armstrong. *A Checklist for the Vascular Plants of Lao PDR.* Edinburgh, UK : Royal Botanic Garden Edinburgh, 2007. https://portals.iucn.org/library/node/9074.

Newman-Norlund, Sarah E., Matthijs L. Noordzij, Roger D. Newman-Norlund, Inge A.C. Volman, Jan Peter de Ruiter, Peter Hagoort, and Ivan Toni. "Recipient Design in Tacit Communication." *Cognition* 111, no. 1 (2009): 46–54. https://doi.org/10.1016/j.cognition.2008.12.004.

Nguyen, C. Thi. "The Seductions of Clarity." *Royal Institute of Philosophy Supplement* 89 (2021): 227–255. https://doi.org/10.1017/S1358246121000035.

Norman, Donald A. *The Design of Everyday Things.* New York: Basic Books, 1988.

Norrick, Neal R. *Conversational Narrative: Storytelling in Everyday Talk.* Amsterdam: John Benjamins, 2000.

Norris, Ray P. "Dawes Review 5: Australian Aboriginal Astronomy and Navigation." *Publications of the Astronomical Society of Australia* 33 (2016). https://doi.org/10.1017/pasa.2016.25.

Nummenmaa, Lauri, Sandra Manninen, Lauri Tuominen, Jussi Hirvonen, Kari K. Kalliokoski, Pirjo Nuutila, Iiro P. Jääskeläinen, et al. "Adult Attachment Style Is Associated with Cerebral μ-Opioid Receptor Availability in Humans: Opioids and Attachment." *Human Brain Mapping* 36, no. 9 (2015): 3621–3628. https://doi.org/10.1002/hbm.22866.

Nunn, Patrick D., and Nicholas J. Reid. "Aboriginal Memories of Inundation of the Australian Coast Dating from More Than 7000 Years Ago." *Australian Geographer* 47, no. 1 (2016): 11–47. https://doi.org/10.1080/00049182.2015.1077539.

Nuttall, Louise. "Transitivity, Agency, Mind Style: What's the Lowest Common Denominator?" *Language and Literature: International Journal of Stylistics* 28, no. 2 (2019): 159–179. https://doi.org/10.1177/0963947019839851.

Oldfield, R. C., and A. Wingfield. "Response Latencies in Naming Objects." *Quarterly Journal of Experimental Psychology* 17, no. 4 (1965): 273–281. https://doi.org/10.1080/17470216508416445.

Origgi, Gloria. *Reputation: What It Is and Why It Matters.* Translated by Stephen Holmes and Noga Arikha. Princeton: Princeton University Press, 2018.

Orwell, George. "Politics and the English Language." *Horizon* 13, no. 76 (1946): 252–265.

Pearce, Eiluned, Jacques Launay, and Robin I. M. Dunbar. "The Ice-Breaker Effect: Singing Mediates Fast Social Bonding." *Royal Society Open Science* 2, no. 10 (2015): 150221. https://doi.org/10.1098/rsos.150221.

Pearce, Eiluned, Rafael Wlodarski, Anna Machin, and Robin I. M. Dunbar. "Variation in the β-Endorphin, Oxytocin, and Dopamine Receptor Genes Is Associated with Different Dimensions of Human Sociality." *Proceedings of the National Academy of Sciences* 114, no. 20 (2017): 5300–5305. https://doi.org/10.1073/pnas.1700712114.

Perry, Susan. "Case Study 4A: Coalitionary Aggression in White-Faced Capuchins." In *Animal Social Complexity*, edited by Frans B. M. de Waal and Peter L. Tyack, 111–114. Cambridge, MA: Harvard University Press, 2003. https://doi.org/10.4159/harvard.9780674419131.c8.

Perry, Susan. "Male-Male Social Relationships in Wild White-Faced Capuchins, *Cebus capucinus.*" *Behavior* 135, no. 2 (1998): 139–172.

Perry, Susan. *Manipulative Monkeys: The Capuchins of Lomas Barbudal.* Cambridge, MA: Harvard University Press, 2008.

Pillet-Shore, Danielle. "Greeting: Displaying Stance Through Prosodic Recipient Design." *Research on Language and Social Interaction* 45, no. 4 (2012): 375–398. https://doi.org/10.1080/08351813.2012.724994.

Pillet-Shore, Danielle. "When to Make the Sensory Social: Registering in Face-to-Face Openings: When to Make the Sensory Social." *Symbolic Interaction*, March 27, 2020. https://doi.org/10.1002/symb.481.

Pillsbury, Walter Bowers. "A Study in Apperception." *American Journal of Psychology* 8, no. 3 (1897): 315–393. https://doi.org/10.2307/1411485.

Pinker, Steven. *The Language Instinct: The New Science of Language and Mind.* London: Allen Lane, Penguin Press, 1994.

Pointer, M. R., and G. G. Attridge. "The Number of Discernible Colours." *Color Research and Application* 23, no. 1 (1998): 52–54. https://doi.org/10.1002/(SICI)1520-6378(199802)23:1<52::AID-COL8>3.0.CO;2-2.

Pomerantz, A. "Agreeing and Disagreeing with Assessments: Some Features of Preferred/Dispreferred Turn Shapes." In *Structures of Social Action*, edited by J. M. Atkinson and J. Heritage, 57–101. Cambridge: Cambridge University Press, 1984.

Pomerantz, A. *Asking and Telling in Conversation.* New York: Oxford University Press, 2021.

Pomerantz, A. "Compliment Responses: Notes on the Co-Operation of Multiple Constraints." In *Studies in the Organization of Conversational Interaction*, edited by J. Schenkein, 79–112. New York: Academic Press, 1978.

Pomerantz, Anita, and Jenny Mandelbaum. "Conversation Analytic Approaches to the Relevance and Uses of Relationship Categories in Interaction." In *Handbook of Language and Social Interaction*, edited by Kristine L. Fitch and Robert E. Sanders, 149–171. Mahwah, NJ: Erlbaum, 2005.

Popper, Karl R. *Objective Knowledge: An Evolutionary Approach.* Oxford: Clarendon Press, 1972.

Proffitt, Dennis, and Drake Baer. *Perception: How Our Bodies Shape Our Minds.* New York: St. Martin's Press, 2020.

Rachels, James, ed. *Moral Problems: A Collection of Philosophical Essays.* New York: Harper, 1971.

Rachels, James, and Frank A. Tillman, eds. *Philosophical Issues.* New York: Harper, 1972.

Reddy, Michael J. "The Conduit Metaphor: A Case of Frame Conflict in Our Language about Language." In *Metaphor and Thought*, edited by Andrew Ortony, 284–324. Cambridge: Cambridge University Press, 1979. https://doi.org/10.1017/CBO9781139 173865.012.

Reines, Maria Francisca, and Jesse Prinz. "Reviving Whorf: The Return of Linguistic Relativity." *Philosophy Compass* 4, no. 6 (2009): 1022–1032. https://doi.org/10.1111 /j.1747-9991.2009.00260.x.

Riou, Marine, Stephen Ball, Teresa A. Williams, Austin Whiteside, Kay L. O'Halloran, Janet Bray, Gavin D. Perkins, et al. "'Tell Me Exactly What's Happened': When Linguistic Choices Affect the Efficiency of Emergency Calls for Cardiac Arrest." *Resuscitation* 117 (2017): 58–65. https://doi.org/10.1016/j.resuscitation.2017.06.002.

Roberson, Debi, Jules Davidoff, Ian R. L. Davies, and Laura R. Shapiro. "Color Categories: Evidence for the Cultural Relativity Hypothesis." *Cognitive Psychology* 50, no. 4 (2005): 378–411. https://doi.org/10.1016/j.cogpsych.2004.10.001.

Roberson, Debi, Ian Davies, and Jules Davidoff. "Color Categories Are Not Universal: Replications and New Evidence from a Stone-Age Culture." *Journal of Experimental Psychology: General* 129, no. 3 (2000): 369–398. https://doi.org/10.1037/0096-3445 .129.3.369.

Roberson, Debi, and R. Hanley. "Relatively Speaking: An Account of the Relationship between Language and Thought in the Color Domain." In *Words and the Mind: How Words Capture Human Experiencee*, edited by Barbara C. Malt and Phillip Wolff, 183–198. New York: Oxford University Press, 2010.

Rosch, Eleanor. "Linguistic Relativity." In *Thinking: Readings in Cognitive Science*, edited by P. N. Johnson-Laird and P. C. Wason, 501–522. Cambridge: Cambridge Univ. Press, 1977.

Rosch, Eleanor. "Principles of Categorization." In *Cognition and Categorization*, edited by Eleanor Rosch and B. B. Lloyd, 27–48. Hillsdale, NJ: Erlbaum, 1978. https://doi .org/10.1016/B978-1-4832-1446-7.50028-5.

Rosch, Eleanor, Carolyn B. Mervis, Wayne D. Gray, David M. Johnson, and Penny Boyes-Braem. "Basic Objects in Natural Categories." *Cognitive Psychology* 8, no. 3 (1976): 382–439. https://doi.org/10.1016/0010-0285(76)90013-X.

Ryle, Gilbert. *The Perception of the Environment Essays on Livelihood, Dwelling and Skill.* London: Hutchinson, 1949.

Sacks, Harvey. *Lectures on Conversation*. Edited by Gail Jefferson. London: Blackwell, 1992.

Sacks, Harvey, Emanuel A. Schegloff, and Gail Jefferson. "A Simplest Systematics for the Organization of Turn-Taking for Conversation." *Language* 50, no. 4 (1974): 40.

Sales, Leigh. *Any Ordinary Day: Blindsides, Resilience and What Happens after the Worst Day of Your Life.* Sydney: Hamish Hamilton, 2019.

Sapir, Edward. *Selected Writings*. Berkeley: University of California Press, 1949.

Scalise Sugiyama, Michelle. "Food, Foragers, and Folklore: The Role of Narrative in Human Subsistence." *Evolution and Human Behavior* 22, no. 4 (2001): 221–240. https://doi.org/10.1016/S1090-5138(01)00063-0.

Scalise Sugiyama, Michelle. "On the Origins of Narrative: Storyteller Bias as a Fitness-Enhancing Strategy." *Human Nature* 7, no. 4 (1996): 403–425. https://doi.org /10.1007/BF02732901.

Scalise Sugiyama, Michelle. "Oral Storytelling as Evidence of Pedagogy in Forager Societies." *Frontiers in Psychology* 8 (2017). https://doi.org/10.3389/fpsyg.2017 .00471.

Scalise Sugiyama, Michelle. "Reverse-Engineering Narrative: Evidence of Special Design." In *The Literary Animal*, edited by J. Gottschall and D. S. Wilson, 177–196. Evanston, IL: Northwestern University Press, 2005.

Scharling, Henrik. *Nicolai's Marriage: A Picture of Danish Family Life.* 2 vols. London: Richard Bentley and Son, 1876.

Schegloff, Emanuel A. *Sequence Organization in Interaction: A Primer in Conversation Analysis.* Cambridge: Cambridge University Press, 2007.

Schegloff, Emanuel A. "Sequencing in Conversational Openings." *American Anthropologist* 70, no. 6 (1968): 1075–1095. https://doi.org/10.1525/aa.1968.70.6.02a 00030.

Schelling, Thomas C. *The Strategy of Conflict.* Cambridge, MA: Harvard University Press, 1960.

Scherer, Aaron M., Laura D. Scherer, and Angela Fagerlin. "Getting Ahead of Illness: Using Metaphors to Influence Medical Decision Making." *Medical Decision Making* 35, no. 1 (2015): 37–45. https://doi.org/10.1177/0272989X14522547.

Scholl, Brian J., and Ken Nakayama. "Causal Capture: Contextual Effects on the Perception of Collision Events." *Psychological Science* 13, no. 6 (2002): 493–498. https://doi.org/10.1111/1467-9280.00487.

Schöner, G., W. Y. Jiang, and J. A. S. Kelso. "A Synergetic Theory of Quadrupedal Gaits and Gait Transitions." *Journal of Theoretical Biology* 142, no. 3 (1990): 359–391. https://doi.org/10.1016/S0022-5193(05)80558-2.

Schooler, Jonathan W., and Tonya Y. Engstler-Schooler. "Verbal Overshadowing of Visual Memories: Some Things Are Better Left Unsaid." *Cognitive Psychology* 22, no. 1 (1990): 36–71. https://doi.org/10.1016/0010-0285(90)90003-M.

Schudson, Michael. *Watergate in American Memory: How We Remember, Forget, and Reconstruct the Past.* New York: Basic Books, 1992.

Schultz, E. *Dialogue at the Margins: Whorf, Bakhtin, and Linguistic Relativity.* Madison: University of Wisconsin Press, 1990.

Searle, John R. *Speech Acts: An Essay in the Philosophy of Language.* Cambridge: Cambridge University Press, 1969.

Sellars, Wilfrid. *In the Space of Reasons: Selected Essays of Wilfrid Sellars.* Edited by Kevin Scharp and Robert Brandom. Cambridge, MA: Harvard University Press, 2007.

Shalvi, S., and C. K. W. De Dreu. "Oxytocin Promotes Group-Serving Dishonesty." *Proceedings of the National Academy of Sciences* 111, no. 15 (2014): 5503–5507. https://doi.org/10.1073/pnas.1400724111.

Shannon, C. E. "A Mathematical Theory of Communication." *Bell System Technical Journal* 27, no. 3 (1948): 379–423. https://doi.org/10.1002/j.1538-7305.1948.tb01338.x.

Sheng, Feng, Yi Liu, Bin Zhou, Wen Zhou, and Shihui Han. "Oxytocin Modulates the Racial Bias in Neural Responses to Others' Suffering." *Biological Psychology* 92, no. 2 (2013): 380–386. https://doi.org/10.1016/j.biopsycho.2012.11.018.

Sher, Shlomi, and Craig R. M. McKenzie. "Framing Effects and Rationality." In *The Probabilistic Mind: Prospects for Bayesian Cognitive Science*, edited by Nick Chater and Mike Oaksford. Oxford: Oxford University Press, 2008.

Sherzer, Joel. "A Discourse-Centered Approach to Language and Culture." *American Anthropologist* 89, no. 2 (1987): 295–309. https://doi.org/10.1525/aa.1987.89.2.02a00010.

Sidnell, Jack. "Action in Interaction Is Conduct under a Description." *Language in Society* 46, no. 3 (2017): 313–337. https://doi.org/10.1017/S0047404517000173.

Sidnell, Jack, and Rebecca Barnes. "Alternative, Subsequent Descriptions." In *Conversational Repair and Human Understanding*, edited by Geoffrey Raymond, Jack Sidnell, and Makoto Hayashi, 322–342. Cambridge: Cambridge University Press, 2013. https://doi.org/10.1017/CBO9780511757464.011.

Sidnell, Jack, and Tanya Stivers, eds. *The Handbook of Conversation Analysis*. Oxford: Wiley-Blackwell, 2013. https://doi.org/10.1002/9781118325001.

Sikveland, Rein Ove, and Elizabeth Stokoe. "Should Police Negotiators Ask to 'Talk' or 'Speak' to Persons in Crisis? Word Selection and Overcoming Resistance to Dialogue Proposals." *Research on Language and Social Interaction* 53, no. 3 (2020): 324–340. https://doi.org/10.1080/08351813.2020.1785770.

Silverstein, M. "Denotation and the Pragmatics of Language." In *The Cambridge Handbook of Linguistic Anthropology*, edited by N. J. Enfield, Paul Kockelman, and Jack Sidnell, 128–57. Cambridge: Cambridge University Press, 2014.

Silverstein, M. "Language Structure and Linguistic Ideology." In *The Elements: A Parasession on Linguistic Units and Levels*, edited by P. Clyne, W. Hanks, and C. Hofbauer, 193–247. Chicago: Chicago Linguistic Society 1979.

Silverstein, M. "The Limits of Awareness." Sociolinguistic working paper 84. Austin, TX: Southwest Education Development Lab, 1981.

Silverstein, M. "Shifters, Linguistic Categories, and Cultural Description." edited by K. Basso and H. Selby, 11–55. Albuquerque: University of New Mexico Press, 1976.

Simon, Herbert A. "Rational Choice and the Structure of the Environment." *Psychological Review* 63, no. 2 (1956): 129–138. https://doi.org/10.1037/h0042769.

Simon, Herbert A. *Reason in Human Affairs*. Stanford, CA: Stanford University Press, 1983.

Simon, Herbert A. *The Sciences of the Artificial*, 2d ed., rev. and enl. Cambridge, MA: MIT Press, 1981.

Slobin, Dan I. "The Role of Language in Language Acquisition." Address presented at the 50th Annual Meeting of the Eastern Psychological Association, Philadelphia, 1979.

Smith, Daniel, Philip Schlaepfer, Katie Major, Mark Dyble, Abigail E. Page, James Thompson, Nikhil Chaudhary, et al. "Cooperation and the Evolution of Hunter-Gatherer Storytelling." *Nature Communications* 8, no. 1 (2017). https://doi.org/10.1038/s41467-017-02036-8.

Somin, Ilya. *Democracy and Political Ignorance: Why Smaller Government Is Smarter*. Stanford, CA: Stanford University Press, 2013.

Sperber, Dan, and Nicolas Baumard. "Moral Reputation: An Evolutionary and Cognitive Perspective: Moral Reputation." *Mind and Language* 27, no. 5 (2012): 495–518. https://doi.org/10.1111/mila.12000.

Sperber, Dan, and Dierdre Wilson. *Relevance: Communication and Cognition*, 2nd ed. Oxford: Blackwell, 1995.

Stefano, G. B., R. Ptáček, H. Kuželová, and R. M. Kream. "Endogenous Morphine: Up-to-Date Review 2011." *Folia Biologica* 58, no. 2 (2012): 49–56.

Stivers, Tanya. "Alternative Recognitionals in Person Reference." In *Person Reference in Interaction*, edited by N. J. Enfield and Tanya Stivers, 73–96. Cambridge: Cambridge University Press, 2007. https://doi.org/10.1017/CBO9780511486746.005.

Sullivan, Philip J., Kate Rickers, and Kimberley L. Gammage. "The Effect of Different Phases of Synchrony on Pain Threshold." *Group Dynamics: Theory, Research, and Practice* 18, no. 2 (2014): 122–128. https://doi.org/10.1037/gdn0000001.

Takahashi, D. Y., D. Z Narayanan, and A. A. Ghazanfar. "Coupled Oscillator Dynamics of Vocal Turn-Taking in Monkeys." *Current Biology* 23 (2013): 2162–2168.

Taleb, Nassim Nicholas. *Antifragile: Things That Gain from Disorder*. New York: Random House, 2012.

Tallis, Raymond. *Not Saussure: A Critique of Post-Saussurean Literary Theory*, 2nd ed. 1988. Reprint, Basingstoke: Macmillan, 1997.

Tauzin, Tibor, and György Gergely. "Communicative Mind-Reading in Preverbal Infants." *Scientific Reports* 8, no. 1 (2018). https://doi.org/10.1038/s41598-018-27804-4.

Tauzin, Tibor, and György Gergely. "Variability of Signal Sequences in Turn-Taking Exchanges Induces Agency Attribution in 10.5-Mo-Olds." *Proceedings of the National Academy of Sciences* 16, no. 31 (2019): 15441–15446.

Thaler, Richard H. and Cass R. Sunstein. *Nudge: Improving Decisions about Health, Wealth, and Happiness*. New Haven: Yale University Press, 2008.

Thibodeau, Paul H., and Lera Boroditsky. "Metaphors We Think With: The Role of Metaphor in Reasoning." Edited by Jan Lauwereyns. *PLoS One* 6, no. 2 (2011): e16782. https://doi.org/10.1371/journal.pone.0016782.

Thibodeau, Paul H., and Lera Boroditsky. "Natural Language Metaphors Covertly Influence Reasoning." Edited by Attila Szolnoki. *PLoS One* 8, no. 1 (2013): e52961. https://doi.org/10.1371/journal.pone.0052961.

Thibodeau, Paul H., Rose K. Hendricks, and Lera Boroditsky. "How Linguistic Metaphor Scaffolds Reasoning." *Trends in Cognitive Sciences* 21, no. 11 (2017): 852–863. https://doi.org/10.1016/j.tics.2017.07.001.

Tomasello, Michael. *Origins of Human Communication*. Cambridge, MA: MIT Press, 2008.

Tomasello, Michael. "Why Don't Apes Point?" In *Roots of Human Sociality: Culture, Cognition, and Interaction*, edited by N. J. Enfield and Stephen C. Levinson, 506–524. London: Berg, 2006.

Tomlin, Russell S. "Focal Attention, Voice, and Word Order: An Experimental, Cross-Linguistic Study." In *Word Order in Discourse*, edited by Pamela A. Downing and Michael Noonan, 517–554. Amsterdam: John Benjamins, 1995.

Truby, John. *The Anatomy of Story*. New York: Farrar, Straus and Giroux, 2007.

Tuchman, G. *Making News*. New York: Free Press, 1978.

Tversky, A., and D. Kahneman. "The Framing of Decisions and the Psychology of Choice." *Science* 211, no. 4481 (1981): 453–458. https://doi.org/10.1126/science.74 55683.

Tversky, Amos, and Daniel Kahneman. "Rational Choice and the Framing of Decisions." *Journal of Business* 59, no. 4 (1986): S251–S278.

Tyack, Peter L. "Dolphins Communicate about Individual-Specific Social Relationships." In *Animal Social Complexity: Intelligence, Culture, and Individualized Societies*, edited by Frans B. M. de Waal and Peter L. Tyack, 342–361. Cambridge, MA: Harvard University Press, 2003.

Uexküll, Jakob von. "The Theory of Meaning." *Semiotica* 42, no. 1 (1982): 25–82.

Waddy, Julie Anne. *Classification of Plants and Animals from a Groote Eylandt Aboriginal Point of View*. Darwin: Australian National University, 1988.

Wasserstrom, Richard A. *Today's Moral Problems*. Riverside, NJ.: Macmillan, 1975.

Webster, A. K. "In Favor of Sound: Linguistic Relativity and Navajo Poetry." In *Texas Linguistic Forum*, edited by M. Siewert, M. Ingram, and B. Anderson, 57. Austin: University of Texas Press, 2014. http://salsa.ling.utexas.edu/proceedings/2014/Webster.pdf.

Weiner, Irving B. *Principles of Rorschach Interpretation*. London: Routledge, 2003.

Weinstein, Daniel, Jacques Launay, Eiluned Pearce, Robin I. M. Dunbar, and Lauren Stewart. "Singing and Social Bonding: Changes in Connectivity and Pain Threshold as a Function of Group Size." *Evolution and Human Behavior* 37, no. 2 (2016): 152–158. https://doi.org/10.1016/j.evolhumbehav.2015.10.002.

Wells, Randall S. "Dolphin Social Complexity: Lessons from Long-Term Study and Life-History." In *Animal Social Complexity: Intelligence, Culture, and Individualized Societies*, edited by Frans B. M. de Waal and Peter L. Tyack, 32–56. Cambridge, MA: Harvard University Press, 2003.

Whiten, Andrew, and Richard W. Byrne, eds. *Machiavellian Intelligence II: Extensions and Evaluations*. Cambridge: Cambridge University Press, 1997.

Whorf, Benjamin Lee. *Language, Thought, and Reality*. Cambridge, MA: MIT Press, 1956.

Whorf, Benjamin Lee. *Language, Thought, and Reality*. 1956. Reprint. Cambridge, MA: MIT Press, 2012.

Wickham, Lee H. V., and Hayley Swift. "Articulatory Suppression Attenuates the Verbal Overshadowing Effect: A Role for Verbal Encoding in Face Identification." *Applied Cognitive Psychology* 20, no. 2 (2006): 157–169. https://doi.org/10.1002/acp.1176.

Wierzbicka, Anna. "Baudouin De Courtenay and the Theory of Linguistic Relativity." In *Jan Niecisław Baudouin de Courtenay a lingwistyka światowa: materiały z konferencji międzynarodowej, Warszawa, 4–7 IX 1979*, edited by Janusz Rieger, Mieczysław Szymczak, Stanisław Urbańczyk, and Polska Akademia Nauk, 51–57. Wrocław: Zakład Narodowy im. Ossolińskich, 1989.

Wierzbicka, Anna. *Lexicography and Conceptual Analysis*. Ann Arbor, MI: Karoma, 1985.

Wierzbicka, Anna. "The Human Conceptualisation of Shape." Plenary paper presented at the International Conference on Cognitive Science, Sydney, July 2003.

Wilbur, Ronnie B., and Laura A. Petitto. "Discourse Structure in American Sign Language Conversations (or, How to Know a Conversation When You See One)." *Discourse Processes* 6, no. 3 (1983): 225–228. https://doi.org/10.1080/01638538309544565.

Wilson, D. *Presupposition and Non-Truth-Conditional Semantics*. New York: Academic Press, 1975.

Winawer, J., N. Witthoft, M. C. Frank, L. Wu, A. R. Wade, and L. Boroditsky. "Russian Blues Reveal Effects of Language on Color Discrimination." *Proceedings of the National Academy of Sciences* 104, no. 19 (2007): 7780–7785. https://doi.org/10.1073/pnas.0701644104.

Winter, Bodo, Marcus Perlman, and Asifa Majid. 2018. "Vision Dominates in Perceptual Language: English Sensory Vocabulary Is Optimized for Usage." *Cognition* 179 (2018): 213–220. https://doi.org/10.1016/j.cognition.2018.05.008.

Wittgenstein, Ludwig. *Philosophical Investigations*. New York: Macmillan, 1953.

Wittgenstein, Ludwig. *Tractatus Logico-Philosophicus*. Translated by C. K. Ogden. London: Kegan Paul, Trench, Trubner & Co., 1922.

Wnuk, Ewelina, Rujiwan Laophairoj, and Asifa Majid. "Smell Terms Are Not Rara: A Semantic Investigation of Odor Vocabulary in Thai." *Linguistics* 58, no. 4 (2020): 937–966. https://doi.org/10.1515/ling-2020-0009.

Wolff, Phillip, and Kevin J. Holmes. "Linguistic Relativity: Linguistic Relativity." *Wiley Interdisciplinary Reviews: Cognitive Science* 2, no. 3 (2011): 253–265. https://doi.org/10.1002/wcs.104.

Wolff, Phillip, Douglas L Medin, and Connie Pankratz. "Evolution and Devolution of Folkbiological Knowledge." *Cognition* 73, no. 2 (1999): 177–204. https://doi.org/10.1016/S0010-0277(99)00051-7.

Wolfram, Stephen. *A New Kind of Science*. Champaign, IL: Wolfram Media, 2002.

Wulf, Friedrich. "Beitrage Zur Psychologic Der Gestalt; vi. Ueber Die Veranderung von Vomellungen (Gedachtnis Und Gestalt)." *Psychologische Forschung* 1 (1922): 333–373.

Yeshurun, Yaara, and Noam Sobel. "An Odor Is Not Worth a Thousand Words: From Multidimensional Odors to Unidimensional Odor Objects." *Annual Review of Psychology* 61, no. 1 (2010): 219–241. https://doi.org/10.1146/annurev.psych.60 .110707.163639.

Youssouf, Ibrahim Ag, Allen D. Grimshaw, and Charles S. Bird. "Greetings in the Desert." *American Ethnologist* 3, no. 4 (1976): 797–824. https://doi.org/10.1525/ae .1976.3.4.02a00140.

Zak, Paul J. "Why Inspiring Stories Make Us React: The Neuroscience of Narrative." *Cerebrum: The Dana Forum on Brain Science* 2 (2015): 2.

Zillmann, Dolf, Steve Rockwell, Karla Schweitzer, and S. Shyam Sundar. "Does Humor Facilitate Coping with Physical Discomfort?" *Motivation and Emotion* 17, no. 1 (1993): 1–21. https://doi.org/10.1007/BF00995204.

Zinken, J. "The Metaphor of "linguistic Relativity." *History and Philosophy of Psychology* 10, no. 2 (2008): 1–10.

Zuckerman, Charles H. P., and N. J. Enfield. "Heavy Sound Light Sound: A Nam Noi Metalinguistic Trope." In *Studies in the Anthropology of Language in Mainland Southeast Asia*, edited by N. J. Enfield, Jack Sidnell, and Charles H. P. Zuckerman, 85–92. Honolulu: University of Hawaii Press, 2020.

Zuckerman, Charles H. P., and N. J. Enfield. "The Unbearable Heaviness of Being Kri: House Construction and Ethnolinguistic Transformation." *Journal of the Royal Anthropological Institute* 28, no. 1 (2022).

Index